THE GOSPEL OF MARK

PUBLISHED VOLUMES

The Parables of Jesus: Red Letter Edition

The Gospel of Mark: Red Letter Edition

THE GOSPEL OF MARK

RED LETTER EDITION

Robert W. Funk
WITH Mahlon H. Smith

SONOMA, CALIFORNIA

Library of Congress Cataloging-in-Publication Data

Funk, Robert Walter, 1926–
    The Gospel of Mark : red letter edition / by Robert W. Funk with
Mahlon H. Smith.
       p.   cm. — (Jesus Seminar series)
    Includes bibliographical references and index.
    ISBN 0-944344-09-7 : $19.95
    1. Jesus Christ—Words. 2. Jesus Christ—Parables. 3. Bible.
N.T. Mark—Controversial literature. 4. Bible. N.T. Mark-
-Sources. I. Smith, Mahlon H. II. Jesus Seminar. III. Title.
IV. Series.
BT306.F865   1990
226.3'0663–dc20   91–11780
                                       CIP

CONTENTS

FIGURES
and
Cameo Essays

ACKNOWLEDGMENTS

The Gospel of Mark: Red Letter Edition is the product of six years of devoted labor on the part of the Fellows and Associates of the Jesus Seminar. The author wishes to acknowledge the contributions of those who wrote papers, attended the twice-yearly sessions, and cast their votes at the conclusion of discussion and debate. The camaraderie between and among participants permitted free and open debate and allowed everyone, upon occasion, to change his or her mind. Yet the conversations were always intense. Those who may have wondered whether the Seminar was merely trading in shopworn information should be warned: the distance traveled by the Seminar since its inception in 1985 is the equivalent of a trip to the moon.

Mahlon H. Smith of Rutgers University has drafted parts of the notes on which this volume is based. He has also been the author's consultant and reviewer late and soon, on matters both great and small.

Several Fellows and Associates read parts of the manuscript and offered suggestions for improvement: John Dominic Crossan, Arthur Dewey, Julian Hills, Roy Hoover, Joan Johnson, Sanford Lowe, Robert Miller, Stephen Patterson, John Rousseau, Daryl Schmidt, Milfred Smith, and Jim Wyrick.

Charlene Matejovsky is responsible for the design of the book, as well as for correcting many infelicities and inaccuracies.

I have attempted to represent the views of the Fellows of the Seminar rather than my own. Needless to say, the generalizations that are to be found here and there in the Introduction, Rules of Evidence, and Notes are my own. I only hope I did not distort the collective wisdom of my colleagues in endeavoring to state simply and briefly the complex issues they sought to resolve.

The Jesus Seminar is sponsored by the Westar Institute located in Sonoma, California.

Robert W. Funk
Westar Institute/Polebridge Press

CATALOGUE
of
Written Gospels

NARRATIVE GOSPELS

Gospel of Matthew. An anonymous author compiled the Gospel of Matthew after the fall of Jerusalem in 70 C.E. and sometime before the Council of Jamnia, 90 C.E. This is the period when the Christian community was seeking its own identity over against Judaism, and when Judaism was attempting to recover from the loss of the center of its worship, the temple. Matthew can be dated to about 85 C.E., give or take a few years.

Matthew was composed in Greek in dependence on Mark and Q, both written in Greek. It is therefore incorrect to identify it with a gospel composed in Hebrew by a disciple of Jesus.

Gospel of Mark. An anonymous author composed the Gospel of Mark shortly after the destruction of the temple in 70 C.E. Mark may be responsible for forming the first chronological outline of the life of Jesus. He may also be responsible for the first connected account of Jesus' passion (Mark 14–16). He reflects the early Christian view that God was about to bring history to an end in an apocalyptic conflagration.

The Gospel of Mark is attributed to John Mark, a companion of Paul and perhaps an associate of Peter. This attribution, like others in the ancient world, is the product of speculation.

Mark's gospel was widely used in the early Christian community as indicated by the fact that Matthew and Luke made use of his text in creating their gospels a few years later.

Gospel of Luke. Luke-Acts, a two-volume work by a single author, depicts the emergence of Christianity on the world stage. It was composed around 85 C.E., during the same period as Matthew. Whereas Matthew was concerned with the Jewish reaction to Christianity, Luke is preoccupied with developments among the gentiles.

The tradition that Luke the physician and companion of Paul was the author of Luke-Acts goes back to the second century C.E. It is improbable that the author of Luke-Acts was a physician and it is doubtful that he was a companion of Paul. As in the case of the other canonical gospels, the author is anonymous.

Gospel of John. The Gospel of John was allegedly written by John, son of Zebedee, one of an inner group of disciples. According to legend, John lived to a ripe old age in Ephesus where he composed the gospel, three letters, and possibly the Book of Revelation. The legend is highly improbable.

The Gospel of John was probably written towards the close of the first century C.E., which makes it a close contemporary of Matthew and Luke. It exhibits evidence of having gone through several editions. Many scholars therefore conclude that John is the product of a "school," which may indeed have been formed by the John of the legend.

Its place of origin is unknown. It was clearly created in a hellenistic city of some magnitude with a strong Jewish community. A city in Asia Minor or Syria, or possibly Alexandria in Egypt, would do.

It is uncertain whether John knew the Synoptics. He almost certainly made use of a "signs" source and possibly a source consisting of lengthy discourses.

SAYINGS GOSPELS

Gospel of Thomas. The Gospel of Thomas contains 114 sayings of Jesus, consisting of wisdom sayings, parables, proverbs, and prophecies attributed to Jesus. It has virtually no narrative content.

Thomas is extant in complete form only in a Coptic translation found among the fifty-two tractates that make up the Coptic Gnostic Library discovered at Nag Hammadi, Egypt, in 1945. Three fragments of the original Greek version of Thomas were discovered at Oxyrhynchus (1, 654, 655) in Egypt around the turn of the century. The fragments can be dated to around 200 c.e. The first edition of Thomas was probably composed around 60 c.e.

Thomas is widely regarded as an independent witness to the sayings of Jesus, comparable in form to so-called Q, a sayings collection believed to function as one of two sources utilized by Matthew and Luke in creating their gospels.

Dialogue of the Savior. The Dialogue of the Savior is a fragmentary and composite document containing dialogues of Jesus with three of his disciples, Judas, Matthew, and Mary. It was found at Nag Hammadi, Egypt, in 1945.

The earlier portions of the Dialogue may be dated to the second half of the first century c.e., while the final form of the Dialogue of the Savior is probably to be dated to the second half of the second century c.e.

Dialogue of the Savior is closely related to the Gospel of Thomas and the Gospel of John.

Apocryphon of James. The Apocryphon of James is a Coptic translation of a Greek original containing a dialogue of Jesus with Peter and James. Apocryphon of James was found among the codices of the Nag Hammadi Library in Egypt in 1945.

Apocryphon of James lacks a narrative framework; like Thomas and Q, it consists entirely of sayings, parables, prophecies, and rules governing the Christian community attributed to Jesus. It is the risen Jesus who speaks. The whole is embedded in a letter purportedly written in Hebrew by James.

Apocryphon of James was probably composed during the course of the second century c.e.

INFANCY GOSPELS

Infancy Gospel of Thomas. Infancy Gospel of Thomas is a narrative of the miraculous works of the young magician-hero, Jesus, prior to his twelfth birthday. Infancy Gospel of Thomas continues the *divine man* tradition of the ancient world: itinerant miracle workers accredited by their amazing deeds.

Infancy Gospel of Thomas is preserved in a Syriac manuscript of the fourth century C.E. and in Greek manuscripts of the fourteenth through the sixteenth centuries C.E. The gospel is based on oral sources and the Gospel of Luke. In its original form it may be as old as the second century C.E.

Infancy Gospel of James.   Infancy Gospel of James is an infancy gospel containing an account of the birth and dedication of Mary and the birth of Jesus. The traditional title *Protevangelium* indicates that the events recorded precede those narrated in the canonical gospels. Infancy James is dated in the period mid-second century C.E. to early third century C.E.

PASSION GOSPELS

Gospel of Peter.   The Gospel of Peter is preserved only as a fragment discovered in upper Egypt in 1886–1887; the language is Greek and the fragment dates to the eighth or ninth century C.E. However, two Greek papyrus fragments from Oxyrhynchus, dating to late second or early third century C.E., may also belong to the Gospel of Peter.

The Gospel of Peter contains a passion narrative, an epiphany story, an account of the empty tomb, and the beginning of a resurrection story.

In its original form, the Gospel of Peter may have arisen in the second half of the first century C.E.

Acts of Pilate.   The Acts of Pilate is an elaborate account of Jesus' trial before Pontius Pilate, his crucifixion and burial, accounts of the empty tomb, and a discussion of his resurrection by a council of Jewish elders. It is an example of early Christian apologetic in narrative form.

The original Acts of Pilate was probably written in Greek sometime during the second or third century C.E. The prologue claims that it was written by Nicodemus in Hebrew shortly after Jesus' death. The Acts of Pilate was eventually incorporated into the Gospel of Nicodemus. It is preserved in several medieval Greek manuscripts.

FRAGMENTS

Egerton Gospel.   An unknown gospel is represented by four fragments of Papyrus Egerton 2 and a fifth fragment designated Papyrus Köln 255. The five fragments are from the same papyrus codex, which can be dated to the second century C.E., perhaps as early as 125 C.E. The Egerton Gospel contains the healing of a leper, a controversy over payment of taxes, a miracle of Jesus by the Jordan, plus two tiny segments closely related to the Gospel of John.

Oxyrhynchus Papyrus 1224.   Oxyrhynchus Papyrus 1224 is the remains of a papyrus codex containing fragments of an unknown gospel. It can be dated to the beginning of the fourth century C.E.

Oxyrhynchus Papyrus 840.   Oxyrhynchus Papyrus 840 is a single leaf of a Greek parchment containing fragments that can be dated to the fourth century C.E. It contains the conclusion of a discourse between Jesus and his disciples and a controversy story involving Jesus and a Pharisaic chief priest in the temple court.

Papyrus Cairensis 10 735.   Papyrus Cairensis may be a fragment of a non-canonical gospel containing the story of Jesus' birth and flight to Egypt. The fragment is dated to the sixth or seventh century C.E. Further identification has not been possible.

Fayyum Fragment. Fayyum Fragment is a fragment of the third century C.E. containing an excerpt from an unknown gospel. The text is too fragmentary to warrant definitive conclusions.

Freer Logion. The Freer logion is a variant reading in codex W acquired by Charles L. Freer of Detroit in 1906 and now lodged in the Freer Museum of the Smithsonian Institution in Washington, D.C. (late fourth or early fifth century C.E.). The variant in question is an insertion in the Gospel of Mark at 16:14.

Secret Gospel of Mark. Secret Mark is a fragment of an early edition of the Gospel of Mark containing a story of the raising of a young man from the dead, a rite of initiation, and an encounter of Jesus with three women in Jericho. These stories are presently embedded in a letter of Clement of Alexandria (second century C.E.), the copy of which dates to the eighteenth century C.E. Secret Mark, however, may go back in its original form to the early second century C.E.

Gospel of the Ebionites. A Jewish-Christian gospel preserved only in quotations by Epiphanius (fourth century C.E.). The original title is unknown. The Ebionites were Greek-speaking Jewish Christians who flourished in the second and third centuries C.E. Their gospel, erroneously called the Hebrew Gospel by Epiphanius, probably dates to the mid-second century C.E.

Gospel of the Egyptians. The Gospel of the Egyptians consists of sayings of Jesus. The few fragments extant are preserved in Greek by Clement of Alexandria (end of the second century C.E.). The gospel appears to be oriented to sexual asceticism, to judge by the few remaining fragments. The Gospel of the Egyptians arose in the period 50–150 C.E.

Gospel of the Hebrews. The Gospel of the Hebrews contains traditions of Jesus' preexistence and coming into the world, his baptism and temptation, a few of his sayings, and an account of his resurrected appearance to James, his brother (1 Cor 15:7). The provenance of the Gospel of the Hebrews is probably Egypt. It was composed sometime between the mid-first century C.E. and mid-second century C.E. The Gospel of the Hebrews has been lost except for quotations and allusions preserved by the Church Fathers.

Gospel of the Nazoreans. The Gospel of the Nazoreans is an expanded version of the Gospel of Matthew. It is preserved in quotations and allusions in the Church Fathers and in marginal notations found in a number of medieval manuscripts. These marginal notations appear to go back to a single "Zion Gospel" edition composed prior to 500 C.E. The Gospel of the Nazoreans is evidently a translation into Aramaic or Syriac of Greek Matthew, with additions.

The Gospel of the Nazoreans is first quoted by Hegesippus around 180 C.E. Its provenance is probably western Syria.

CATALOGUE
of
Select Greek Manuscripts

IN CHRONOLOGICAL ORDER

Designation	Date	Contents	Location/Notes
Greek Papyri			
PEgerton 2	100–150	Unknown gospel frags.	London
PKöln 255	100–150	Unknown gospel frags.	Cologne
𝔓52	ca. 125	John frag.	Manchester
𝔓75	175–225	Luke & John frags.	Cologny
POxy 2949	ca. 200	Peter frags.	Oxford
POxy 1	ca. 200	Thom frag.	Oxford
POxy 655	ca. 200	Thom frag.	Cambridge, Mass.
𝔓64 & P67	ca. 200	Matt frag.	Oxford; Barcelona
𝔓66	ca. 200	John frags.	Cologny; Dublin
𝔓77	II/III	Matt 23:30–39	Oxford
𝔓1	III	Matt frags.	Philadelphia
𝔓4	III	Luke frags.	Paris
𝔓45	200–250	Gospels & Acts	Dublin
𝔓53	III	Matt & Acts frags.	Ann Arbor, Mich.
𝔓69	III	Luke frags.	Oxford
𝔓70	III	Matt frags.	Oxford
𝔓37	III/IV	Matt 26:19–52	Ann Arbor, Mich.
𝔓88	IV	Mark 2:1–26	Milan
Greek Uncials			
ℵ	IV	e, a, p, r	British Museum; only complete copy of Greek New Testament in uncial script.
B	IV	e, a, p	Vatican Library
A	V	e, a, p, r	British Museum
C	V	e, a, p, r	Paris
D	V	e, a	Cambridge
W	V	e	Washington, D.C.
Θ	IX	e	Tiflis, Georgia, USSR
0212	III	e	New Haven, Conn.

Definitions: All dates are C.E. Roman numerals indicate centuries. Papyrus is a writing material made from Egyptian reeds. Parchment is a writing material made from animal skins. Uncial is a form of writing using all capital letters. *Codes:* e=gospels; a=Acts; p=letters; r=Revelation.

STORY
of
The Jesus Seminar

Ten o'clock scholars

The scene is a group of academics seated around a huge U-shaped conference table. They are gospel specialists. They teach at leading colleges, universities, and seminaries in the U.S. and Canada. They come from every major Christian denomination and tradition. Jewish scholarship is also represented. They are passing small covered boxes from hand to hand, into which they are dropping red, pink, gray, and black beads through small holes in the top. The tally of the beads will determine the color in which the parable of the Unmerciful Servant in Matt 18:23–34 will be printed in *The Parables of Jesus: Red Letter Edition,* and in *Five Gospels: Red Letter Edition.* (It will be pink.)

Some critics quickly labelled the scene blasphemous. Other detractors joked about determining the truth by democratic vote. But the Fellows of the Jesus Seminar are undeterred. They are certain of the merits of the project. They do not think for a moment that they will determine historical truth by vote, nor are they tampering with the word of God, as some fundamentalists claim. Their purpose is elementary: They want to learn whether a scholarly consensus exists as to what Jesus really said, and they want to report the results of their deliberations to a broad public in some relatively simple, lucid form.

The Jesus Seminar is the place of their joint deliberations and *Five Gospels: Red Letter Edition* the form of their final report. Interim reports will be issued on the parables, on each of the gospels including Thomas, and on the five gospels taken together.

This is the story of how it all came about.

King James and Bible scholars

A King James Bible bound in black, imitation leather, with gilt edges, was the coffee table centerpiece in the home of my youth. In that sacrosanct volume, the words of Jesus were printed in red. It was a red letter edition. Many years later I was to come back to that simple and omnipresent version of the Bible that has had such profound influence on the shaping of what Americans think about the Bible. Meanwhile, it was not long before I learned that the Bible scholars working for King James had very limited tools and severely restricted knowledge: the King James version rested on inferior

Hebrew and Greek manuscripts and the translators had little knowledge of the ancient world. In addition, the English its translators wrote and spoke has since become archaic.

In the university I attended, one of my instructors taught me that scholars have been studying the gospels using the scientific methods of modern critical scholarship for more than two hundred years. I soon learned the difference between a literalist view of the text and a critical approach. A literalist insists that everything written in the scriptures is literally true or it is not true at all. A critical scholar is one whose conclusions are determined, not by prior religious convictions, but by the evidence. As in the case of many other students, my naive piety was no match for the facts. I came to see that Jesus, like many other sages in the ancient world, became a repository of common lore in a predominantly oral culture. Although I didn't know it then, a critical red letter edition lay way off in my future.

I have been a student of the gospels for more than forty years. I am acutely aware that longevity, or even piety, does not necessarily mean competence. No amount of service, or good will, or even devotion, can substitute for proper training, extensive learning, and tough peer review. Like all other students who aspired to join the professional guild of critical scholars, I was required to pass through years of rigorous training, four academic degrees, and endless papers and dissertations. Along the way I had to master more than one ancient language, along with a few modern languages and a vast array of secondary literature in those tongues. I mention these details because many Americans are unaware of what a proper education in the field of biblical studies entails.

Yet examinations were not over when I finished seminary and graduate school. As a working scholar in the field of biblical studies, I was obliged to put my ideas, my translations, my interpretations, my theories, into the public domain of scholarship by means of essays and books. The examinations got tougher, rather than easier, as time went by. My professional colleagues were tough on me: they corrected, chided, counseled—and encouraged. Occasionally I was rewarded with applause and approval. This is the way of critical scholarship: propose, review, reformulate, publish, test, test, test. A half-dozen books and more than one hundred articles later, I am still forced to run the gauntlet of criticism each time I open my mouth or turn on my computer.

The mills of scholarship grind slowly, but they grind exceedingly small. I have been subject to no small amount of grinding.

The end product of this process is something called the scholarly consensus. Every scholar aspires to contribute to that consensus and to become a representative of it.

After thirty-three years of teaching—college, seminary, graduate school—I decided to embark on the great venture and write a book on Jesus. This is the ambition of many who have spent their lives investigating the gospels. I thought I would endeavor to sum up everything I have learned about Jesus from my colleagues, past and present, and from my own research. I wanted to contribute in some small way to the modification of the existing scholarly consensus and yet affirm its dominant direction. This modest resolve was to lead me in surprising new directions and to open challenging and exciting vistas. In academic life one should never be too old to learn.

Here is what happened.

The cupboard was bare

The first step was to compile a list of the things Jesus said and the things he did. A raw list would then of course have to be refined in the light of the history of gospel scholarship and a new, critical list created. This second list would be the data base from which I would work in writing my sketch of Jesus.

It is the way of scholarship to begin by going to the library and reviewing everything written on the subject. I hoped to find both raw and refined lists among the dusty tomes housed there. Here is where surprise and astonishment set in.

In the first instance, I could find no raw lists of words or deeds that could serve as my raw data base. So far as I have been able to discover, no one had ever compiled such a list of all the words attributed to Jesus in the first three hundred years following his death.

Astonishment began to grow when, among the many scholarly books written on Jesus in the last century and more (my beginning point was about 1880), I could find no critical list of sayings and deeds on which a particular scholar had based his or her picture of Jesus. A few partial lists turned up, but nothing exhaustive. Although scholars of the gospels regularly make the distinction between authentic and inauthentic materials, they are not in the habit of revealing the results explicitly. In quizzing contemporary colleagues, I was equally surprised to learn that no one had compiled a raw list, or worked up a critical list, of Jesus materials. This in spite of the fact that most of them lecture or write about Jesus nearly every day. I felt destiny beckoning.

The Tom Sawyer approach to fence painting

When one has a picket fence to paint, the best strategy is to enlist help. I did just that. I sat down and wrote letters to thirty of my colleagues in gospel studies and invited them to join me in forming the Jesus Seminar. Eventually the membership was to grow to more than two hundred, more or less equally divided between established academic scholars (Fellows) and interested non-specialists (Associates).

We agreed to meet twice a year. The original thirty Charter Fellows nominated additional Fellows and Associates. The membership grew. No one has ever been refused membership in the Seminar. However, one Fellow lost his academic post because of his participation, and others are unable to acknowledge publicly that they belong. In spite of these problems, the group has developed a strong sense of mission and achievement as it has pursued its agenda. It has now completed its sixth year of deliberations.

The aims of the Seminar were two: (1) we were to compile a raw list of all the words attributed to Jesus in the first three centuries (down to 300 c.e.). These sayings and parables were to be arranged as parallels, so that all versions of the same item would appear side by side on the page for close comparison and study. We decided to defer listing the deeds of Jesus until a second phase of the Seminar. (2) We were then to sort through this list and determine, on the basis of scholarly consensus, which items probably echoed or mirrored the voice of Jesus, and which items belong to subsequent stages of the Jesus tradition.

These aims seem simple enough. But leave it to scholars to complicate what appears to be simple and straightforward.

Heresy and harrassment

This is the best point at which to insert warnings that should go on the label of the Jesus Seminar.

This is what I said to the original Charter Fellows in March, 1985:

> We are about to embark on a momentous enterprise. We are going to inquire simply, rigorously after the voice of Jesus, after what he really said.
>
> In this process, we will be asking a question that borders the sacred, that even abuts blasphemy, for many in our society. As a consequence, the course we shall follow may prove hazardous. We may well provoke hostility. But we will set out, in spite of the dangers, because we are professionals and because the issue of Jesus is there to be faced.

We have indeed provoked controversy and been subject to hostile attacks. But the Seminar has also attracted the attention of the news media and we have found wide and enthusiastic support.

Academic folk are a retiring lot. They like noiseless libraries and private sanctuaries for reflection. They prefer books to lectures, and solitude to public display. To this disposition, I am inspired to say: We have too long buried our considered views of Jesus and the gospels in technical jargon and in obscure journals. We have hesitated to contradict what TV evangelists and pulp religious authors have to say about the Bible for fear of political reprisal and public controversy. And the charge of popularizing or sensationalizing biblical issues is anathema to promotion and tenure committees in the institutions of higher learning where we work. It is time for us to quit the library and study and speak up.

The level of public knowledge of matters biblical borders on the illiterate. The church has failed in its historic mission to educate the public in the fourth "R," religion. Many Americans cannot even name the four canonical gospels. The public is poorly informed about any of the assured results of critical scholarship, although those results are commonly taught in colleges, universities, and seminaries. In this vacuum, drugstore books and magazines play on the fears and ignorance of the uninformed. Radio and TV evangelists indulge in platitudes and pieties. In contrast, the Jesus Seminar is a clarion call to enlightenment. It is for those who prefer facts to fancies, history to histrionics, science to superstition, where Jesus and the gospels are concerned.

Yet one should heed the warning on the label: a seventeenth-century view of the Bible will not long remain intact in the face of a little knowledge. As I have frequently warned my students over the years, learning has a way of opening up new vistas and eroding uninformed opinion.

When you see white smoke from the chimney . . .

The Seminar made good progress in compiling the basic inventory of words attributed to Jesus. J. Dominic Crossan, a leading gospels scholar, author of numerous well-known books and essays, professor at DePaul University, took the lead in creating *Sayings Parallels.* This workbook contains more than a thousand versions of 503 items, classified in four categories: parables, aphorisms, dialogues, and stories incorporating words attributed to Jesus. It covers all intracanonical and extracanonical sources in the first three hundred years. *Sayings Parallels* became the official workbook of the Jesus Seminar, together with the original language texts.

Now the fun was to begin. We formed specific agendas of items to be reviewed and evaluated at each of our semiannual meetings. Scholarly essays were prepared and distributed in advance on each item. The meetings themselves were devoted to argument and debate. The question then became: how shall we determine whether a scholarly consensus exists on a particular item? And how shall we measure the magnitude of that consensus?

My bold suggestion was that we vote on each item. There were two reasons for so doing. First, scholars are prone to put off making decisions until they have had time for further study, or until they have read the latest article or heard the most recent argument, or just because they are trained to hold issues open to further knowledge. The essence of scholarship is attention to endless detail and the patience of Job in weighing evidence.

Caution has to be balanced with the willingness to make tough decisions, even for humanists. Knowledge of literature, or art, or the Bible, should be good for something. Yet I know academics well enough to know we will not readily come to decision unless we agree in advance to a decision-making procedure. Further, in the case of the Jesus Seminar, we needed the means to report the results of our deliberations to a broad public. But we had not decided on how that could be done. A critical red letter edition of the gospels seemed the best way to make a report readily comprehensible to the non-specialist reader browsing in the local bookstore or library.

Voting to me was a way to ascertain whether a scholarly consensus existed. After all, committees creating critical texts of the Greek New Testament, such as the one responsible for the United Bible Societies Greek Testament, vote in the course of their deliberations about whether to print this or that text and about what to consign to variants in the notes. And translation committees, such as the one creating the *Revised Standard Version*, vote in the course of their work on which translation proposal to adopt. In so doing, they are only attempting to discover whether the members around the table agree on a point and the extent of that agreement. Of course, they do not thereby determine the ultimate truth; they only learn what the majority among them think is the truth. Similarly, I deemed it entirely consonant with such procedures to ask members of the Jesus Seminar, after appropriate preparation and review, to decide whether, in their collective judgment, a given item did or did not permit the voice of Jesus to be heard. The old model of the red letter edition—here I go back to my childhood—suggested to me that a given item should be labelled either red (Jesus did say it or something like it) or black (he did not).

But my colleagues resisted making matters so simple. We ended by adopting four categories. In addition to red, we permitted a pink vote for those who were not quite sure of red, or thought red was too strong. And for those who did not quite want to print an item in black, we permitted a gray vote. Four colors means that our report will not be a simple red letter edition; it will be a color-coded edition in red, pink, gray, and black.

In a sense, the formation of a scholarly consensus customarily takes place by "voting," although the voting occurs covertly and over a long period of time. One scholar discovers a fact, or proposes a theory, publishes that work, and other scholars approve and adopt that work or disapprove and reject it, all normally in writing. Eventually, the body of scholars generally agrees to such proposals and a consensus is formed, or disagrees and a different proposal is advanced.

In the Jesus Seminar, as in textual and translation committees, we are merely trying to shorten the cycle by asking scholars to express their minds on specific items under consideration. Surgery committees in hospitals, with the patient lying in bed, have to decide whether to operate or not, at the time; they cannot afford to publish their opinions in the *New England Journal of Medicine* and wait for letters to the editor. It is equally appropriate, though perhaps less urgent, to ask biblical scholars to state what they think, at this point, on a given topic, particularly when that topic is of widespread public interest and concern. On a radio talk show recently, a caller asked me whether there was a hell. I responded: Do you want to know whether Jesus thought there was a hell? The caller insisted on the general question as one that troubled her deeply and immediately. She was not interested in the history of the concept; she just wanted to know whether there was one, yes or no. I gave her my answer: there is not a hell, certainly not in the mythological sense depicted in the Bible. Scholars of the Bible have the responsibility to tell the public what they know, or think they know, just as do politicians, medical experts, economists, anthropologists, chemists, ecologists, and other experts, where knowledge impinges on the public good.

My book on Jesus has been postponed. It awaits the complete reports of the Jesus Seminar. Following on *The Parables of Jesus: Red Letter Edition* and this volume will come similar reports on the gospels of Thomas, Matthew, Luke, John, and the sayings gospel Q. Finally, we will issue *The Five Gospels: Red Letter Edition.*

VOTING
Procedures and Interpretation

The goal of the Jesus Seminar has been to evaluate all the parables and sayings attributed to Jesus in the first three centuries (more than 1500 items). The next task was to arrange them on a scale from those Jesus almost certainly said to those he almost certainly did not say. The ranking was to be determined by scholarly consensus.

Using the traditional red letter editions of the New Testament as the model, the Fellows decided to make red and black the basic categories: words that approximate the words of Jesus were to be printed in red, in accordance with the red letter tradition. Words not representative of Jesus were to be left in black—the customary way the text of books is printed. Two intermediate categories were also created. Pink, which is a lighter form of red, was to be the color given to items that echo the voice of Jesus, while gray was to be a step up from black: gray items preserve ideas close to Jesus, but do not approximate his words or echo his voice. The Seminar employed colored beads dropped into voting boxes in order to permit all members to vote in secret.

The Seminar adopted two official interpetations of the four colors (see p. xxii). Individuals could elect either one for their own guidance. An unofficial but helpful interpretation of these categories by one member led to this formulation:

red: That's Jesus!
pink: Sure sounds like Jesus.
gray: Well, maybe.
black: There's been some mistake.

The Seminar did not insist on uniform standards for balloting.

The ranking of items is determined by weighted vote. Since most Fellows of the Seminar are professors, they are accustomed to grade points and grade point averages. So they decided on the following scheme:

red   = 3
pink   = 2
gray   = 1
black = 0

The points on each ballot are added up and divided by the number of votes in order to determine the weighted average. While the scale is zero to three, it was decided to convert the weighted averages to percentages—to employ a scale of 100 rather than a scale of 3.00. The result is a scale divided into four quadrants:

red: .7501 up
pink: .5001 to .7500
gray: .2501 to .5000
black: .0000 to .2500

We instructed the computer to carry the averages out to four decimal places, but we have rounded the numbers off to two decimal places in the voting tables found in an appendix to this volume.

In voting on general questions, the Fellows had to employ a slightly different interpretation of the scale. General questions were put in the form of statements with which each Fellow was to agree or disagree:

red: strongly agree
pink: agree
gray: disagree
black: strongly disagree

The results of six years of deliberations and voting are being reported in the Red Letter Series:

The Parables of Jesus: Red Letter Edition (1988)
The Gospel of Mark: Red Letter Edition (1991)
The Sayings Gospel (Q): Red Letter Edition
The Gospel of Thomas: Red Letter Edition
The Gospel of Matthew: Red Letter Edition
The Gospel of Luke: Red Letter Edition
The Gospel of John: Red Letter Edition

Each of the volumes will contain text, parallels, and notes for each saying or parable.

The results will then be summed up in:

The Five Gospels: Red Letter Edition

CODES
and
Abbreviations

Fellows and Associates of the Jesus Seminar are asked to cast ballots in one of four categories for each item in the inventory of sayings attributed to Jesus. However, there are two options under which ballots may be cast. They are as follows:

Option 1

Red: I would include this item unequivocally in the data base for determining who Jesus was.

Pink: I would include this item with reservations (or modifications) in the data base for determining who Jesus was.

Gray: I would not include this item in the primary data base, but I might make use of some of the content in determining who Jesus was.

Black: I would not include this item in the primary data base for determining who Jesus was.

Option 2

Red: Jesus undoubtedly said this or something very like it.

Pink: Jesus probably said something like this.

Gray: Jesus did not say this, but the ideas contained in it are close to his own.

Black: Jesus did not say this; it represents the perspective or content of a later or different tradition.

J1, O2, W3, etc., refer to the rules in the essay "Rules of Evidence."	
⟨ ⟩	Words are supplied by the translator to complete an expression or fill a gap in the manuscript.
[ ]	A doubtful textual variant.
[[ ]]	A reading that certainly did not belong to the original text but is included here for ease of reference.
//	One gospel text parallels another.
100	Totals in the voting tables do not always add up to 100 because of rounding.
v. (vv.)	Verse(s)
B.C.E.	Before the Common Era
C.E.	Common Era
Barn	Barnabas, a letter of uncertain authorship, 1st or 2nd cent. C.E.

1 Clem   1 Clement, a letter from Clement of Rome to the church at Corinth, ca. 95 C.E.

2 Clem   2 Clement, a sermon attributed to Clement of Rome, ca. 150 C.E.

Did   Didache, a compendium of teachings or catechetical work attributed to the apostles, 2nd cent. C.E.

Herm   Shepherd of Hermas, an apocalyptic work, 1st or 2nd cent. C.E.

Man   Hermas, Mandates
Sim   Hermas, Similitudes
Vis   Hermas, Visions

Ign Eph   A letter from Ignatius, bishop of Antioch in Syria, to the church at Ephesus, 2nd cent. C.E.

Pol Phil   A letter from Polycarp, bishop of Smyrna in Asia Minor, to the Philippians, mid-2nd cent. C.E.

INTRODUCTION

THE PROBLEM OF THE HISTORICAL JESUS

The historical Jesus—Jesus as he actually lived and taught in Palestine in the first decades of the common era—is to be distinguished from the pictures drawn of him in the earliest surviving sources. Those sources include the four **canonical** gospels, Mark, Matthew, Luke, and John, as well as numerous extracanonical gospels. What we know about Jesus comes almost entirely from the gospel records. But the evangelists have so modified, re-shaped, and extended the material that the historical figure is obscured by a curtain of Christian piety and storytelling. On this judgment all **critical** scholars are agreed.

> *Canon:* a collection or authoritative list of books accepted as holy scripture.

> *To be critical* means "to exercise careful, considered judgment." Biblical critics belong to the same category as art critics and literary critics.

The problem of the historical Jesus was provoked initially by the revolutionary worldview produced by the rise of modern science and critical reason. The radical shift in worldview required an equally revolutionary approach to the question of Christian origins on the part of the intellectually honest biblical scholar, who could no longer submit historical judgments to the dictates of ecclesiastical dogma. The impact of this shift is explored further below in the section on research methods.

The discrepancy between the historical Jesus and the picture presented by the gospels led the great biblical scholars of the nineteenth century, such as **Albert Schweitzer**, to embark on a quest of the historical Jesus.

> *Albert Schweitzer* (1875–1965), world renowned organist, biblical scholar, medical doctor, and recipient of the Nobel Peace Prize, gave up a brilliant academic career to found a mission hospital in Africa.

Why are critical biblical scholars universally convinced that the historical Jesus differs in important respects from the accounts given of him in the gospels?

This question has been at the center of more than two centuries of scientific research and scholarly debate. During this period, scholars have established certain basic facts, and formed, collectively, a number of fundamental hypotheses or theories, which are designed to account for those facts.

1

Scholars disagree of course on many of the details, but they are united on the major **premises** that underlie all critical work on the gospels. Those premises fall broadly into four categories: (1) premises that underlie the scholarly approach to Jesus as a historical person; (2) premises related to the oral transmission of the Jesus tradition; (3) premises that function as the foundation of the study of the written gospels; and (4) premises concerning methods of study.

> A *premise* may be a statement of fact, a hypothesis, or a combination of the two.

Premises supporting the scholarly conviction that the gospels offer heavily gilded portraits of the historical Jesus will be explored in this introduction and particularized as rules of evidence in the following chapter. At the conclusion of each section we will summarize the premises sketched in that section. The premises are numbered consecutively.

The first premise is the crowning premise of the sixty-three premises to follow. It is the collective result of the modern critical study of the gospels. It is an axiom shared by all critical scholars of whatever theological persuasion.

PREMISE 1: *The historical Jesus is to be distinguished from the gospel portraits of him.*

THE SCHOLARLY APPROACH TO JESUS

Jesus, the oral teacher

The Jesus tradition is an oral tradition. Both at its inception with Jesus and in its formative years with his disciples, the words of Jesus came to life and were passed around by word of mouth. The gospels portray Jesus as one who speaks, not as one who writes.

Jesus wrote nothing, so far as we know. Indeed, we do not know for certain that Jesus could write; we are not even positive that he could read. Similarly, many of his first followers were technically illiterate, so that writing did not become a significant part of the Christian movement until later. Jesus himself taught his followers by means of the spoken word: his verbal vehicles consisted primarily of **parables** and short, provocative sayings termed **aphorisms.** His disciples also responded to his teaching orally: they repeated his most memorable words, to each other and to others they hoped would join their movement.

> A *parable* is a brief narrative or picture. It is also a metaphor or simile drawn from nature or the common life, arresting the hearer by its vividness or strangeness, and leaving the mind in sufficient doubt about its precise application to tease it into active thought.

> *Aphorisms* and *proverbs* are striking one-liners. An aphorism is a short, provocative saying that challenges the established, accepted view of things. A proverb embodies common sense.

Information about Jesus—what he did and said—was probably preserved in oral form only for at least two decades after Jesus' death.

Oral tradition is fluid. Jesus no doubt altered his aphorisms and parables from time to time, from occasion to occasion, adapting them each time to his audience. His students like-

> *The Gospel of Thomas* is a new and important source for the sayings and parables of Jesus. See the *Catalogue of Written Gospels* and pages 10–11.

wise improvised as they went, all in the name of Jesus. Occasionally, the surviving records provide us with glimpses of this fluidity. An instructive example is found in Mark 2:21 and its parallels in Luke 5:36 and **Thomas** 47:5. Mark has Jesus speak this aphorism or proverb:

Nobody sews a piece of unshrunk cloth on an old garment,
otherwise the new, unshrunk patch pulls away from the old
and creates a worse tear.

Matthew agrees with Mark precisely, but Luke has a slightly different form of the saying:

Nobody tears a piece from a new garment and puts it on an old one,
since the new will tear and the piece from the new will not match the old.

The Markan saying concerns the damage that results from patching an old garment with a piece of unshrunk cloth. Luke has a garbled version, which pictures the illogical process of tearing a piece from a new garment to fix an old garment. Moreover, Luke does not account for the reason the new tears as a result of being used as a patch, so he, or the oral tradition before him, adds the bit about mismatching the two—a point quite different than the one made by the Markan version.

Thomas has yet another version:

An old patch is not sewn onto a new garment, for there would be a tear.

Thomas has the relationship in the canonical gospels reversed: an *old* patch is not sewn onto a *new* garment, rather than a new or unshrunk patch not being sewn onto an old garment.

Transmitters of oral tradition do not necessarily remember the exact words they intend to quote. Rather, they remember the core or gist of the saying or parable, together with the key terms, and then frequently put the matter in their own words.

Oscar Wilde is reported to have remarked: "People would not worry so much about what others think of them if they realized how little they did." I have put that saying in quotation marks, although I am not at all certain I have quoted Wilde word-for-word. I have never seen Wilde's original statement in print. But I have heard it said, and I have repeated it from time to time, but rarely, I think, in precisely the same words. However, once the organization and point are firmly in mind, it is possible to rephrase freely.

This is what happened with the words of Jesus. His disciples may remember the formal organization, which they can then manipulate in their own words, for the occasion. But if the saying is an enigma, or subtle, they may not get the point exactly right, or they may reorganize the saying for some new point. These revised and reorganized versions also enter the tradition and may be preserved in writing. There are many examples in the written records of just this kind of fluidity.

Aramaic and Greek

Another issue connected with the Jesus tradition concerns its original language. It is certain that Jesus' mother tongue was Aramaic. If Jesus spoke only Aramaic, his actual words have been lost forever, with some exceptions: for example, the term, *Abba,* is Aramaic for "father" and is Jesus' way of addressing God. There are a few other Aramaic words and phrases recorded in the gospels that may derive from Jesus. But it is possible that Jesus was bilingual. He may have learned Greek from the many merchants and wandering teachers who traveled in and through Galilee during his youth. As a consequence of the conquest of Alexander the Great three centuries earlier, the common language in Jesus' world was Greek, and it was necessary for those who engaged in commerce or taught philosophy to know that language. Recent archaeological excavations in Galilee indicate that Greek influence was more widespread in Jesus' day than scholars once thought. If Jesus learned Greek as a second language, it is possible that the Jesus tradition of sayings and parables preserved for us in the Greek gospels actually originated with him. But if Jesus spoke only Aramaic, we have lost access to the words of the historical Jesus, and someone other than Jesus is responsible for their shape in the Greek gospels.

Jesus as itinerant

It is also clear to scholars that Jesus was an itinerant. He had no permanent home, although he seems to have headquartered in Capernaum for a time and perhaps returned to other localities repeatedly at other times. But basically, he wandered around from town to town, teaching from his repertoire of wisdom, which he revised and remodeled for each occasion, as did many another itinerant sage in his time.

Jesus was an oral teacher, he was possibly bilingual, and he was itinerant. These three features of Jesus' life tell scholars that at its inception the sayings tradition of Jesus was fluid, unstable, uncodified. They indicate that it was created for the occasion and remodeled for the occasion as Jesus traveled about. They suggest Jesus and his first followers may have had to work between two languages. Jesus' disciples followed suit: they passed the sayings around exclusively by word of mouth and revised and rephrased sayings and parables as each new situation demanded.

Scarcity of biographical information

The discussion of premises concerning Jesus has thus far made no mention of biographical data. The reason for the omission is that the oral tradition had very little interest in biographical data. The evidence for this assertion is the written gospels: they record virtually no personal data about Jesus for its own sake.

The tradition tells us nothing of Jesus' physical appearance, his educational or religious background (other than legends about his youth), his personal dispositions and eccentricities beyond those captured incidentally in anecdotes related to his teaching. His family is obscure: we don't know what happened to his father, Joseph, and we don't know for sure how many brothers and sisters he had. We have only the sketchiest information about his closest associates, both male and female. Biographical data reported in the written gospels is limited to his public life and is confined to a very brief period, perhaps as short as one year and certainly no more than three years. In speaking of the oral tradition, then, we are speaking predominantly of Jesus' teachings and his public performances as healer and exorcist. The former are the subject of this report; the latter will form the agenda of the second phase of the Jesus Seminar.

Summary of premises concerning Jesus:

PREMISE 2: *Jesus taught his disciples orally; Jesus wrote nothing.*

PREMISE 3: *Traditions about Jesus were circulated by word of mouth for many years after Jesus' death.*

PREMISE 4: *Oral tradition is fluid.*

PREMISE 5: *The oral mentality remembers, not the precise words, but the core of what was said.*

PREMISE 6: *Jesus' mother tongue was Aramaic; the gospels were written in Greek.*

PREMISE 7: *Jesus possibly spoke Greek as a second language.*

PREMISE 8: *Jesus was itinerant: he moved around and adapted his sayings and parables to the occasion.*

PREMISE 9: *Jesus' disciples were oral and itinerant: they moved around and revised his sayings and parables as the situation demanded.*

PREMISE 10: *The oral tradition exhibits little interest in biographical data about Jesus.*

THE STUDY OF THE WRITTEN GOSPELS

The first records

The first Christians began to produce written records about 50 C.E.—two decades after Jesus' death. But the first canonical gospel to survive was not written until later, probably not

> C.E. stands for Common Era, B.C.E. for Before the Common Era.

until 70 C.E., give or take a few years. There is thus a gap of some forty years, more or less, between the death of Jesus and the Gospel of Mark, the first of the canonical gospels.

The gospels were published originally without indication of author, date, or place of composition. In short, they were anonymous documents. Names were attached to the gospels at a later time as titles; in most cases they do not provide any significant information about authorship or origin. Some of the lore surrounding the naming of the Gospel of Mark is given on pp. 27–28: *How Mark Got Its Name.*

The surviving written gospels fall into one of five categories: (1) narrative gospels, (2) sayings gospels, (3) infancy gospels, (4) passion gospels, and (5) fragments of unknown gospels and other gospel fragments. Narrative gospels provide a connected narrative of the public life of Jesus. Sayings gospels are collections of sayings and parables with a minimal amount of narrative connection between and among sayings and groups of sayings. Infancy gospels are collections of stories about the young Jesus. Passion gospels tell the story of Jesus' arrest, trial, and crucifixion; the passion of Jesus in the narrow sense refers to his suffering on the cross. Fragments may of course belong to any of the four categories. For a list and description of each gospel, see the *Catalogue of Written Gospels* (pp. viii–xi).

Mark

Mark was the first of the canonical gospels to be written. It was created around 70 C.E., just before or just after the fall of Jerusalem (the particulars are provided in the notes on Mark 13:2). In the judgment of most critical scholars, Mark was written by someone who was not an eyewitness of the events he reports. The author makes numerous errors about Palestinian geography. He writes for gentile readers, as his explanations of Aramaic terms and Jewish customs demonstrate. He develops a sharp polemic against unbelieving Jews, which suggests that Judaism and Christianity are in the process of separating. It is sometimes claimed that his point of view is that of Peter, who was a disciple of Jesus, but this claim cannot be substantiated. Mark's gospel itself portrays Peter as one who does not understand Jesus. Further, Peter was the brunt of heavy criticism in circles in which Mark was popular (particulars are provided in the comments on Mark 14:27–34).

The synoptic gospels: Mark, Matthew, and Luke

Mark, Matthew, and Luke are called synoptic gospels because they share a common view of Jesus (*synoptic* means 'to see together'). When laid out in a **gospel parallels** or **synopsis**, the similarities between and among the three are striking. One way in which they correspond is the extensive ver-

> In a *parallels* or *synopsis* the gospels are arranged in parallel columns with matching materials opposite each other.

bal agreement involving all three. This verbal agreement can be observed, for example, in the parable of the Mustard Seed (Mark 4:31–32 and parallels) or in the story of Jesus curing a leper (Mark 1:40–45 and parallels).

How to account for these close parallels is termed the synoptic problem. The commonly accepted explanation of the synoptic problem is that Matthew and Luke made use of Mark in creating their gospels. Matthew reproduces about 90% of Mark, Luke about 50%. Very little of Mark is not paralleled in one form or another in either Matthew or Luke.

A powerful argument for the commonly accepted solution to the synoptic problem rests on the fact that the agreement between Matthew and Luke begins where Mark begins (with the appearance of John the Baptist) and ends where Mark ends (with the empty tomb): Matthew and Luke diverge dramatically in the birth and childhood narratives and in the resurrection stories. This singular relationship to Mark applies also to smaller units within Mark: here, too, Matthew and Luke agree with each other where Mark begins and ends; otherwise they diverge. This convergence and divergence can be observed in any good gospel parallels. In addition to verbal agreements, another type of evidence links Matthew and Luke to Mark: the order of events and sayings. Matthew and Luke in general follow Mark's order when they are copying from him. Mark's chronology thus provides the outline of events for both Matthew and Luke.

The synoptic sayings gospel: Q

A second form of extensive verbal agreement links Matthew to Luke, where there is no corresponding text in Mark. Agreement of this order may be observed in the parable of the Leaven (Matt 13:33, Luke 13:20–21) or in the account of the teaching of John the Baptist (Matt 3:7–10, Luke 3:7–9).

The remarkable agreements among the three synoptic gospels, in the first place, and the equally impressive agreements between Matthew and Luke, in addition, have led scholars

> Q stands for the German word *Quelle*, which means "source." Q is the source on which Matthew and Luke draw, in addition to Mark.

to conclude that Matthew and Luke copied (1) from Mark and (2) from a second written source no longer directly available to us. This second source is known as the synoptic sayings gospel or **Q**.

The theory of gospel relationships that posits Mark and Q as the two primary sources for Matthew and Luke is known as the **two source hypothesis**.

To be sure, Matthew and Luke also have knowledge of still other traditions about Jesus which they incorporate into their gospels. For want of a better name, scholars refer to this material as special Matthew (designation in charts and graphs: M) and special Luke (L). M and L do not necessarily represent written sources; the material each adds probably derives from oral tradition.

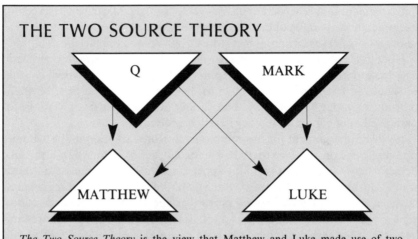

THE TWO SOURCE THEORY

The Two Source Theory is the view that Matthew and Luke made use of two written sources—Mark and the Sayings Gospel Q—in composing their gospels.

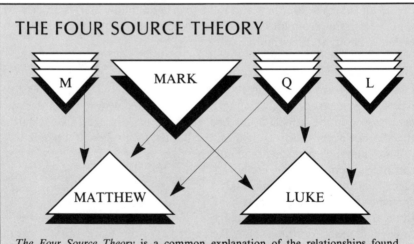

THE FOUR SOURCE THEORY

The Four Source Theory is a common explanation of the relationships found among the Synoptic Gospels. Matthew used Mark, Q, and his own special source called M. Luke also used Mark and Q, but had another source called L, that Matthew did not have. The material in M and L probably comes from oral tradition.

The theory that posits M and L in addition to Mark and Q as sources for Matthew and Luke is known, understandably, as the **four source hypothesis.**

Matthew and Luke are not merely extended versions of Mark and Q. They are brand new compositions, each with a distinctive point of view. When incorporating older materials into their gospels, the authors have assembled them in new configurations and edited to shape them into new wholes.

Instructive examples of editing and shaping are provided by two narrative incidents. The first concerns the call of the first disciples. Mark records the story in two brief narratives in Mark 1:16–20; he is followed closely by Matthew (4:18–22). In the Markan version, Jesus calls Simon and Andrew, James and John, while at their occupation as fishermen. Luke has an entirely different version in 5:1–11: Jesus calls Peter, James, and John after a miraculous catch of fish. John has yet another version in 1:35–51: the four called under different circumstances are Andrew and Peter, Philip and Nathanael.

In Mark 14:3–9, a woman enters the house of Simon the leper and anoints Jesus' head with a jar of expensive myrrh. Matthew again copies Mark closely. This same story or one very like it is found in Luke 7:36–40. Jesus is now in the house of a Pharisee and the woman is a 'sinner.' She washes Jesus' feet with her tears, dries them with her hair, and anoints his feet with myrrh. Yet another version of this same story occurs in John 12:1–8. In this account, Mary, Martha, and Lazarus are involved. Mary anoints Jesus' feet and wipes them with her hair. Judas complains at the waste, we are told, but does so because he is a thief.

Chronology

Mark alone is responsible for our earliest chronology of the life of Jesus. Matthew and Luke are dependent on the chronological outline of Mark; their gospels do not indicate that they knew an outline of Jesus' life that was independent of Mark's. This is supported by the fact that when they draw on Q, they differ about where items should be placed in the Markan outline. The relative sequence of certain events is of course not in doubt: for example, events in Galilee precede the arrest, trial, and crucifixion in Jerusalem. But Mark has arbitrarily arranged the order of events in the story of Jesus, as is proved by the fact that he often arranges his material in clusters by form or theme: 2:1–3:6, for example, consists of a series of conflict stories; parables are gathered into 4:1–34. We do not know when or where items in these complexes actually occurred. Numerous incidents have only a vague temporal or geographical connection with what precedes (note the cure of the leper in 1:40–45).

The Q-source also lacks chronology. Q is a collection of the sayings of Jesus arranged much like the book of Proverbs. It contains very little biographical material. It has no birth and childhood stories, and, what is even more remarkable, it has no passion narrative. It is a sayings gospel, much like the Gospel of Thomas.

Summary of premises concerning the narrative gospels and Q:

PREMISE 11: *At least two decades separate the death of Jesus from the first written records.*

PREMISE 12: *Forty years elapsed after the death of Jesus before the first canonical gospel was composed.*

PREMISE 13: *Mark was the first of the canonical gospels to be written.*

PREMISE 14: *Mark was not an eyewitness of the events he reports.*

PREMISE 15: *The synoptic gospels—Mark, Matthew, Luke—share a common view of Jesus in contrast to the Gospel of John.*

PREMISE 16: *Between them Matthew and Luke incorporate nearly all of Mark into their gospels, often almost word-for-word.*

PREMISE 17: *Matthew and Luke make use of a sayings gospel, known as Q, often almost word-for-word.*

PREMISE 18: *Matthew and Luke each make use of additional material unknown to Mark, Q, and each other.*

PREMISE 19: *Mark has arbitrarily arranged the order of events in his story of Jesus.*

PREMISE 20: *Matthew and Luke have no independent knowledge of the order of events in the story of Jesus.*

PREMISE 21: *Q is a collection of sayings without a narrative framework.*

Gospel of Thomas

The discovery of the Gospel of Thomas has provided a new and important source for the Jesus tradition.

Three Greek fragments of what was then an unknown gospel were discovered in Egypt around 1900 (known in **papyrus** inventories as Papyrus Oxyrhynchus [POxy] 1, 654, and 655). A complete copy of the Gospel of Thomas was discovered among the fifty-two tractates that make up the Coptic Gnostic Library found

> *Papyrus* is the predecessor of modern paper. It was made from Egyptian reeds that were cut in strips, dried, and glued together to form sheets.

near Nag Hammadi, Egypt, in 1945. With that discovery scholars learned that the Greek fragments belonged to the Gospel of Thomas. The three Greek fragments are all from different copies of Thomas, so we know Thomas was frequently duplicated at an early date. The fragments date from around 200 C.E. The Coptic text is from a fourth-century manuscript.

The Gospel of Thomas is a sayings gospel: it consists of 114 items—aphorisms, proverbs, parables, and prophecies—attributed to Jesus. It has no miracle stories, no account of the passion or resurrection, and no narrative connectives. It is thus similar in form to the Q-source. Before the discovery of Thomas, some scholars opposed the Q-hypothesis because they doubted the existence of a "gospel" made up entirely of the words of Jesus. The discovery of Thomas has erased that doubt.

Because Thomas provides no narrative settings for the words of Jesus, because the author only occasionally appends interpretive words or allegories to parables, and because the author has arranged sayings into groups less frequently, Thomas represents an earlier stage of the tradition than do the canonical gospels. Thomas also records items not found in other gospels.

Some but not all of these items have a **gnostic** tinge.

> *Gnosticism* gets its name from the Greek word *gnosis* meaning knowledge or insight. For gnostics the world is divided into realms of darkness and light. *Gnosis* is the means of salvation for the selected few; it is the means of finding one's way back to the realm of light above.

Thomas parallels the synoptic gospels at numerous points. Some scholars espouse the view that Thomas is dependent on the canonical gospels and is therefore later than they. Most Fellows of the Jesus Seminar, however, hold that Thomas is an independent witness to the Jesus tradition and is not dependent on the synoptic gospels. There are four reasons for this view:

(1) There is no pattern of relationships between Thomas and the synoptics that would require Thomas' dependence on them (contrast Matthew and Luke in relation to Mark).
(2) The order of items in Thomas is random in comparison with the synoptics.
(3) The material in the synoptics that is clearly the product of editorial activity on the part of the evangelists is uniformly missing in Thomas. Thomas never reproduces the special theological perspectives of the synoptics. This suggests that the oral tradition behind Thomas was reduced to writing before the synoptic tradition achieved its final form.
(4) Thomas sometimes appears to be closer to an original version of a saying or parable. The parable of the Leased Vineyard (Wicked Tenants) in Thomas 65, for example, is shorter than the synoptic version and has none of the allegorizing elements introduced into those later versions.

Most Fellows agree that Thomas is an independent and valuable witness to the sayings and parables of Jesus.

Summary of premises concerning Thomas:

PREMISE 22: *The Gospel of Thomas has provided a new and important source for the Jesus tradition.*

PREMISE 23: *The Gospel of Thomas consists of 114 sayings without a narrative framework.*

PREMISE 24: *Thomas represents an earlier stage of the tradition than do the canonical gospels.*

PREMISE 25: *Thomas represents an independent witness to the Jesus tradition.*

Gospel of John

One powerful reason for the scholarly conviction that the gospel portraits of Jesus differ from the historical Jesus is that the Gospel of John differs so markedly from the synoptics. Both pictures cannot be historically accurate.

In the Gospel of John, the public ministry of Jesus lasts for three years; in the synoptics it is concluded in one year. In John, the cleansing of the temple takes place early in Jesus' ministry; in the synoptics it occurs at the beginning of the final week in Jerusalem. In place of the synoptic account of the institution of the eucharist at the last supper (Mark 14:12–26), John has the story of the foot washing (John 13:1–20). John begins his story with the creation, while Matthew and Luke begin with the miraculous birth of the messiah. In contrast, Mark begins with the appearance of John the Baptist. As the tradition matured, it seems, the beginning date is moved back in time.

In the synoptics and Thomas, Jesus speaks in aphorisms and parables. In John, Jesus is represented as giving long, involved discourses, in which no parables and only an occasional aphorism appear. Thus in the synoptics and Thomas, Jesus is a sage while, in John, Jesus is a philosopher, lecturer, and mystic. The difference in themes is also remarkable: in the synoptics Jesus espouses the causes of the poor and downtrodden, the afflicted and oppressed, but has relatively little to say about himself. In John, by contrast, Jesus reflects extensively on his own mission and person and has little to say about the poor and oppressed.

For all these reasons, scholars agree that the picture drawn of Jesus in the synoptics and Thomas is more faithful to the historical person as a teacher than the portrait provided by the fourth evangelist. The Gospel of John, consequently, is not a reliable source for what Jesus said, although it may provide other valuable information.

Summary of premises concerning the Gospel of John:

PREMISE 26: *The portrait of Jesus in the Fourth Gospel differs markedly from that drawn by the synoptics.*

PREMISE 27: *In the Gospel of John Jesus speaks in long monologues, in which only an occasional aphorism and no parables appear.*

PREMISE 28: *In the Gospel of John Jesus reflects extensively on his own mission and purpose and has little to say about the poor and oppressed.*

PREMISE 29: *John is a less reliable source than the other gospels for the sayings of Jesus.*

Stratification of the gospels

Determining the history of the gospels and their relationship to each other would be a much simpler task if the surviving gospels were not themselves made up of various layers or strata of tradition, the source and final form of which have to be determined individually. This appears to be true of all gospels of any length.

The conviction that the gospels consist of strata or are layered is universally shared by critical scholars, even by those who do not accept the theory of gospel relationships sketched in this introduction.

One of the basic principles of gospel research undergirds the view that the gospels are stratified: close verbal and structural parallels permit scholars to identify the minimal texts of common sources. Put differently, close parallels of Matthew and Luke to Mark indicate that the two evangelists are copying Mark; close parallels of Matthew and Luke to each other but not to Mark permit scholars to identify the source Q, which appears to have been a compendium of the sayings of Jesus. The identification of independent and derivative sources, and the relative chronology of the gospels, are based on this basic principle. It follows that what is left over when common sources have been extracted is either derived from oral tradition, from other written sources unknown to us, or is the work of the individual evangelist.

There are other tell-tale signs of layering in our written sources. More prominent among these signs are indications that the written text has been pieced together: breaks or seams in the flow of the discourse suggest that the evangelist is weaving together written and perhaps oral sources in creating a new narrative or a new composite of sayings or parables, such as the little apocalypse in Mark 13. Seams of this sort betray themselves in the following ways:

(1) An arbitrary change in grammatical construction within a text indicates a seam in the discourse.
(2) An abrupt shift in the person addressed or in the speaking subject suggests a seam in the story or discourse.
(3) A break in the flow of the story or in the sequence of thought often points to a join in the discourse.
(4) A rupture in the formal rhetorical structure may betray a seam in the discourse.

Seams in the texts of the gospels, taken together with close verbal and structural parallels, function as a detailed guide to the stratification of the gospels. The results of research on the stratification of the gospels can be indicated here in summary form for each document.

Stratification in Q. Scholars who have specialized in the study of Q are inclined to the view that Q contains at least two and probably three layers. The first layer consists of wisdom materials (Q¹); the second layer consists of an **apocalyptic** overlay (Q²); the third layer provides introductory material

> *Apocalypticism* is the view that history will come to an end and a new age begin following a cosmic catastrophe.

about John the Baptist (Q³). Q exhibits more compositional organization than does the Gospel of Thomas. When Matthew and Luke made use of Q, the document was already complete.

Stratification in Mark. Many scholars believe that Mark went through at least two editions and thus has two layers. Secret Mark, an edition of Mark containing two additional narrative fragments, may have been the earlier of the two. Slight discrepancies in the use of Mark by Matthew and Luke suggest that they may have known yet another version, which antedates both canonical Mark and Secret Mark.

Stratification in Thomas. While the study of Thomas is still in its infancy, it is highly probable that Thomas also underwent development. Fellows of the Jesus Seminar have divided Thomas into two stages by assigning sayings with parallels in other gospels to the first edition, the balance of the sayings to the second edition. To simplify references, we may refer to the two editions as Thomas[1] and Thomas[2]. The organization of Thomas is exceedingly simple: the sayings of Jesus are linked by means of theme, word, or phrase.

Stratification in Matthew and Luke. Scholars have exposed the layers in Matthew and Luke with considerable success. Both evangelists have taken Mark as the narrative framework for their gospels. Into this narrative framework they have inserted sayings material derived from Q, distributing those sayings in the Markan outline in different ways. Finally, each has added his own collection of unique sayings, parables, and stories, as indicated above. Matthew is therefore made up of three different strata, as is Luke.

Stratification in John. The Gospel of John is also stratified, in the judgment of most scholars. The fourth evangelist has made use of a source, called the **signs gospel.** Scholars have reconstructed this hypothetical source in much the same way they have reconstructed Q, except, in this case, they have only a single gospel to work from. The author made use of the signs gospel in creating the first edition of the gospel, which consisted of

> *Signs gospel:* This view is based on two prominent miracle stories in John, the miracle at Cana (2:1–11) and the cure of the nobleman's son (4:46–54), which are numbered one and two (2:11, 4:54). Several other miracle stories in John are believed to have derived from this source.

most of chapters 1–20 (designated John[1]). Later, someone from the Johannine school enlarged the gospel, possibly adding chapter 21 and parts of chapters 13–17 (designated John[2]).

Summary of premises concerning the stratification of the gospels:

PREMISE 30: *The gospels are made up of layers or strata of tradition.*

PREMISE 31: *Close verbal and structural parallels permit scholars to identify the minimal texts of common sources.*

PREMISE 32: *The synoptic saying gospel, Q, appears to consist of three layers: Q[1], Q[2], and Q[3].*

PREMISE 33: *The Gospel of Mark probably went through two or more editions, one of which is known as Secret Mark.*

PREMISE 34: *The Gospel of Thomas has been divided provisionally by scholars into two strata: Thomas[1] and Thomas[2].*

PREMISE 35: *Matthew has three strata: Q, Mark, and special Matthew (M). Luke likewise has three strata: Q, Mark, and special Luke (L).*

PREMISE 36: *The fourth evangelist made use of a book of signs in creating the first edition of his gospel (John[1]). John was subsequently enlarged by additions in chapters 13–17 and 21 (John[2]).*

Age of the written gospels

Scholars speculate that the original versions of Q and Thomas were composed around 50–60 c.e., a scant two or three decades after Jesus' death. They would thus be contemporary with the letters of Paul. The authors are unknown.

As noted earlier, Mark was composed by an unknown author shortly before or just after the destruction of Jerusalem (70 c.e.). Matthew and Luke made use of Mark barely a decade later in creating their own gospels, so Mark's gospel must have become established relatively quickly.

Someone compiled the Gospel of Matthew after the fall of Jerusalem (70 c.e.), during the period when the Christian community was seeking its own identity over against Judaism, and when Judaism was attempting to recover from the loss of the temple, the center of its national religious life. Matthew mirrors the pain suffered

> The Judaism centered in Jerusalem and the temple was replaced by *rabbinic Judaism* following destruction of city and temple in 70 c.e.

by Christians when they were excluded from the synagogue (Matt 5:10–13). This period of adjustment for both Christianity and Judaism took place between 70 c.e. and the Council of Jamnia in 90 c.e., when **rabbinic Judaism** took shape. Matthew can therefore be dated to about 85 c.e., give or take a few years.

Luke–Acts, a two-volume work by a single author, depicts the emergence of Christianity on the world stage. It belongs to the same period as Matthew. Whereas Matthew was concerned with the Jewish reaction to Christianity, Luke is preoccupied with developments among the gentiles. The first volume begins with a formal dedication to a Greek nobleman, Theophilus, and the second concludes with Paul preaching in the first city of the Mediterranean world, Rome.

Some scholars hold the view that John is dependent in some minor ways on the synoptic gospels and thus is the last of the gospels to be composed. Other scholars hold that John is an entirely independent source and is roughly contemporary with Matthew and Luke. In either case, John makes use of a collection of miracles (signs gospel) in creating the first edition of his gospel, probably between 80 and 100 c.e. The signs gospel was created during the period 60–80 c.e. The revised and enlarged edition of John was edited after 100 c.e.

Summary of premises concerning the dates of the gospels:

PREMISE 37: *Q and Thomas were composed during the period 50–60 c.e.*
PREMISE 38: *Mark was written about 70 c.e.*
PREMISE 39: *Matthew was composed about 85 c.e.*
PREMISE 40: *Luke–Acts was created around 90 c.e.*

PREMISE 41: *The signs gospel embedded in the Gospel of John was composed during the period 60–80 C.E.*

PREMISE 42: *The first edition of John appeared between 80 and 100 C.E.*

Independent and derivative gospels

A table of independent and derivative gospels, as determined by the premises articulated above, may be combined with the chronological periods into which the gospels are grouped.

Time	30–60	60–80	80–120	120–150
Independent	Q^1 Thomas^1 Q^2 Q^3	Secret Mark Mark Thomas^2 Signs Gospel		
Derivative			Matthew Luke John^1	John^2

The division into independent and derivative sources, and the chronology of the written gospels, enable us to formulate two additional basic premises:

PREMISE 43: *The major independent sources of information about Jesus are Q (all three stages), Thomas (first edition), Mark, and the signs gospel embedded in the Gospel of John.*

PREMISE 44: *The earliest sources are Q^1 and Thomas^1. The second and third editions of Q follow closely.*

Assessment of written sources

The evangelists arranged materials with great freedom and interpreted the same sayings, parables, stories in quite different ways. They were not simply conserving or reporting the traditions about Jesus, but adapting them to new needs. Each of the gospels was written for a particular audience in a specific locale in the ancient Christian world, which was spread out over the Mediterranean basin from Egypt to Greece and from Syria to Rome, perhaps even to Gaul and Spain.

The nature of the written gospels and the literary relationships between and among them prompt scholars to be extremely cautious in identifying specific bits of tradition as historical.

The polls taken among Fellows of the Jesus Seminar on given items indicate that scholarly judgments are rarely uniform. Nevertheless, the trend of critical assessment is abundantly clear: only a very small portion of the words attributed to Jesus actually go back to him. The proportion of authentic parables is perhaps higher than is the case with the short sayings.

The parables, it seems, were more difficult to imitate because they were less widely used in the ancient world and because Jesus achieved a consummate artistry in creating them. The greater part of the sayings tradition was created by those who transmitted the oral tradition. The transmitters frequently coined sayings in Jesus' style and put them on his lips, or they borrowed them from common lore and attributed them to him. Although the Jesus Seminar has yet to consider the deeds of Jesus, it would not be imprudent to forecast that a similar reservation will be recorded about the many deeds ascribed to Jesus in the written gospels. The recognition of such discrepancies between the picture of Jesus presented by the written gospels and Jesus as he actually lived and taught in Palestine has become an axiom of modern, critical biblical scholarship.

Summary of premises concerning the assessment of the tradition:

PREMISE 45: *Only a small portion of the sayings attributed to Jesus in the gospels was actually spoken by him.*

PREMISE 46: *A larger portion of the parables goes back to Jesus because the parables were harder to imitate.*

PREMISE 47: *The greater part of the sayings tradition was created or borrowed from common lore by the transmitters of the oral tradition and the authors of the gospels.*

Surviving copies of the gospels

The original copies of the gospels (called autographs) penned by their authors or scribes have long since disappeared. The earliest fragment of any of the gospels is a tiny fragment of the Gospel of John—$\mathfrak{P}^{52}$ is the inventory number—which can be dated to about 125 C.E. Contemporary with it is a group of fragments from an unknown gospel, designated the Egerton Gospel after the donor of the fund used to purchase it. But these fragments provide very little information about Jesus.

The earliest copy of any part of Mark in existence today is in $\mathfrak{P}^{45}$, a papyrus **codex**, which is dated to about 225 C.E. The earliest complete copy of Mark is in the codex Sinaiticus, written on **parchment**, which belongs to the fourth century C.E. If we give Sinaiticus the earliest possible date—

> The *codex* is a stack of sheets the same size bound or tied on one side. It replaced the scroll in the first century C.E.

around 325 C.E.—it comes 295 years after the death of Jesus and 255 years after Mark was composed. If we were to compare this distance with comparable events in American history, it would be as though the Declaration of Independence were not written down until about 1815 and

> *Parchment* is made from the skins of animals, usually sheep or goats, prepared to receive writing.

no copies of this first edition survive. The first fragmentary copy would date from 1900, and the first complete text will have been published only in the year 2000. This vast distance in a culture that was able to make only handwritten copies of documents suggests that the Greek text we have of the gospels may not represent the original entirely accurately.

The earliest surviving fragments of Matthew and Luke are usually dated to around 200 C.E., as are the earliest Greek fragments of the Gospel of Thomas. An important fragment of John also comes from the same period. To put the matter pointedly, virtually none of the surviving copies of any of the gospels was made before about 200 C.E. Then another century passed before the creation of the first complete copies of the gospels that have survived to modern times. To place the matter in its historical frame of reference, an interest in creating and preserving copies of biblical texts arose at the time Christianity emerged on the world stage as a state religion with the edict of Constantine in 313 C.E.

It sometimes comes as a surprise to students of the Bible to learn that no two copies of the Bible, or any part of the Bible, are exactly alike prior to the invention of the printing press by Johannes Gutenberg in 1454 C.E. Copies of books were made by hand, usually with one scribe dictating and other scribes making copies by ear. In the copying process, the chance for error was comparatively high and the inclination to improve the text indulged. Textual modifications of all kinds are referred to by textual critics as "corruptions." Naturally, improvements are as unwelcome as errors when the aim is to establish the original text.

Of the hundreds of thousands of variants in copies of the gospels made by hand prior to Gutenberg, only a few thousand are really significant, and of those, only a few hundred make a substantial difference in the gospel record. Even so, there are some very important discrepancies—like the longer and shorter endings attached to the Gospel of Mark—which suggest to scholars that the Greek text may have been subject to some flux during its early existence.

Summary of premises concerning surviving copies of the gospels:

PREMISE 48: *The original manuscripts of the gospels have disappeared.*

PREMISE 49: *The earliest small surviving fragments of any gospels date from about 125 C.E.*

PREMISE 50: *The earliest major surviving fragments of the gospels date from about 200 C.E.*

PREMISE 51: *The earliest complete copy of the gospels dates from about 300 C.E.*

PREMISE 52: *Prior to 1454 C.E., no two surviving copies of the same gospel are exactly alike.*

PREMISE 53: *In the copying process, copies of the gospels were both "improved" and "corrupted."*

PREMISE 54: *Scholars cannot assume that the Greek text they have in modern critical editions is exactly the same text that was penned by the evangelists.*

RESEARCH METHODS

Revolt against dogma

The modern critical study of the Bible begins with the revolt of scholarship against the theological tyranny of the churches. Scientists like Galileo and Kepler had suffered because their findings contradicted established dogmas or doctrines of the church. But the revival of learning that was part of the Renaissance was not to be denied: it would eventually culminate in the Enlightenment, towards the close of the seventeenth century, when reason displaced dogma. Thereafter the physical sciences advanced rapidly, as did the study of history, since for the first time scientists and historians did not have to reach conclusions that were compatible with the teachings of the church.

Scholars of the Bible were in the forefront of this revolution and the first remarkable shift to take place was with respect to the Bible. The Bible, it was argued, should be studied like other ancient texts, in its original languages and without regard to theological claims made by the church and its theologians. From this perspective, the books of the Bible were merely other books that had survived from antiquity, such as those ascribed to Homer, Plato, Aristotle, and Caesar. Like other books, the gospels had been written on papyrus and parchment in languages widely used for other purposes, copied by professional copyists, and preserved in secular and monastic libraries—or lost, as the case may be, through the accidents of history. The doctrine of inspiration—whatever that is alleged to mean—did not protect the gospels from textual corruption, from the loss of individual pages, or from devastation by insects and moisture.

It followed from this premise and from the axioms of the emerging sciences that Jesus, too, deserved to be studied like other persons known from history. His home was Nazareth, a town known from other sources, and he belonged to a particular time. He was a Jew and regarded everything he did as consonant with Judaism. It is often forgotten that Jesus remained a Jew. In other words, just as Luther was not the first Lutheran, and Wesley was not the first Methodist, Jesus was not the first Christian. The movement of the early creeds is towards emphasizing the divinity of Jesus at the expense of his humanity. The so-called **Apostles' Creed**, like the **Nicene Creed**, has an

> The so-called *Apostles' Creed* is alleged to have been created by the twelve apostles, each of them contributing one of the twelve articles. In its present form, the creed goes back only to the sixth century C.E., although its content may be much older.

> The *Nicene Creed* was formulated at the first Council of Nicea in 325 C.E. at the direction of the Emperor Constantine to combat theological strife in the church.

empty center: It is affirmed that Jesus was born and that he suffered and died, but nothing is prescribed for the time between birth and death. Christian orthodoxy came dangerously close to the heresy of docetism—the view that Jesus only seemed to be human, while in fact he was a god masquerading as a human being. The emergence of critical scholarship represented a movement back towards the humanity of Jesus. As a consequence, great emphasis was placed on the historical Jesus—Jesus as he might be recovered, freed, disentangled, from the mists of Christian piety.

Summary of premises concerning methods of study:

PREMISE 55: *The same methods of study should be applied to the Bible that are used in the study of other ancient texts.*

PREMISE 56: *The Bible should be studied without being bound to theological claims made by the church.*

PREMISE 57: *Copies of books of the Bible suffered from textual corruption, loss of leaves, devastation by insects and moisture.*

PREMISE 58: *Jesus should be studied like other historical persons.*

PREMISE 59: *Jesus was not a Christian; he was a Jew.*

The new historiography

The foundations of the new approach to the Bible, to the gospels, to Jesus, lay in the emerging historiography—the ground rules for determining what was historical and what not. These rules were articulated forcefully by Ernst Troeltsch, a prominent German theologian, who wrote towards the close of the nineteenth century. According to Troeltsch, historians must carry out their work on the basis of three principles: probability, analogy, and correlation.

The probability principle means that historians can never be absolutely sure of their interpretation of a given historical event; they can only arrive at a high degree of probability. Another way of saying this is: there is always something more to be learned about particular persons and events in the past. The present state of our knowledge is therefore not final.

The second principle is analogy. Historians measure the unknown by the known. They compare persons, events, things from the same or comparable contexts and periods. It was on this basis that the comparative study of religion was erected. The Mosaic law was compared with other legal systems in the ancient world, and Jesus was set alongside other sages, miracle workers, and exorcists of his time. Scholars of the Bible learned a great deal from this process. One of the things scholars of the gospels learned is that Jesus is portrayed much in the same way other so-called 'divine men' were portrayed in his day. Perhaps the most notable example is Apollonius of

Flavius Philostratus (ca. 170–245) belonged to a literary circle in Rome patronized by Julia Domna, wife of Emperor Septimius Severus. He wrote The Life of Apollonius at her suggestion.

Tyana, a contemporary of Jesus, whose story has been recorded for us by **Philostratus**. In writing his own account, Philostratus also makes use of previous records prepared by another follower of Apollonius by the name of Damis.

The third principle is that of correlation. Every event that occurs takes place within a continuum of events, so that every event is related to every other. Anything that happens within that nexus, that network of happenings, affects everything else. The principle of correlation also means that an event occurs only once. Each event is unique in that it is not repeatable in exactly the same form. Taken together, these features mean that each event is an individual event and is relative to all other events.

The principle of correlation is the basis upon which any possibility of recovering the historical Jesus rests: Jesus was a unique person in the history of the world, in the same sense that every person is unique. The desire to identify a specific profile, a single face in a Galilean crowd, is founded upon the proposition that no human being can be reduced, without remainder, to the environmental circumstances that molded him or her. At the same time, the principle of correlation prevents historians from tearing Jesus out of his first-century, Jewish, Galilean context: he was and remains irrevocably tied to that time and place. Who and what he was is linked to the customs, to the history, to the language, to the symbols and concepts, to the aspirations of that era.

These principles apply, not only to persons and events from the past being studied, but also to the investigator—the historian. The historian likewise is caught up in the flux of time and so is not the same observer from one moment to the next. Moreover, the historian, like other mortals, is subject to the perspectives of his or her own time and place. The consequence of all this is that neither the object being investigated nor the investigator can be known except on the principles of probability, analogy, and correlation.

Upon these principles rest the human sciences. While many historians are no longer entirely satisfied with either the method or the results of scientific historiography, they are committed to the method because it has been exceptionally productive. In addition, it has provided the basis for a common approach to historical questions; Christian, Jewish, and secular historians can now address historical problems on a common basis, with the expectation that they will reach comparable results.

Summary of premises concerning the new historiography:

PREMISE 60: *Historians can approach but never achieve certainty in historical judgments on the probability principle.*

PREMISE 61: *Historians measure the unknown by the known on the principle of analogy.*

PREMISE 62: *Historians assume that biblical events occur within a continuum of historical happenings but that each event or person is historically unique.*

Specialization

The new historiography began to produce ever higher degrees of specialization. The more one can learn about a period, or person, or series of events, the more likely one can reconstruct an objective picture of one or the other of those items. In order to amass the data required for a given period, specialization became necessary. Some scholars specialized in textual criticism, by means of which they hoped to recover the earliest and most reliable texts of ancient documents. Other scholars concentrated on language—grammar and lexicography—in order to create new grammars and dictionaries. Still other researchers compiled comparative materials. When archaeology emerged as a new historical science late in the nineteenth century, the Near East became the focus of many expeditions. The result was a flood of new material that ranged from the thousands of papyri recovered from the sands of Egypt to the identification and excavation of many important biblical sites. The development of pottery chronology enabled archaeologists to date the occupation of particular sites to within decades, sometimes within years, of their occupation. Archaeology led to further specialization: numismatics, the study of ancient coins; palaeography, the study of the style of handwriting, by which scholars were able to date the copying of documents very precisely; papyrology, the study of all phases of many papyrus documents and fragments found in Egypt; and many other specialities. It is common presently for a scholar to give an entire career to the mastery of one or two of these areas of specialization.

The consequence of these exhilirating developments is that scholarship has become much more collegial. The lonely scholar sitting in a drafty attic with a pile of foolscap and a quill pen before him or her has become rare. It is now essential to draw on the great research libraries of the world for pertinent information that one does not have the time or the resources to gather for oneself. And one must test one's theories and ideas in the marketplace of scholarship in order to be confident of one's ground. Information is gathered in such great quantity, now that the computer is available to everyone, and the reconstructions of historians change so rapidly, that nothing short of constant consultation with other specialists is adequate to the historical task.

Summary of premises concerning specialization:

PREMISE 63: *Modern critical scholarship is based on cooperation among specialists.*

NEW SOURCES AND MATERIALS

The excitement of historical work has been heightened in the modern period by the repeated discovery of sensational new sources and materials. Among the many that have changed our views of first-century Palestine and its environs forever are the following four.

Codex Sinaiticus

The first is the discovery, by accident, of the great Codex Sinaiticus by Count Tischendorf at the monastery of St. Catherine at the foot of Mount Sinai in the Arabian desert. Tischendorf visited the monastery in May of 1844 and stumbled on a basket of old and tattered parchment sheets which were to be burned for heat. Two similar baskets had already been burned. Would that monks were better trained in biblical studies! To his delight, Tischendorf found in the basket 129 leaves of a copy of the Greek Old Testament that he eventually dated to the fourth century. He revisited the monastery in 1853 and again in 1859, when he was shown the leaves he had left behind fifteen years earlier, plus a complete New Testament, including the Shepherd of Hermas and the letter of Barnabas. These leaves proved to belong to one codex produced by several different hands and corrected by still others. It is the earliest complete copy in existence of what eventually came to be recognized as the New Testament. It revolutionized our knowledge of the Greek text of the New Testament far beyond the few late manuscripts on which the King James version (first published in 1611) is based. The odyssey of this great find is an amazing story in itself. Codex Sinaiticus eventually wound up in the British Museum where it rests today.

Papyri from the trash dumps of Egypt

Finds like the Sinaiticus stimulated other explorations in the Near East. One of the most remarkable developments was the discovery of thousands of papyrus fragments dating from the Greco-Roman period (roughly 300 B.C.E. to 300 C.E.). These discarded scraps came from dumps at several important sites, the most important of which was Oxyrhynchus, an important Roman city 120 miles south of Cairo. The papyri were retrieved from the dry sands and brought back, for the most part, to museums and libraries in Europe and North America over several decades. Their study requires intense specialization. Among these illuminating texts are bills of sale, bills of lading, legal documents consummating marriages and divorces, scores of letters, invitations to dinner, tax lists, and sundry other written documents. Of course, there also appeared fragments of classical texts—scraps of Homer are common—and Christian documents. Papyri are given an inventory number related to the site in which they were found. Thus, Papyrus Oxyrhynchus 1, 654, 655 are inventory numbers of scraps found at that site during excavations that began in 1883. As it turns out, these important little scraps are fragments of three different manuscripts of the Greek version of the Gospel of Thomas. They can be dated to about 200 C.E., which makes them among the earliest fragments of any gospel we possess. These fragments were not identified until the discovery of the Coptic text of Thomas near Nag Hammadi a half century later.

A second group of fragments, now known as the Egerton Gospel, also came from Egypt, possibly Oxyrhynchus, but were named for the British Museum fund which purchased them. More recently, another scrap from the same papyrus codex was discovered among unidentified papyri at Cologne, Germany. Papyrus Egerton 2 is the designation of the first group, and Papyrus Köln 255 is the inventory number given to the second. Together they form a piece of an unknown gospel, termed the Egerton Gospel.

The interesting thing about the Egerton Gospel is that the fragments can be dated to the second century, possibly as early as 125 C.E., which would make them as early as the tiny fragment of the Gospel of John, known as $\mathfrak{P}^{52}$, which can also be dated to the early second century.

Yet the most important aspect of the papyrus finds is not the discovery of a few fragments of Christian texts, but the enormous amount of detail scholars have learned about everyday life and commerce in the period contemporary with Jesus. It is difficult to exaggerate the amount of data these papyri have furnished the serious student of history in the Mediterranean basin for the six hundred years from the death of Alexander to the edict of Constantine in 313 C.E.

Dead Sea Scrolls

"The greatest manuscript discovery in modern times" is the way **W. F. Albright** characterized the appearance of the Dead Sea Scrolls. They have in

> *W. F. Albright* was for many years preeminent among Old Testament scholars in the world.

fact provided an enormous amount of information about the history of the text of the Old Testament, about the diversity of Palestinian Judaism between the Maccabean revolt in 167 B.C.E. and the fall of Jerusalem in 70 C.E., and they have thrown considerable light on the background of the New Testament, although nothing specifically Christian has been found at Qumran.

The Dead Sea Scrolls began to appear in 1947. The first finds were in caves along the walls of the Wadi Qumran, just above the Qumran monastic community located on the shores of the Dead Sea. There are eleven caves altogether. It would take hundreds of entries just to list the scrolls and fragments that have been identified. In addition, there are thousands of fragments from Cave 4 that have yet to be published. The texts discovered at Qumran can be dated approximately to the period beginning in the third century B.C.E. and ending in 70 C.E.—the period especially helpful for the study of John the Baptist and Christian origins.

Prior to the appearance of the scrolls, the oldest text extant of any part of the Hebrew Bible was from 895 C.E. With the discovery of the Isaiah scroll from cave one, the date jumped back almost 1,000 years: the Isaiah scroll was written about 100 B.C.E.

The Jewish sect that occupied Qumran has been identified as a branch of the Essenes, also described by **Josephus.** The scrolls found in the caves constituted their library, probably hidden away when the community was threatened by the Tenth Roman Legion in 68 c.e. Included among the

Josephus was a writer and historian, a near contemporary of Jesus (born 37/ 38, died after 100 c.e.).

documents is a *Manual of Discipline,* which amounts to a rule book governing the life of the sect. A *War Scroll* describes the conflict between the heavenly forces and those of evil. A collection of hymns was among the documents and several commentaries or fragments of commentaries on biblical texts. The Scrolls have thrown light on how early Christians made use of Old Testament texts, on titles and expressions employed by Christian writers, and on the origins of Christian monasticism.

Nag Hammadi library

Just prior to the first appearance of the Dead Sea Scrolls, a farmer found another library buried near Nag Hammadi, a town in upper Egypt. The town has given the library its name. The library consists of thirteen papyrus codices containing more than fifty tractates or treatises. The Nag Hammadi texts did not become known immediately, even though they were found earlier than the Scrolls. In the years following, however, the Nag Hammadi documents were rapidly published, while the publication of the Scrolls is not complete more than forty years after their discovery.

The Nag Hammadi texts represent a library put together by an unknown group. Some texts give evidence of a non-Christian **gnosticism** in the first two centuries of the common era. Other documents supply valuable information about a Christianized gnosticism. Among the books are secular treatises, such as *The Sentences of Sextus* and a short piece from Plato's *Republic.* Of special interest to gospel specialists are the three sayings gospels: *Gospel of Thomas, Apocryphon of John,* and *Dialogue of the Savior.* The Gospel of Thomas especially has been significant in helping scholars chart the history of the Jesus tradition.

The Nag Hammadi texts are written in Coptic, the late form of Egyptian written in Greek capitals, but they are undoubtedly translations of older Greek texts. The Coptic copies themselves were made in the fourth century. Some of the texts are much older, some perhaps going back to the first century, such as the earliest layer of Thomas.

Just as the Dead Sea Scrolls reveal much about the history of Judaism in the period 200 b.c.e.–70 c.e., so the Nag Hammadi library tells us a great deal about the development of Christianity in Egypt in the first three centuries c.e.

These new sources and materials, along with many other discoveries too numerous to mention, have altered our perceptions of the rise of Christianity in untold ways.

Summary of premises concerning new sources and materials:

PREMISE 64: *The study of the Bible in the twentieth century has been trans-formed by the discovery of new sources and materials.*

The premises that underlie the critical study of the gospels should enable the uninformed student to read the gospels with new eyes. A 20/20 reading of the gospels will make it possible to see what is actually there—more, much more, than was supposed. At the same time, an informed reading will dispel the pious fog that can obscure the historical truth.

HOW MARK
Got Its Name

The title "according to Mark" appears for the first time in copies of Greek Mark in the fourth century. In earlier times, copies of the gospels apparently had no titles. Of course, manuscripts of the gospels that can be dated prior to 300 C.E. are relatively rare, so the data we have may not be representative.

THE NAME MARK

Eusebius of Caesarea (260–339 C.E.), friend and advisor to Emperor Constantine and prominent participant in the Council of Nicea (325 C.E.), quotes Bishop Papias of Hierapolis in Asia Minor (135–40 C.E.), who, in turn, quotes an elder or presbyter by the name of John: This John used to say that Mark, the interpreter of Peter, was the author of the second gospel. The works of Papias have been lost, except as they are quoted by Eusebius; the reports of John the elder were oral.

This same elder also said that Mark had not been an auditor or follower of Jesus. And Papias makes it clear that he himself had not been a student or observer of the apostles, but received his knowledge of the Christian faith 'from those who had known the apostles.'

The trail of reports from which we get the name Mark is thus three times removed from the original source: Eusebius, Papias, John the elder, the apostles.

JOHN MARK

The tradition of the name Mark does not itself settle the question of the identification of the author. After all, Mark was an exceedingly common name.

The Mark of the tradition is customarily identified with John Mark, a companion of Paul (Acts 12:12, 25, 13:5, 15:36–41, Phlm 24, Col 4:10, 2 Tim 4:11) and a cousin of Barnabas (Col 4:10). This Mark may also have been an associate of Peter (1 Pet 5:13).

Paul and Mark are linked to Rome in 2 Timothy, which, however, is almost certainly a later letter attributed to Paul.

Mark and Peter are linked to Rome in 1 Peter, which is also almost certainly written by someone other than Peter. In addition, the link with Rome is cryptic: "She [the church?] who is in Babylon [Rome?] sends you greetings."

In a fragmentary letter of Clement of Alexandria (about 150–215 C.E.), it is said that Mark wrote his gospel during the time Peter was in Rome, and then later revised and expanded it in Alexandria, using his own and Peter's notes. This letter was discovered only in 1958.

In his *Ecclesiastical History* (6.14.5–7), Eusebius of Caesarea (died 339 C.E.) also quotes Clement to the effect that Mark had followed Peter for a long time and so, during their time together in Rome, Mark made a record of what Peter had said. This record is known as the Gospel of Mark.

THE AUTHOR OF THE GOSPEL

The second gospel itself does not provide any specific information about its author. The gospel was probably written, however, around 70 C.E. and was addressed to gentile Christians, as his explanations of Aramaic terms and Jewish customs demonstrate. The author makes mistakes about Palestinian geography. He develops a sharp polemic against unbelieving Jews, which suggests that Judaism and Christianity are in the process of separating. Mark portrays Peter as someone who does not understand Jesus. Further, Peter was the brunt of heavy criticism in circles in which Mark was popular (Mark 14:27–31, 54, 66–72). These and other features of Mark make it unlikely that Mark directly reflects Peter's perspective on Jesus. Indeed, they make it unlikely that the gospel was composed by a companion of Peter; it certainly was not composed by a companion of Paul, since the gospel reflects nothing of the Pauline view of the Christian message.

The legend that connects the name Mark with the second gospel, and the identification of that Mark with the John Mark of the New Testament, are both so tenuous that it is better to conclude that the second gospel was written by an anonymous author. As is often the case, legend and speculation have filled in what history left blank.

RULES OF EVIDENCE

Fellows of the Jesus Seminar employ rules of evidence in determining what Jesus actually said. The rules formulated in the following essay were gleaned from the essays and debate of the Seminar over a six-year period. As a result, they are not hypothetical rules; they represent actual practice.

Rules of evidence are standards by which evidence is evaluated. A standard is a criterion—a measure or test of the reliability of certain kinds of information. More than two centuries of critical biblical scholarship have produced a significant array of rules or criteria for judging the reliability of the evidence offered by the gospels, which are, after all, reports of what Jesus did and said.

HEARSAY EVIDENCE

The evidence provided by the written gospels is hearsay evidence. In a court of law, hearsay evidence is the narration by one person of evidence given him or her by another. Hearsay evidence is sometimes barred in legal proceedings because the source of the information is not available for cross-examination. In the case of the gospels, all we have is hearsay evidence: the author of the Gospel of Mark is reporting something Jesus said (or did) as it was related to him by a third party; the author of Mark was not an ear or eyewitness of the words and events he records. The reports Mark records came to him by word of mouth: his sources are anonymous. Indeed, Mark may be recording evidence that has passed through several persons, who of course are not permitted to speak for themselves and who are not available for further interrogation.

Because the evidence afforded by the gospels is hearsay evidence, scholars must be extremely cautious in taking the data at face value.

KINDS OF EVIDENCE

Scholars have divided the kinds of evidence into several broad categories with correlative rules.

The wit and wisdom of Jesus (J)	Rules of attestation (A)
Rules of oral evidence (O)	Rules of narration (N)
Rules of written evidence (W)	General rules of evidence (G)

29

The first category consists of characteristic features of Jesus' discourse. These features are derived from sayings and parables that have been isolated from other elements in the tradition with the help of other, more general rules of evidence. Into the second category are collected rules governing the transmission of oral tradition. Rules in the third category are derived from the nature of the written gospels. Rules of attestation concern the number and value of the sources of data. Rules of narration cover the difference between narrative fiction and narrative history. And general rules of evidence represent a compendium of axioms useful in evaluating historical data of all types.

In the following sketch, we have presented the rules of evidence in the six categories listed above. Each rule is preceded by an identifying letter: J stands for Jesus; O for oral evidence; W for written evidence; A for rules of attestation; N for the rules that apply to narration; and G stands for general rules of evidence. The rules are numbered consecutively within each category (J1, J2, J3, etc.). This reference system will be utilized in the *Notes* in Red Letter Mark; it will also enable the reader to locate the discussion of each rule in this sketch.

THE WIT AND WISDOM OF JESUS

Whatever else Jesus was, he was a sage, a teacher in the Jewish and oriental wisdom tradition. The evidence of the gospels puts that much beyond dispute. At the same time, his voice has been muffled to a greater or lesser extent by those who revered him: the first Christians have gathered and edited all sorts of lore which they have then attributed to his name.

The first eight criteria have been gleaned from decades of close scholarly analysis in the attempt to distinguish the voice of Jesus from other voices in the gospels.

The oral test

J1. *Jesus said things that were short, provocative, memorable.*

Unless sayings or parables were brief, condensed, striking, they would not have survived the twenty- or thirty-year period of oral transmission that separates the public activity of Jesus (death: about 30 c.e.) from the earliest written texts (about 50–60 c.e.).

The form test

J2. *Jesus' best remembered forms of speech were aphorisms and parables.*

No other forms are characteristic of Jesus; no other forms are likely to have survived the oral period. If items do not meet either of these first two rules—

what may be called the *oral* test and what may be called the *form* test—they are not likely to go back to Jesus.

Mark 10:25 preserves a saying that satisfies perfectly these two criteria for the saying or aphorism:

> It is easier for a camel to squeeze through a needle's eye, than for a wealthy person to get into God's domain.

A good example of a short, tightly conceived, memorable parable is found in Mark 4:30–32:

> To what should we compare God's imperial rule, or what parable should we use for it?
> Consider the mustard seed: When it is sown on the ground, though it is the smallest of all the seeds on the earth,—yet when it is sown, it comes up, and becomes the biggest of all garden plants, and produces branches, so that the birds of the sky can nest in its shade.

Jesus' response to a question, his reaction to a challenge or criticism, or his comment on a situation may also have survived in oral lore. That response, reaction, or comment would of course have taken the form of either an aphorism or parable and so would meet the test of the first two criteria.

These first two rules of evidence are not arbitrary. If we examine the surviving gospel records closely—including the Gospel of Thomas and the hypothetical document Q—it is readily observed that Jesus speaks regularly in adages or aphorisms, or in parables, or in witticisms formulated as rebuff or retort in the context of dialogue or debate. It is clear that he did not speak in long monologues of the type found in the Gospel of John. The aphorism and the parable have been established as the speech forms most characteristic of Jesus.

Distinctive talk

J3. *Jesus' talk was distinctive.*

The proverb, it is said, reflects collective wisdom, ancestral authority. The aphorism, on the other hand, embodies personal insight, individual authority. "The early bird catches the worm" is a piece of proverbial lore. Jesus' pronouncement, "The sabbath day was created for Adam, not Adam for the sabbath day," is a statement of direct insight into the order of creation. It is not something that one could put on a bumper sticker, or include in a collection of mom's favorite sayings, or even find in the book of Psalms.

Since Jesus was an aphorist, we might expect him to have found his own voice, to have achieved a certain level of distinctive talk. His formulations would have struck his auditors as singular, as odd, perhaps even as strange—certainly unlike street talk, and probably unlike much other wise and learned talk they may have heard on rare occasions. His listeners would have known that he was not quoting from the Psalms or from the book of Proverbs, or from the wisdom of Jesus ben Sira. Had Socrates been familiar to Jesus' contemporaries, they would have instantly recognized "Know yourself" as a Socratic adage and not a saying of Jesus. On the other hand, Jesus may have sounded like one of the Cynic sages who wandered through Galilee from time to time peddling bits of learned lore. But even in that case, Jesus probably struck his followers as different.

Against the grain

J4. *Jesus' sayings and parables cut against the social and religious grain.*

If Jesus said that those who do not hate mother and father, and brother and sister, cannot be his disciples (Luke 14:26), we have something with a powerful social or religious edge. To have an edge means to cut against the common social or religious grain. If he enjoined his disciples to let the dead bury their own dead (Matt 8:21–22), he was challenging the rules for basic religious and moral behavior. If he congratulated the poor on their poverty (Luke 6:20), he was not saying the ordinary thing. Sayings with an edge are more likely to go back to Jesus: As the Christian movement matured it would have tended to soften such radical injunctions in order to align them with the mainstream of social life (cf. O4) and thus open the new movement to a wider participation. The term for this process is domesticating the tradition.

Reversal and frustration

J5. *Jesus' sayings and parables surprise and shock: they characteristically call for a reversal of roles or frustrate ordinary, everyday expectations.*

This criterion is based on several of the great narrative parables, such as the Good Samaritan (Luke 10:30–35), the Laborers in the Vineyard (Matt 20:1–15), and the Prodigal Son (Luke 15:11–32), as well as on aphorisms like the beatitudes (Luke 6:20–23) or the injunction to lend to those from whom one can expect no return (Thom 95), neither principal nor capital.

The man in the ditch does not expect the Samaritan to come to his aid. The younger son who has squandered his inheritance on frivolous things does not expect to be welcomed home. Those who were hired at the end of the day cannot expect to receive the full day's wage. Yet in all three cases, their expectations were reversed. At the same time, those who were hired early in the day complained because their hope of greater reward was frustrated. The older son griped because he had not squandered his father's estate and yet had never been given a dinner party. And the priests and the Levites in Jesus' audience are incensed because the legal basis of their excuse for not stopping to aid the victim in the ditch is brushed aside.

This substantive criterion has turned out to be exceptionally durable in the quest for authentic sayings of Jesus.

Extravagance, humor, and paradox

J6. *Jesus' sayings and parables are often characterized by exaggeration, humor, and paradox.*

There is extravagance, exaggeration, humor in the parable in which a servant was forgiven a debt of $10,000,000 by his king, but sent a fellow servant to prison because he could not come up with an obligation of $10 (Matt 18:23–35). It is comical to imagine people with logs sticking out of their eyes trying to pick specks out of the eyes of their brothers (Matt 7:3–5).

The first beatitude (Luke 6:20) is a paradox: "Congratulations you poor! God's domain belongs to you" is an apparent contradiction in terms. "Love your enemies" (Matt 5:44) is another paradox: enemies that are loved are no longer enemies.

Vivid images, unspecified application

J7. *Jesus' images are concrete and vivid, his sayings and parables customarily metaphorical and without explicit application.*

Jesus' figures of speeches are drawn from the ordinary, everyday world: a master calling his steward to account, a dinner party, a harvest of grapes, a buried treasure. Yet these images may represent only what folk take to be typical: younger sons are prodigal, village idlers never seek work, the rich are completely indifferent to the needs of others. Listeners nod their heads in naive agreement.

The figures as Jesus presents them, however, arrest the hearer by their vividness and strangeness. The leaven is surprisingly employed as a figure for the holy (leaven is normally considered evil), everyone refuses the dinner invitation, the mustard plant pokes fun at the mighty cedar of Lebanon, the symbol of great secular power. The listener is struck by the surprising twist in the story, the odd image, the inverted symbol.

Jesus' auditors undoubtedly clamored for explanations, for conclusions, for explicit instructions. In return, Jesus gave them more questions, more parables with unclear references, more responses that waffle: "Pay the emperor whatever belongs to the emperor, and pay God whatever belongs to God" (Mark 12:17).

The serene, self-effacing sage

J8.　A. *Jesus does not as a rule initiate dialogue or debate, nor does he offer to cure people.*

B. *Jesus rarely makes pronouncements or speaks about himself in the first person.*

The sage is laconic, slow to speech, a person of few words. The sage does not precipitate encounters. In addition, the miracle worker does not hang out a shingle or advertise services. As a rule, the sage is self-effacing, modest, unostentatious.

It is a commonplace in the comparative study of miracle stories that the prophet or holy man does not initiate cures or exorcisms. This is characteristic of both the Old Testament prophets and Jesus. Those who need help either petition in person or have someone petition for them. The holy man is often reluctant to give help even when asked (an example is the story of the Greek woman's daughter, Mark 7:24–30).

In a comparable way, Jesus apparently does not initiate debates or controversies. He is passive until a question is put to him, or until he or his disciples are criticized. Stories in which Jesus initiates the argument are thought to be creations of the storyteller.

In a similar vein, the evangelists occasionally turn you-statements into I-statements.

In Matt 10:27 we find this quatrain:

What I tell you in the dark,
　　utter in the light;
and what you hear whispered,
　　proclaim from the housetops.

The first line must originally have read "What you are told in the dark" as the second couplet suggests. The saying is taken from Q. The parallel in Luke reads:

Whatever you have uttered in darkness
　　will be heard in the light.
and what you have whispered in private
　　will be proclaimed from the housetops.

It is evident that the I-form does not belong to the original form of this saying. Yet the tendency to add the authority of Jesus' voice will occasionally cause an *I* to displace a *you*.

It is difficult to imagine the sage who declared, "The last will be first, the first last" (Matt 20: 16), to be self-assertive—unless, of course, he thought nothing of what he said applied to himself.

The first eight criteria add up to something that might be termed Jesus' wit and wisdom, his mode of teaching, his style. In sorting out the swirl of lore that gathered around Jesus' name, the characteristics of Jesus as a teacher distilled from an enormous amount of research have turned out to be an extremely useful tool.

ORAL EVIDENCE

In examining the gospels, scholars are actually examining the memories of the first generation or two of Christians. The examination requires that we pose two questions: What did they remember? How did they remember? The 'what' has been the focus of the J-rules, just sketched. The 'how' is as important as the 'what' and will be the primary focus of the O-rules in this section on oral evidence. The orality of Jesus and his followers is considered in the *Introduction*, pp. 2–4.

One core, different performances

O1. *In the oral transmission of Jesus' words, his disciples remembered only the core or gist of his sayings and parables, not his precise words.*

As an aphorist and sage, Jesus spoke his aphorisms and parables on many different occasions and in many different versions. His disciples likewise repeated his aphorisms and parables on different occasions and in different versions.

A simple saying may serve as an example. The saying about ears for hearing occurs numerous times in the gospels and in a variety of contexts. It appears in several different forms, which have been translated in the Scholars Version as follows:

> Whoever has two good ears should use them.
> Whoever has good ears should use them.
> If anyone has two good ears, use them!
> If anyone has a good ear, use it!
> If anyone has an ear, use it!
> Whoever has an ear should pay attention.

It will be conceded that these sentences are six versions of the same saying. We may call the hypothetical version that underlies them all the *core* of the saying; each of the six variations would then be a *performance*.

The aphorism recorded in Matthew 20:16 provides a second example.

Thus the last will be first, and the first last.

This aphorism appears in slightly modified form elsewhere:

Luke 13:30	And look out! Last are those who will be first, and first are those who will be last.
Mark 10:31//Matt 19:30	Many of the first will be last, and of the last many will be first.
POxy654 4:2–3	For many of the first will be last and the last first, and will become one.
Thom 4:2–3	For many of the first will be last and will become a single one.

In this set there are five different performances. Yet the underlying core is evident: basic to three of the five is the reversal of the first and last. In the two Thomas versions (POxy654 is a Greek fragment of Thomas), the second line has been replaced by a new conclusion: the last will become (a single) one, which is probably a gnosticizing addition. The versions in Matt 20:16 and Luke 13:30 are closer to the original form because they express a simple reversal with no qualifications (cf. J5, O3). In Mark 10:31//Matt 19:30 the qualifer "many" has been added, which is very likely a softening touch added as the community entered the mainstream of everyday life (cf. O4). In this instance, as in many others, scholars search for the underlying core of the saying (or parable). It is only this core that can be attributed to Jesus with any confidence. We cannot be sure that any of the performances actually go back to him.

Single aphorisms and parables

O2. *The bedrock of the sayings tradition is made up of single aphorisms and parables that once circulated independently.*

Aphorisms and parables do not lend themselves to long speeches. By definition the sage is a person of few words. Accordingly, Jesus probably did not collect his sayings into extended discourses such as we find in the sermon on the mount (Matthew 5–7) or in the Gospel of John. In any case, his disciples did not remember them that way. They remembered them as single aphorisms and parables, or at most as a couplet or a brief series. The proof of this assertion lies in the fact that the same sayings and parables often appear in different contexts in the several gospels. The oral memory, in short, is not context-specific. At the earliest stage of the tradition we should expect to find single aphorisms and parables and not extended clusters or discourses.

The simpler, the earlier

O3. A. *The simpler forms of sayings and parables are more likely to be original with Jesus.*

B. *More complicated forms may mask earlier and simpler forms.*

In Matt 5:3, the first beatitude reads:

Congratulations to the poor in spirit, for Heaven's domain belongs to them.

The Lukan form of the same beatitude (Luke 6:20) is simpler and addresses the poor directly:

Congratulations you poor, for God's domain belongs to you.

Luke has probably retained the form he found in Q, while Matthew has 'spiritualized' the beatitude, and in so doing has moved it away from its original, concrete sense: the poverty stricken (cf. J4, O4). In addition, he has depersonalized it.

Hard is softened

O4. *Hard sayings are frequently softened in the process of transmission to adapt them to the conditions of daily living.*

Matthew's version of the aphorism, "The last will be first and the first last" (Matt 20:16), is softened in Mark 10:31 to "*Many* of the first will be last, and of the last *many* will be first."

Jesus advises the rich young man to sell all his goods and give the proceeds to the poor. He is understandably stunned by this advice (Mark 10:21–22). Jesus then tells his disciples that it is easier for a camel to squeeze through a needle's eye than for a rich person to get into God's domain (Mark 10:25). But the disciples and Mark find this a hard saying. So Mark appends a qualifer, probably taken from common lore: "Everything's possible for God" (Mark 10:27). So the paradox of the needle's eye is softened by God's un-limited grace. Modern interpreters have been in the softening business too: some have located a narrow caravan pass, called the needle's eye, which a camel can squeeze through with difficulty; others have imagined a tight gate in the wall of Jerusalem, through which a camel can barely pass. These are feeble and misguided attempts to take the sting out of the aphorism and rob Jesus' words of their edge (cf. J4).

Words on the lips of Jesus

O5. *Words are frequently borrowed from the fund of common lore or from the Old Testament and put on the lips of Jesus.*

The many variations reported in the aphorisms and parables of Jesus demonstrate that his disciples did not hesitate to formulate sayings and attribute them to him. They put words on Jesus' lips by giving new per-formances of the aphorisms and parables they remembered, by formulating new statements in his style and spirit, or by attributing to him proverbs and other lore they thought appropriate for the new movement. The other lore may include words, phrases, or sentences from the Greek Old Testament (LXX). It also includes secular proverbs and adages. This is the way of oral tradition: it indulges in free quotation, it invents in the name of the patron as a way of honoring him or her, and it knows nothing of plagiarism so it borrows freely from the fund of common lore.

The Greek Old Testament (LXX) played a special role in the development of the Jesus tradition. The Christian community soon began to search the scriptures for proof that Jesus was truly the messiah. The tendency of the gospel writers, especially Matthew, was to make the event fit the prophecy. In addition, the gospel writers did not hesitate to put words taken from the Old Testament on the lips of Jesus, because those words, too, were sacred words. It is for this reason that the Jesus Seminar consistently labelled words ascribed to Jesus on the cross black: they are borrowed from the Old Testament scriptures.

The proverb in Mark 2:17 is attested in secular sources (Plutarch and Diogenes Laertes, for example):

Since when do the able-bodied need a doctor? It's the sick who do.

Jesus was not the only one to say it.

In the parallel to this Markan passage, Matthew adds a sentence taken from the Old Testament (9:13):

Go and learn what this means, 'I desire mercy and not sacrifice.'

The words, borrowed from Hos 6:6, are attributed to Jesus.

WRITTEN EVIDENCE

How scholars study the written gospels is sketched in the *Introduction,* pp. 5–18. That sketch is essential background for rules pertaining to written evidence.

Clusters and complexes

W 1. *The evangelists frequently group sayings and parables in clusters and complexes that did not originate with Jesus.*

As it matures, the tradition tends to group sayings and parables into simple clusters at the oral stage and then into more extended complexes in the written stage. Clustering aphorisms and short parables makes them easier to remember, provided some kind of memory device is employed. Groups were created out of common themes, or forms, or by the use of a key word, often called a "catchword." The group of beatitudes in the great sermon is an example of clustering by form. The materials in Mark 10:17–34 were collected around the theme of wealth. Association by catchword is often subtle and not particularly logical:

Mark 9:48   where the worm never dies
             and the fire never goes out!
      9:49   As you know, everyone there is salted by fire.
      9:50   Salt is good ⟨and salty⟩
             —if it becomes bland,
             with what will you renew it?

The mention of fire in v. 48 attracts the saying in v. 49. The mention of salt in the second saying becomes a magnet for the saying about bland salt. These sayings did not originally belong together, in all probability. Matthew and Luke do not reproduce the cluster, and the third saying (Mark 9:50) appears in quite different contexts in Matthew and Luke.

Since the tradition tended to group sayings and parables as it matured, it also tended to interpret one saying by another, to append an aphorism to a parable in order to fix interpretation, or to link parables and sayings in such a way that they interpret each other. The tendency to cluster and compound often obscures the original sense of particular sayings or parables. Clustering is a way of giving a saying an invented context, although not a narrative context.

Narrative contexts

W2. *The evangelists frequently invent narrative contexts for sayings and parables.*

Another way to give a saying or parable a context is to embed it in a narrative. The most common form of this technique is the pronouncement story or chreia, which consists of a short anecdote that climaxes in a witticism. Pronouncement stories may contain historical reminiscences, but most of the settings are contrived.

The pronouncement story in Mark 2:23–28 furnishes a good example of the contrived context. In this story, the Pharisees criticize Jesus' disciples for harvesting grain on the sabbath. Criticism directed at the disciples probably betrays the later historical context in which this story is being told. The scribes, rather than the Pharisees, were Jesus' original opponents; the Pharisees probably do not play a role in Galilee until after Jesus' death (cf. W10). Moreover, the response of Jesus involves quoting the story of David and his associates from the Old Testament—another telltale sign of the community's search in the scriptures for legitimacy (cf. O5). And finally, we cannot be sure that the concluding aphoristic couplet originally went with this story: Mark's "and he continued" and Luke's "and he used to say to them" suggests that the aphorism was joined belatedly to the narrative.

The setting or context in which Jesus' responses have been preserved is less likely to have been remembered and reiterated than the response itself. The reason for this is simple: the Christian community would have applied the words of Jesus to situations relevant to its own life and thus have adapted the original setting to its own situation. That is probably the reason so many anecdotes involving responses of Jesus begin in the written gospels as criticisms directed against the disciples: at the time the gospels were being written, they, and not Jesus, were under fire. Originally, Jesus is likely to have borne the brunt of criticism (cf. W5).

In all probability, Jesus' first disciples did not remember the many occasions on which he uttered a particular saying. At all events, they did not preserve those original contexts, except perhaps in rare instances. Most of Jesus' sayings are recorded without narrative or descriptive setting. For other sayings the evangelists, or the transmitters of the oral tradition before them, invented plausible narrative settings, which in many cases are imagined typical scenes. In so doing, they were guided by vague memories, they imitated secular parallels, they drew on their own experience, and they were influenced by the requirements of their own context to which Jesus was now made to speak.

Expansion and interpretive overlay

W3. *The evangelists often expand sayings or parables, or provide them with an interpretive overlay or comment, which may take the form of allegory.*

The disciples of John the Baptist and the Pharisees and their followers were in the habit of fasting. Jesus and his followers apparently did not fast. When asked why his disciples did not fast, Jesus responded (Mark 2:19):

The groom's friends can't fast while the groom is with them, can they?

This aphorism, which may well go back to Jesus, is followed by a Christian expansion (2:20):

But the days will come when the groom is taken away from them, and then they will fast, on that day.

The addition accounts for the rise of Christian fasting, when Jesus and his disciples did not fast (cf. W9).

To the secular proverb,

Since when do the able-bodied need a doctor? It's the sick who do.

Mark, or the tradition before him, has appended:

I did not come to enlist decent folks but sinners!

The latter is a Christian interpretation of the former; it is almost certainly secondary (cf. W8).

Similarly, to the parable of the Vineyard Laborers (Matt 20:1–16) Matthew has appended an aphorism—in this case probably an aphorism of Jesus:

So the last will be first, and the first last.

Yet the aphorism does not go with the parable: the point of the parable is that all are paid the same wage, not that the last were paid first (cf. W1).

Editorial style and viewpoint

W4. *The evangelists frequently compose or revise and edit both sayings and narrative contexts to make them conform to their own individual language, style, or viewpoint, or to make saying and context conform to each other.*

Mark, or someone before him, created the collection of parables and sayings found in Mark 4:1–34. The principle ingredient around which the collection was made is the parable of the sower (4:3–8). This parable, according to the editorial frame Mark has given it, holds the secret of God's imperial rule, which Jesus must explain to his disciples in private (4:10–12). This technique—public teaching, private explanation—plays a prominent role in Mark elsewhere (7:17–22, 9:28–29, 13:3–37). Both the technique and the theme are Markan creations. Consequently, 4:11–12 was composed by Mark to suit his secrecy theory. The allegorical interpretation of the sower likewise is Markan (4:13–20): it reveals the secret to those inside. Because the parables and sayings of Jesus are hard to understand, according to Mark, the author keeps admonishing the reader to pay attention and to listen: 4:9, 12, 15, 16, 18, 23, and 24.

This is but one complex example of how the evangelists compose or revise and edit to make the material conform to their editorial themes and goals.

Brunt of criticism

W5. *A criticism of, or attack on, Jesus often becomes a criticism of, or attack on, Jesus' disciples in the later tradition.*

As tradition was passed on, the tendency was to adapt settings that might plausibly go with Jesus' public life to settings more immediately relevant to life in the young Christian community. One of the consequences of this tendency was to shift the point of attack or criticism from Jesus to his disciples. After all, it was they, not Jesus, who were presently under fire by other Jews as the two segments of Judaism began to separate.

In Mark 2:18–22, Jesus is asked why his disciples don't fast. Presumably, the question originally concerned Jesus' behavior as their leader. Yet he is no longer the point of attack. A similar shift has taken place in the argument over harvesting grain on the sabbath in Mark 2:23–28.

Difficult sayings

W6. *Variations in difficult sayings often betray the struggle of the early Christian community to interpret or adapt sayings to its own situation.*

An example of such a difficult saying is found in Mark 3:28–29 and parallels. The saying concerns the unforgivable sin. According to the tradition, a word spoken against the holy spirit is not forgivable. Matthew and Luke also permit a word spoken against the son of Adam to be forgiven; Mark is silent. The difficult question here is whether blasphemy against the son of Adam—here understood by Matthew and Luke in its messianic sense to refer to Jesus—was different from the blasphemy against the holy spirit.

Jesus as spokesman

W7. *The evangelists frequently attribute their own statements to Jesus.*

In Mark 1:15, the author summarizes what he takes to be Jesus' proclamation in his own words (for details, see the *Notes* on this verse). Matthew has Jesus announce the great commission for him: Matt 28:18–20. Luke puts his own outline of the advancement of the gospel—the one he uses as the outline of his gospel and the book of Acts—onto the lips of Jesus in Luke 24:46–49. All of these passages are composed in language typical of the respective evangelists but attributed to Jesus.

Christian language

W8. A. *Sayings and parables expressed in "Christian" language are the creation of the evangelists or the oral tradition before them.*

B. *Sayings or parables that contrast with the language or viewpoint of the gospel in which they are embedded reflect older tradition.*

The earliest version of the oral gospel preserved for us in written records is the "gospel" of Paul. In 1 Cor 15:3–5, he summarizes it in two steps:

Christ died for our sins
   according to the scriptures,

and was buried,
and rose up on the third day
according to the scriptures.

Both events take place because the scriptures said they would.

Paul's gospel was in general circulation when Mark composed his story of Jesus. In the three predictions of the passion, Mark betrays his knowledge of this oral gospel:

> 8:31 He started teaching them that the son of Adam must suffer a great deal, and be rejected by the elders and ranking priests and the scribes, and be killed, and after three days rise up.
>
> 9:31 The son of Adam will be turned over to human agents, and they will end up killing him. And three days after he is killed he will rise up!
>
> 10:33 The son of Adam will be turned over to the ranking priests and the scribes, and they will sentence him to death, and turn him over to the gentiles,
>
> 34 and they will make fun of him, and spit on him, and flog him, and kill ⟨him⟩. Yet after three days he will rise!

The formulations of Mark indicate that he knew the oral gospel quoted by Paul. Both versions are composed in "Christian" terminology.

The development of a specifically Christian way of speaking about Jesus in the decades after Jesus' death often influenced formulations in the gospels, acts, and letters, because the memories of the disciples were completely colored by the Easter faith. The testimony of non-believers and enemies left virtually no imprint on the records. As a consequence, scholars must be on the alert for biased testimony: for words attributed to Jesus that simply reflect the later Christian point of view. The inclination of the evangelists and other Christians was to make Jesus affirm what they themselves had come to believe.

The axiom bears repeating: Jesus was not the first Christian. However, he was made to talk like a Christian by his devoted followers. The contrast between Christian language or viewpoint and the language and viewpoint of Jesus is often a very important clue to the real voice of Jesus. The language of Jesus was distinctive, as was his style and viewpoint (J3, J6, J7). That distinctiveness will still be evident, if the evangelists have not effaced it and replaced it with their own language and viewpoint (W4).

Christian social practice

W9. A. *Sayings and narrative that reflect the social practice of the emerging Christian community were formulated or edited by the evangelists or the oral tradition before them.*

B. *Sayings and parables that contrast with the social context and interests of the emerging Christian community reflect older tradition.*

This rule of evidence has proved to be very useful. Since Jesus was not an institution builder but an itinerant, the circle of his disciples probably did not form a settled community during his lifetime. The early Christian movement, however, did begin to form social groups at an early date. Evidences of community formation in sayings or parables suggest to scholars that the budding church has reinterpreted the Jesus tradition to assist in determining community boundaries—deciding who is in and who is out—and in providing for rites of initiation, such as baptism. Moreover, traces of the shift from a rural to an urban setting occasionally betray intrusive elements. The contrast between earlier and later social contexts thus often provides clues to the earliest levels of the tradition.

It is also helpful to note that the memories of the first disciples, and those who followed, were highly selective: they remembered the things Jesus did and said that were relevant to them. They tended to forget things that did not apply to their changing situations. The selection of words attributed to Jesus will therefore mirror, to a greater or lesser extent, the social, economic, and religious situations of the Christian communities scattered around the eastern end of the Mediterranean in the second half of the first century.

Post-mortem events

W 10. *Sayings and narratives that reflect knowledge of events that took place after Jesus' death are the creation of the evangelists or the oral tradition before them.*

The sayings attributed to Jesus in the "little apocalypse" (Mark 13:–34) occasionally reflect events that took place after Jesus' death. The advice to the disciples to look out for themselves because they will be beaten in synagogues and hauled up before governors and kings (Mark 13:9) reflects events that took place beginning with Paul. The goal to announce the good news to the whole world (Mark 13:10) was developed by Paul, Mark, and others in the early days of the new movement. The betrayal of family members by family members (Mark 13:12–13) probably echoes the terrible events of the siege of Jerusalem, 66–70 C.E.

Whenever scholars detect detailed knowledge of post-mortem events in sayings and parables attributed to Jesus, they are inclined to the view that the formulation of such sayings has been influenced by actual events.

Defamatory statements

W 11. *Neither the evangelists nor the oral tradition before them would have invented statements that cast aspersions on Jesus' character or contradicted their own viewpoint.*

In Luke 7:33–34, Jesus is reported to have said:

³³For John the Baptist appeared on the scene, eating no bread and drinking no wine, and you say, 'He is demented.' ³⁴The son of Adam appeared on the scene both eating and drinking, and you say, 'There is a glutton and a drunk, friend of toll collectors and sinners!'

It is difficult to conceive the evangelists or earlier followers of Jesus inventing slurs on either John the Baptist or their venerated leader. To describe the saintly ascetic John the Baptist as demon-possessed would have been unthinkable. To describe Jesus as a glutton and drunkard is even more improbable. And the term 'son of Adam' used by Jesus to refer to himself in the third person cannot readily be attributed to the followers who thought 'son of Adam' referred to the heavenly figure to come on clouds at the end of time. These formulations, consequently, almost certainly derive from Jesus, who apparently did not hesitate to quote such slurs and poke fun at them (cf. J6).

RULES OF ATTESTATION

In examining the surviving gospels for evidence of the first or oral stage of the tradition, scholars are looking for hard evidence—evidence that rests on relatively objective criteria. The best evidence that can be found meets one or more of the following three very basic rules:

Independent sources

A 1. *Sayings or parables that are attested in two or more independent sources are likely to be old.*

If a saying is attested in two independent sources, scholars know that the item in question has entered the tradition at different points and has survived along different textual trajectories. The testimony of two independent sources almost guarantees that the saying or parable was present in the oral tradition. Provided they are not identical, two independent attestations, moreover, provide scholars with additional control in analyzing the development of that piece of tradition: Differences often provide clues to the development of the item.

A list of independent and derivative gospels is provided in the Introduction, p. 16.

Different contexts

A2. *Sayings or parables that are attested in two different contexts probably circulated independently at an earlier time.*

If a saying is attested in two different contexts, the item in question probably once circulated independently: it is not bound to either of the contexts in which it appears in written texts. Items that are not context-bound probably originated in the oral tradition. The contexts, on the other hand, are almost certainly secondary, and thus are not of much use in interpreting the saying.

Different forms

A3. *The same or similar content attested in two or more different forms has a life of its own and therefore may stem from old tradition.*

If the same content appears in more than one form, for example, in both an aphorism and a parable, scholars learn two things: (a) the content was deemed sufficiently important to warrant repeating; (b) the content is not bound up with a particular form. Content that transcends form signals a theme or topic deemed important to the first purveyors of the oral tradition.

Unwritten tradition

A4. *Unwritten tradition that was captured by the written gospels relatively late may preserve very old memories.*

A caveat should be issued against the three preceding rules of attestation.

The methodological skepticism of critical scholars regarding words attributed to Jesus is warranted because of what we know of the creation and transmission of oral tradition in the ancient world. Nevertheless, a word of caution is in order. The oral mode of transmitting traditions about Jesus remained lively and robust well down into the second century, so that oral tradition developed alongside of, and occasionally in competition with, the written gospels. Of course, we have no direct record of the living oral tradition, except as early theologians of the church talk about it, or as bits and pieces of unwritten lore find their way into the written tradition. These bits and pieces of stray and unwritten tradition are sometimes extremely valuable. For example, many of the great narrative parables of Jesus are not found in our earliest written sources, Mark, Q, and Thomas; they are not captured in writing until Matthew and Luke framed their gospels in the 80s of the first century C.E. Had it not been for the special material recorded by Matthew and Luke, in addition to their use of Q and Mark, we would not have known the parables of the Good Samaritan, the Laborers in the Vineyard, the Prodigal Son, and the Unmerciful Servant.

RULES OF NARRATION

In evaluating a narrative for historical detail, scholars follow a number of common sense guidelines.

Quoted words

N 1. *Only words reported as directly quoted speech are eligible to be considered words of Jesus.*

The Seminar agreed at the outset to consider only words that are reported as directly quoted speech—the kind enclosed by quotation marks in printed texts. In Greek texts, which do not have quotation marks, it is sometimes difficult to tell the difference between directly quoted speech and indirectly quoted speech. Indeed, three kinds of reported speech have to be distinguished. They are: quoted speech, indirectly quoted speech, and free indirect speech.

The instructions Jesus gives the twelve when he sends them out in pairs are given in Luke 9:3 as direct discourse:

He said to them, "Take nothing for the road: neither staff, nor bread, nor knapsack, nor money; no one is to take two tunics."

The same instructions, more or less, are recorded in Mark 6:8 but in indirect discourse:

And he instructed them not to take anything on the road, except a staff: no bread, no knapsack, no spending money, but to wear sandals and to wear no more than one tunic.

The Markan instructions are not in quotation marks because Jesus is being quoted indirectly. We could perhaps reconstruct some form of direct discourse from the indirect provided by Mark, but the direct might not agree precisely with the direct form provided by Luke (aside from differences in content). To put the matter pointedly, when dealing with indirect discourse, scholars cannot be certain of the original formulations.

We can imagine a free indirect form of the same report:

Jesus gave the disciples instructions for the road.

It is not possible, given the free indirect form, to reconstruct even approximately what Jesus actually said.

As a rule, the Jesus Seminar confined its evaluations to directly quoted speech. It did not attempt to reconstruct the direct from the indirect. One exception is the case where the indirect form in one gospel is paralleled by the direct form in another; in such instances the Fellows considered all parallel forms. A second exception was made in rare instances in which the Fellows voted on some hypothetical core saying (cf. O1).

Context-bound speech

N2. *Quoted speech that is entirely context-bound is probably the product of the storyteller.*

When Jesus is reported to have said to the leper, "Okay—you're clean!" (Mark 1:40), he was making a statement specific to the story of the cure of the leper. The pronouncement makes no sense outside that story context, and the saying could not have circulated independently (cf. O2). It is therefore context-bound.

Context-bound speech is sometimes determined, to a greater or lesser extent, by the form stories normally take. Stories about Jesus, such as healing stories or exorcisms, follow their hellenistic models, as a rule. The outline of such stories is well known: the healer's attention is called to the sufferer; the sufferer is introduced and the gravity of the malady is indicated; in full forms of the story, a dialogue follows between the healer and the patient or the patient's agent; one or more of the following elements may then conclude the account: healing word, healing technique, healing affirmation, and demonstration that the healing (or exorcism) has been effected. In following the standard form, storytellers will provide the usual elements in verbal exchanges. It is possible, of course, that Jesus said some of the ordinary things reported in such stories.

Such stories are the product of the Christian troubadour, who is casting Jesus in a role well known among secular raconteurs. Scenes of this type are both fictional and typical: they are fictional in the sense that the narrator has formed them on the established pattern, and they are typical in that they represent how the hellenistic healer behaved. The words attributed to Jesus in such stories are context-bound, for the most part: the words, "Shut up and get out of him!" (Mark 1:25) are pointless outside the exorcism in which they appear; they belong to the story as an integral part of it. They can only be evaluated as part of the story to which they belong.

Absence of auditors

N3. *Statements made by Jesus when a second party was not present are not historically verifiable.*

Words attributed to Jesus during his lonely vigil in the wilderness must be the product of the early Christian imagination, since no one was present to overhear his private conversations. Similarly, the prayers he is reported to have uttered in the garden on the night of his arrest were not overheard by another human being, according to the narrative itself. Words attributed to Jesus in the absence of an auditor are assumed to be the fiction of the storyteller and cannot be used to determine what Jesus said.

The post-historical Jesus

N4. *Statements attributed to the risen Jesus are not admissible as evidence for the historical Jesus.*

Statements ascribed to the *risen* Jesus, by definition, are not attributable to the *historical* Jesus. Statements made to Paul in his vision on the Damascus road, or statements made to the author of the Book of Revelation in his dream-vision, are accordingly omitted. In addition, if the Jesus Seminar were to admit such statements, the inventory of possible Jesus sayings would grow interminably. A Los Angeles visionary, for example, recently submitted to the Jesus Seminar for evaluation a list of 800 sayings allegedly spoken by Jesus in a dream.

GENERAL RULES OF EVIDENCE

In addition to rules of evidence related directly to the written and oral stages of the gospel tradition, gospel specialists have adopted several general rules that are applied to every saying and parable.

Base of evidence

G1. A. *The convergence of two or more rules on a single piece of evidence greatly strengthens the case for or against that piece of evidence.*

B. *A major conclusion cannot rest on a single piece of evidence.*

Since the Jesus Seminar is searching for clues to the historical Jesus in a haystack of reports, claims, and admonitions, it will be cautious of any conclusion that does not rest on a broad base of evidence.

The plausibility test

G2. *A plausible reading or interpretation for a historical context in Jesus' public life is required for sayings and parables that are to be correctly attributed to Jesus.*

In the proceedings of the Jesus Seminar, when Fellows tackle especially difficult sayings and parables, they ask themselves whether someone can provide a plausible interpretation of a saying that fits the historical circumstance of Jesus' life. For example, the saying attributed to Jesus in Luke 10:18:

I watched Satan fall like lightning from the sky.

is problematic. What can this statement mean? There are at least two possibilities. One is to read it as the content of a vision in which Jesus sees Satan cast out of heaven in accordance with the old myth (recounted in Revelation

12). In this case, Jesus is presumably speaking from the standpoint of his position at the Father's right hand prior to creation when rebellious angels were expelled from heaven (note the allusions to this standpoint in John 1:1–18). A second way to read the text is to take it as a reference to the exorcism of demons or evil spirits at the hands of his disciples. This is the context in which Luke places the saying.

The Fellows of the Seminar were able to give this saying a pink designation on the basis of the plausibility of the second reading. Had they decided on the first reading, they would most certainly have voted black.

The more difficult reading

> **G3.** A. *The saying or parable which is the more difficult—which least suits the tendencies of the unfolding tradition—is likely to be the earlier.*
>
> B. *The saying or parable that best accounts for any confusion or variation that arose in the development of the tradition is probably the more original.*

The next battery of tests borrows two rules from the practices of textual criticism. In determining the more original reading of the Greek text of the New Testament, textual critics adopt (a) that reading (or variant) which is the more difficult, or (b) that reading which best explains the rise of all other variants.

The principle in the case of the first is this: the tendency of the scribes who copied the texts was to smooth, explain, clarify. The more difficult reading is therefore likely to be the earlier one. In the case of the second, the principle is: that reading is more original that best explains how the confusion or variation arose. Variations arise for some reason. When they do, the reading that best explains how they arose and thus accounts for them is likely to be more original.

Scholars who probe the gospels for the more original reading of words ascribed to Jesus are inclined to look for sayings that are more difficult or which best explain variations or contradictions in the tradition.

Canonical and extracanonical

> **G4.** *Canonical boundaries are irrelevant in critical assessments of the various sources of information about Jesus.*

Critical scholars are not inclined to give special weight to the canonical gospels—the gospels eventually included in the New Testament. Since two extracanonical gospels, Q and Thomas, are our earliest independent sources, scholars accord them the preeminent place they deserve by virtue of their independence and their age. For the critical scholar, inclusion in the canon does not guarantee historical accuracy. Every gospel is considered in its own right and on its own merits as a source for information about Jesus. This principle is widely accepted by scholars and indicates why the Scholars Version of the gospels includes both intracanonical and extracanonical works.

Coherence

G5. *The emerging body of primary data (items voted red or pink) should be reasonably coherent.*

The pre-eminent danger is that the sayings and parables identified as reflecting the voice of Jesus will be *too* coherent. If so, the proof that led to them will probably be circular: we got only what we were looking for. On the other hand, the data cannot be grossly contradictory: the test of coherence is a test of method. If the method produces "garbage," the method is flawed.

Loose ends

G6. *Beware of the profile of Jesus that accounts for all the data.*

In concert with the previous rule, the Fellows must ask whether they have stray data—sayings, parables—that do not fit the pattern, the profile, the emerging image. What does not fit? If everything fits, historians should beware. History has a way of eluding those who attempt to reduce persons and events to clean categories and exhaustive theories.

A lovable Jesus

G7. *Beware of a congenial Jesus.*

In retrospect, scholars will want to ask: Did I get a Jesus I like, one who is congenial to me? If so, I was probably not looking very circumspectly. The business of critical scholars of the gospels is not to find a pleasant, or useful, or compatible Jesus; their business is to find a Jesus that is historically plausible in the context of first-century Galilee. That Jesus, in all probability, will undermine the picture we currently hold. He will be a Jesus with whom we may not be entirely comfortable. A Jesus we may not wish to acknowledge may turn out to be the historical Jesus, the real Jesus.

In the quest for a specific Jesus, scholars must be on guard against their own theological biases. The inclination to demonstrate that Jesus is unique is easily confused with a high christology, in which the divinity of Jesus is the underlying motivation. The opposite tendency, to fit Jesus fully into his time and place, particularly in relation to Judaism, represents a drift to the other end of the Chalcedonian definition, that Jesus was fully human. This inclination may be motivated by a rejection of the fundamentalist position (Jesus is naively identified with God), or by guilt arising out of the holocaust (Jesus was simply a Jew).

Some critics of the Jesus Seminar have alleged that the Seminar has discovered a non-apocalyptic Jesus because an apocalyptic Jesus, who thought the world was to come to an end in his own time, is an embarrassment to modern scholars. It is of course the case that the fundamentalist Jesus is thoroughly apocalyptic and that scholars are embarrassed by the fundamentalist conception of the Bible. But Fellows of the Jesus Seminar have discovered a non-apocalyptic Jesus for quite a different reason: it is the best explanation of the two contrary positions found in the gospel texts: on the one hand, God's imperial rule was expected to arrive in the near future, ushered in by the son of Adam who would arrive on clouds; on the other, God's reign was already present in the words and deeds of Jesus: "But if it is by the finger of God that I drive out demons, then for you God's imperial rule has arrived" (Luke 11:20). Of the two, the first is more likely to be the popular, everyday expectation to which the Christian community immediately reverted once Jesus' unusual notion died away with his words. Jesus' view that God's rule was arriving without being noticed was too subtle for the average believer to retain.

Scholars, like everyone else, have to hold their christological anxieties, their guilt, their apologetic interests, and their own critical proclivities at bay when attempting to locate Jesus among the welter of attributions and characterizations found in the surviving gospel texts. It is not a task for the light-hearted or the faint of heart; it is a rigorous discipline to be undertaken only by the stout of heart.

ORIGINAL SAYINGS
in
The Gospel of Mark

There are one hundred eleven sayings put on the lips of Jesus in the Gospel of Mark, not counting words attributed to Jesus that cannot be divorced from their narrative contexts. Of the 111 items considered by the Jesus Seminar, only seventeen (17) of them were designated red or pink by weighted average. That's about 15% of the total—perhaps a little less than we anticipated when the Seminar began.

If we add three more sayings on which members of the Seminar were evenly divided—the weighted average is precisely .50—that brings the total to 20 and the percentage of the total to almost 18%. Since a weighted average of .50 can be counted either way, to include those three additional items in the data base will not compromise the integrity of the Seminar.

The result may strike the reader unacquainted with critical biblical scholarship as insignificant. But, in fact, it is a very substantial result. Never before has a group of scholars gathered around a table, analyzed and debated the gospel texts in detail, and then come to a collegial decision item by item. Our differences on many matters great and small pale into insignificance in comparison with the firm results achieved—not just on items to be included in the data base for determining who Jesus is, but also on a body of those *not* to be utilized in forming a profile of the historical Jesus.

If we assign gray items to a special category—gray means that the item in question contains ideas that may go back to Jesus—there are about sixty sayings that fall into the black spectrum. The Jesus Seminar has thus agreed that a little more than half of the sayings attributed to Jesus in Mark do *not* represent him.

One saying in five in the Gospel of Mark can therefore be used in giving that particular face in a Galilean crowd a definite profile. About three sayings in five should not be so employed.

In the list to follow, we have provided the name of the saying or parable, its location in Mark, its color designation, its weighted average, the percentage of red, pink, gray, and black votes, and the independent sources in which that item is attested.

K stands for Mark (we have adopted the last letter of the name since M is taken by Matthew). The percentages of votes in each category do not always add up to a hundred because we have rounded to the nearest whole number. The translation given is the Scholars Version.

RED AND PINK SAYINGS
By Weighted Average

1. God & the emperor   Mk 12:17   K, T, EgerG   R P G B Av.
Pay to the emperor whatever belongs to the emperor,   50 45 5 0 .82 **R**
and to God whatever belongs to God!

2. Mustard seed   Mk 4:30–32   K, Q, T   R P G B Av.
To what should we compare God's imperial rule, or   43 36 21 0 .74 **P**
what parable should we use for it? Consider the mustard
seed: When it is sown on the ground, though it is the
smallest of all the seeds on the earth,—yet when it is
sown, it comes up, and becomes the biggest of all garden
plants, and produces branches, so that the birds of the
sky can nest in its shade.

3. What comes out   Mk 7:14–15   K, T   R P G B Av.
Listen to me, all of you, and try to understand! It's not   39 39 14 7 .70 **P**
what goes into a person from the outside that can defile;
rather it's what comes out of the person that defiles.

4. Eye of the needle   Mk 10:25   K, GNaz   R P G B Av.
It's easier for a camel to squeeze through a needle's eye,   28 40 28 4 .64 **P**
than for a wealthy person to get into God's domain!

5. Placing the lamp   Mk 4:21   K, Q, T   R P G B Av.
Since when is a lamp brought in to be put under the   27 47 17 10 .63 **P**
bushel basket or under the bed? It's put on the lamp-
stand, isn't it?

6. Honors & salutations   Mk 12:38–39   K, Q   R P G B Av.
Look out for the scribes who like to parade around in   25 42 25 8 .61 **P**
long robes, and insist on being addressed properly in the
marketplaces, and prefer important seats in the synagogues and the best couches at banquets.

7. Powerful man   Mk 3:27   K, Q   R P G B Av.
No one can enter a powerful man's house to steal his   24 45 14 17 .59 **P**
belongings unless he first ties him up. Only then does he
loot his house.

8. Prophet's hometown   Mk 6:4   K, T, J   R P G B Av.
No prophet goes without respect, except in his home-   21 38 38 4 .58 **P**
town and among his relatives and at home!

9. Bland salt   Mk 9:50a   K, Q   R P G B Av.
Salt is good ⟨and salty⟩—if salt becomes bland, with   33 33 8 25 .58 **P**
what will you renew it?

10. Groom's friends   Mk 2:19   K, T, (J)

The groom's friends can't fast while the groom is with them, can they? So long as the groom is around, you can't expect them to fast.

R	P	G	B	Av.	
31	19	38	13	.56	P

11. Lord of Sabbath   Mk 2:27–28   K

The sabbath day was created for Adam, not Adam for the sabbath day. So, the son of Adam lords it even over the sabbath day.

R	P	G	B	Av.	
15	50	21	15	.55	P

12. Hard for rich   Mk 10:23   K, GNaz

How difficult it is for those who have money to enter God's domain!

R	P	G	B	Av.	
16	40	36	8	.55	P

13. Sower   Mk 4:3–8   K, T

Listen to this! Here is a sower who went out to sow. While he was sowing, some seed fell along the path, and the birds came and ate it up. Other seed fell on rocky ground where there wasn't much soil, and it came up right away because the soil had no depth. But when the sun came up it was scorched, and because it had no root it withered. Still other seed fell among thorns, and the thorns came up and choked it, so that it produced no fruit. Finally, some seed fell on good earth and started producing fruit. The seed sprouted and grew: one part had a yield of thirty, another part sixty, and a third part one hundred.

R	P	G	B	Av.	
28	38	3	31	.54	P

14. Let the children   Mk 10:14   K, T

Let the children come up to me, don't try to stop them. After all, God's domain is peopled with such as these.

R	P	G	B	Av.	
16	36	36	12	.52	P

15. Able bodied & sick   Mk 2:17a   K

Since when do the able-bodied need a doctor? It's the sick who do.

R	P	G	B	Av.	
7	60	13	20	.51	P

16. Have & receive   Mk 4:25   K, Q, T

In fact, to those who have, more will be given, and from those who don't have, even what they do have will be taken away!

R	P	G	B	Av.	
0	61	30	9	.51	P

17. Wineskins   Mk 2:22   K, T

Nobody pours young wine into old wineskins, otherwise the wine will burst the skins, and destroy both the wine and the skins. Instead, young wine is for new wineskins.

R	P	G	B	Av.	
9	50	27	14	.51	P

18. First & last   Mk 10:31   K, T

Many of the first will be last, and of the last many will be first.

R	P	G	B	Av.	
33	17	17	33	.50	G

19. Forgiveness   Mk 11:25   K, Q, 1 Clem, Pol   R P G B Av.
And when you stand up to pray, if you are holding   14 36 36 14 .50 **G**
anything against anyone, forgive them, so your father in
heaven may forgive your misdeeds.

20. No stone   Mk 13:2   K   R P G B Av.
Take a good look at these monumental buildings! You   31 23 12 35 .50 **G**
may be sure one stone won't remain on another! They
will all certainly be knocked down!

THE GOSPEL
OF
MARK

𝔓88, one of the oldest fragments of the Gospel of Mark, contains
Mark 2:2–26 and dates to the fourth century C.E. It came to light only
recently in the library of the Catholic University, Milan, Italy. Where
and when it was first discovered are unknown. Shown above are the two
outside pages containing Mark 2:20–26 (left) and Mark 2:2–8 (right).
Photo courtesy of Catholic University of the Sacred Heart, Milan, Italy.

1 The good news of Jesus the Anointed begins ²with what Isaiah the prophet wrote: "Here is my messenger, whom I send on ahead of you to prepare your way! ³A voice of one in the wilderness shouting: 'Make ready the way of the Lord, make straight his paths.'" ⁴So, John the Baptizer appeared in the wilderness calling for baptism and a change of heart that lead to forgiveness of sins. ⁵And everyone from the Judean countryside and all the residents of Jerusalem streamed out to him and were baptized by him in the Jordan river, acknowledging their sins. ⁶And John was dressed in camel hair [and wore a leather belt around his waist] and lived on locusts and raw honey. ⁷And he began his proclamation by saying: "One more powerful than I will succeed me, whose sandal straps I am not fit to bend down and untie. ⁸I have been bap-

---

Mark 1:14–15

Source. Mark is the source of the tradition recorded in Mark 1:15. Matthew takes it over, abbreviates it, and also attributes it to John the Baptist (Matt 3:2). Luke pointedly omits, because of its anticipation that the end of the age is near, which does not suit his notion of the "good news" or "gospel" (but note Luke 10:9, 11, where Jesus has his disciples announce this theme).

Attribution. Jesus is remembered to have spoken in aphorisms, parables, and in the style of a challenge followed by verbal retort (J2). Mark 1:15 does not belong to any of these categories.

Most scholars hold the view that some, perhaps most, of the Greek vocabulary of Mark 1:15 is Markan. Mark apparently summarizes in his own words what he believes Jesus to have said (W7). The question is whether Mark preserves a tradition, admittedly in his own words, that goes back to Jesus.

Issues arising out of this text are: (a) Did Jesus proclaim that "the time is up"? (b) Did Jesus speak of God's rule (in traditional language: the kingdom of God)? Did he announce that the end of the age was closing in? (c) Did Jesus call on people to change their ways (in traditional language: to repent)? (d) Did Jesus call on his followers to "put their trust in the good news"?

(a) If the claim that the time is ripe means that certain prophecies of the Hebrew Bible were being realized, Jesus probably did not make that claim. Such a claim would be characteristic of the emerging community seeking to establish its claims by quoting scripture (O5).

(b) The Fellows of the Seminar are convinced that Jesus used the language and conceptuality of God's rule or domain (kingdom). At the same time, they generally doubt that Jesus expected the end of the world in his lifetime or soon thereafter. The conclusion they evidently draw is that, for Jesus, the rule of God was not the beginning of a new age within history or the end of history following a cosmic catastrophe. Nor did Jesus speak of God's rule in the nationalistic sense as a revival of David's kingdom. Rather, Jesus must have spoken of God's rule as close or already present but hidden, and

tizing you with water, but he will baptize you with holy spirit."

⁹During that same period Jesus came from Nazareth in Galilee and was baptized in the Jordan by John. ¹⁰And just as he got up out of the water, he saw the skies torn open and the spirit coming down toward him like a dove. ¹¹There was also a voice from the skies: "You are my favored son—of you I fully approve."

¹²And right away the spirit drives him out into the wilderness, ¹³where he remained for forty days, being put to the test by Satan. While he was living there among the wild animals, the angels looked after him.

¹⁴After John was locked up, Jesus came to Galilee proclaiming God's good news. ¹⁵His message went: "**The time is up: God's imperial rule is closing in. Change your ways, and put your trust in the good news!**"

God's Imperial Rule

Saying	Percentage				Wgt.
	R	P	G	B	Av.
Mk 1:15	0	16	28	56	.20 **B**
Mt 4:17	0	16	36	48	.23 **B**
Mt 3:2	0	17	21	62	.18 **B**

Matt 4:17 ➡ Mark 1:14–15
¹⁷From that time Jesus began to proclaim in these words: "**Change your ways, for Heaven's imperial rule is closing in.**"

Matt 3:1–2 ➡ Mark 1:14–15
¹In due course John the Baptist appeared in the wilderness of Judea, ²calling out: "**Change your ways, for Heaven's imperial rule is closing in.**"

thus in a way that frustrates ordinary expectations (J5). This is what he does in the parables of the leaven (Matt 11:33) and the treasure hidden in a field (Matt 11:44). Although God's imperial rule was closing in for Jesus, he warned people, "You cannot detect the coming of God's imperial rule. Nor can people say, 'Look, here it is!' or 'Look, there!' For the reign of God is in your presence" (Luke 17:20).

Mark, on the other hand, thinks of God's rule as a dramatic public event connected with some cosmic upheaval (Mark 8:34–9:1; 13: 1–34). This represents Mark's own apocalyptic view. The Seminar thought that Mark 1:15 more likely originated with Mark than with Jesus. In this gospel, as in others, the author has Jesus speak for him (W7).

(c) The call to repentance is charac-teristic of the message of John the Baptist (Matt 3:7–12; Luke 3:7–14), but it may not have been an ingredient carried forward by Jesus. The term is rarely attributed directly to Jesus.

(d) A majority of the Jesus Seminar holds the view that "trust in the good news" reflects the terminology of the established Christian community (W8a): "good news" refers to the "good news" about Jesus as the Christ (in traditional terms, gospel), and the call for trust in him would be integral to that notion. They therefore accorded the form in Matt 4:17 a slightly higher ranking than Mark 1:15, since Matthew lacks that phrase.

For all these reasons nothing in Mark 1:15 and parallels can be attributed to Jesus. ■

Fishing for People

Saying	Percentage				Wgt. Av.	
	R	P	G	B		
Mk 1:17	8	20	24	48	.29	**G**
Mt 4:19	8	20	24	48	.29	**G**
Lk 5:4,10	0	12	8	80	.11	**B**
Jn 21:5,etc.	0	8	0	92	.05	**B**
GEbi 2	0	0	4	96	.01	**B**

[16]As he was walking along by the Sea of Galilee, he saw Simon and Andrew, Simon's brother, casting ⟨their nets⟩ into the sea—since they were fishermen—[17]and Jesus said to them: "Become my followers and I'll have you fishing for people!" [18]And right then and there they left their nets and followed him.

Matt 4:18–22 ➡ Mark 1:16–20

[18]As he was walking by the Sea of Galilee, he saw two brothers, Simon, the one who is called Peter, and Andrew his brother, casting a net into the sea, since they were fishermen. [19]And Jesus says to them, "Become my followers and I'll have you fishing for people!" [20]So right then and there they left their nets and followed him.

[21]When he had gone on from there, he caught sight of two other brothers, James the son of Zebedee and his brother John, in the boat with Zebedee their father, mending their nets. He then called out to them. [22]They left their boat and their father right then and there and followed him.

Luke 5:1–11 ➡ Mark 1:16–20

[1]One day when the crowd pressed him to hear the word of God, he was standing by the lake of Gennesaret. [2]He noticed two boats moored there at the bank; the fishermen had left them and were washing their nets. [3]He got into one of the boats, the one belonging to Simon, and asked him to pull out a little from the shore. Then he sat down and began to teach the crowds from the boat.

[4]When he had finished speaking, he said to Simon, **"Pull out into deep water and lower your nets for a catch."** [5]But Simon replied, "Master, we worked hard all night and took nothing. But if you say so, I will lower the nets." [6]On doing this, they caught such a huge number of fish that their nets began to tear apart. [7]They signaled to their partners in the other boat to come and lend a hand. They came and loaded both boats until they nearly sank. [8]At the sight of this, Simon Peter fell to his knees in front of Jesus and said, "Have nothing to do with me, Master, as undeserving as I am." [9]For he and his companions were stunned at the catch of fish they had made, [10]as were James and John, sons of Zebedee and partners of Simon. Jesus said to Simon, **"Have no fear; from now on you will be catching people."** [11]They then brought their boats to shore, left everything, and followed him.

John 21:1–14 ➡ Mark 1:16–20

[1]Some time after these events, Jesus again presented himself to his disciples by the Sea of Tiberias. This is how he did it. [2]Simon Peter and Thomas, the one known as 'The Twin,' were together, along with Nathaniel from Cana in Galilee, the sons of Zebedee, and two other of his disciples. [3]Simon Peter says to them, "I'm going fishing." "We're coming with you," they reply. They went down and got into the boat. But that night they didn't catch a thing.

[4]It was already getting light when Jesus appeared there on the beach. However, the disciples did not recognize that it was Jesus. [5]Jesus now addresses them: **"Friends,"** he says, **"You haven't caught any fish, have you?"** "No," they replied to him. [6]He says to them, **"Cast your net on the starboard side of the boat and you will have better**

luck." They do as he instructs and are no longer able to haul it in because of the weight of the fish. [7]The disciple whom Jesus loved then exclaims to Peter, "It's the lord!" When Peter heard this, he tied his cloak around him, since he was naked, and threw himself into the sea. [8]The rest of them came in the boat, dragging the net full of fish. They were not far from land, only about a hundred yards offshore.

[9]When they get to shore, they see a charcoal fire burning, with fish cooking on it, and some bread. [10]Jesus says to them, **"Bring some of the fish you have just caught."** [11]And so Simon Peter went aboard and hauled the net full of huge fish ashore—one hundred fifty-three of them. Even though there were so many of them, the net was not torn. [12]Jesus says to them, **"Come and eat."** None of the disciples had the courage to ask, "Who are you?" They knew it was the lord. [13]Jesus comes, takes the bread, and gives it to them, and he treats the fish in the same way.

[14]This was now the third time Jesus was made to appear to his disciples following his resurrection from the dead.

GEbi 2 ➡ Mark 1:16–20

At any rate, in the gospel that is called by them "according to Matthew," which is not complete but adulterated and mutilated—they call it the "Hebraic" (gospel)—the following is found:

There was a certain man by the name of Jesus, about thirty years of age, who chose us. And when he came to Capernaum, he entered the house of Simon, whose surname was Peter, and opening his mouth, he said:

"As I was walking alongside the lake of Tiberias, I chose John and James, the sons of Zebedee, and Simon and Andrew, and ⟨ Philip and Bartholomew, James the son of Alphaeus and Thomas⟩ Thaddeus and Simon the Zealot and Judas Iscariot, and I called you, Matthew, while you were sitting at the customs booth, and you followed me. Therefore, I wish you to be twelve apostles as a sign of Israel."

Epiphanius, *Haer.* 30.13.2

Mark 1:16–20

Sources. Matthew is evidently copying Mark, whereas Luke has woven Mark's call story together with the account of a miraculous catch of fish, which John locates as a post-resurrection story (21:1–14). There is thus a single independent tradition, with its Lukan variation.

Attribution. Since the saying did not, in all probability, ever circulate independently (O2), it is once again the question of whether a genuine Jesus metaphor lies behind the formulation: Did Jesus challenge disciples to change their occupation to "catch" people? Or, was the saying composed along with the scene?

Mark 1:16–20 reflects Markan vocabulary and style (W4). As a result, many Fellows hold the view that Mark is the author of both story and saying.

Disciples. From time to time, the Jesus Seminar considered general questions. Fellows were asked to respond to statements in one of four forms: YY = strongly agree; Y = agree; N = disagree; NN = strongly disagree. In response to the statement *Jesus recruited disciples*, 54% of the Fellows voted Y or YY, 46% N or NN. They were thus evenly divided. On the statement, *A group of disciples traveled with Jesus* the vote was decisive: 81% responded Y or YY, only 19% N or NN. A strong majority believes Jesus was accompanied by disciples, although he may not have actively recruited them. These votes correlate well with the decision regarding Mark 1:17 and parallels. Conclusion: the scene and saying were created by Mark, but they dimly reflect a historical circumstance. ■

[19]When he had gone a little farther, he caught sight of James, son of Zebedee, and his brother John mending their nets in the boat. [20]Right then and there he called out to them as well, and they left their father Zebedee behind in the boat with the hired hands and accompanied him.

[21]Then they come to Capernaum, and on the sabbath day he went right to the synagogue and started teaching. [22]They were astonished at his teaching, since he would teach them on his own authority, unlike the scribes. [23]Now right there in their synagogue was a person possessed by an unclean spirit, which shouted, [24]"What do you want with us, Jesus, you Nazarene? Have you come to get rid of us? I know you, who you are: God's holy man!" [25]But [Jesus] yelled at it, **"Shut up and get out of him!"** [26]Then the unclean spirit threw the man into convulsions, and letting out a loud shriek it came out of him. [27]And they were all so amazed that they asked

An Unclean Spirit

Saying	Percentage				Wgt.
	R	P	G	B	Av.
Mk 1:25	0	0	0	100	.00 **B**
Lk 4:35	0	0	0	100	.00 **B**

Luke 4:31–37 ➡ Mark 1:21–28

[31]He went down to Capernaum, a town in Galilee, and he would teach them on the sabbath day. [32]They were astonished at his teaching because his message had authority. [33]Now in the synagogue there was a person who had an unclean demon, which shouted in a loud voice, [34]"Hey! What do you want with us, Jesus, you Nazarene? Have you come to get rid of us? I know you, who you are: God's holy man." [35]But Jesus yelled at it, **"Shut up and get out of him!"** Then the demon threw the man down in full view ⟨of everyone⟩ and came out of him without doing him any harm. [36]And amazement came over them all and they would say to one another, "What kind of message is this? With authority and power he gives orders to unclean spirits, and they leave." [37]So rumors about him began to spread to every corner of the surrounding region.

Mark 1:21–28

Attribution. We frequently meet words of Jesus in the gospels that are context-bound. To be context-bound means that words attributed to Jesus cannot be divorced from the narrative of which they are a part. "Shut up and get out of him!" (Mark 1:25) is meaningless outside the account of the exorcism (N2). Furthermore, such words could not have had a life of their own: they would not have circulated independently (O2). As a consequence, the Jesus Seminar regularly designated such words black. The second phase of the Jesus Seminar, which will consider the deeds of Jesus, may modify that decision after its deliberations.

All the words in Mark 1:21–28 are context-bound and hence designated black. ∎

themselves, "What's this? A new kind of teaching backed by authority! He gives orders even to unclean spirits and they obey him!" [28]So his fame spread rapidly everywhere throughout Galilee and even beyond.

[29]They left the synagogue right away and entered the house of Simon and Andrew along with James and John. [30]Simon's mother-in-law was in bed with a fever, and they told him about her right away. [31]He went up to her, took hold of her hand, raised her up, and the fever left her. Then she started looking after them.

[32]In the evening, at sundown, they would bring all the sick and demon possessed to him. [33]And the whole city would crowd around the door. [34]On such occasions he healed many people afflicted with various diseases and drove out many demons. He would never let the demons speak, because they realized who he was.

To Other Places

Saying	Percentage R P G B	Wgt. Av.
Mk 1:38	5 26 21 47	.30 **G**
Lk 4:43	0 21 21 58	.21 **B**

[35]And rising early, while it was still very dark, he [went outside and] stole away to an isolated place where he started praying. [36]Then Simon and those with him hunted him down. [37]When they had found him they say to him, "They're all looking for you." [38]But he replies: "Let's go somewhere else, to the neighboring villages, so I can speak there too, since that's what I came for." [39]So he went all around Galilee speaking in their synagogues and driving out demons.

Luke 4:42–44 ➡ Mark 1:35–39

[42]The next morning he went outside and withdrew to an isolated place. Then the crowds came looking for him, and when they got to him they tried to keep him from leaving them. [43]He said to them, "**I must declare God's imperial rule to the other cities as well, for this is why I was sent.**" [44]And he continued to speak in the synagogues of Judea.

Mark 1:35–39

Source. The sole source for this narrative is Mark. Luke has evidently taken the saying about God's imperial rule from Mark 1:15 and conflated it with what Mark says in 1:38b in formulating Luke 4:43. Luke's formulation has a decidedly "Christian" ring to it (W8a) (cf. the notes on Mark 1:15). Matthew also draws on Mark, but omits the particulars of the story and generalizes.

Attribution. It is doubtful that the saying in Mark 1:38b could ever have circulated independently (O2). It is neither an aphorism nor a parable (J2). It is quite possible that the saying was created as part of the narrative summary and thus is a product of the primitive Christian community (W2).

On the other hand, there are also signs that the saying reflects pre-Markan tradition, which Mark has edited to suit his narrative context. Evidence that the underlying tradition may be older than Mark: (a) the absence of the language of God's rule (W8b) (again, contrast Mark 1:15); (b) the enigmatic character of the saying (J7): SV translates, "came for," that is, came to this place: did Jesus leave Capernaum simply to go on a speaking tour of Galilee? Luke clarifies by having Jesus "sent" to declare God's rule (W4, W8a); (c) the ministry of Jesus retains its local character, rather than taking on the broader scope it assumes in Luke-Acts, which envisions a world mission (W8b); (d) the absence of obvious Christian features (W8b). These are arguments for a pre-Markan tradition.

The Fellows evidently did not find the arguments convincing that the saying was based on something Jesus said. They were predominantly inclined to the view that even the Markan saying reflects very little of the voice of Jesus, but suggests rather the missionary purpose of the early church (W8a). ■

⁴⁰Then a leper comes up to him, pleads with him, falls down on his knees, and says to him, "If you want to, you can make me clean." ⁴¹Although Jesus was indignant, he stretched out his hand, touched him, and says to him, **"Okay—you're clean!"** ⁴²And right away the leprosy left him, and he was made clean. ⁴³And Jesus snapped at him, and dismissed him curtly ⁴⁴with this warning, **"See that you don't tell anyone anything, but go, and let the priest examine ⟨your skin⟩. Then offer for your cleansing what Moses commanded, as evidence of your cure."** ⁴⁵But after he went out, he started telling everyone and spreading the story, so that Jesus could no longer enter a city openly, but had to stay out in the countryside. Yet they continued to come to him from everywhere.

Jesus Cures a Leper

Saying	Percentage				Wgt.
	R	P	G	B	Av.
Mk 1:41,44	0	0	0	100	.00 **B**
Mt 8:3,4	0	0	0	100	.00 **B**
Lk 5:13,14	0	0	0	100	.00 **B**

Matt 8:1–4 ➡ Mark 1:40–45

¹When he came down from the mountain, huge crowds followed him. ²Just then a leper appeared, bowed down to him, and said, "Sir, if you want to, you can make me clean." ³And he stretched out his hand, touched him, and says, **"Okay—you're clean!"** At once his leprosy was cleansed away. ⁴Then Jesus warned him, **"See that you don't tell anyone, but go, and let the priest examine ⟨your skin⟩. Then offer the gift that Moses commanded, as evidence of your cure."**

Luke 5:12–16 ➡ Mark 1:40–45

¹²And it so happened while he was in one of the towns, just then a man covered with leprosy appeared. Seeing Jesus, he knelt with his face to the ground and begged him, "Sir, if you want to, you can make me clean." ¹³Jesus stretched out his hand, touched him, and says, **"Okay—you're clean!"** And at once the leprosy left him. ¹⁴He ordered him to tell no one. **"But go, and let the priest examine ⟨your skin⟩. Then make an offering, as Moses commanded, for your cleansing, as evidence of your cure."** ¹⁵Yet the story about him spread around all the more. Great crowds would gather to hear him and to be healed of their sicknesses. ¹⁶But he would withdraw to the countryside and pray.

Mark 1:40–45
All the words in this story are context-bound and hence designated black (N2). ■

Power to Forgive

Saying	Percentage				Wgt. Av.
	R	P	G	B	
Mk 2:10	6	17	23	54	.25 **B**
Mt 9:6	6	15	21	59	.23 **B**
Lk 5:24	6	15	21	59	.23 **B**
Mk 2:5,etc.	6	6	26	63	.18 **B**
Mt 9:2,etc.	0	9	29	62	.16 **B**
Lk 5:20,etc.	0	11	26	63	.16 **B**
Jn 5:6,etc.	0	9	21	71	.13 **B**

2 Some days later he went back to Capernaum and was rumored to be at home. ²And many people crowded around so there was no longer any room, even outside the door. Then he started speaking to them. ³Some people then show up with a paralytic being carried by four people. ⁴And when they were not able to get near him on account of the crowd, they removed the roof above him. After digging it out, they lowered the mat on which the paralytic was lying. ⁵When Jesus noticed their trust, he says to the paralytic, "**Child, your sins are forgiven.**" ⁶Some of the scribes were sitting there

---

Matt 9:1–8 ➡ Mark 2:1–12

¹After he got on board the boat, he crossed over and came to his own city. ²Just then some people appeared, bringing a paralytic lying on a bed to him. When Jesus noticed their trust, he said to the paralytic, "**Take courage, child, your sins are forgiven.**" ³At that some of the scribes said to themselves, "This fellow blasphemes!" ⁴Because he perceived their thoughts, Jesus said, "**Why do you harbor evil thoughts? ⁵For which is easier: to say, 'Your sins are forgiven,' or to say, 'Get up and walk'? ⁶But so that you may realize that on earth the son of Adam has authority to forgive sins,**" he then says to the paralytic, "**Get up, pick up your bed and go home.**" ⁷And he got up and went to his home. ⁸When the crowds saw this, they became fearful, and glorified God, who had given such authority to humans.

Luke 5:17–26 ➡ Mark 2:1–12

¹⁷And it so happened one day, as he was teaching, that the power of the Lord was with him to heal. Now Pharisees and teachers of the Law, who had come from every village of Galilee and Judea and from Jerusalem, were sitting around. ¹⁸Just then some men appeared, bringing a paralyzed person on a bed. They attempted to bring him in and lay him before Jesus. ¹⁹But finding no way to bring him in on account of the crowd, they went up onto the roof and lowered him on his cot through the tiles into the middle of the crowd in front of Jesus. ²⁰When he noticed their trust, he said, "**Man, your sins have been forgiven you.**" ²¹And the scribes and the Pharisees began to raise questions: "Who is this who utters blasphemies? Who can forgive sins except God alone?" ²²Because Jesus was aware of their questions, he responded to them, "**Why do you entertain such questions? ²³Which is easier: to say, 'Your sins have been forgiven you,' or to say, 'Get up and walk'? ²⁴But so that you may realize that on earth the son of Adam has authority to forgive sins,**" he said to the paralyzed man, "**You there, 'Get up, pick up your cot and go home.'**" ²⁵And immediately he stood up in front of them, picked up what he had been lying on, and went home praising God. ²⁶They all became ecstatic, and they began to glorify God, but they were also filled with fear and exclaimed, "Today we have seen incredible things!"

and silently wondering: [7]"Why does that fellow say such things? He's blaspheming! Who can forgive sins except the one God?" [8]And right away, because Jesus sensed in his spirit that they were raising questions like this among themselves, he says to them: "**Why do you entertain questions about these things?** [9]**Which is easier, to say to the paralytic, 'Your sins are forgiven,' or to say, 'Get up, pick up your mat and walk'?** [10]**But so that you may realize that [on earth] the son of Adam has authority to forgive sins,**" he says to the paralytic, [11]"**You there, get up, pick up your mat and go home!**" [12]And he got

---

John 5:1–9 ➡ Mark 2:1–12

[1]After these events, a Jewish feast was to take place and Jesus went up to Jerusalem. [2]There is in Jerusalem by the Sheep Gate a pool known in Hebrew as Bethzatha, which has five porticoes. [3]Among these ⟨porticoes⟩ was lying a multitude of invalids—blind, lame, paralyzed—waiting for some movement of the water. [[4]For an angel of the Lord would bathe in the pool occasionally and agitate the water. Then the first one who got in after the waters were agitated would be cured of whatever disease that person had.]

[5]One person was there who had been an invalid for thirty-eight years. [6]When Jesus caught sight of this fellow lying there, and when he realized that he had been ⟨sick⟩ a long time already, he says to him, "**Do you want to be cured?**" [7]The invalid replied, "Sir, I have no one to put me in the pool when the waters have been agitated. When I try to go, someone beats me to it." [8]Jesus says to him, "**Get up, take up your mat, and walk around.**" [9]And the fellow was cured at once, and he picked up his mat and began to walk around. Now that was a sabbath day.

Mark 2:1–12

Sources. Stories of Jesus healing a paralytic are found in all four canonical gospels. Matthew and Luke are dependent on Mark: Matthew characteristically condenses Mark's version; Luke just as typically provides a paraphrase. Although the Johannine version differs substantially from the synoptic account, the two have enough in common to convince most scholars that they derive from a common tradition (for example, "You there, get up, pick up your mat and go home," or something similar, appears in both versions).

The dispute over the forgiveness of sins (Mark 2:5b–10) occurs only in the synoptic account. Matthew and Luke reproduce what is in Mark. The discussion of the authority to forgive sins is not an integral part of the story: it is not found in the parallel in John.

Mark's insertion. Most scholars regard 2:5b–10 as a Markan insertion. There are eight instances in the Gospel of Mark where the author appears to insert one block of material into the midst of another block. Such insertions are called *intercalations* by scholars. In this case, Mark repeats "he said to the paralytic" in

up, picked his mat right up, and walked out as everyone looked on. So they all became ecstatic, gave God the glory, and exclaimed, "We've never seen the likes of this!"

[13]Again he went out by the sea. And, with a big crowd gathered around him, he started teaching.

---

v. 10, which indicates the extent of the insertion. Insertions of this type are a feature of Mark's style (W4).

Intercalations in Mark
  Mark 2:1–5b/5c–10b/10c–12
  Mark 3:1–3/4–5c/5d–6
  Mark 3:20–21/22–30/31–35
  Mark 5:1–24a/24b–34/35–43
  Mark 6:7–13/14–29/30–34
  Mark 11:12–14/15–19/20–25
  Mark 14:53–54/55–65/66–72
  Mark 15:1–15/16–20/21–32

Details of Mark 2:5b–10 are typically Markan, especially the description of the amazed response on the part of some scribes to Jesus' authority (cf. Mark 1:22, 27, 3:15, 6:7) (W4). Further, it is difficult to think that any of the statements attributed to Jesus in this passage could have circulated independently in their present form (O2). The conclusion many scholars draw is that the whole passage is a Markan creation.

Old tradition. On the other hand, some scholars are inclined to the view that Mark 2:10 is based on a pre-Markan "son of Adam" saying that can be traced back to Jesus. Although there is no Jewish precedent for the claim that human beings have the authority to forgive sin, such a conclusion may be inferred from Old Testament texts. Forgiveness is frequently claimed to characterize the God of Israel (Exod 34:7, Num 14:18, Ps 86:5, 99:8). And that humans were created to be like God was basic Jewish teaching (Gen 1:26, Ps 8:4–6). Accordingly, some members of the Seminar view the claim made in 2:10 as a radical reinterpretation of the Jewish tradition (J4): on earth "the son of Adam"—which means, any human being—has the authority to forgive sin. This reading seems to accord with the claim that the sabbath was an institution created for the sake of humankind, not the other way around (Mark 2:27–28). On this view, "son of Adam" has a generic reference: son of Adam is any human person, just as the phrase, "son of a prophet," means any prophet. Matt 9:8 in particular supports this interpretation: God gives this authority to humankind.

Attribution. Other scholars think "son of Adam" refers here to an apocalyptic figure and accordingly attribute the saying to the Christian community or to Mark, who gives an apocalyptic interpretation to the saying (W8a).

Although a majority of the Seminar agreed that Jesus accepted sinners, most were not persuaded that Jesus pronounced forgiveness on sinners as a matter of course (but note Luke 7:48 and the story of the woman taken in adultery, John 8:2–11). In the absence of a verifiable setting within Jesus' ministry for incidents of this type, most Fellows of the Seminar doubt that the saying in Mark 2:10 is correctly attributed to Jesus. ∎

¹⁴As he was walking along, he caught sight of Levi the son of Alphaeus sitting at the toll booth, and he says to him, "**Follow me!**" And Levi got up and followed him.

Toll Taker Called

Saying	Percentage				Wgt.
	R	P	G	B	Av.
Mk 2:14	0	0	0	100	.00 **B**
Mt 9:9	0	0	0	100	.00 **B**
Lk 5:27	0	0	0	100	.00 **B**
GEbi 2	0	0	0	100	.00 **B**

Matt 9:9 ➡ Mark 2:14

⁹As Jesus was walking along there, he caught sight of a man sitting at the toll booth, one named Matthew, and he says to him, "**Follow me!**" And he got up and followed him.

Luke 5:27–28 ➡ Mark 2:14

²⁷After these events he went out and observed a toll collector named Levi sitting at the toll booth. He said to him, "**Follow me!**" ²⁸Leaving everything behind, he got up, and followed him.

GEbi 2 ➡ Mark 2:14

At any rate, in the gospel that is called by them "according to Matthew," which is not complete but adulterated and mutilated—they call it the "Hebraic" (gospel)—the following is found:

There was a certain man by the name of Jesus, about thirty years of age, who chose us. And when he came to Capernaum, he entered the house of Simon, whose surname was Peter, and opening his mouth, he said:

As I was walking alongside the lake of Tiberias, I chose John and James, the sons of Zebedee, and Simon and Andrew, and ⟨Philip and Bartholomew, James the son of Alphaeus and Thomas⟩ Thaddeus and Simon the Zealot and Judas Iscariot, and I called you, Matthew, while you were sitting at the customs booth, and you followed me. Therefore, I wish you to be twelve apostles as a sign of Israel.

Epiphanius, *Haer.* 30.13.2

Mark 2:14

The remarks on Mark 1:16–20, Fishing for People, also apply to Mark 2:14 and parallels, the call of Levi, with adjustments for the differences in the two accounts: the saying probably never circulated alone (O2) and probably does not go back to Jesus. The Fellows found it unnecessary to take a separate vote on the saying embedded in this story; it was designated black by consensus. ■

Able-bodied and Sick

Saying	Percentage				Wgt.
	R	**P**	**G**	**B**	**Av.**
Mk 2:17a	7	60	13	20	.51 P
Mt 9:12	7	60	13	20	.51 P
Lk 5:31	7	60	13	20	.51 P
POxy1224 3	7	60	13	20	.51 P

[15]Then Jesus happens to recline at table in ⟨Levi's⟩ house, along with many toll collectors and sinners and Jesus' disciples (remember, there were many of these people and they were all following him). [16]And whenever the Pharisees' scribes saw him eating with sinners and toll collectors, they would question his disciples: "What's he doing eating with toll collectors and sinners?" [17]When Jesus overhears, he says to them: "Since when do the able-bodied need a doctor? It's the sick who do. I did not come to enlist religious folks but sinners!"

Matt 9:10–13 ➡ Mark 2:15–17

[10]And it so happened while he was dining in ⟨Levi's⟩ house, that many toll collectors and sinners surprisingly appeared and dined with Jesus and his disciples. [11]And when the Pharisees saw this, they would question his disciples: "Why does your teacher eat with toll collectors and sinners?" [12]When Jesus overheard, he said: "Since when do the able-bodied need a doctor? It's the sick who do. [13]Go and learn what this means, 'I desire mercy and not sacrifice.' For I did not come to enlist religious folks but sinners!"

Luke 5:29–32 ➡ Mark 2:15–17

[29]And Levi gave him a great banquet in his house, and a large group of toll collectors and others were dining with them. [30]The Pharisees and their scribes complained to his disciples: "Why do all of you eat and drink with toll collectors and sinners?" [31]In response Jesus said to them: "Since when do those in good health need a doctor? It's the sick who do. [32]I have not come to enlist religious folks to change their hearts, but sinners!"

POxy 1224 3 ➡ Mark 2:15–17

[3]When the scribes [and Pharise]es and priests observ[ed hi]m, they became angry [because he reclined in the com]pany of sin[ners]. And when Jesus heard, [he said: "Since when do] those in good h[ealth need a doctor?] [It's the sick who do.]"

Luke 19:1–10 ➡ Mark 2:15–17

[1]He had entered Jericho and was passing through it. [2]There was a man there named Zacchaeus who was a chief toll collector and a rich man. [3]He was trying to see who Jesus was, but could not, because of the crowd, for he was short. [4]So he ran on ahead to where Jesus was going to pass by and climbed a sycamore tree to see him. [5]When Jesus came to the place, he looked up and said to him, "Zacchaeus, hurry and come down, for I have to stay at your house today." [6]So he came down in a hurry, and welcomed him joyfully. [7]But all who saw this murmured, "He has gone to be the guest of a sinner." [8]But Zacchaeus stood there and said to the Lord, "Look, sir, I will give half of my possessions to the poor, and if I have gotten anything from anyone by extortion, I will pay it back four times over." [9]Jesus said to him, "Today salvation has come to this house, for this man too is a son of Abraham. [10]For the son of Adam came to seek out and to save what was lost."

Religious Folks and Sinners

Saying	R	P	G	B	Av.	Wgt.
Mk 2:17b	13	20	40	27	.40	G
Mt 9:13b	13	20	40	27	.40	G
Lk 5:32	13	20	40	27	.40	G
2Clem 2:4	13	20	40	27	.40	G
Mt 9:13a	7	13	27	53	.24	B
Barn 5:9	0	25	8	67	.19	B
Lk 19:10	0	0	36	64	.12	B
1Tim 1:15	0	0	8	92	.03	B

1 Tim 1:15 ➡ Mark 2:15–17

[15]This saying is accurate and deserves full endorsement: **"Christ Jesus came into the world to save sinners."** And among sinners I hold first rank.

2 Clem 2:4 ➡ Mark 2:15–17

[4]Another text also reads, "I did not come to enlist religious folks but sinners."

Barn 5:9 ➡ Mark 2:15–17

[9]When he selected his own apostles who were about to proclaim his gospel, he selected those who were exceptionally sinful in order to indicate that he **'did not come to enlist the religious folks but sinners,'** and thus to demonstrate that he was God's son.

Mark 2:15–17

Sayings. There are two distinct sayings in Mark 2:17: the first is a secular proverb to the effect that it is not the able-bodied who need a doctor, but the sick. Matt 9:12, Luke 5:31, and POxy 1224 3 are versions of this proverb.

The second is a related saying that apparently interprets the first in more theological terms: those in good health stand for decent folks—those who fulfill their religious obligations faithfully— while the sick represent the sinners. Jesus is made to say that he came not to enlist religious folks but sinners. The remaining passages in the list above are versions of the second saying.

Stages of the tradition. The key question in coming to a decision on these two sayings is: Were Mark 2:17a and 2:17b originally two independent sayings out of which the story in 2:16–17 with its dialogue was developed, or: Was 2:17b a conclusion appended by Mark to the exchange in 2:16–17a, which originally ended with the secular proverb?

Scholarly opinion generally opposes the view that Mark 2:17a and b were linked from the beginning and go back to Jesus. There are several reasons for this view.

(1) Mark 2:15 in the judgment of many commentators has been supplied by Mark as an editorial comment linking the story in 2:16–17a to the call of Levi (W2). The link is awkward: the ambiguity about whose house it is is clarified in Luke, who has Levi give Jesus a banquet. The tendency was to smooth the narrative as the tradition developed (G3a).

(2) If the connection between the call of Levi and the exchange with the scribes is secondary, then the exchange must have had an independent existence in the oral tradition (O2).

(3) It is sometimes held that the secular proverb about the need for a doctor goes back to Jesus, whereas the exchange in which it is embedded was created to go with the proverb. Some Fellows argue, however, that it is impossible to conceive the proverb as an independent aphorism

spoken by Jesus without some setting. They therefore conclude that the criticism of Jesus eating with toll collectors and sinners is one example of a typical problem incident in the life of Jesus that has attracted a saying as its conclusion.

(4) It is also alleged that the version in POxy 1224 3 is the earliest form. Insofar as the mutilated nature of the papyrus fragment permits a judgment, it has only a positive form: "Those in good health don't need a doctor." In addition to the argument that the simpler form is the more original (O3a), it is often observed that the question in POxy 1224 is directed to Jesus, whereas in Mark the question is addressed to Jesus' disciples. In the primitive community it would have been the disciples who bore the brunt of criticism, whereas during Jesus' public ministry it would have been he who attracted criticism (W5). POxy 1224 may therefore represent the earliest form of this saying.

(5) The second saying is an interpretation of the first, and in specifically Christian terms (W3, W8a). Further, statements made in the first person (I-statements) attributed to Jesus come under suspicion (J8b). Although there is no good reason why Jesus could not have used the first person pronoun, the tradition exhibits the tendency to add first person introductions (Matt 10:27):
What I tell you in the dark,
    utter in the light;
and what you hear whispered,
    proclaim from the housetops.
The first line in this double couplet must

originally have read: What *you* are told in the dark. Since the proverb about the doctor is metaphorical, it would have attracted a Christian interpretation (W3), and that interpretation might well have been put into the mouth of Jesus as an I-saying. The equation of Jesus with the Father leads eventually to the form we find in Justin, *First Apology* 15:

> For Christ did not call the righteous or the temperate to repentance, but the ungodly and incontinent and unrighteous. So he said: "I have not come to call the righteous but sinners to repentance." For the Heavenly Father wishes the repentance of a sinner rather than his punishment.

Attribution. The secular proverb received a pink designation by a slim margin: it is always difficult to determine whether a piece of secular wisdom was actually spoken by Jesus or merely attributed to him (O5). But the Fellows were inclined to the view that Jesus might have responded to a situation like the one depicted with a secular proverb and not with a more theological reply. However, the Christian interpretation appended by Mark in 2:17b is not inimical to Jesus' disposition: He did think of himself as related to religious outcasts and not decent folk. The second saying was therefore judged to contain some of the ideas of Jesus but not to have been spoken by him. It was appropriately designated gray. Fellows did not doubt that Jesus typically ate with toll collectors and sinners upon occasion. ■

¹⁸John's disciples and the Pharisees were in the habit of fasting, and they come and ask him, "Why do the disciples of John fast and the disciples of the Pharisees fast, but your disciples don't?" ¹⁹And [Jesus] said to them: "The groom's friends can't fast while the groom is with them, can they? So long as the groom is around, you can't expect them to fast. ²⁰But the days will come when the groom is taken away from them, and then they will fast, on that day.

Groom's Friends Don't Fast

Saying	Percentage				Wgt. Av.
	R	P	G	B	
Mk 2:19	31	19	38	13	.56 P
Mt 9:15a	31	19	38	13	.56 P
Lk 5:34	31	19	38	13	.56 P
Th 104:2	0	0	0	100	.00 B
Mk 2:20	0	0	13	88	.04 B
Mt 9:15b	0	0	13	88	.04 B
Lk 5:35	0	0	13	88	.04 B
Th 104:3	0	13	13	75	.13 B

Matt 9:14–15 ➡ Mark 2:18–20

¹⁴Then the disciples of John come up to him, and ask: "Why do we and the Pharisees fast a lot, but your disciples don't?" ¹⁵And Jesus said to them, "The groom's friends can't mourn as long as the groom is with them, can they? But the days will come when the groom is taken away from them, and then they will fast."

Luke 5:33–35 ➡ Mark 2:18–20

³³They said to him, "The disciples of John fast often and offer prayers, and so do those of the Pharisees, but yours eat and drink." ³⁴And Jesus said to them, "You can't make the groom's friends fast as long as the groom is with them, can you? ³⁵But the days will come when the groom is taken away from them, and then they will fast in those days."

Thom 104:1–3 ➡ Mark 2:18–20

¹They said to Jesus, "Come, let us pray today, and let us fast."

²Jesus said, "What sin have I committed, or how have I been undone? ³Rather, when the bridegroom leaves the wedding chamber, then let people fast and pray."

Mark 2:18–20

Saying. Fasting and a wedding celebration are simply incompatible, according to the saying in Mark 2:19: Guests cannot fast as long as the bridegroom is present.

Attribution. Fellows of the Jesus Seminar evidently think that this saying, in some approximate form, goes back to Jesus.

The saying is embedded in a dialogue in both the Synoptics and Thomas. However, different parties raise the question about fasting (W2). The question in response, on the other hand, is virtually identical in the Synoptics: "Can the wed-

ding guests fast while the bridegroom is with them?" The question is repeated as a statement in the second half of v. 19b in Mark. It is uncertain whether this addition, omitted by both Matthew and Luke, goes with the question.

Mark 2:20 and parallels appear to be a Christian expansion: It justifies the subsequent practice of the Christian community (W9a). Jesus' style would have been to leave the matter hanging as a provocative question (J7).

Thomas offers a slightly different dialogue setting (W2), and Jesus' response has apparently already been "Christianized" (W8a). ∎

Patches and Wineskins

| Saying | Percentage | | | | Wgt. |
	R	P	G	B	Av.
Mk 2:21	8	33	50	8	.47 G
Mt 9:16	8	33	50	8	.47 G
Lk 5:36	8	33	46	13	.46 G
Th 47:5	0	29	46	25	.35 G
Mk 2:22	9	50	27	14	.51 P
Mt 9:17	8	42	38	13	.49 G
Lk 5:37–38	9	50	27	14	.51 P
Th 47:4	4	57	30	9	.52 P

²¹Nobody sews a piece of unshrunk cloth on an old garment, otherwise the new, unshrunk patch pulls away from the old and creates a worse tear. ²²And nobody pours young wine into old wineskins, otherwise the wine will burst the skins, and destroy both the wine and the skins. Instead, young wine is for new wineskins."

Matt 9:16–17 ➡ Mark 2:21–22

¹⁶"Nobody puts a piece of unshrunk cloth on an old garment, since the patch pulls away from the garment and creates a worse tear. ¹⁷Nor do they put young wine into old wineskins, since the wineskins burst, the wine runs out, and the wineskins are destroyed. Instead, they put young wine in new wineskins and both are preserved."

Luke 5:36–39 ➡ Mark 2:21–22

³⁶He then gave them a proverb: "Nobody tears a piece from a new garment and puts it on an old one, since the new will tear and the piece from the new will not match the old. ³⁷And nobody puts young wine into old wineskins, otherwise the young wine will burst the wineskins, it will spill out, and the wineskins will be destroyed. ³⁸Instead, young wine must be put into new wineskins. ³⁹Besides, nobody wants young wine after drinking aged wine; for one says, 'The aged is fine.'"

Thom 47:1–5 ➡ Mark 2:21–22

¹Jesus said, "A person cannot mount two horses or bend two bows. ²And a servant cannot serve two masters, otherwise ⟨that servant⟩ will honor the one and offend the other. ³Nobody drinks aged wine and immediately wants to drink new wine. ⁴New wine is not poured into old wineskins, lest they break, and aged wine is not poured into a new wineskin, lest it spoil. ⁵An old patch is not sewn onto a new garment, since it would create a tear."

Mark 2:21–22

Sayings. There are two different sayings in this complex: one concerns unshrunk cloth and an old garment, the other concerns young wine and old wineskins. A third saying preserved in Luke 5:39//Thom 47:3 did not find its way into the Markan tradition and is therefore also omitted by Matthew. It will be considered in a later report.

Stages of the tradition. The sequence in Mark and parallels affords some interesting insights into the history of the tradition.

Mark has apparently combined the two sayings in 2:21 and 2:22 with the preceding cluster (2:19–20) in order to create a complex of sayings with a common figure and theme. The figure concerns the impropriety of combining certain things. The theme combines the principal ingredients of a wedding: good food, appropriate dress, adequate wine. Mark has thus created a thematic cluster.

The cluster is probably Mark's creation because Thomas preserves the two groups of sayings (Mark 2:19–20, 21–22) in different places: Thomas 104, 47:3–5. Accordingly, the two groups were originally transmitted as separate oral units, in all probability.

Attribution. Both of these sayings, in

the judgment of Fellows, are probably secular proverbs. That observation does not, however, settle the question of whether Jesus made use of them or whether they were reinterpreted by the evangelists.

It is possible that the Christian community imported them and put them on the lips of Jesus (O5). In so doing, it interpreted them in accordance with its own perspectives. That perspective involves the contrast between the old (Judaism) and the new (Christianity). That interpretive overlay (W3) created problems for the underlying secular proverb, which had to do with what things go together. Just as oil and water don't mix, so unshrunk cloth (a new piece of cloth) does not go with an old garment, and new wine does not go with old wineskins and the reverse. The proverbs thus were "Christianized" (W8a).

The least Christianized version of the wine/wineskins proverb is Thom 47:4; there the 'old' is the 'good,' so the Christian contrast with Judaism has not yet taken over. As a consequence, 47:4 drew the highest vote. The versions in Mark 2:22 and Luke 5:37–38 were not far behind and were designated pink also.

It is difficult to determine whether Jesus may actually have uttered such proverbs. The context in which he may have said them has been lost. Several Fellows nevertheless argued that Jesus must have made use of some common wisdom; these two proverbs are among the few that scholars could imagine Jesus saying. The Seminar was obviously divided on the issue. The plausibility (G2) and coherence tests (G5) produced this suggestion: good food, appropriate dress, adequate wine in the context of the wedding would not have been distasteful to the one who came eating and drinking (Luke 7:33–34) or who may have liked to attend weddings (John 2:1–11).

Garbled versions. The proverb about patch and garment has been garbled in Thom 47:5—an old patch on a new garment, when it should be a new patch on an old garment. This version therefore drew the least positive vote. Luke has attempted to remodel the same saying, with unsatisfactory results. The form in Mark 2:21 and Matt 9:16 appears to be more satisfactory. But all versions of the same aphorism drew gray designations. ■

Adam Over the Sabbath

Saying	Percentage				Wgt. Av.
	R	P	G	B	
Mk 2:25–26	6	25	6	63	.25 B
Mt 12:3–7	6	25	6	63	.25 B
Lk 6:3–4	6	25	6	63	.25 B
Mk 2:27–28	15	50	21	15	.55 P
Mt 12:8	9	32	21	38	.37 G
Lk 6:5	9	32	21	38	.37 G

²³It so happened that he was walking along through the grainfields on the sabbath day, and his disciples began to strip heads of grain as they walked along. ²⁴And the Pharisees started to argue with him: "See here, why are they doing what's not permitted on the sabbath day?" ²⁵And he says to them: "**Haven't you ever read what David did when he found it necessary, when both he and his companions were hungry? ²⁶He went into the house of God, when Abiathar was high priest, and ate the consecrated bread, and even gave some to his men to eat. No one is permitted to eat this bread, except the priests!**" ²⁷And he continued: "The sabbath day was created for Adam, not Adam for the sabbath day. ²⁸So, the son of Adam lords it even over the sabbath day."

Matt 12:1–8 ➡ Mark 2:23–28

¹On that occasion Jesus walked through the grainfields on the sabbath day. His disciples were hungry and began to strip heads of grain and eat. ²When the Pharisees saw this, they said to him, "See here, your disciples are doing what's not permitted on the sabbath day." ³He said to them, "**Haven't you read what David did when he and his companions were hungry? ⁴He went into the house of God, and ate the consecrated bread, which neither he nor his companions were permitted to eat, except the priests alone! ⁵Or haven't you read in the law that the priests violated the sabbath day on the sabbath in the temple and were held blameless? ⁶Yet I say to you, one greater than the temple is here. ⁷And if you had known what this means, 'I prefer mercy and not sacrifice,' you would not have con-** demned those who are blameless. ⁸For the son of Adam lords it over the sabbath day."

Luke 6:1–5 ➡ Mark 2:23–28

¹It so happened that he was walking through grainfields on a sabbath day, and his disciples would strip some heads of grain, rub them in their hands, and eat them. ²Some of the Pharisees said, "Why are you doing what's not permitted on the sabbath day?" ³And Jesus answered them, "**Haven't you read what David did when he and his companions were hungry? ⁴He went into the house of God, took and ate the consecrated bread himself, and gave some to his men to eat? No one is permitted to eat this bread except the priests alone!**" ⁵And he used to say to them, "The son of Adam lords it over the sabbath day."

Mark 2:23–28

Sayings. There are two distinct sets of sayings in this passage. The first, Mark 2:25–26, is a recap of the story of what David did when he entered the temple and ate the consecrated bread because he was hungry (1 Sam 21:2–7). The second is a couplet in aphoristic style (Mark 2:27–28). The two sayings need to be treated separately.

Stages of the tradition. In the gospels, Jesus is frequently charged with profaning the sabbath by not observing traditional limits on "work": in addition to the present passage, note Mark 3:1–6 and parallels, Luke 13:10–17, John 5:10–18. Who was originally accused of violating the sabbath, Jesus or his followers? Some scholars interpret Mark 2:23–28 and parallels as evidence that it was Jesus' disciples who first violated the sabbath observance: it is they and not Jesus who pluck the grain on the sabbath. Other scholars trace the dispute back to Jesus himself. If it was the disciples who first violated sabbath regulations, the dispute probably arose in the primitive church. If it was Jesus, then the dispute probably originated with him.

Attribution. The incident reported by Mark, expanded by Matthew, and condensed by Luke, appears to reflect the social context of the post-crucifixion community, rather than the life of Jesus (W9a). Mark seems to have been particularly concerned with practices among the disciples that deviated from those of other Jews (cf. Mark 2:18–20, 7:1–8); other writers do not introduce them except when they are drawing on Mark. The criticism ascribed to the "Pharisees" in general against the followers of Jesus mirrors the later period: it is the disciples rather than Jesus who are the object of such criticisms (W5); nevertheless, Mark regularly introduces a saying of Jesus to resolve matters (W7). Further, the practice of citing the Hebrew scriptures directly, as in Mark 2:25–26, reflects common early Christian practice and is not characteristic of Jesus (O5). On the whole, the evidence indicates that Mark has created the story out of the experience of the primitive church. Accordingly, Mark 2:25b–26 and parallels were voted black by the Seminar.

The sayings recorded in 2:27–28 are a different matter, however. It is quite possible that these sayings originally circulated independently (O2). They are aphoristic in style (J2) and are memorable (J1). In them Jesus does not quote scripture (O5). Rather, he gives a radical reinterpretation of the creation story (Gen 1:26; Ps 8:4–8): the dominion God gave humankind over all earthly beings is extended even to the sabbath (J4). On this interpretation, the phrase, "the son of Adam," is generic: it is parallel with "human being" in v. 27 and means the same thing—a member of the human race. Of course, it is also clear that Mark, along with Matthew and Luke, understood the phrase as a title of Jesus. This may be the reason Matthew and Luke record only v. 28; or, their copy of Mark may have lacked v. 27. But the parallel lines in Mark give the origin of the saying away: Jesus is rearranging the priorities: humankind comes before the institution of the sabbath in the economy of God. The apocalyptic son of Adam plays no role in this reordering.

The majority of the Seminar were of the opinion that this type of radical and indirect reinterpretation of Jewish practice was typical of Jesus rather than of the ancient church (J4, W8b). The couplet in Mark received a pink vote, as a consequence, while the Seminar designated the truncated version in Matthew and Luke as gray simply because the two evangelists have obscured the original horizon of the saying by taking only the second member and understanding the phrase "son of Adam" as a messianic title (W4, W8b). ∎

THE SON OF ADAM

Jesus does not customarily speak about himself in the first person (as "I"). The few exceptions are found in sayings that the Fellows of the Jesus Seminar do not think originated with Jesus. For example, "Can you drink the cup I am drinking?" (Mark 10:38) was designated black. And Jesus' response to the question of the high priest about whether Jesus were the Anointed, "I am!" (Mark 14:62) was likewise voted black. The response given by Matthew, "If you say so." (Matt 26:64) sounds more authentically like the Jesus who is either silent or gives evasive answers at his trial.

A more characteristic way of referring to himself is when Jesus speaks about himself in the third person, as though he were another individual.

In the Gospel of Mark the phrase "son of Adam" appears thirteen times in what look to be indirect references of Jesus to himself or to a third person. This phrase is traditionally translated "son of man." The phrase appears in twenty-three additional sayings in Matthew and Luke and another thirteen in John. Jesus is virtually the only person in the gospels who uses this phrase (exceptions in Acts and Revelation).

The traditional translation is apt to be misleading. In ordinary English, "man" refers primarily to males of the species. But the Greek word (*anthropos*) means "human," as distinct from beast or god. It is a generic term that can apply to any member of the human species. *Anthropology* is thus the study of the behavior of all humans, male and female.

The phrase was not in common use in first-century Greek. But it was used to translate passages from the Hebrew Bible where the original Semitic subject was described as an offspring of Adam. Consequently, it is a phrase that has been colored by the Old Testament. The Hebrew word *Adam* was a term for humanity or humankind, rather than the name of a particular male individual. The male orientation of ancient societies prompted many speakers and writers to refer to the progeny of Adam as "sons of Adam." The Scholars Version has decided to use "son of Adam" as the basic phrase in order to call attention to the scriptural link with the creation story in Genesis and to the generic sense of the Hebrew noun, *Adam*. Some members of the translation panel preferred "child of Adam," but that phrase was ultimately rejected because the term "child" seems generally restricted to immature persons.

In the Hebrew Bible, the phrase is used in three different senses.

1. *Son of Adam: Insignificant Earthling*

The phrase is employed to refer to the human species as insignificant creatures in the presence of God:

> How can a human be right before God?
> Look, even the moon is not bright,
>   and the stars are not pure in his sight;
> How much less a human, who is a maggot,
>   and a *son of Adam*, who is a worm!   Job 25:4–6

2. *Sons of Adam: A Little Lower than God*

The phrase was also used to identify human beings as next to God in the order of creation:

> When I look at the heavens, the work of your fingers,
> the moon and the stars that you set in place;
> what are humans that you should regard them,
> and *sons of Adam* that you attend them?
> You made them a little lower than God
> and crowned them with glory and honor;
> you gave them rule over the works of your hands
> and put all things under their feet. Ps 8:3–6

3. *Son of Adam: the Apocalyptic Figure*

The Jewish scriptures portray the human being as the agent to exercise control over every living creature (Gen 1:28). This ideal decisively shaped Jewish visions of the end of history:

> As I looked on, in a night vision,
> I saw one like a *son of Adam* coming with heaven's clouds.
> He came to the Ancient of Days and was presented to him.
> Dominion and glory and rule were given to him.
> His dominion is an everlasting dominion that will not pass away,
> and his rule is one that will never be destroyed. Daniel 7:13–14

The phrase "son of Adam" is employed in three different senses in the Gospel of Mark: (a) To refer to the heavenly figure who is to come; (b) To refer to one who is to suffer, die, and rise; (c) To refer to human beings.

(a) References to the figure who is to come in the future on clouds of glory to judge the world are found in Mark 8:38, 13:26, and 14:62. This usage is derived from Daniel 7 (sense 3 above). On the lips of Jesus these references to the apocalyptic figure of the future are not self-references but allusions to a third person. Since Jesus distinguishes himself from the apocalyptic son of Adam, some scholars hold the view that these are old tradition and go back to Jesus. Other scholars take the view that the Christian community coined these sayings after they had identified Jesus with this heavenly figure following his death.

(b) References to the figure who is to suffer, die, and rise are scattered through Mark beginning in chapter 8: 8:31, 9:9, 12, 31, 10:33, 45, 14:21 (twice). There is no hint of a second coming in these formulations. They refer to unique events in the story of Jesus' suffering and death, so that "son of Adam" seems to be only a roundabout way of saying "I." Mark is the source of these sayings.

(c) Two sayings highlight the authority of the "son of Adam" on earth, in one instance, to forgive sin (Mark 2:10), in a second, to "lord it" over the sabbath (Mark 2:28). These sayings appear to conform to the first two senses drawn from the Hebrew Bible mentioned earlier.

The confusion in how this phrase is to be understood owes to the fact that the Christian community tended to understand the phrase messianically or apocalyptically. The original senses derived from the Hebrew Bible were lost or suppressed. As a result, it is necessary to consider more than one level of meaning wherever this phrase appears.

Except for sense c just sketched, Fellows of the Jesus Seminar are inclined to think that the son of Adam sayings in the gospels are all the product of the early Christian community.

Hand and Sabbath

Saying	Percentage				Wgt.
	R	P	G	B	Av.
Mk 3:3,etc.	0	0	0	100	.00 B
Lk 6:8,etc.	0	0	0	100	.00 B
Mt 12:11–12	4	38	17	42	.35 G
Lk 14:5	4	38	17	42	.35 G

3 Then he went back to the synagogue, and a fellow with a withered hand was there. ²So they kept an eye on him, to see whether he would heal the fellow on the sabbath day, so they could denounce him. ³And he says to the fellow with the withered hand, "**Get up here in front of everybody.**" ⁴Then he asks them, "**On the sabbath day is it permitted to do good or to do evil, to save life or to destroy it?**" But they maintained their silence. ⁵And looking right at them with anger, exasperated at their obstinacy, he says to the fellow, "**Hold out your hand!**" He held it out and his hand was restored. ⁶Then the Pharisees went right out with the Herodians and hatched a plot against him, to get rid of him.

Matt 12:9–14 ➡ Mark 3:1–6

⁹And when he had moved on, he went into their synagogue. ¹⁰Just then a fellow with a withered hand appeared and they asked him, "Is it permitted to heal on the sabbath day?" so they could denounce him. ¹¹He asked them, "Which one of you who has a single sheep does not grab it and pull it out if it falls into a ditch on the sabbath? ¹²A person is worth considerably more than a sheep. So, it's permitted to do good on the sabbath day!" ¹³Then he says to the fellow, "**Hold out your hand!**" He held it out and it was restored to health like the other.

¹⁴ The Pharisees went out and hatched a plot against him to get rid of him.

Luke 6:6–11 ➡ Mark 3:1–6

⁶On another sabbath day, he entered the synagogue and taught. A fellow was there whose right hand was withered. ⁷And the scribes and the Pharisees watched him carefully, to see if he would heal on the sabbath day, in order to find some means to denounce him. ⁸However, he knew their motives, and

he said to the fellow with the withered hand, "**Get up and stand here in front of everybody.**" And he rose and stood there. ⁹Then Jesus queried them, "**I ask you, on the sabbath day is it permitted to do good or to do evil, to save life or to destroy it?**" ¹⁰And he looked right at all of them, and said to him, "**Hold out your hand!**" He did and his hand was restored. ¹¹But they were filled with rage and discussed among themselves what they might do to Jesus.

Luke 14:1–6 ➡ Mark 3:1–6

¹And it so happened one sabbath, when Jesus went to dinner at the house of a prominent Pharisee, that they were watching him closely. ²Now, there was a man in front of him who had dropsy. ³Jesus spoke to the lawyers and Pharisees, saying, "**Is it permitted to heal on the sabbath, or not?**" ⁴But they were silent. He took the man, healed him, and let him go. ⁵Then he said to them, "Suppose your son or your ox falls down a well—which of you would not immediately pull him up on the sabbath day?" ⁶And they could not reply to this.

⁷Then Jesus withdrew with his disciples to the sea, and a huge crowd from Galilee followed. When they heard what he was doing, a huge crowd from Judea, ⁸and from Jerusalem and Idumea and across the Jordan, and from around Tyre and Sidon, collected around him. ⁹And he told his disciples to have a small boat ready for him on account of the crowd, so they would not mob him. ¹⁰(After all, he had healed so many, that all who had diseases were pushing forward to touch him.) ¹¹The unclean spirits also, whenever they faced him, would fall down before him and shout out, "You son of God, you!" ¹²But he always warned them not to disclose his identity.

Mark 3:1–6

Sayings and sources. The words ascribed to Jesus in this pericope (Mark 3:3, 4, 5//Luke 6:8, 9, 10) belong to the fabric of the story. They did not have an independent existence outside this narrative (N2). As a consequence, they cannot be traced back to Jesus (O2).

The saying in Matt 12:11–12//Luke 14:5 is derived from Q. Fellows evidently concluded that the Q words were also context-bound (N2) and so could not have circulated independently during the oral period (O2).

Narrative context. The account of the healing of the man with the withered hand surprises the discerning reader on a number of counts:

(1) Did the Pharisees really credit Jesus with the power to heal? Verse 2 indicates that they did and that is surprising. However, we do not learn until v. 5 that Pharisees are involved; originally it may have been a different group of opponents (W10).

(2) The Pharisees are accused of hardness of heart (v. 5), so that not even the miracle of healing moved them. Does this not reflect the bitterness of the struggle between the later Christian community and Judaism, at the time the former was attempting to define itself

over against the latter? If so, Mark has either created a story or revised an earlier tradition to reflect circumstances current in his day (W9a).

(3) Jesus would not have killed the man with the withered hand, as v. 4 suggests, had he waited until the sabbath day was over to perform his cure. The dichotomy set up by v. 4 thus appears contrived (W4).

(4) Jesus does not in fact break the sabbath law: he does not perform a physical act not permitted on the sabbath.

(5) The plot being hatched in v. 6 goes together with the plot of Mark's gospel: note Mark 8:31–33, 9:30–32, 10:32–34 (W4).

Taken together, these features suggest that Mark has created the story himself or has heavily edited a healing story that came down to him in the tradition.

In either case, the Fellows of the Seminar designated the words ascribed to Jesus in the Markan version, together with their parallels in Matthew and Luke, black by consensus. Nevertheless, the vote on Mark 2:27–28 (pink) indicates that Jesus probably challenged sabbath regulations, in the judgment of Fellows (see notes on that saying). Whether he did so in connection with an incident like this one is difficult to determine. ■

¹³Then he goes up on the mountain and summons those he wanted, and they came to him. ¹⁴He formed a group of twelve to be his companions, and to be sent out to speak, ¹⁵and to have authority to drive out demons.

¹⁶And to Simon he gave the nickname Rock, ¹⁷and to James, the son of Zebedee, and to John, his brother, he also gave a nickname, Boanerges, which means "Thunder Brothers"; ¹⁸and Andrew and Philip and Bartholomew and Matthew and Thomas and James son of Alphaeus and Thaddeus and Simon the Canaanite, ¹⁹and Judas Iscariot, who, in the end, turned him in.

²⁰Then he goes home, and once again a crowd gathers, so they could not even grab a bite to eat. ²¹When his relatives heard about it, they came to get him (you see, they thought he was out of his mind). ²²And the scribes, who had come down from Jerusalem, were saying, "He is under the control of Beelzebul" and "He drives out demons in the name of the head demon!"

Preface to Mark 3:20-35

Mark 3:20-21 is a Markan construction: The introduction of Jesus' family anticipates the scene in 3:31-35 and the saying on true relatives; and the theme, *he is out of his mind* (v. 21), anticipates the charge by the scribes that he is demon possessed. Mark has thus created a literary envelope structure (3:20-21, 31-35) to frame a cluster of sayings (W4).

The setting for the Beelzebul controversy in Matthew and Q is the exorcism of a demon from a mute, whereas in Mark the occasion consists of the appearance of his family and the scribes from Jerusalem (W2). A compendium of sayings follows in Q, as it does in Mark, but the two compendia vary in content, as the following table demonstrates (W1). Since Matthew and Luke agree at most points against Mark, they must be drawing on Q rather than on Mark.

The cluster of sayings ascribed to Jesus that underlay Mark and Q in all probability consisted of the following:

1. An accusation leveled against Jesus: Jesus is in collusion with God's enemy
2. Jesus' three-part reply:
   a. Government divided
   b. Household divided
   c. Satan divided
3. Comparison with the powerful man's house

This cluster appeared in Mark and Q, which means that the cluster was formed in the earliest decades of the Jesus movement, if it doesn't go back to Jesus himself. The cluster was then elaborated in different ways in the two sources, Mark and Q. Apparently Luke more faithfully represents Q, whereas Matthew has conflated Mark and Q, as he sometimes does elsewhere. ■

JESUS AS EXORCIST

In response to the general question, *Jesus exorcized what were thought to be demons,* 95% of the Fellows agreed; only 5% disagreed. But in response to the statement, *There were and are such things as demons,* 84% disagreed. Fellows evidently permit themselves to be guided by what was taken to be real in the ancient world (demons were generally taken for granted) and what is understood to be real in the modern world (demonology is not a standard part of either medical or psychological practice).

The statement, *Gospel stories of Jesus' exorcisms are fictional,* drew a negative vote of 90%; only 10% thought they were fictions. Yet they were divided on the assertion: *The gospel stories preserve only general memories of Jesus' exorcisms.* Forty-five percent agreed; 55% disagreed. The question here had to do with the particular: About half of the Fellows hold the view that narratives of this sort reflect only typical or general memories, but do not preserve the detail of specific events. Stories that reflect the typical or the general are nevertheless not to be understood as entirely fictional. The other half of the Fellows think that stories of exorcisms may contain some particularized historical memory.

THE BEELZEBUL CLUSTER

	Mark	Matthew	Luke
Setting:	Appearance of family 3:20–21	Dumb demoniac 12:22–23	Dumb demoniac 11:14
Scene:	Beelzebul Controversy 3:22–26	Beelzebul Controversy 12:24–26	Beelzebul Controversy 11:15–18
Sayings:		Your People 12:27	Your People 11:19
		God's Rule 12:28	God's Rule 11:20
	Powerful Man 3:27	Powerful Man 12:29	Powerful Man 11:21–22
		With & Against 12:30	With & Against 11:23
	Blasphemies 3:28–30	Blasphemies 12:31–32	Blasphemies 12:10
	True Relatives 3:31–35	[True Relatives] [12:46–50]	[True Relatives] [8:19–21]

Satan Divided

Saying	Percentage				Wgt.	
	R	P	G	B	Av.	
Mk 3:23–26	10	45	13	32	.44	G
Mt 12:25–26	10	50	20	20	.50	G
Lk 11:17–18	10	70	0	20	.57	P

Powerful Man's House

Saying	Percentage				Wgt.	
	R	P	G	B	Av.	
Mk 3:27	24	45	14	17	.59	P
Mt 12:29	24	45	14	17	.59	P
Lk 11:21–22	24	41	17	17	.57	P
Th 35:1–2	24	45	14	17	.59	P

[23]And after calling them over, he would speak to them in riddles: "How can Satan drive out Satan? [24]After all, if a government is divided against itself, that government cannot endure. [25]And if a household is divided against itself, that household will not be able to survive. [26]So if Satan rebels against himself and is divided, he cannot endure but is done for. [27]No one can enter a powerful man's house to steal his belongings unless he first ties him up. Only then does he loot his house.

Matt 12:25–26 ➡ Mark 3:23–26
[25]But he knew how they thought, and said to them: "Every government divided against itself is devastated, and every city or house divided against itself will not survive. [26]So if Satan drives out Satan, he is divided against himself. In that case, how will his domain endure?"

Luke 11:17–18 ➡ Mark 3:23–26
[17]But he knew what they were thinking, and said to them: "Every government divided against itself is devastated, and a house divided against a house falls. [18]If Satan is divided against himself—since you say I drive out demons by Beelzebul—how will his domain endure?"

Matt 12:29 ➡ Mark 3:27
[29]"Or how can someone enter a powerful man's house and steal his possessions, unless he first ties him up? Only then does he loot his house."

Luke 11:21–22 ➡ Mark 3:27
[21]"When a powerful man is fully armed and guards his courtyard, his possessions are safe. [22]But when a stronger man attacks and overpowers him, he takes the weapon on which he was relying and divides the loot."

Thom 35:1–2 ➡ Mark 3:27
[1]Jesus said, "One cannot enter the house of the strong and take it by force without tying the person's hands. [2]Then one will loot the person's house."

Mark 3:23–26
Setting. Fellows of the Seminar generally agree that Jesus did exorcize demons. It is highly probable that he was accused of being demon possessed (cf. John 8:48, 52, 10:20). So the circumstance depicted in Matt 12:22–24//Luke 11:14–15 is not improbable.
Attribution. The response of Jesus to this accusation strikes some scholars as a piece of everyday, ordinary wisdom and not at all characteristic of Jesus' witticisms elsewhere. On the other hand,

Jesus' response may be understood as ironic (J6; compare W11): Jesus adopts the view of his opponents as his own and then follows its logic out. 'If,' as you say, 'I am in league with Satan, then Satan's domain is divided against itself. In that case, Satan is coming to an end by his own hand working through me. Is that what you intend to say?' Making his opponents say something like the opposite of what they intend has more of an authentic ring to it.
The balance of arguments means that

²⁸I swear to you, all offenses and whatever blasphemies humankind might blaspheme will be forgiven them. ²⁹But whoever blasphemes against the holy spirit is never ever forgiven, but is guilty of an eternal sin." ³⁰(Remember, it was they who had started the accusation, "He is controlled by an unclean spirit.")

Blasphemies

Saying	Percentage				Wgt.
	R	P	G	B	Av.
Mk 3:28-29	0	15	24	62	.18 B
Mt 12:31-32	0	18	15	68	.17 B
Lk 12:10	6	9	18	68	.18 B
Th 44:1-3	0	15	9	76	.13 B
Did 11:7b	0	9	12	79	.10 B

Matt 12:31-32 ➡ Mark 3:28-29
³¹"That is why I tell you, every offense and blasphemy will be forgiven humankind, but the blasphemy of the spirit won't be forgiven. ³²And everyone who speaks a word against the son of Adam will be forgiven. But the one who speaks a word against the holy spirit won't be forgiven, either in this age or in the one to come."

Luke 12:10 ➡ Mark 3:28-29
¹⁰"And everyone who speaks a word against the son of Adam will be forgiven. But the one who blasphemes against the holy spirit won't be forgiven."

Thom 44:1-3 ➡ Mark 3:28-29
¹Jesus said, "Whoever blasphemes against the Father will be forgiven, ²and whoever blasphemes against the son will be forgiven, ³but whoever blasphemes against the holy spirit will not be forgiven, either on earth or in heaven."

Did 11:7b ➡ Mark 3:28-29
⁷"You must not test or examine any prophet who is speaking under the influence of the spirit. For, every sin will be forgiven, but this sin will not be forgiven."

the Fellows of the Seminar are sharply divided on whether any of the sayings in this group go back to Jesus. Votes hover around the dividing line between gray and pink (weighted average of .50). The vote on Mark 3:23-26 yielded a weighted average of .44 (G), although nearly 55% of the Fellows voted red or pink: a substantial black vote pulled the average down. Only the formulation of Luke in 11:17-18 made it into the pink category by a slim margin.

Whether one reads this cluster of sayings as proverbial wisdom (O5) or as subtle irony (J7) goes together with how one assesses the series. Both readings are possible, hence the close vote. ■

Mark 3:27
Attribution. It is difficult to conceive that the early Christian community attributed this robust and colorful figure of speech to Jesus if he did not in fact say it (J6, J7, O4). To compare the conquest of

Satan through exorcism to house breaking and entering is a bold stroke, not unlike the strategy employed in the parable of the Dishonest Steward (Luke 16:1-9) or the parable of the Assassin (Thomas 98), in which God's rule is compared to a dishonest or a violent act. The Fellows gave the Dishonest Steward a red vote, the figure of the Powerful Man's House and the parable of the Assassin pink votes. ■

Mark 3:28-29
Variations. The great variation in the wording of sayings on the subject of blasphemies indicates how difficult this issue was even for early Christians (W6). There appear to be three distinct versions of the saying: Mark, Q (= Luke 12:10), and Thomas. Matthew combines a modified version of Mark with Q. The only point all three versions have in common is that blasphemy against the holy spirit will not be forgiven. But what constitutes such

³¹Then his mother and his brothers arrive. While still outside, they send in and ask for him. ³²A crowd was sitting around him, and

---

blasphemy is left obscure. And the sources differ in identifying which blasphemies (or sins) can be forgiven.

The Markan version states that all human offenses and blasphemies are forgivable, except for slander directed against the holy spirit. Since it is this spirit that inhabits Jesus, Mark's saying is a severe rebuttal of those who claim that Jesus' spirit is *unclean* (Mark 3:30). In effect, Mark insists that any criticism of Jesus is unforgivable. The Q version, however, contrasts speaking against the *son of Adam* with speaking against the *holy spirit*: *Son of Adam* must originally have meant *humankind* in general, since in Judaism all sins against humankind were forgivable, even though sins against God were not. In this respect, the version in Thomas supports the Q version: blasphemy of the *son* is forgivable. If *son of Adam* refers to generic human beings, then the dictum is a common Jewish axiom.

The canonical gospels, however, regularly understand the phrase *son of Adam* in a christological sense: the *son of Adam* is the heavenly figure who comes on clouds of glory to judge the world. In that case, *son of Adam* as adopted by Luke and Matthew must mean Jesus. The Q version then contradicts Mark: blasphemy against Jesus is forgivable. It is difficult to imagine any followers of Jesus inventing a saying that tolerated, perhaps even encouraged, criticism of him. As Paul puts it:

> I want you to understand that no one says 'Jesus be damned,' while speaking in the spirit, and no one is able to confess, 'Jesus is Lord,' except under the guidance of the holy spirit.
> —1 Cor 12:3

If criticism of Jesus was not to be tolerated, then *son of Adam* can only be taken in the generic sense.

Attribution. Votes by the Fellows of the Seminar depended on how each one took this saying in its historical development. Some thought it a common affirmation of Jewish doctrine (contrast between slander of humankind with that of the divine), others took it as a legal formula of the early church (cf. Didache 11:7b) that came to be ascribed to Jesus (blasphemy of Jesus is not permitted). The majority of Fellows did not find the saying distinctive enough to ascribe it to Jesus (J3); others were of the opinion that it originated in the primitive church (O5). Votes tended to fall on the black end of the spectrum. ∎

Mark 3:33–35

Elements. This scene contains three discrete parts:

1. The concluding aphorism (Mark 3:35)
2. The dialogue (Mark 3:32–34)
3. The narrative setting (Mark 3:31, with 3:20–21)

There are four possibilities to be considered:

(a) Did the aphorism in Mark 3:35 circulate as a separate oral unit at an earlier stage of the tradition? Was the dialogue then created as a setting for the aphorism?

(b) Did the dialogue (Mark 3:32–34)—which may be thought of as an enacted parable—circulate independently? Was the concluding aphorism then created by the Christian community as a generalized version of Jesus' response in the dialogue?

(c) Were the dialogue and the concluding saying integral to each other at the earliest stage of the tradition?

(d) Is the entire scene a figment of someone's imagination? In this connection, it should be noted that the narrative

they say to him, "Look, your mother and your brothers [and sisters] are outside looking for you." [33]In response he says to them: "My mother and brothers—who ever are they?" [34]And looking right at those seated around him in a circle, he says, "Here are my mother and my brothers. [35]Whoever does God's will, that's my brother and sister and mother!"

True Relatives

| Saying | Percentage | | | | Wgt. |
	R	P	G	B	Av.
Mk 3:33–35	21	28	10	41	.43 G
Mt 12:48–50	30	40	10	20	.60 P
Lk 8:21	10	50	20	20	.50 G
Th 99:2	22	44	0	33	.52 P
Th 99:3	4	16	36	44	.27 G
2 Clem 9:11	22	22	33	22	.48 G
GEbi 5b	22	22	22	33	.44 G

Matt 12:48–50 ➡ Mark 3:33–35
[48]In response he said to the one speaking to him, "Who ever is my mother and who ever are my brothers?" [49]And he stretched out his hand over his disciples and said, "Here are my mother and my brothers. [50]For whoever does the will of my Father in heaven, that's my brother and sister and mother."

Luke 8:21 ➡ Mark 3:33–35
[21]He replied to them, "My mother and my brothers are those who hear the message of God and do it."

Thom 99:2–3 ➡ Mark 3:33–35
[2]He said to them, "Those here who do the will of my Father are my brothers and my mother. [3]They are the ones who will enter the domain of my Father."

2 Clem 9:11 ➡ Mark 3:33–35
For the Lord said, "My brothers are those who do the will of my Father."

GEbi 5 ➡ Mark 3:33–35
Moreover, they deny that he was human, I suppose on the basis of what the Savior said when it was reported to him:
"Behold, your mother and your brothers are standing outside." "Who are my mother and brothers?" And stretching out his hand to his disciples, he said, "These are my brothers and mother and sisters, who do the will of my Father."
Epiphanius, *Haer.* 30.14.5

setting provided by Mark 3:20–21, 31 is undoubtedly the work of Mark (W2), as comparison with the version in Thomas makes evident.
Sources. There are at least two independent versions, Mark and Thomas (A1). Mark's is more fully developed and suggests to many scholars the later controversy over the admission of gentiles to the Christian community: Jesus' relatives stand for the Jews; his disciples stand for the gentiles (W9a). One can imagine that Christians reading this text in the 80s and 90s of the first century c.e. understood

the scene in precisely this way.
Thomas has the simpler version (O3a), although it reflects the same structural elements: the scene of Jesus' mother and brothers standing outside the circle of followers and his response.
Some Fellows are of the opinion that the contrast between Jesus' relatives and his disciples mirrors the tension in the primitive community between unrelated disciples and Jesus' relatives, some of whom may have been leaders in the church (W9a). It is possible, of course, that both the opening of the fellowship to

4 Once again he started to teach beside the
sea. An enormous crowd gathers around him,
so he climbs into a boat and sits there on the
water facing the huge crowd on the shore.

²He would then teach them many things in
parables. In the course of his teaching he would
tell them: ³"Listen to this! Here is a sower who
went out to sow. ⁴While he was sowing, some
seed fell along the path, and the birds came and
ate it up. ⁵Other seed fell on rocky ground where
there wasn't much soil, and it came up right
away because the soil had no depth. ⁶But when
the sun came up it was scorched, and because it
had no root it withered. ⁷Still other seed fell
among thorns, and the thorns came up and

The Sower

| Saying | Percentage | | | | Wgt. |
	R	P	G	B	Av.
Mk 4:3–8	28	38	3	31	.54 **P**
Mt 13:3–8	28	38	0	34	.53 **P**
Lk 8:5–8a	21	43	0	36	.50 **G**
Th 9:1–5	21	46	0	32	.52 **P**
1 Clem 24:5	0	4	21	75	.10 **B**

gentiles and the conflict between
disciples and relatives originated with
Jesus.

Attribution. In support of this last
view, some scholars argue that neither
the setting nor the saying are likely to
have been invented by Mark or anyone
else. Jesus' seeming rebuke to his mother
is eyebrow-raising, to say the least. It puts
him in sharp conflict with the command
to honor and obey one's parents, common to both Judaism and Christianity
(Exodus 20:12, Col 3:20, Eph 6:1) (J4).
However, his quip about his mother may
have been made with deliberate irony
(J6, J7), inasmuch as Jesus responds to
the notice of his mother outside by
referring to *his Father.* And his identification of his followers is almost as
radical, especially in a Jewish context
where a teacher regularly addressed
disciples as *my sons* rather than as *my
brothers* (J4). The passage thus calls into
question traditional attitudes to two
kinds of social relationships: to followers
or disciples; to parents and siblings (J4).

Most members of the Jesus Seminar
were of the opinion that versions of the
saying that refer to *my Father* (Matthew
and Thomas) were older than those with
the term *God* (Mark and Luke). When
Jesus referred to God, he probably al-

ways did so as his Father. Fellows were
divided on whether Jesus would have
asked about his true mother as reported
in the Markan version: the term most
commonly employed in the early church
for other members of the Christian fellowship was *brothers* (note the version in
2 Clem 9:11). The addition of *sisters* in
some early manuscripts seems to have
been a move to make the concluding saying more inclusive.

Voting procedures may well have
determined the fate of this passage. The
Seminar voted on Thom 99:3 separately.
A clear majority thought the saying secondary. The group awarded a pink designation to Thomas 99:2. The Seminar
then voted on the Markan passage (3:33–
35) as a whole: it did not command a
pink vote, possibly because v. 35 was
linked with vv. 33–34. The corresponding passage in Matthew (12:48–50) did
garner a pink vote, apparently because
Matthew refers to *my Father* and not
God. The Seminar was evenly divided on
Luke 8:21.

In this case, as in many others, Fellows
were torn between evidence and arguments supporting the antiquity of the
dialogue and concluding saying and those
that placed its origin in the early Christian community. ∎

choked it, so that it produced no fruit. [8]Finally, some seed fell on good earth and started producing fruit. The seed sprouted and grew: one part had a yield of thirty, another part sixty, and a third part one hundred."

Matt 13:3–8 ➡ Mark 4:3–8
[3]He told them many things in parables. "Here is a sower who went out to sow. [4]While he was sowing, some seed fell along the path, and the birds came and ate it up. [5]Other seed fell on rocky ground where there wasn't much soil, and it came up right away because the soil had no depth. [6]When the sun came up they were scorched, and because they had no roots they withered. [7]Still other seed fell among thorns, and the thorns came up and choked them. [8]Other seed fell on good earth and started producing fruit. One part had a yield of one hundred, another a yield of sixty, and a third a yield of thirty."

Luke 8:5–8a ➡ Mark 4:3–8
[5]"A sower went out to sow his seed; and while he was sowing, some seed fell along the path, and was trampled under foot, and the birds of the sky ate it up. [6]Other seed fell on the rock; when it grew, it withered because it lacked moisture. [7]Still other seed fell among thorns; the thorns grew with it and choked it. [8]Other seed on fertile earth;

and when it matured, it produced fruit a hundredfold."

Thom 9:1–5 ➡ Mark 4:3–8
[1]Jesus said, "Look, the sower went out, took a handful (of seeds), and scattered (them). [2]Some fell on the road, and the birds came and gathered them. [3]Others fell on rock, and they did not take root in the soil and did not produce heads of grain. [4]Others fell on thorns, and they choked the seeds and worms ate them. [5]And others fell on good soil, and it produced a good crop: it yielded sixty per measure, even one hundred twenty per measure."

1 Clem 24:5 ➡ Mark 4:3–8
[5]The sower went out and threw each of his seeds on the ground. They fall to the ground parched and bare and begin to decay. Then the Master, out of his magnanimous providence, causes them to spring up out of their decay. Each single seed produces many more, which also ⟨in their turn⟩ produce grain.

Mark 4:3b–8
Sources. Matthew's version is derived from Mark. Luke may have known an independent tradition, but he also knew Mark. Thomas represents another independent source. We thus have three (or two, if Luke does not reflect an independent version) independent sources for the parable of the sower (A1).
Location in the sources. Mark has located the Sower in a collection of seed parables (4:1–34), which may, in fact,

have been formed prior to Mark and taken over by him. Others take the view that Mark created the sequence or formal period that begins with 4:1 and ends with 4:33–34.

Mark's collection of parables (4:1–34) interrupts the narrative flow of that gospel. The only other long discourse in Mark is the so-called little apocalypse in chap. 13, with which 4:1–34 shares some common themes (e.g., persecution, defection).

In Mark, the parable holds the secret of God's imperial rule (4:11), which Jesus must explain to his disciples in private. This technique plays a prominent role in Mark elsewhere (7:17–22, 9:28–29, 13:3–37) (W4).

Matthew also uses the Sower to introduce an extended discourse (13:1–52) made up principally of parables, although in Matthew the collection includes more parables and is differently arranged (W1, W2).

Luke does not form a long discourse around the Sower, unlike Matthew and Mark. However, Luke, like Mark, links the aphorism about the lamp (cf. 8:16–17 with Mark 4:21–23) to the Sower and its interpretation (W2).

In Thomas, the Sower (9) occurs in the first part of the gospel where seeking and finding are prominent themes. The Sower does not suit those themes particularly well (W8b).

One core, different performances. The original structure of the parable was probably triadic: there were three episodes of failure, each of which probably had three phrases or elements. There was also a brief introduction: "A sower went out," and a conclusion consisting of three levels of yield.

The seeds "fall" in each episode—a threefold repetition, which is characteristic of oral discourse.

The introduction and the first episode share the same structure in all versions. Although Luke alters "the birds came" to "was trodden under foot," he nevertheless has three elements.

The original triadic structure of the second episode is best preserved by Thomas (9:3):

> Others fell on rock,
> and they did not take root in the soil
> and did not produce heads of grain.

Mark, on the other hand, has considerably expanded his version: He has inserted the role of the sun between the twin phrases, "since it had no," (4:5, 6), which betrays Mark's insertion technique (called intercalations: insertions are placed between identical phrases, the second of which is Mark's addition, along with the intervening material.) Further, the phrase in 4:5b, "where there wasn't much soil," is lacking in both Luke and Thomas. This lack suggests that the phrase is an explanatory gloss on the preceding, "fell on rocky ground." With these insertions omitted, the episode in Mark runs: fell on rocky ground, sprang up, withered—a triadic structure.

Luke also preserves the triadic structure, although Luke gives lack of moisture as the cause of withering, rather than thinness of soil. As is often the case, Matthew follows Mark closely.

To the third episode Mark has added a fourth element, "and it produced no fruit," to go with his notice in 4:19. Otherwise all versions reflect a simple, triadic arrangement: fell, grew up, choked.

To the conclusion Mark has added two verbs, "came up and grew," in conformity with his habit of doubling elements (W4). In the judgment of many scholars, Mark's threefold yield is original because it is triadic and because it lacks symmetry (30/60/100) and closure (it does not have

a conclusion: other seed may have produced other quantities), both of which are characteristic of Jesus' parabolic discourse. The conclusion to the versions in Thomas and Luke have been simplified and rounded off, thus creating closure.

Attribution. It is evident from these observations that the three basic versions (Mark, Thomas, Luke) all offer important evidence in reconstructing the history of the tradition. All three are close to the original structure, yet all three have undergone significant modification. As a consequence, Fellows' evaluations of the versions fell in the lower pink range, and no version merited a red designation. The difference in weighted averages among the five gospels is insignificant. Luke falls on the dividing line and so is designated gray, but in fact Luke's version differs only slightly from the other three.

1 Clement may represent an independent tradition, yet Clement provides a good example of a parable being modified to support a theological point. ■

Who Has Ears

Saying	Percentage				Wgt.
	R	P	G	B	Av.
Mk 4:9	13	33	13	40	.40 **G**
Mt 13:9	13	33	13	40	.40 **G**
Lk 8:8	13	33	13	40	.40 **G**
Mk 4:23	13	33	13	40	.40 **G**
Mt 11:15	13	33	13	40	.40 **G**
Mt 13:43	13	33	13	40	.40 **G**
Lk 14:35	13	33	13	40	.40 **G**
Th 8:4	13	33	13	40	.40 **G**
Th 21:10	13	33	13	40	.40 **G**
Th 24:2	13	33	13	40	.40 **G**
Th 63:4	13	33	13	40	.40 **G**
Th 65:8	13	33	13	40	.40 **G**
Th 96:3	13	33	13	40	.40 **G**
Rev 2:7	7	13	0	80	.16 **B**
Rev 2:11	7	13	0	80	.16 **B**
Rev 2:17	7	13	0	80	.16 **B**
Rev 2:29	7	13	0	80	.16 **B**
Rev 3:6	7	13	0	80	.16 **B**
Rev 3:13	7	13	0	80	.16 **B**
Rev 3:22	7	13	0	80	.16 **B**
Rev 13:9	13	33	13	40	.40 **G**

"Whoever has two good ears should use them!"

[10]Whenever he went off by himself, those close to him with the twelve would ask him about the parables. [11]And he would say to them: **"To you the secret of God's imperial rule has been granted; but to those outside everything is presented in parables, [12]so that 'They may look with eyes wide open but never quite see, and may listen with attentive ears but never quite understand, otherwise they might turn around and find forgiveness'!"**

Secret of God's Imperial Rule

Saying	Percentage				Wgt.
	R	P	G	B	Av.
Mk 4:11	0	4	32	64	.13 **B**
Mt 13:11	0	8	24	68	.13 **B**
Lk 8:10	0	4	32	64	.13 **B**
Th 62:1	0	0	12	88	.04 **B**

Matt 13:9 ➡ Mark 4:9

[9]"Whoever has two ears should use them. **[If you have a mind, put it to work.]**"

Luke 8:8b ➡ Mark 4:9

[8]". . . During his discourse, he would call out, "Whoever has two good ears should use them."

Matt 13:11 ➡ Mark 4:11

[11]In response he said to them, "To you it has been granted to know the secrets of Heaven's imperial rule, but to everyone else it has not been granted."

Luke 8:10 ➡ Mark 4:11

[10]He replied, "To you it has been granted to know the secrets of God's imperial rule; but to the rest there are **only parables,** so that 'They may look but not see, listen but not understand.'"

Thom 62:1 ➡ Mark 4:11

[1]Jesus said, "I disclose my mysteries to those [who are worthy] of [my] mysteries."

Matt 13:13–15 ➡ Mark 4:12

[13]"Therefore I speak to them in parables, **because 'When they look they don't see and when they listen they don't hear or understand.' [14]Moreover, it fulfills for them the prophecy of Isaiah, which says, 'You listen closely, yet you will never understand, and you look intently but never see. [15]For the mind of this people has grown dull, and their ears are hard of hearing, and they have shut their eyes, lest they see with their eyes, and hear with their ears, and understand with their minds, and turn back and I heal them."**

Luke 8:10 ➡ Mark 4:12

[10]He replied, "To you it has been granted to know the secrets of God's imperial rule; but to the rest there are only parables, **so that 'They may look but not see, listen but not understand.'"**

Unhearing Ears

Saying	Percentage					Wgt. Av.
	R	P	G	B		
Mk 4:12	0	0	0	100	.00	**B**
Mt 13:13b–15	0	0	0	100	.00	**B**
Lk 8:10	0	0	0	100	.00	**B**

Mark 4:9

Sources. This saying occurs repeatedly in the gospels and the Book of Revelation (A1). It also occurs in the *Sophia of Jesus Christ,* a Nag Hammadi tractate in the form of a revelation discourse addressed by the risen Christ to his followers. There was a tendency, furthermore, for scribes to insert the admonition in the gospels, especially as the conclusion to parables (Mark 7:16, Matt 25:29, 30, Luke 8:15, 12:21, 13:9, 21:4).

One core, different performances. There are two noteworthy variations in the saying. Sometimes the catchword *hear* is doubled: literally, "The one who has ears to hear should hear." The Scholars Version has rendered this doubling as: "Whoever has two good ears (= ears that function) should use them (= to hear)." When the catchword *hear* is not doubled, the translation is: "Whoever has two ears should use them." The other variation is between plural (two) ears and a singular ear. The singular occurs in the Book of Revelation and in the *Sophia of Jesus Christ* (but not in the Greek fragment of that work, POxy 1081). Other variations are grammatical and of no particular significance.

Use. The saying is often appended to parables as a conclusion. It appears elsewhere in the gospels after sayings that are obscure, or are difficult to understand, or were thought to be difficult to understand (W1). Parables often fall in this category, as do many aphorisms. Note particularly those instances where Jesus explains to his followers (Mark 4:9, 7:16); Luke 14:35 is a good example of the admonition following a difficult aphorism.

Attribution. The appearance of the saying in the gospels drew a uniformly gray vote. Fellows were guided by two consid-

erations. First, the saying is not particularly distinctive and so could have been said by any sage (J3). Consequently, it does not tell us much about Jesus. The second consideration is more complex.

Many scholars believe that Mark 4:1–34 is a Markan creation; others hold that it is a pre-Markan composition. In either case, it does not go back to Jesus. Specifically, Mark has assembled three parables (Sower, Seed and Harvest, and Mustard Seed), to the first of which he has appended an allegorizing interpretation, almost certainly not inspired by Jesus (W3). And then in the middle of this composition he has assembled a cluster of aphorisms (4:21–25) (W1). The theme that runs through the composition is that of "hearing, listening, comprehending" (4:3, 9, 12, 15, 18, 20, 23, 24, 33) (W4). The conclusion in 4:33–34 refers to the entire essay and so functions as a conclusion to the whole (W2).

If the theme of "hearing" is Markan, it is possible that Mark has introduced the saying about two good ears into his complex (W2). Other evangelists subsequently made use of it elsewhere and it was taken up and scattered around in the tradition. Against this view of the aphorism, however, stands the Gospel of Thomas, which affords a strong and independent attestation apart from Mark's use of it. Nevertheless, Fellows elected to follow their own axiom: Put into the primary data base those items which echo the distinctive voice of Jesus (J3). "Whoever has two good ears should use them" did not strike the majority of Fellows as meeting that criterion. ∎

Mark 4:11–20

It has already been observed, in the discussion of Mark 4:3–8 and 4:9, that

Understanding the Sower

	Percentage				Wgt.
Saying	R	P	G	B	Av.
Mk 4:13–20	0	0	0	100	.00 B
Mt 13:18–23	0	0	0	100	.00 B
Lk 8:11–15	0	0	0	100	.00 B

[13]Then he says to them: "**You don't get this parable, so how are you going to understand other parables?** [14]**The 'sower' is 'sowing' the message.** [15]**The first group are the ones 'along the path': here the message 'is sown,' but when they hear, Satan comes right along and steals the message that has been 'sown' into them.** [16]**The second group are the ones sown 'on rocky ground.' Whenever they listen to the message, they receive it with instant joy.** [17]**Yet they do not have their own 'root' and so are short-lived. When distress or persecution comes because of**

---

the composition of Mark 4:1–34 cannot go back to Jesus. It remains to inquire whether 4:11, 12, and 13–20 are elements within that composition that could go back to Jesus, or whether they are elements created along with the composition.

Attribution. The Fellows of the Seminar were virtually unanimous in all three cases: Mark's 'hardening theory' in 4:11–12 (W4) and the allegorical interpretation of the Sower in 4:14–20 (W3) are the formulations of second and third generations of Christians.

Mark and others in the early church recognized that the parables of Jesus were difficult to understand owing to their non-literal language. As a consequence, interpretations were necessary. On this basis, Mark, or someone before him, theorized that those *on the inside* knew the correct interpretation of the parables—knew the secret of God's imperial rule—while those *on the outside* did not have access to that information. The inside/outside dichotomy suggests the process of group formation in the later church (W9a). However, Mark endeavors to maintain the centrality of the parable tradition by making the disciples, who do not grasp the meaning of the parables, into outsiders. Nevertheless, to the reader he makes the promise: you have the secret of God's imperial rule.

While all of this is removed from the

style of Jesus' discourse, Mark has echoed the original function of the parables: the parable itself moves the line between insider and outsider around, so that those who think they are on the inside are actually on the outside, and those who fear they are on the outside are actually inside (J5, J7). The fourth evangelist puts the matter succinctly: "I have come into this world for judgment, that those who do not see may see and those who do see may become blind" (John 9:39). This saying in John probably did not originate with Jesus in its present form, but it does express Jesus' ideas well.

The allegorical interpretation of the parable of the Sower (Mark 4:14–20, Matt 13:18–23, Luke 8:11–15) is the product of the church (W3). The Thomas version proves that the parable once circulated without interpretation (O3a). Further, the allegory is ill-suited to the parable and is inconsistent within itself: the seed is the word, the gospel, while the crop represents different classes of hearers. The possible failure of Christian proclamation is a problem for the second and third generations, when the Christian community experienced different responses to its evangelistic efforts.

Fellows of the Seminar did not find it necessary to hear special papers and vote on the allegorical interpretation, so firm were they in their judgments. The loose

the message, such a person becomes easily shaken right away. [18]And the third group are those sown 'among the thorns.' These are the ones who have listened to the message, [19]but the worries of the age and the seductiveness of wealth and the yearning for everything else come and 'choke' the message and they become 'fruitless.' [20]And the final group are the ones sown 'on good earth.' They are the ones who listen to the message and take it in and 'produce fruit, here thirty, there sixty, and there one hundred.'"

Matt 13:18–23 ➡ Mark 4:13–20

[18]"You there, pay attention to the interpretation of the sower. [19]When anyone listens to the message of ⟨ Heaven's⟩ imperial rule and does not understand it, the evil one comes and steals away what was sown in the heart: this is the one who is sown 'along the path.' [20]The one who is sown 'on rocky ground' is the one who listens to the message and receives it with instant joy. [21]However this one lacks its own root and so is short-lived. When distress or persecution comes because of the message, such a person becomes easily shaken right away. [22]And the one sown 'into the thorns' is the one who listens to the message, but the worries of the age and the seductiveness of wealth 'choke' the message and it becomes 'fruitless.' [23]The one who is sown 'on the good earth' is the one who listens to the message and understands, who really 'produces fruit and yields here a hundred, there sixty, and there thirty.'"

Luke 8:11–15 ➡ Mark 4:13–20

[11]"Now this is the interpretation of the parable. The 'seed' is God's message. [12]Those 'along the path' are those who have listened to it, but then the devil comes and steals the message from their hearts, lest they believe and be saved. [13]Those 'on the rock' are those who, when they listen to the message, receive it with joy. But they 'have no root': they believe for a short time and fall away in time of testing. [14]"What fell into the thorns' represents those who listen, but as they go on, they are 'choked' by the worries and riches and pleasures of life, and they do not come to maturity. [15]But the seed 'in good earth' stands for those who listen to the message and hold on to it with a good and fertile heart, and 'produce fruit' through perseverance."

---

quotation from Isaiah 6:9–10 reproduced in Mark 4:12 and parallels drew a unanimous black vote (O5). The vote on Mark 4:11 was no less decisive. Indeed, Fellows were generally agreed that Mark 4:10–20 was all the product of the later community and consequently did not represent Jesus. ∎

²¹And he would say to them: "Since when is the lamp brought in to be put under the bushel basket or under the bed? It's put on the lampstand, isn't it?

Placing the Lamp

Saying	Percentage				Wgt.
	R	P	G	B	Av.
Mk 4:21	27	47	17	10	.63 P
Mt 5:15	27	47	17	10	.63 P
Lk 8:16	27	47	17	10	.63 P
Lk 11:33	27	47	17	10	.63 P
Th 33:2–3	27	47	17	10	.63 P

Matt 5:15 ➡ Mark 4:21

¹⁵"Nor do they light a lamp and put it under a bushel basket but on the lampstand, and it sheds light for all those in the house."

Luke 8:16 ➡ Mark 4:21

¹⁶"No one lights a lamp and covers it with a pot or puts it under a bed; rather, one puts it on a lampstand, so that those who come in can see the light."

Luke 11:33 ➡ Mark 4:21

³³"No one lights a lamp and then puts it in a cellar or under a bushel, but rather on a lampstand so that those who enter can see the light."

Thom 33:2–3 ➡ Mark 4:21

²"After all, no one lights a lamp and puts it under a basket, nor does one put it in a hidden place. ³Rather, one puts it on a lampstand so that all who come and go will see its light."

Preface to Mark 4:21–25

Composition of Mark 4:21–25. The cluster of sayings in Mark is composed of two subclusters of two aphorisms each (4:21–22, 24–25), joined together (W1).

Placing the Lamp (4:21) has been joined by *Hidden Brought to Light* (4:22) to form a thematic cluster around the topic: *light.* The second subcluster is formed out of *Measure for Measure* (4:24) and *Have and Receive* (4:25), which focus on the theme: *measure.*

Mark has framed the two subclusters with similar introductory sentences: "And he would say to them" (4:21a, 24a) and the admonition to listen (4:23, 24b). The second aphorism in each subcluster is linked to the first by means of an inferential term (Greek *gar* = "after all" or "indeed").

Sources. The four aphorisms in the Markan cluster are independently attested in at least three sources (A1), as the following table indicates:

Placing the Lamp

Mark:	Mark 4:21 // Luke 8:16
Q:	Luke 11:33 // Matt 5:15
Thom:	Thom 33:2–3

Hidden Brought to Light

Mark:	Mark 4:22 // Luke 8:17
Q:	Luke 12:2 // Matt 10:26
Thom:	Thom 5:2 // Thom 6:5–6
	POxy654 5:2 // 6:5

Measure for Measure

Mark:	Mark 4:24
Q:	Luke 6:37–38 // Matt 7:1–2
1Clem:	1 Clem 13:2
PolPhil:	PolPhil 2:3

Have and Receive

Mark:	Mark 4:25 // Luke 8:18b–e //
	Matt 13:12
Q:	Luke 19:26 // Matt 25:29
Thom:	Thom 41:1–2

The evidence presented in this table demonstrates that each of the four aphorisms once circulated independently

(O2). Each of the four was taken up into both Mark and Q but in different contexts (A2), and three of the four appear also in Thomas. ■

Mark 4:21b–e

Sources. This saying is attested by Q (Luke 11:33//Matt 5:15), Thomas (33:2–3), and, of course, Mark (A1).

Form. In Mark, the adage consists of two rhetorical questions, the answers to which everyone knows. It therefore reflects a kind of folk wisdom the application of which would vary from situation to situation (O5). It is no longer possible to say how Jesus used it, if he did.

Markan themes. Mark has joined the next saying to the questions about the lamp to emphasize the importance of correct hearing—a theme that runs through the collection of parables in 4:1–34 (W4). The gospel is a mystery, but it can be heard correctly: "If anyone has two good ears, use them!" (4:23). The fact that Mark has pressed a saying about light into service for his hearing theme—and thereby mixes his metaphors—shows that the saying about the lamp originally occurred in a different context. Indeed, this saying occurs in different contexts in Matthew, Luke (11:33), and Thomas (W2, but also A2).

Attribution. In spite of the variations in both the content of the saying and its placement in the gospels, Fellows of the Seminar thought the saying ought to be included in the data base for determining what Jesus said. The reasons for this judgment are: (a) it is Jesus' style to speak in figures that cannot be taken literally (J7); (b) the application of the saying is left ambiguous (J7); (c) the saying is well attested (A1); (d) the saying is short and memorable (J1). ■

Hidden Brought to Light

| Saying | Percentage | | | | Wgt. |
	R	P	G	B	Av.
Mk 4:22	0	20	75	5	.38 G
Mt 10:26	0	65	30	4	.54 P
Lk 8:17	0	65	30	4	.54 P
Lk 12:2	0	70	26	4	.55 P
POxy654 5:2	0	74	22	4	.57 P
Th 5:2	0	74	22	4	.57 P
POxy654 6:5	0	68	27	5	.55 P
Th 6:5–6	0	70	26	4	.55 P
POxy654 5:3	0	13	4	83	.10 B

²²After all, there is nothing hidden except to be brought to light, nor anything secreted away that won't be exposed.

²³If anyone has two good ears, use them!"

²⁴And he went on to say to them: "Pay attention to what you hear! The measure you use will be the measure used on you, and then some.

²⁵In fact, to those who have, more will be given, and from those who don't have, even what they do have will be taken away!"

Matt 10:26 ➡ Mark 4:22

²⁶"So don't be afraid of them. After all, there is nothing veiled that will not be unveiled and hidden that will not be made known."

Luke 8:17 ➡ Mark 4:22

¹⁷"After all, there is nothing hidden that will not be brought to light, nor secreted away that will not be made known and exposed."

Luke 12:2 ➡ Mark 4:22

²"There is nothing concealed that will not be revealed, nothing hidden that will not be made known."

POxy654 5:2–3 ➡ Mark 4:22

²"For there is nothing hidden that will not become manifest, ³and nothing buried that will not be raised."

Thom 5:2 ➡ Mark 4:22

²"After all, there is nothing hidden that will not be revealed."

Thom 6:5–6 ➡ Mark 4:22

⁵"For there is nothing hidden that will not be revealed, ⁶and there is nothing covered up that will remain undiscovered."

POxy 654 6:5 ➡ Mark 4:22

⁵"For there is nothing hidden that will not be manifest."

Mark 4:22

Sources. This saying is found in varying forms in Mark, Q, and Thomas (A1) It is also preserved in different contexts (A2).

Stages of the tradition. The simplest form is found in Thom 5:2//POxy654 6:5 (O3a): here it is a single saying. It has been expanded to a couplet in Thom 6:5–6 and POxy654 5:2–3 (W3). It also has the form of a couplet in Q: Luke 12:2// Matt 10:26. The form in Mark 4:22// Luke 8:17 has become garbled: People do not generally hide things in order to make them known. In fact, Mark has remodelled the saying to make it fit the context into which he has placed it: he has appended 4:22 to 4:21 as a way of

interpreting it (W1): the mysterious gospel—his theme—is not intended to be hidden, but to be brought to light (W4).

If the saying goes back to the historical Jesus, the original context has been lost.

Attribution. Fellows were inclined on balance to agree that this saying is correctly attributed to Jesus, even in its expanded form. Those who ranked it gray or black did so in part because they judged this saying a part of folk wisdom (O5) and not particularly enlightening about Jesus (J3). In this instance, as in many other comparable cases, a piece of proverbial wisdom of a general nature is extremely difficult to interpret without a context. On the other hand, the paradox expressed is not unlike other paradoxical

Measure for Measure

Saying	R	P	G	B	Av.
Mk 4:24	13	13	23	50	.30 G
Mt 7:2	13	13	23	50	.30 G
Lk 6:38c	13	13	23	50	.30 G
1 Clem 13:2	13	13	23	50	.30 G
PolPhil 2:3e	13	13	23	50	.30 G

Percentage / Wgt. headers above columns R P G B Av.

Have and Receive

Saying	R	P	G	B	Av.
Mk 4:25	0	61	30	9	.51 P
Mt 13:12	0	57	35	9	.49 G
Mt 25:29	0	57	35	9	.49 G
Lk 8:18	0	61	30	9	.51 P
Lk 19:26	0	57	35	9	.49 G
Th 41:1–2	0	61	30	9	.51 P

Matt 7:2 ➡ Mark 4:24

²"For the judgment you hand out will be the judgment you receive, and the measure you use will be the measure used on you."

Luke 6:38 ➡ Mark 4:24

³⁸"Give, and it will be given to you: good measure, pressed down, shaken together, overflowing, will be poured into your lap. For the measure you use will be the measure used on you."

1 Clem 13:2 ➡ Mark 4:24

². . . "The measure you give will be the measure you get."

PolPhil 2:3 ➡ Mark 4:24

³. . . "The measure you give will be the measure you get back."

Matt 13:12 ➡ Mark 4:25

¹²"In fact, to those who have, more will be given, and then some; and from those who don't have, even what they do have will be taken away!"

Matt 25:29 ➡ Mark 4:25

²⁹"To everyone who has it will be added and then some, and from the one who does not have, even what he has will be taken from him."

Luke 8:18 ➡ Mark 4:25

¹⁸"So pay attention to how you're listening! In fact, to those who have more will be given, and from those who don't have, even what they do have will be taken away."

Luke 19:26 ➡ Mark 4:25

²⁶He said, "I tell you, to everyone who has, more will be added; but from those who have not, even what they have will· be taken away."

Thom 41:1–2 ➡ Mark 4:25

¹Jesus said, "Whoever has something in hand will be given more, ²and whoever has nothing will be deprived of even the little that person has."

statements made by Jesus (J6). It was evidently this quality that induced many Fellows to vote pink. ■

Mark 4:24

Attribution. The saying *Measure for Measure* is basically a legal precept announcing God's judgment. Without modification, it appears inimical to Jesus' fundamental announcement of God's unlimited love and expansive mercy (G5). However, Luke has linked

the saying to "give, and it will be given to you," which brings it more into line with Jesus' emphasis on reciprocity ("Forgive, and you will be forgiven," Luke 6:37). Luke's "They'll put in your lap a full measure, packed down, sifted and overflowing" appears to be echoed in Mark's addition, "and then some"; both are probably Christian expansions (W8a). Fellows generally held that the bare saying tells us nothing distinctive about Jesus (J3). ■

Seed and Harvest

Saying	Percentage				Wgt.
	R	P	G	B	Av.
Mk 4:26–29	4	28	48	20	.39 G
Th 21:9	0	52	24	24	.43 G

[26]And he would say: "God's imperial rule is like this: Suppose someone sows seed on the ground, [27]and sleeps and rises night and day, and the seed sprouts and matures, although one is unaware of it. [28]The earth produces fruit on its own, first a shoot, then a head, then mature grain on the head. [29]But when the grain ripens, all of a sudden ⟨that farmer⟩ sends for the sickle, because it's harvest time."

Thom 21:9 ➡ Mark 4:26–29
[9]"When the crop ripened, that one came quickly with sickle in hand and harvested it."

Mark 4:25

Attribution. In Q the saying *Have and Receive* appears as the conclusion to the parable of the Money Given in Trust (Matt 25:29//Luke 19:26) (W1). For this reason, many scholars think the adage belonged originally to legal language and thus was a legal precept like the saying in Mark 4:24: it seems to have that same judgmental ring to it. If this dictum is a saying borrowed from judicial language and made to serve in a context of eschatological judgment, it probably does not go back to Jesus.

On the other hand, the saying is preserved independently in both Mark and Thomas (A1), and thus need not be connected with the parable as it is in Q. This saying reverses the system of rewards and punishments in place for the ordinary person—those who have it will lose out, and those who lack it will get it—and so turns ordinary expectations on their head (J5). In this respect, the saying has an authentic ring to it.

The weighted averages indicate that the vote was almost evenly divided: only a few points separate the pink from the gray. Like other proverbial sayings of this sort, it is extremely difficult to interpret without a specific context. ■

Mark 4:26–29

Source. The parable of Seed and Harvest appears only in Mark. Neither Matthew nor Luke reproduces it, possibly because they considered it difficult to understand, and, unlike the Sower, it was not accompanied by an interpretation.

The allusion in Thom 21:9 is to Joel 4:13 (LXX; MT 3:13), which provides a weak connection of Thomas with Mark 4:29: Mark has probably been influenced by the same passage in Joel (O5). At all events, Mark is the sole source for this parable.

Matthew, however, records a similar parable, The Planted Weeds, which does have an interpretation appended (Matt 13:24–30, 36–43). The same parable appears in Thom 57 without the appended explanation (O3a).

Core. The Seed and Harvest is tightly narrated in four steps or stages:

the farmer sows
the seed sprouts and grows
the earth produces blade, ear, and grain
the farmer reaps.

The farmer acts only at the beginning and end; the seed grows without the farmer being aware of it and it produces grain on

³⁰And he would say: "To what should we compare God's imperial rule, or what parable should we use for it? ³¹Consider the mustard seed: When it is sown on the ground, though it is the smallest of all the seeds on the earth, ³²—yet when it is sown, it comes up, and becomes the biggest of all garden plants, and produces branches, so that the birds of the sky can nest in its shade."

Mustard Seed

Saying	Percentage				Wgt.
	R	P	G	B	Av.
Mk 4:30–32	43	36	21	0	.74 P
Mt 13:31–32	38	31	24	7	.67 P
Lk 13:18–19	36	39	21	4	.69 P
Th 20:2–4	39	50	11	0	.76 R

Matt 13:31–32 ➡ Mark 4:30–32
³¹He put another parable before them with these words: "Heaven's imperial rule is like a mustard seed, which a man took and sowed in his field. ³²Though it is the smallest of all seeds, yet when it has grown up, it is the largest of garden plants, and becomes a tree, so that the birds of the sky come and roost in its branches."

Luke 13:18–19 ➡ Mark 4:30–32
¹⁸Then he would say, "What is the imperial rule of God like? To what should I compare it? ¹⁹It is like a mustard seed which a man took and tossed into his garden. It grew and became a tree, and the birds of the sky roosted in its branches."

Thom 20:1–4 ➡ Mark 4:30–32
¹ The disciples said to Jesus, "Tell us what heaven's imperial rule is like."

²He said to them, "It is like a mustard seed. ³⟨It⟩ is the smallest of all seeds, ⁴but when it falls on prepared soil, it produces a large plant and becomes a shelter for birds of sky."

its own—without the farmer's help. Only at the end, at harvest time, does the farmer reenter the picture with his sickle. That moment arrives *all of a sudden.*

Interpretation. If God's rule is to be compared with the seed, some interpreters hold that God's domain is internal, secretly at work. If the parable illustrates the process of growth, then God's rule is a growing, vital thing, unaided by human effort. If God's rule is to be likened to the harvest, the parable can be understood apocalyptically to refer to the judgment at the end of history. But the parable is probably to be taken as a whole to refer to God's rule. In that case, the parable emphasizes the contrast between what the seed and earth achieve on their own in comparison with the minor contributions of humankind to the process.

Attribution. The Fellows of the Semi-nar took the parable to be reminiscent of a figure of speech Jesus used (J7), but held that it was not originally a metaphor for the domain of God. In considering the parable since the publication of Red Letter Parables, the Fellows downgraded it from pink to gray. The allusion in Thom 21:9 is only remotely connected to the parable and occurs in a different context. ■

Mark 4:30–32
Sources. The Mustard Seed is recorded in three independent sources: Mark, Q, and Thomas. Most scholars think the Q version is best preserved in Luke (A1). In that case, Luke and Thomas have the briefest and simplest versions (O3a). Matthew appears to take elements from both Q and Mark in creating his version.

In Q the parables of the Mustard Seed

³³And with the help of many such parables he would speak his message to them according to their ability to comprehend. ³⁴Yet he would not say anything except in parables, but would spell everything out in private to his own disciples.

---

and Leaven were apparently linked (Matthew and Luke both link them). Mark does not know the Leaven. Thomas has both parables, but they appear in widely separated places (Mustard Seed in 20; Leaven in 96). It seems likely that the two were joined for the first time in Q (W1).

Structure. The Mustard Seed has a simple four-part structure. God's imperial rule is like:

   a. a mustard seed (the smallest of all seeds)
   b. which when sown (falls, is tossed) on the ground (field, garden, prepared soil)
   c. becomes a big plant (tree) (with branches)
   d. and birds of the sky nest (roost) under or in its branches.

(a) In all versions the seed is the mustard seed, proverbial for its smallness. It is not certain whether mention of the size of the seed is original with the parable (Thomas, Mark) or whether it is just assumed (Luke). (c) The mustard plant is clearly a shrub and not a tree. It is an annual, grows often to four feet or more in height, and proliferates readily. But it has to start over each season. Yet in Luke it becomes a tree, as it does in Matthew after it has become the largest of garden plants. In Mark, too, it becomes the biggest of all garden plants and produces branches. Only in Thomas does it remain a large plant. (d) The mustard then serves as a haven for the birds of the sky, either by furnishing shade (shelter) or by developing branches in which the birds roost.

The mustard seed and the apocalyptic tree. Jesus apparently employed a surprising figure of speech for God's domain in using the mustard seed (J5). In everyday parlance, something great would be appropriate for comparison to the work of God, not something small. As the tradition was passed on, it fell under the influence of two figures: that of the mighty cedar of Lebanon as a metaphor for a towering empire (Ezek 17:22–23); and that of the apocalyptic tree of Daniel 4:12, 20–22 (O5). In Daniel, the crown of the tree reaches to heaven and its branches cover the earth; under it dwell the beasts of the field and in its branches nest the birds of the sky. These well-known figures undoubtedly influenced the transmission and reshaping of the original parable.

In the original parable Jesus surprises his listeners by comparing the domain of God to a lowly garden plant. The Mustard Seed is thus a parody of the mighty cedar of Ezekiel and the apocalyptic tree of Daniel (J6).

Attribution. In the judgment of Fellows, the extant version closest to the original is Thomas. It was therefore given a red designation. The three synoptic versions have given way to a greater degree to the apocalyptic tree theme and so were designated pink. This parable is a good example of how the original Jesus tradition, perhaps shocking in its modesty or poorly understood (J5), is revised to accommodate living and powerful mythical images drawn from the Hebrew scripture (O5). ∎

³⁵Later in the day, when evening had come, he says to them, **"Let's go across to the other side."** ³⁶After sending the crowd away, they took him along since he was in the boat, and other boats accompanied him. ³⁷Then a great squall comes up and the waves begin to pound against the boat, so that the boat suddenly began to fill up. ³⁸He was in the stern sleeping on a cushion. And they wake him up and say to him, "Teacher, don't you care that we are about to drown?" ³⁹Then he got up and rebuked the wind and said to the sea, **"Be quiet, shut up!"** The wind then died down and there was a great calm. ⁴⁰He said to them: **"Why are you so cowardly? You still don't trust, do you?"** ⁴¹And they were completely terrified and would say to one another, "Who can this fellow be, that even the wind and the sea obey him?"

Jesus Rebukes Wind and Sea

Saying	Percentage				Wgt.
	R	P	G	B	Av.
Mk 4:35,etc.	0	0	0	100	.00 **B**
Mt 8:26	0	0	0	100	.00 **B**
Lk 8:22,etc.	0	0	0	100	.00 **B**

Matt 8:18, 23–27 ➡ Mark 4:35–41

¹⁸When Jesus saw the crowds around him, he gave orders to cross over to the other side. . . .

²³When he got into the boat, his disciples followed him. ²⁴And just then a great storm broke on the sea, so that the boat was enveloped by the waves, but he was asleep. ²⁵And they came and woke him up, and said to him, "Master, save us! We are about to drown! ²⁶He says to them, **"Why are you so cowardly, you of little trust?"** Then he got up and rebuked the winds and the sea, and there was a great calm. ²⁷And everyone marveled, saying, "What kind of person is this, that even the winds and the sea obey him?"

Luke 8:22–25 ➡ Mark 4:35–41

²²One day it so happened that Jesus and his disciples got into a boat, and he said to them, **"Let's go across to the other side of the lake."** So they cast off, ²³and as they sailed he fell asleep. A squall came down on the lake, and they were being swamped, and were in danger. ²⁴And they came and woke him up, saying, "Master, master, we are about to drown!" He got up and rebuked the wind and the rough water; and they ceased, and there was calm. ²⁵Then he said to them, **"Where is your trust?"** Although they were terrified, they marveled, saying to one another, "Who can this fellow be, that he commands even winds and water [and they obey him]?"

Mark 4:35–41

All the sayings appearing in this story are context-bound (N2) and so designated black by consensus. ∎

5 And they came to the other side of the sea, to the region of the Gerasenes. ²And when he got out of the boat, suddenly a person controlled by an unclean spirit came from the tombs to accost him. ³This man had his home in the tombs, and no one was able to bind him, not even with a chain, ⁴because, though he had often been bound with fetters and with chains, he would break the fetters and pull the chains apart, and nobody had the strength to subdue him. ⁵And day and night he would howl in the tombs and in the hills and keep bruising himself on the stones. ⁶And when he saw Jesus from a distance, he ran up and knelt before him ⁷and shouting in a loud voice, he says, "What do you want with me, Jesus, you son of the most high God? For God's sake, don't torment me!" ⁸—because he had been saying to it: **"Come out of that fellow, you filthy spirit!"** ⁹And ⟨Jesus⟩ started questioning him, **"What's your name?"** "My name is Legion," he says, "for there are many of us." ¹⁰And it kept begging him over and over not to expel them from their territory.

¹¹Now over there by the mountain a large herd of pigs was feeding. ¹²And so they bargained with him: "Send us over to the pigs so we may enter them!" ¹³And he agreed. And then the unclean spirits came out and entered the pigs, and the herd rushed down the bluff into the sea, about two thousand of them, and

The Demon of Gerasene

Saying	Percentage				Wgt.
	R	P	G	B	Av.
Mk 5:8,etc.	0	0	0	100	.00 **B**
Mt 8:32	0	0	0	100	.00 **B**
Lk 8:30,etc.	0	0	0	100	.00 **B**

Matt 8:28–34 ➡ Mark 5:1–20

²⁸And when he came to the other side, to the region of the Gadarenes, there met him two demoniacs who came out from the tombs. They were very hard to deal with so that no one was powerful enough to pass along that road. ²⁹And just then they shouted, "What do you want with us, you son of God? Did you come here ahead of time to torment us?" ³⁰And a large herd of pigs was feeding off in the distance. ³¹And the demons kept bargaining with him: "If you drive us out, send us into the herd of pigs." ³²And he said to them, **"Be gone!"** And they came out and went into the pigs, and suddenly all the herd rushed down the bluff into the sea and died in the water. ³³The herdsmen fled, and went into town and reported everything, especially about the demoniacs. ³⁴And what do you know, all the city came out to meet with Jesus. And when they saw him, they begged him to move on from their district.

drowned in the sea. ¹⁴And the herdsmen ran off and reported it in town and out in the country.

And they went out to see what had happened. ¹⁵And they come to Jesus and notice the demoniac sitting with his clothes on and with his wits about him, the one who had harbored Legion, and they were scared. ¹⁶And those who had seen told them what had happened to the demoniac, and all about the pigs. ¹⁷And they started begging him to go away from their region. ¹⁸And as ⟨Jesus⟩ was getting into the boat, the ex-demoniac kept pleading with him to let him go along. ¹⁹And he would not let him, but says to him, **"Go home to your people and tell them what your patron has done for you—how he has shown mercy to you."** ²⁰And he went away and

---

Luke 8:26–39 ➡ Mark 5:1–20

²⁶They sailed to the region of the Gerasenes, which lies directly across from Galilee. ²⁷As he stepped out on land, a certain man from the town who had demons met him. For a long time he had not worn clothes and hadn't stayed in a house but in the tombs instead. ²⁸When he saw Jesus, he shouted out and fell down before him, and said with a loud voice, "What do you want with me, Jesus, you son of the most high God? I beg of you, do not torment me." ²⁹For he was about to command the unclean spirit to come out of the human being. (⟨The demon⟩ had taken control of him many times; ⟨the man⟩ had been kept under guard and bound with chains and fetters, but he would break the bonds and be driven by the demon into the wilderness.) ³⁰Jesus questioned him: **"What is your name?"** "Legion," he said, for many demons had entered him. ³¹They begged him not to order them to depart into the abyss. ³²Now over there a large herd of pigs was feeding on the mountain; and they bargained with

him to let them enter those pigs. And he did. ³³Then the demons came out of the fellow and entered the pigs, and the herd rushed down the bluff into the lake and was drowned.

³⁴When the herdsmen saw what had happened, they fled and reported it in town and out in the country. ³⁵And they went out to see what had happened. They came to Jesus and found the fellow from whom the demons had gone, sitting at the feet of Jesus, with his clothes on and his wits about him; and they were scared. ³⁶Those who had seen how the ex-demoniac had been saved reported it to them. ³⁷Then the entire populace of the Gerasene region asked him to leave them; for they were gripped by a great fear. So he got into a boat and went back. ³⁸The man from whom the demons had gone begged to be with him; but he dismissed him, saying, ³⁹**"Return home, and recount what God has done for you."** And he went away, proclaiming throughout the whole city what Jesus had done for him.

started proclaiming in the Decapolis what Jesus had done for him, and everybody would marvel.

²¹When Jesus had again crossed over to the other side, a large crowd gathered around him, and he was beside the sea. ²²And one of the synagogue officials comes, Jairus by name, and as soon as he sees him, he falls at his feet ²³and pleads with him and begs, "My little daughter is on the verge of death, so come and put your hands on her so she may be cured and live!" ²⁴And ⟨Jesus⟩ set out with him.

Mark 5:1–20

The sayings attributed to Jesus in the account of the demon of Gerasene are all context-bound (N2) and thus never circulated independently as aphorisms or parables (O2). They were designated black by general consent. ∎

Mark 5:24b–34

The sayings attributed to Jesus in the story of the woman with the vaginal flow are neither aphorisms nor parables (J2); they did not circulate in the oral tradition as separate items (O2). The Fellows agreed by general consent to designate them black. ∎

And a large crowd started following and shoving against him. ²⁵And there was a woman who had had a vaginal flow for twelve years, ²⁶who had suffered much under many doctors, and who had spent everything she had, but hadn't been helped at all, but instead had gotten worse. ²⁷When ⟨this woman⟩ heard about Jesus, she came up from behind in the crowd and touched his cloak. ²⁸(No doubt she had been figuring, "If I could just touch his clothes, I'll be cured!") ²⁹And the vaginal flow stopped instantly and she sensed in her body that she was cured of her illness. ³⁰And suddenly, because Jesus realized that power had drained out of him, he turned around and started asking the crowd, **"Who touched my clothes?"** ³¹And his disciples said to him, "You see the crowd jostling you around and you're asking, 'Who touched me?'?" ³²And he started looking around to see who had done this. ³³Although the woman was afraid and trembling, since she realized what she had done, she came and fell down before him and told him the whole truth. ³⁴He said to her, **"Daughter, your trust has cured you. Go in peace, and farewell to your illness."**

Woman with a Vaginal Flow

Saying	Percentage				Wgt.
	R	P	G	B	Av.
Mk 5:30,etc.	0	0	0	100	.00 **B**
Mt 9:22	0	0	0	100	.00 **B**
Lk 8:45,etc.	0	0	0	100	.00 **B**

Matt 9:20–22 ➡ Mark 5:24b–34

²⁰And just then a woman who had suffered from ⟨vaginal⟩ bleeding for twelve years came up from behind and touched the hem of his cloak. ²¹She had been saying to herself, "If I only touch his cloak, I will be cured." ²²When Jesus turned around and saw her, he said, **"Take courage, daughter, your trust has cured you,"** and the woman was cured from that hour.

Luke 8:42b–48 ➡ Mark 5:24b–34

⁴². . . As ⟨Jesus⟩ went, the crowd milled around him. ⁴³A woman who had a vaginal flow for twelve years, and had found no one able to heal her, ⁴⁴came up behind him, and touched the hem of his cloak. Immediately her flow of blood stopped. ⁴⁵Then Jesus said, **"Who touched me?"** When everyone denied it, Peter said, "Master, the crowds are pressing in and jostling you!" ⁴⁶But Jesus said, **"Someone touched me; I can tell that power has drained out of me."** ⁴⁷And when the woman saw that she had not escaped notice, she came forward trembling, and fell down before him. In front of all the people she told why she had touched him, and how she had been immediately healed. ⁴⁸Jesus said to her, **"Daughter, your trust has cured you; go in peace."**

Jairus Begs for Jesus' Help

Saying	Percentage				Wgt.
	R	P	G	B	Av.
Mk 5:36,etc.	0	0	0	100	.00 B
Mt 9:24	0	0	0	100	.00 B
Lk 8:50,etc.	0	0	0	100	.00 B

³⁵While he was still speaking, the synagogue official's people approach and say, "Your daughter has died; why keep bothering the teacher?" ³⁶When Jesus overheard this conversation, he says to the synagogue official, "**Don't be afraid, just have trust!**" ³⁷And he wouldn't let anyone follow along with him except Peter and James and John, James' brother. ³⁸When they come to the house of the synagogue official, he notices a lot of clamor and people crying and wailing, ³⁹and he goes in and says to them, "**Why are you carrying on like this? The child hasn't died but is asleep.**" ⁴⁰And they started laughing at him. But he runs everyone out and takes the child's father and her mother and his companions and goes in where the child is. ⁴¹And he takes the child by the hand and says to her, "*talitha koum*" (which means, "'Little girl,' I say to you, 'Get up!'"). ⁴²And the little girl got

---

Matt 9:18–19, 23–26

➡ Mark 5:21–24a, 35–43

¹⁸While he was speaking these things to them, just then one of the officials came, kept bowing down to him and saying, "My daughter has just died. But come and put your hand on her and she will live." ¹⁹And Jesus got up and followed him, along with his disciples.

²³And when Jesus came into the home of the official and saw the flautists and crowd making a disturbance, ²⁴he said, "**Go away; the girl hasn't died but is asleep.**" And they started laughing at him. ²⁵When the crowd had been thrown out, he came in and took her by the hand and raised the little girl up. ²⁶And his fame went out into that whole land.

Luke 8:40–42a, 49–55

➡ Mark 5:21–24a, 35–43

⁴⁰Now when Jesus returned, the crowd welcomed him, for they were all waiting for him. ⁴¹Just then a man named Jairus, a ruler of the synagogue, came up to Jesus. He fell at Jesus' feet and begged him to come to his house, ⁴²because his only child, a twelve-year old daughter, was dying.

⁴⁹While he was still speaking, someone from the synagogue ruler's house came and said, "Your daughter is dead; do not bother the teacher further." ⁵⁰When Jesus heard this, he answered him, "**Don't be afraid; just have trust, and she will be cured.**" ⁵¹When he arrived at the house, he allowed no one to go in with him except Peter and John and James, and the child's father and mother. ⁵²Everyone was crying and mourning her, but he said, "**Don't cry; she hasn't died but is asleep.**" ⁵³But they started laughing at him, knowing that she had died. ⁵⁴He took her by the hand and called out, "**Child, get up!**" ⁵⁵Her breath returned and she immediately got up. He ordered them to give her something to eat.

right up and started walking around. (Incidentally, she was twelve years old.) And they were downright ecstatic. [43]And he gave them strict orders that no one should learn about this, and he told them to give her something to eat.

Mark 5:21–24a, 35–43

  The sayings attributed to Jesus in the story of Jairus could not have circulated at one time as independent aphorisms (O2); the words are therefore context-bound (N2). They were designated black by general consent. ∎

6 Then he left that place, and he comes to his hometown, and his disciples follow him. [2]When the sabbath day arrived, he started teaching in the synagogue; and many who heard him were astounded and said so: "Where's he getting this?" and "What's the source of all this wisdom?" and "Who gave him the right to perform such miracles? [3]This is the carpenter, isn't it? Isn't he Mary's son? And who are his brothers,

---

Matt 13:53–58 ➡ Mark 6:4

[53]And it happened when Jesus had finished these parables, he departed from there. [54]And he came to his hometown and taught them in their synagogue, so that they were astounded and said, "What's the source of this wisdom and these miracles? [55]This is the carpenter's son, isn't it? Isn't his mother called Mary? And aren't his brothers James and Joseph and Simon and Judas? [56]And aren't all his sisters neighbors of ours? So where do all these things come from?" [57]And they were resentful of him. Jesus said to them, "No prophet goes without respect, except in his hometown and at home!" [58]And he was unable to perform many miracles there because of their lack of trust.

Luke 4:16–30 ➡ Mark 6:4

[16]When he came to Nazareth, where he had been brought up, he went to the synagogue on the sabbath day, as was his custom. He stood up to do the reading [17]and was handed the scroll of the prophet Isaiah. He unrolled the scroll and found the place where it was written: [18]"**The spirit of the Lord is upon me, because he has anointed me to bring good news to the poor. He has sent me to announce pardon for prisoners and recovery of sight to the blind; to set free those who are oppressed,** [19]**to**

proclaim the acceptable year of the Lord." [20]Rolling up the scroll, he gave it back to the attendant, and sat down; and the attention of everyone in the synagogue was riveted on him. [21]He began to say to them, "**Today this scripture has come true as you listen.**" [22]And they would all speak well of him, and would marvel at the pleasing speech which he delivered; and would say, "Isn't this Joseph's son?" [23]And he said to them, "**Doubtless you will quote me that proverb, 'Doctor, cure yourself,' and tell me, 'Do here in your hometown what we have heard you did in Capernaum.'**" [24]Then he said, "You know as well as I, no prophet is respected in his hometown. [25]**I assure you, there were many widows in Israel in Elijah's time, when the sky was closed up for three and a half years, and there was a great famine throughout the land. [26]Yet Elijah was not sent to any of them, but to a widow in Zarephath near Sidon. [27]There were also many lepers in Israel in the prophet Elisha's time; yet none of them was made clean, except Naaman the Syrian.**" [28]Everyone in the synagogue was filled with rage when they heard ⟨him⟩ say this. [29]They rose up, ran him out of town, and led him to the brow of the hill on which their town was built, intending to hurl him over it. [30]But he slipped away through the throng and went on his way.

if not James and Judas and Simon? And who are his sisters, if not our neighbors?" And they were resentful of him. ⁴Jesus used to tell them: "No prophet goes without respect, except in his hometown and among his relatives and at home!" ⁵He was unable to perform a single miracle there, except that he did heal a few by laying hands on them, ⁶though he was always shocked at their lack of trust. And he used to go around the villages teaching in a circuit.

⁷Then he summoned the twelve and started sending them out in pairs and giving them

No Respect at Home

Saying	Percentage				Wgt.
	R	P	G	B	Av.
Mk 6:4	21	38	38	4	.58 P
Mt 13:57	21	42	33	4	.60 P
Lk 4:24	42	33	21	4	.71 P
Jn 4:44	33	38	25	4	.67 P
POxy1 31:1	29	38	29	4	.64 P
Th 31:1	50	29	13	8	.74 P
POxy1 31:2	0	17	71	13	.35 G
Th 31:2	0	17	71	13	.35 G

John 4:43–45 ➡ Mark 6:4

⁴³Two days later Jesus left there for Galilee. ⁴⁴(You see, Jesus had observed: "In his hometown a prophet gets no respect.") ⁴⁵When he arrived in Galilee, the Galileans gave him a welcome, since they had observed everything he had done in Jerusalem on the occasion of the festival. (Remember, they, too, had gone to the festival.)

POxy1 31:1–2 ➡ Mark 6:4

¹Jesus says, "A prophet is not well received in the prophet's own town, ²nor does a doctor effect cures on those who know the doctor."

Thom 31:1–2 ➡ Mark 6:4

¹Jesus said, "A prophet is not well received in the prophet's own town; ²a doctor does not cure those who know the doctor."

Mark 6:1–6

Sources. The saying about a prophet lacking respect is independently attested in Thomas, Mark, and John (A1). It thus has a firm place in the tradition.

Stages of the tradition. The earliest form of the saying is probably the single-member aphorism found in POxy1 31:1, Thom 31:1, Luke 4:24, John 4:44 (O3a). Such an adage would be typical of the type of sage Jesus apparently was (J1). The image of the doctor was probably taken from common lore (O5) and the original aphorism expanded (W3): POxy1 31:2 and Thom 31:2. Luke is also acquainted with the figure of the doctor (4:23): "Doctor, cure yourself." However, Luke has not linked the saying about the doctor to the saying about the prophet, and his form of the adage is only distantly related to Thom 31: "A doctor does not cure those who know him."

Mark has adapted the saying to his own narrative context (W4): Jesus' relatives apparently do not respect him (3:20) and at one point come to get him (3:31–35), so Mark adds the remarks about relatives and home. Matthew omits this Markan detail (13:57). Luke has inserted the saying into a different context (W4), where the figure of the prophet is appropriate (Jesus quotes Isaiah and then expounds the text, 4:1–30) (O5).

Attribution. A majority of the Fellows of the Seminar were of the opinion that the simple proverb was plausible in the context of Jesus' public work, in connection with the rejection of him in his own village (G2). Accordingly, it merited a pink designation, although the Thomas version (31:1) came very close to a red vote (weighted average: .74). ∎

Instructions for the Road

Saying	Percentage				Wgt.
	R	P	G	B	Av.
Mk 6:8–9	5	32	36	27	.38 G
Mt 10:9	0	0	0	100	.00 B
Mt 10:10a	4	43	30	22	.43 G
Lk 9:3	4	48	30	17	.46 G
Lk 10:4	0	35	39	26	.36 G

authority over unclean spirits. [8]And he instructed them not to take anything on the road, except a staff: no bread, no knapsack, no spending money, [9]but to wear sandals, and to wear no more than one tunic. [10]And he went on to say to them: "Wherever you enter someone's house, stay there until you leave town. [11]**And whatever place does not welcome you or listen to you, get out of there and shake the dust off your feet as evidence against them.**" [12]So they went

---

Matt 10:1–15 ➡ Mark 6:8–11

[1]And summoning his twelve disciples he gave them authority over unclean spirits, to drive them out and to heal every disease and every ailment. [2]The names of the twelve apostles were these: first Simon who is called Rock, and Andrew his brother and James the son of Zebedee and John his brother, [3]Philip and Bartholomew, Thomas, and Matthew the toll collector, James the son of Alphaeus, and Thaddaeus, [4]Simon the Canaanite and Judas of Iscariot, the one who, in the end, turned him in.

[5]Jesus sent out these twelve after he had commanded them, "Don't travel gentile roads and don't enter a Samaritan city, [6]but go rather to the lost sheep of the house of Israel. [7]Go and announce: 'Heaven's imperial rule is closing in.' [8]Heal the sick, raise the dead, cleanse the lepers, drive out demons. You have received freely, so give freely. [9]**Don't get gold or silver or copper coins for spending money,** [10]don't take a knapsack for the road, or two tunics, or sandals, or a staff; **for the worker deserves to be fed.** [11]**Whichever town or village you enter, find out who is deserving; stay there until you leave.** [12]**When you enter a house, greet it.** [13]And if the house is deserving, give it your peace blessing, **but if it is un-**

worthy, withdraw your peace blessing. [14]**And if anyone does not welcome you, or listen to your words, as you are going out of that house or city shake the dust off your feet. [15]I swear to you, it will be more bearable for the land of Sodom and Gomorrah on the judgment day than for that city."**

Luke 9:1–6 ➡ Mark 6:8–11

[1]He called the twelve together and gave them power and authority over all demons and to heal diseases. [2]He sent them out to announce God's imperial rule and to heal the sick. [3]He said to them, "Take nothing for the road: neither staff nor knapsack, neither bread nor money; no one is to take two tunics. [4]And whichever house you enter, stay there and leave from there. [5]**And wherever they do not welcome you, leave the city and shake the dust from your feet as evidence against them."** [6]And they left and went from village to village, bringing good news and healing everywhere.

Luke 10:1–16 ➡ Mark 6:8–11

[1]After this the Lord appointed seventy(-two) others and sent them on ahead of him in pairs to every town and place that he himself intended to visit. [2]He said to them, "The harvest is abundant, but the workers are few; so implore the lord of the harvest to dis-

Instructions for Lodgings

Saying	Percentage				Wgt.
---	R	P	G	B	Av.
Mk 6:10	5	19	33	43	.29 **G**
Mt 10:10b–12	0	10	38	52	.19 **B**
Mt 10:13a	5	19	33	43	.29 **G**
Mt 10:13b	5	15	30	50	.25 **B**
Lk 9:4	5	19	38	38	.30 **G**
Lk 10:5–6	5	19	33	43	.29 **G**
Lk 10:7a	25	31	19	25	.52 **P**
Lk 10:7b–c	5	10	43	43	.25 **B**
Th 14:4	8	56	16	20	.51 **P**

Instructions for the Town

Saying	Percentage				Wgt.
---	R	P	G	B	Av.
Mk 6:11	0	10	24	67	.14 **B**
Mt 10:14–15	5	5	24	67	.16 **B**
Lk 9:5	0	10	24	67	.14 **B**
Lk 10:8	0	14	19	67	.16 **B**
Lk 10:9	0	14	19	67	.16 **B**
Lk 10:10–12	0	14	19	67	.16 **B**

patch workers to his harvest. ³Get going; look, I am sending you out like lambs among wolves. ⁴Carry no purse, no bag, no sandals. Do not greet anyone on the road. ⁵Whenever you enter a house, first say, 'Peace to this house.' ⁶If a peaceful person lives there, your peace will rest on him. But if not, it will return to you. ⁷Stay at that one house, eating and drinking what they provide, **for the worker deserves his pay. Do not move from house to house. ⁸Whenever you enter a town and they receive you, eat what is set before you. ⁹Cure the sick there and say to them, 'God's imperial rule is closing in.' ¹⁰But whenever you enter a town and they do not receive you, go out into its streets and say, ¹¹'Even the dust of your town that sticks to our feet, we wipe off against you. But know this: God's imperial rule is closing in.' ¹²I tell you, on that day it will be more** bearable for Sodom than for that town.

¹³"Too bad for you, Chorazin! Too bad for you, Bethsaida! If the miracles done among you had been done in Tyre and Sidon, they would have sat in sackcloth and ashes and changed their ways long ago. ¹⁴But it will be more bearable in the judgment for Tyre and Sidon than for you. ¹⁵And you, Capernaum, you don't think you will be exalted to heaven, do you? No, you will go down to Hades.

¹⁶"Whoever hears you hears me, and whoever rejects you rejects me, and whoever rejects me rejects the one who sent me."

Thom 14:4 ➡ Mark 6:10

⁴"When you go into any country and walk from place to place, when the people receive you, eat what they serve you and cure the sick among them."

Preface to Mark 6:8–11

Sources. This set of instructions that was to govern the disciples as they traveled about comes from two independent sources: Mark and Q. The usual assumption is that Matthew has conflated Mark and Q in 10:1–15, while Luke has preserved two versions, the one in 9:1–6 deriving principally from Mark, the other dependent upon Q (10:1–12). In any case, there are clearly two independent sources for a set of instructions that have a common origin and share a common pattern. In addition, one of the sayings is paralleled in Thom 14:4 (A1).

Stages of the tradition. The differences in detail have occasioned heated debate among scholars. For example, Mark advises the disciples to wear sandals; Matthew (10:10) and Luke (10:4) advise them not to take sandals along. Does this minor difference indicate varying practice among early itinerant prophets? It is more probable that Mark represents a

out and announced that people should turn their lives around, ¹³and they often drove out demons, and they anointed many sick people with oil and healed ⟨them⟩.

¹⁴King Herod heard about it (by now, ⟨Jesus'⟩ reputation had become well known),

---

softening of the tradition: wear sandals, the road is long and rocky, whereas Matthew and Luke, in copying from Q, have preserved the more primitive and stringent restrictions (O4). The latter and not the former are more likely to go back to Jesus or to a very early period.

Some scholars take these instructions as evidence that Jesus and his disciples were wandering beggars. Other scholars hold the view that these instructions were given for a few specific missions to nearby Galilean villages. Still others hold that these guidelines were created by early Christian practice as it sought to shape the new movement. In general, scholars are agreed that these admonitions are old and did not originate with the evangelists. Yet opinion was divided on whether any of them can be traced directly back to Jesus. ■

Mark 6:8-9

Stages of the tradition. This is a startling set of instructions for the travelers since it is basically a list of things *not* to take with them. Mark 6:8-9//Matt 10:9–10//Luke 10:4 agree that the emissaries are to travel light: they are to take no knapsack (in which to carry provisions) and are to go out penniless, without money belt or purse. Matthew and Luke prohibit sandals as well, while Mark advises sandals for the road. Bare feet were not uncommon, and hellenistic Cynic philosophers, who went around teaching, made a point of going unshod. Given the rocky roads and rough terrain of Galilee, however, people going any distance usually wore sandals. Mark's deviation on this point suggests that he is thinking of the longer, more extended journey (O4). Matthew and Luke probably reflect the

more primitive Q tradition.

Matthew and Luke also agree that the staff is prohibited, while Mark makes an exception. The staff was useful over rough terrain or in a climb, as hikers both ancient and modern attest. Here, again, Mark has probably modified an older tradition in order to make travel more practical (O4, W4). However, Luke 10:4 makes no mention of the staff. If Luke 10 is closer to Q, it is unclear whether Q prohibited the staff.

Attribution. It was generally agreed that Luke 9:4//Matt 10:10 exhibit few pragmatic considerations and is therefore likely to be the more primitive. It is difficult to imagine later emissaries inventing such restrictions; on the contrary, it is more likely that the stringencies of a new movement would gradually be relaxed as time went by (O4). The question that divided the group was whether these radical instructions came from Jesus or were adopted by the first itinerant emissaries as they set out on the first limited tours.

Many of the Fellows of the Jesus Seminar held that these instructions in their more stringent form were in line with the simple life style Jesus generally advocated. Others took the view that such instructions were not compatible with the Jesus who came eating and drinking (G5). In either case, the variation in details suggests that each of the evangelists has modified the instructions on this or that point (W4). For both of these reasons, the majority of the Fellows believe that we cannot trace these admonitions directly back to Jesus. ■

and people kept saying that John the Baptizer had been raised from the dead and that, as a consequence, miraculous powers were at work in him. [15]Some spread the rumor that he was Elijah, while others reported that he was a prophet like one of the prophets. [16]When Herod

---

Mark 6:10

Attribution. The Seminar has considered this compendium of sayings on more than one occasion and the debate has been warm and extended. One can only say that the vote, for most sayings in this complex, hovers between gray and black, with one exception. Thom 14:4// Luke 10:7a have attracted a pink vote. The reader should bear that in mind as the discussion unfolds.

Mark 6:10//Luke 9:4 contain vague yet simple instructions: Wherever you stop, stay put. No further instructions about lodging are given.

Luke 10:5–6//Matt 10:11–13 provide additional rules, including some ritual. The traveler is to greet the house with the usual Jewish greeting, "Shalom." The concept of a peace that returns to the speaker if it is not deserved is quite primitive (Luke 10:6). The greeting has been toned down in Matthew (10:12) (O4).

Luke 10:7 also includes instructions to eat whatever the host provides; similar advice is given in the next verse. This injunction is attested independently in Thom 14:2 (A1). Matthew's reason for omitting the advice to eat food that is not kosher was evidently the pressure of Jewish dietary regulations (Matt 5:18–19). On the other hand, Luke may have had good reason to insert such advice (note Acts 10:9–16). Nevertheless, scholars are inclined to the view that Luke is closer to Q on this point. And Thomas provides independent attestation that this part of the tradition is old.

The injunction to eat whatever is set before one is a radical injunction for those living in a Jewish world with its strict dietary regulations. Jesus himself was accused of eating with 'sinners'—with non-observant Jews—according to Mark 2:16 and Q (Luke 7:34//Matt 11:19). So a radical injunction of this order might well have come from Jesus (J4). In Acts, long after the crucifixion, Peter does not seem to have been aware of such advice (Acts 10:14). He must learn the lesson all over again through a vision. This is taken by some scholars as evidence that the advice to eat food that was non-kosher was a decision of the early Christian community, which Q has put on the lips of Jesus (W7). In this case, however, the Fellows gave the admonition a pink vote, which indicates that the majority of Fellows are of the opinion that this particular injunction goes back to Jesus in some form. ■

Mark 6:11

Attribution. The act of shaking dust from the feet is a graphic Jewish gesture of disassociation; what is shaken off is usually foreign soil. Used here against Jewish towns that did not accept Jesus' followers, it has prophetic symbolic connotations: the Christian movement is in the process of separating from Judaism. This aspect of the gesture is less explicit in Mark 6:11 than it is in Q (Matt 10:14–15//Luke 10:8–10), where the comparison with Sodom and Gomorrah (Gen 19) is especially ominous.

Since this text refers to the Jewish rejection of Jesus' disciples, most scholars hold that it probably reflects their frustration over the failure of their mission among Jewish towns, long after the crucifixion (W10). Few Fellows of the Seminar thought that it was based on anything Jesus thought, much less said. ■

got wind of it, he started declaring, "John, the one I beheaded, has been raised!" [17]Earlier Herod himself had sent someone to arrest John and put him in chains in a dungeon, on account of Herodias, the wife of his brother Philip, because he had married her. [18]For John had said to Herod, "It is not right for you to have your brother's wife!" [19]So Herodias nursed a grudge against him and wanted to eliminate him, but she couldn't manage it, [20]because Herod was afraid of John. He knew that he was an upright and holy man, and so protected him, and although he listened to him frequently, he was very confused, yet he listened to him eagerly. [21]Now a festival day came, when Herod gave a banquet on his birthday for his courtiers, and his commanders, and the leading citizens of Galilee. [22]And the daughter of Herodias came in and captivated Herod and his dinner guests by dancing. The king said to the girl, "Ask me for whatever you wish and I'll grant it to you!" [23]Then he swore an oath to her, "I'll grant you whatever you ask for, up to half my domain!" [24]She went out and said to her mother, "What should I ask for?" And she replied, "The head of John the Baptist!" [25]She promptly hastened back and made her request: "I want you to give me the head of John the Baptist on a platter, right now!" [26]The king grew regretful, but didn't want to refuse her because of his oaths and the dinner guests. [27]So right away the king sent for the executioner and commanded him to bring his head. And he went away and beheaded ⟨John⟩ in prison. [28]He brought his head on a platter and presented it to the girl, and the girl gave it to her mother. [29]When his disciples heard about it, they came and got his body and put it in a tomb.

³⁰Then the apostles regroup around Jesus and they reported to him everything that they had done and taught. ³¹And he says to them: **"You come privately to an isolated place and rest a little."** (Remember, many were coming and going and they didn't even have a chance to eat.) ³²So they went away in the boat privately to an isolated place. ³³But many noticed them leaving and figured it out and raced there on foot from all the towns and got there ahead of them. ³⁴When he came ashore, he saw a huge crowd and was moved by them, because they 'resembled sheep without a shepherd,' and he started teaching them at length.

³⁵And when the hour had already grown late, his disciples would approach him and say, "This place is desolate and it's late. ³⁶Send them away so that they can go to the farms and villages around here to buy something to eat."

The Twelve Report

Saying	Percentage				Wgt.
	R	P	G	B	Av.
Mk 6:30	0	0	0	100	.00 **B**

Matt 14:13–14 ➡ Mark 6:30–34

¹³When Jesus heard ⟨their report⟩, he departed from there in a boat privately to an isolated place. And the crowds heard ⟨of it⟩, and followed him on foot from the cities. ¹⁴And he went ashore and saw a huge crowd and was moved by them and healed their sick.

Luke 9:10–11 ➡ Mark 6:30–34

¹⁰On their return the apostles reported to him what they had done. Taking them along, Jesus withdrew privately to a town called Bethsaida. ¹¹But the crowds found this out and followed him. He welcomed them, spoke to them about God's imperial rule, and cured those in need of treatment.

Mark 6:30–34

The quoted speech, "You come privately to an isolated place and rest a little," belongs to the fabric of the narrative (N2) and so is the product of the storyteller. ■

Loaves and Fishes for 5,000

Saying	Percentage				Wgt.
	R	P	G	B	Av.
Mk 6:37,etc.	0	0	0	100	.00 **B**
Mt 14:16,etc.	0	0	0	100	.00 **B**
Lk 9:13,etc.	0	0	0	100	.00 **B**
Jn 6:5,etc.	0	0	0	100	.00 **B**

[37]But in response he said to them: "**Give them something to eat yourselves!**" And they say to him: "Are we to go out and buy half a year's wages worth of bread and donate it for their meal?!" [38]So he says to them: "**How many loaves do you have? Go look.**" And when they find out, they say, "Five, and two fish." [39]Next he instructed them all to sit down and eat, some over here, some over there, on the green grass. [40]So they sat down group by group, in hundreds and in fifties. [41]And he took the five loaves and the two fish, looked up to the sky, gave a blessing,

---

Matt 14:15–21 ➡ Mark 6:35–40

[15]When it was evening the disciples approached him, and said, "This place is desolate and it's already late. Send the crowd away so that they can go to the villages and buy food for themselves." [16]Jesus said to them, "**They don't need to leave; give them something to eat yourselves!**" [17]But they say to him, "We have nothing here except five loaves of bread and two fish." [18]He said, "**Bring them here to me.**" [19]And he told the crowd to sit down on the grass, and he took the five loaves and two fish, and looking up to the sky he gave a blessing, and breaking it apart he gave the bread to the disciples, and the disciples ⟨gave it⟩ to the crowd. [20]And everyone ate and had their fill, and they picked up twelve full baskets of leftovers. [21]The number of men who had eaten came to about five thousand, not counting women and children.

Luke 9:12–17 ➡ Mark 6:35–40

[12]As the day began to draw to a close, the twelve approached him and said, "Send the crowd away, so that they can go to the villages and farms around here and find food and lodging; for we are in a desolate place here." [13]But he said to them, "**Give them something to eat yourselves.**" They said, "All we have are five loaves and two fish—unless we go ourselves and buy food for all these people." [14](There were about five thousand men.) He said to his disciples, "**Have them sit down in groups of about fifty.**" [15]They did so, and got them all seated. [16]Then he took the five loaves and two fish, looked up to the sky, gave a blessing, [and broke them,] and started giving them to the disciples to pass around to the crowd. [17]And everybody ate and had their fill. Then the leftovers were collected, twelve baskets full of them.

John 6:1–5 ➡ Mark 6:35–40

[1]After these events, Jesus crossed the sea of Galilee, ⟨also known as⟩ Tiberias. [2]A huge crowd kept following him, because they would observe the signs he was performing on the sick. [3]Jesus went up on the mountain and sat down there with his disciples. [4]It was about time for Passover, the feast of the Jews.

[5]Jesus looks up and sees a huge crowd approaching him, and he says to Philip, "**Where are we going to get bread to feed this mob?**"

and broke the bread apart, and started giving it to his disciples to pass around to them, and even the two fish they shared with everybody. [42]Everybody ate and had their fill, [43]and they picked up twelve baskets full of leftover bread and pieces of fish. [44]And the number of men who ate bread came to five thousand.

[45]And right away he made his disciples embark in the boat and go ahead to the opposite shore toward Bethsaida, while he himself dispersed the crowd. [46]And once he got away from them, he went off to the mountain to pray.

Mark 6:35–44
This account seems to be a duplication of the story of the loaves and fishes in Mark 8:1–10 and parallels. In any case, all the words attributed to Jesus are context-bound (N2) and so cannot be used to determine what Jesus said. ■

Jesus Walks on the Sea

Saying	Percentage				Wgt.
	R	P	G	B	Av.
Mk 6:50	0	0	0	100	.00 **B**
Mt 14:27,etc.	0	0	0	100	.00 **B**
Jn 6:20	0	0	0	100	.00 **B**

[47]When evening came, the boat was in the middle of the sea, and he was alone on the land. [48]When he saw they were having a rough time making headway, since the wind was against them, at about three o'clock in the morning he comes to them walking on the sea and intending to go past them. [49]But when they saw him walking on the sea, they thought he was a ghost and they cried out. [50]By now they all saw him and were terrified. But right away he spoke with them and says to them: **"Be brave, it's me! Don't be afraid."** [51]And he climbed into the boat with them, and the wind died down. By this time they were completely dumbfounded. [52](You see, they hadn't understood about the loaves; they were being obstinate.)

Matt 14:24–33 ➡ Mark 6:47–52

[24]Now the boat was already some distance from the land and was being buffeted by waves because the wind was against them. [25]About three o'clock in the morning he came to them walking on the sea. [26]But when the disciples saw him walking on the sea, they were terrified, and said, "It is a ghost," and they cried out in fear. [27]Right away Jesus spoke to them, saying, **"Be brave, it's me! Don't be afraid."** [28]In response Peter said, "Master, if it is you, command me to come to you across the water." [29]He said, **"Come."** And Peter got out of the boat and walked on the water and came to Jesus. [30]But facing the strong wind, he became afraid. And when he started to sink, he cried out, "Master, save me." [31]Right away Jesus extended his hand and took hold of him and says to him, **"You with not enough trust, why did you doubt?"** [32]And when they had climbed into the boat, the wind died down. [33]Then those in the boat paid homage to him saying, "You really are God's son."

John 6:16–21 ➡ Mark 6:47–52

[16]As evening approached, his disciples went down to the sea. [17]They embarked in a boat and were trying to cross the lake to Capernaum. It had already gotten dark, and Jesus had not yet joined them. [18]A strong wind began to blow and the sea was getting rough. [19]When they had rowed about three or four miles, they catch sight of Jesus walking on the sea and coming towards the boat. [19]They were frightened, [20]but he says to them, **"Don't worry! It's me."** [21]Then they wanted to take him into the boat, and suddenly the boat arrived at the shore toward which they had been going.

Mark 6:47–52

Once again the words attributed to Jesus in this story are the creation of the narrator (N2). They constitute neither an aphorism or parable (J2) and so could not have circulated independently during the oral period (O2). ■

⁵³Once they had crossed over to land, they landed at Gennesaret and dropped anchor. ⁵⁴As soon as they had gotten out of the boat, people recognized him right away, ⁵⁵and they ran around over the whole area and started bringing those who were ill on mats to wherever he was rumored to be. ⁵⁶And wherever he would go, into villages, or towns, or onto farms, they would lay out the sick in the marketplaces and beg him to let them touch the fringe of his cloak. And all those who managed to touch it were cured!

WHAT IS
A CRITICAL
RED LETTER EDITION

In the traditional red letter Bible, all the words ascribed to Jesus in the whole of the New Testament are printed in red. Jesus is not only made to say, "If any one strikes you on the right cheek, turn to him the other also" (Matt 5:39), he is also represented as saying, "Behold, I will throw her [the woman Jezebel] on a sickbed, and those who commit adultery with her I will throw into great tribulation, unless they repent of her doings; and I will strike her children dead" (Rev 2:22–23). The stark contrast in content makes one wonder whether the same Jesus is speaking.

In some red letter versions, the words ascribed to Jesus in the Book of Revelation are not printed in red. Ecclesiastical officials, who generally control these decisions, are understandably hesitant to identify the bloodthirsty figure of Revelation with the peacemaker of the gospels. They probably also want to distinguish words spoken by Jesus in public from those spoken by a heavenly figure privately, usually in dreams or visions, and reported by third parties. And they may be concerned to segregate the words of the earthly Jesus from those allegedly spoken by an ethereal Jesus. In other words, they are attempting to circumscribe what may be credited as words spoken by Jesus of Nazareth.

Unless limits are placed on the process, there would be no end in principle to what may be reported as words of Jesus. In the first days of the Jesus Seminar, an individual in Los Angeles submitted a thick document to the Seminar for critical review. The document contained thousands of words revealed directly to that person, allegedly by Jesus. Fortunately, the Seminar had already decided to limit its review and evaluation to words reported in written documents in the first three centuries C.E.

In distinguishing words ascribed to Jesus in the four gospels from words attributed to Jesus in the Book of Revelation, the editors of some traditional red letter editions are producing a "critical" edition. A critical edition is nothing more or less than an edition in which certain discriminations are made.

7 The Pharisees gather around him, along with some of the scribes, who had come from Jerusalem. ²When they notice some of his disciples eating their meal with defiled hands, that is to say, without washing their hands ³(you see, the Pharisees and the Jews generally wouldn't think of eating without first washing their hands in a particular way, thus observing the

---

Preface to Mark 7:1–23

The issue that sparks the controversy reported in Mark 7:1–13—one of the longest reports of such controversies in Mark—is eating with unwashed hands. It is not simply a matter of having children wash their hands after playing outside and before they come to the table; it is a much more serious matter: it concerns the contrast between holiness and purity, on the one hand, and pollution and defilement, on the other. Regulations governing holiness and purity concern the preservation of values and meanings supporting a specific way of life. The 'clean' defends that way of life; the 'unclean' permits assimilation to an alien social system.

The purity regulations observed by particular groups influence their practices, define their limits, and thus determine their relationship with outsiders. Different purity standards are a source of friction and divisiveness in every society. The Mosaic code established purity codes that were intended to set Israel apart from all other peoples. Yahweh was 'holy' and all that approached him must be 'clean.' Disagreement on what constituted holiness and purity divided Jew from Samaritan, Pharisee from Sadducee, and the Essene from them all. Each group had intricate maps of the sources of pollution and strategies for purification. One inviolable principle concerned table fellowship: to eat with those who were considered unclean was polluting; to eat with hands not ritually washed was equally defiling. At issue was not merely concern for personal

hygiene but also membership in the Jewish community.

In the controversy reported by Mark, scribes from Jerusalem are represented as challenging the presence among Jesus' followers of some who do not properly observe the official definition of clean hands. Jesus rebuts their challenge in detail. He does so in order to defend the presence of non-Pharisees in his group and to establish his authority to determine the standards of pollution and purity required by God. The scene is a classic example of verbal fencing in the challenge/riposte manner: Jesus deflects the challenge with a counterthrust that gives his disciples the advantage over their opponents.

Mark places this controversy between his two accounts of the *feeding* of the multitudes (6:30–44, 8:1–10) and immediately before Jesus' encounter with the Greek woman, the conversation with whom concerns eating. Such literary artistry as Mark exhibits here leads scholars to question whether the conflict between Jesus and the Pharisees took place during Jesus' lifetime, or whether it was a conflict between Jesus' disciples and the Pharisees at a later time. After all, Jesus himself is not accused of eating with unwashed hands; it is his disciples who are guilty. And it is possible that the Pharisees and their scribes were not active in Galilee during the earlier period. But it is certain that the Pharisees were in conflict with the Christian community on matters such as this after the fall of Jerusalem and the emergence of Pharisaic Judaism as the dominant form of that tradition. ■

Unwashed Hands

Saying	Percentage				Wgt. Av.
	R	P	G	B	
Mk 7:6–8	11	11	0	79	.18 **B**
Mk 7:9–13	11	11	0	79	.18 **B**
Mt 15:3–9	11	22	11	56	.30 **G**
EgerG 3:5–6	0	25	0	75	.17 **B**

tradition of the elders, [4]and they won't eat when they get back from the marketplace without washing again, and there are many other traditions they cherish, such as the washing of cups and jugs and kettles), [5]the Pharisees and the scribes start questioning him: "Why don't your disciples live up to the tradition of the elders, instead of eating bread with defiled hands?" [6]And he answered them: "**How accurately Isaiah prophesied about you phonies when he wrote: 'This people honors me with their lips, but their heart stays far away from me. [7]Their worship of me is empty, because they insist on teachings that are human commandments.' [8]You have set aside God's commandment and hold fast to human tradition!**" [9]Or he would say to them: "**How expert you've become at putting aside God's commandment to estab-**

Matt 15:1–9 ➡ Mark 7:1–13

[1]Then the Pharisees and scribes from Jerusalem come to Jesus, and say, [2]"Why do your disciples deviate from the traditions of the elders? For they do not wash their hands when they eat bread." [3]In response he said to them, "Why do you also break God's commandment because of your tradition? [4]For God said, 'Honor your father and mother' and 'Those who curse their father or mother will surely die.' [5]But you say, 'If people say to their father or mother, "Whatever I might have spent to support you has been consecrated to God," [6]they certainly should not honor their father [or mother].' You thereby invalidate God's word because of your tradition. [7]You phonies, how accurately Isaiah prophesied about you, when he said, [8]"This people honors me with their lips, but their heart stays far away from me. [9]Their worship of me is empty, because they insist on teachings that are human commandments.'"

EgerG 3:1–6 ➡ Mark 7:1–13

[1]They come to him and put him to the test by examination. [2]They ask, "Teacher, Jesus, we know that you are from God, since the things you do put you above all the prophets. [3]Tell us, then, is it permitted to pay to rulers what is due them? Should we pay them or not?" [4]Jesus knew what they were up to, and became indignant. [5]Then he said to them, "**Why do you pay me lip service as a teacher, but pay no attention to what I say? [6]How accurately Isaiah prophesied about you when he said, 'This people honors me with their lips, but their heart stays far away from me; they worship me in vain, [because they insist on teachings that are human] commandments . . .**'"

lish your own tradition. [10]For instance, Moses said, 'Honor your father and your mother' and 'Those who curse their father or mother will surely die.' [11]But you say, 'If people say to their father or mother, "Whatever I might have spent to support you is *korban*"' (which means 'consecrated to God'), [12]you no longer let those persons do anything for their father or mother. [13]So you end up invalidating God's word with your own tradition, which you then perpetuate. And you do all kinds of other things like that!"

Mark 7:1–13

Mark 7:6–8. Jesus' first response to the charge that his disciples do not observe the tradition of the elders by not washing their hands before meals is a quotation from Isa 23:19 (vv. 6–7). His own conclusion is in v. 8. The text he cites does not have to do with purity regulations, but with the claim that the Pharisees have interpreted the law so as to avoid some of its basic precepts. This response prepares the way for the second part of his rejoinder in vv. 9–13.

Searching the scriptures for proof of the Christian way was undertaken with great vigor and imagination by the primitive congregation. Most, perhaps all, quotations from the Greek version of the Hebrew Bible put on the lips of Jesus are secondary, in the judgment of many Fellows (O5). In addition, Old Testament texts played a significant role in the formation of gospel stories. The vote on Mark 7:6–8 and parallel was accordingly black.

Mark 7:9–13. The Pharisaic interpretation of the law permitted property and goods pledged to God to be exempted from the commandment to honor father and mother: goods so pledged did not have to be used to support parents in their old age. According to the story, the Pharisees pose as obedient sons of Israel but in fact are ungrateful children who connive to deprive their aging parents of

the real 'honor' they deserve. Thus the charge that the Pharisees set aside the commandment in order to hold to traditions ordained by themselves.

The repartee reflected in this passage seemed to many Fellows to be the kind in which Jesus frequently indulged. However, his rejoinders tended to be more of a secular nature, rather than subtle arguments about the law. The Hebrew word *korban*, which Mark has to explain, indicates that the debate is a technical point of law and that the original location of the argument was probably Palestine. Yet, prophetic condemnations of Israel were more typical of Greek-speaking Christians, such as we find attributed to Stephen in Acts 7:1–53 and on the lips of Paul in Acts 28:25–28. Moreover, the emphasis on honoring one's parents does not seem appropriate for Jesus in view of other aphorisms that probably go back to him: Mark 3:31–35; Luke 14:26; and the injunction to a would-be disciple to let the dead bury the dead, when the fellow wanted leave to bury his father (Luke 9:59–60). In the last analysis, the Fellows decided that the attempt to discredit Pharisaic tradition in principle fits better into the competitive environment of the later community, after the destruction of the temple and after Jesus had been made the supreme teaching authority in the church. ■

Not What Goes In

Saying	Percentage				Wgt.
	R	P	G	B	Av.
Mk 7:14–15	39	39	14	7	.70 **P**
Mt 15:10–11	11	67	22	0	.63 **P**
Th 14:5	25	50	25	0	.67 **P**

[14]Once again he summoned the crowd and would say to them: "Listen to me, all of you, and try to understand! [15]It's not what goes into a person from the outside that can defile; rather it's what comes out of the person that defiles. [16][If anyone has two good ears, use them!]"

Matt 15:10–11 ➡ Mark 7:14–15

[10]And he summoned the crowd and said to them, "Listen and try to understand. [11]It's not what goes into the mouth that defiles a person; rather, it's what comes out of the mouth that defiles a person."

Thom 14:5 ➡ Mark 7:14–15

[5]"For what goes into your mouth will not defile you; rather, it is what comes out of your mouth that will defile you."

Mark 7:14–15

Sources. The aphorism in 7:15 is independently attested in Thom 14:5 in a different configuration of sayings. This fact alone alerts us to the possibility that 7:15 once circulated independently (A1, O2).

Stages of the tradition. To this observation we must add others about the composition of 7:1–23. Mark's transitional phrases are clearly evident in 7:9, 14, 17, 20 ("Or he would say to them," etc.). These connectives suggest that Mark has put the entire composition together out of disparate parts. That impression is substantiated by a closer examination of the subject matter (W1, W4).

The first section, 7:1–13, treats the criticism, 'eating with unwashed hands.' The second segment, 7:14–15, concerns eating: not what goes into the mouth, but what comes out. The aphorism in 7:15 is then divided into two parts: 'what goes in' and 'what comes out.' The first is repeated in 7:18 and a commentary or explanation for the disciples follows in 7:19. The second is reiterated in 7:20, with an explanation following in 7:21–23. The first subsection retains the theme of unclean foods (problem: what can and cannot be eaten), but the second subsection abandons this theme and turns to 'what comes from the heart': evil deeds and words—these are what really defile.

This sketch of the structure of 7:1–23 makes it clear that Mark has created the whole. Only the aphorism in 7:15 can be isolated from the rest. And because it is independently attested in Thomas, it may well be older than either gospel (A1).

Attribution. The aphorism—not what goes in but what comes out defiles—is a categorical challenge to the laws governing pollution and purity. Since the saying need not be taken entirely literally—although it certainly has a literal dimension with respect to foods—it can also be made to apply to other forms of pollution, as Mark has explained. As a simple aphorism, it may well go back to Jesus (O2): it challenges the everyday, the inherited, the established, and erases boundaries taken to be sacrosanct (J4,J5). If Jesus taught that there is nothing taken into the mouth that can defile, he was undermining a whole way of life. That, in the judgment of the Fellows, sounds like Jesus. All three versions of the aphorism were accordingly designated pink. ∎

¹⁷When he entered a house away from the crowd, his disciples started questioning him about the riddle. ¹⁸And he says to them: "Are you as slow-witted as the rest? Don't you realize that nothing from outside can defile by going into a person, ¹⁹because it doesn't get to the heart but passes into the stomach, and comes out in the outhouse?" (This is how everything we eat is purified.) ²⁰And he went on to say: "It's what comes out of a person that defiles. ²¹For from out of the human heart issue wicked intentions, sexual immorality, thefts, murders, ²²adulteries, envies, wickedness, deceit, promiscuity, an evil eye, blasphemy, arrogance, lack of good sense. ²³All these evil things come from the inside out and defile the person."

What Comes Out

| Saying | Percentage | | | | Wgt. |
	R	P	G	B	Av.
Mk 7:18–19	20	30	15	35	.45 G
Mk 7:20–23	5	0	5	90	.07 B
Mt 15:16–20	11	11	22	56	.26 G

Matt 15:16–20 ➡ Mark 7:18–19

¹⁶He said, "Are you still as slow-witted as the rest? ¹⁷Don't you realize that everything that goes into the mouth passes into the stomach and comes out in the outhouse? ¹⁸But the things that come out of the mouth come from the heart, and those things defile a person.

¹⁹For out of the heart emerge evil intentions, murders, adulteries, sexual immorality, thefts, false witnesses, blasphemies. ²⁰These are the things that defile a person. However, eating with unwashed hands does not defile a person."

Mark 7:18–19

Attribution. Jesus' categorical pronouncement that nothing ingested can contaminate a person is clarified by pointing out the purgative role of the alimentary tract. Manuscript variants make it unclear whether the last part of v. 19 is supposed to be understood as words of Jesus or whether they are a parenthetical remark by Mark. The Scholars Version takes the second option as the correct one.

The Seminar was divided on whether this part of the explanation can be traced back to Jesus. On the one hand, the explanation goes well with the aphorism and fits appropriately with a Jewish context. On the other hand, the transitional remarks of Mark play on a well-known Markan theme, the obtuseness of the disciples (7:18) (W4).

The Fellows were virtually unanimous in rejecting 7:20–23 as coming from Jesus. The list of sins is similar to others found in early Christian texts, such as in Rom 1:28–32. And it appears to have been introduced here to spiritualize and thus soften the previous reference to bodily defecation. An allegorical interpretation of a saying or parable of Jesus is typical of the unfolding tradition (W3). Compare, for example, the allegory of the Sower in Mark 4:13–20. ∎

The Children's Bread

| Saying | Percentage | | | | Wgt. |
	R	P	G	B	Av.
Mk 7:27,29	0	0	0	100	.00 B
Mt 15:24,etc.	0	0	0	100	.00 B

24From there he got up and went away to the regions of Tyre. Whenever he visited a house he wanted no one to know, but he could not escape notice. 25Instead, suddenly a woman whose daughter had an unclean spirit heard about him, and came and fell down at his feet. 26The woman was a Greek, by race a Phoenician from Syria. And she started asking him to drive the demon out of her daughter. 27He responded to her like this: **"Let the children be fed first, since it isn't good to take bread out of children's mouths and throw it to the dogs!"** 28But as a rejoinder she says to him: "Sir, even the dogs under the table get to eat scraps dropped by children!" 29Then he said to her: **"For that retort, be on your way, the demon has come out of your daughter."** 30She returned home and found the child lying on the bed and the demon gone.

Matt 15:21–28 ➡ Mark 7:24–30

21And Jesus left there, and withdrew to the district of Tyre and Sidon. 22And behold a Canaanite woman from those parts appeared and cried out, "Have mercy on me, sir, you son of David. My daughter is severely possessed." 23But he did not respond at all. And his disciples came and began to complain: "Get rid of her because she is crying after us." 24But in response he said, **"I was not sent except to the lost sheep of the house of Israel."** 25She came and bowed down to him, saying, "Sir, help me." 26In response he said, **"It is not good to take bread out of children's mouths and throw it to the dogs."** 27But she said, "Of course, sir, but even the dogs eat the scraps that fall from their master's table." 28Then in response Jesus said to her, **"My good woman, your trust is enormous! Let your wish be fulfilled."** And her daughter was cured at that moment.

Mark 7:24–30

It is highly probable that the words attributed to Jesus in this story were created along with the story (N2). They are not independently attested elsewhere (A1, O2). If they do represent an aphorism that had an independent existence, Fellows of the Seminar doubt that they can be traced back to Jesus. Statements about the extent of his mission, such as Matt 15:24 ("I was not sent except to the lost sheep of the house of Israel"), are all taken to be secondary (W8a). ∎

³¹Then he left the regions of Tyre and traveled through Sidon to the Sea of Galilee, through the middle of the region known as the Decapolis. ³²And they bring him a deaf mute and plead with him to lay his hand on him. ³³Taking him aside from the crowd in private, he stuck his fingers into the man's ears and spat and touched his tongue. ³⁴And looking up to the sky, he groaned and says to him, "*ephphatha*" (which means, "Be opened!"). ³⁵And his ears opened up, and right away his speech impediment was removed, and he started speaking properly. ³⁶Then he ordered them to tell no one. But no matter how much he enjoined them, they spread it around all the more. ³⁷And they were completely dumbfounded. "He's done everything and has done it quite well," they said; "he even makes the deaf hear and the mute speak!"

Cure of a Deaf Mute

Saying	Percentage				Wgt.
	R	P	G	B	Av.
Mk 7:34	0	0	0	100	.00 **B**

Matt 15:29–31 ➡ Mark 7:31–37

²⁹And Jesus left there and went to the sea of Galilee. And he went up on the mountain and sat there. ³⁰And huge crowds came to him and brought with them the lame, the blind, the maimed, the mute, and many others, and they crowded around his feet and he healed them. ³¹Consequently, the crowd was astonished when they saw the mute speaking, the maimed made strong, and the lame walking and the blind seeing. And they glorified the God of Israel.

Mark 7:31–37
The word attributed to Jesus in this story is context-bound (N2) and thus does not go back to Jesus. ∎

8 And once again during that same period, when there was a huge crowd without anything to eat, he calls the disciples aside and says to them: ²"I feel sorry for the crowd, because they have already spent three days with me and haven't had anything to eat. ³If I send these people home hungry, they will collapse on the road—in fact some of them have come from quite a distance." ⁴And his disciples answered him, "How can anyone feed these people bread out here in this desolate place?" ⁵And he started asking them, "How many loaves do you have?" They replied, "Seven." ⁶Then he orders the crowd to sit down on the ground. And he took the seven loaves, gave thanks, and broke them into pieces, and started giving ⟨them⟩ to his disciples to hand out; and they passed them around to the crowd. ⁷They also had a few small fish. When he had blessed them, he told them to hand those out as well. ⁸They ate and had their fill, and they picked up seven big baskets of leftover scraps. ⁹There were about four thousand people there. Then he started sending them away. ¹⁰And he got right into the boat with his disciples and went to the Dalmanoutha district.

Loaves and Fish for 4,000

Saying	Percentage				Wgt.
	R	P	G	B	Av.
Mk 8:2,etc.	0	0	0	100	.00 **B**
Mt 15:32,etc.	0	0	0	100	.00 **B**

Matt 15:32-39 ➡ Mark 8:1-10

³²Then Jesus called his disciples aside and said: **"I feel sorry for the crowd because they have already spent three days with me and haven't had anything to eat. And I do not want to send these people away hungry lest they collapse on the road."** ³³And the disciples say to him, "How can we get enough bread here in this desolate place to feed so many people?" ³⁴Jesus says to them, **"How many loaves do you have?"** They replied, "Seven, and a few fish." ³⁵And he gave orders to the crowd to sit down on the ground. ³⁶And he took the seven loaves and the fish and gave thanks and broke them into pieces, and started giving ⟨them⟩ to the disciples, and the disciples ⟨started giving them⟩ to the crowds. ³⁷And everyone ate and had their fill. And they picked up seven baskets of leftover scraps. ³⁸Those who had eaten numbered 4,000 men, not counting women and children. ³⁹And after he sent the crowds away, he got into the boat and went to the Magadan region.

¹¹The Pharisees came out and started to argue with him. To test him, they demanded a heavenly sign. ¹²He groaned under his breath and says: "Why does this generation insist on a sign? I swear to God, no sign will be given this generation!" ¹³And leaving them behind, he got back in the boat and crossed over to the other side.

No Sign for This Generation

	Percentage				Wgt.	
Saying	R	P	G	B	Av.	
Mk 8:12	6	20	23	51	.27	**G**
Mt 16:4	3	17	20	60	.21	**B**
Mt 12:39	0	6	19	75	.10	**B**
Mt 12:40	0	0	9	91	.03	**B**
Lk 11:29	0	20	17	63	.19	**B**
Lk 11:30	0	14	23	63	.17	**B**

Matt 16:1–4 ➡ Mark 8:11–12

¹And the Pharisees and Sadducees came, and to put him to the test they asked him to show them a heavenly sign. ²In response he said to them, "[When it is evening, you say, it will be fair weather because the sky looks red. ³Early in the morning, ⟨you say,⟩ the day will bring winter weather because the sky looks red and dark. You know how to read the face of the sky, but you can't discern the signs of the times.] ⁴An evil and immoral generation seeks a sign, yet no sign will be given it except the sign of Jonah." And he left them behind and went away.

Matt 12:38–40 ➡ Mark 8:11–12

³⁸Then some of the scribes and Pharisees answered him, saying, "Teacher, we would like to see a sign from you." ³⁹In response he said to them, "An evil and immoral generation demands a sign, but no sign will be given it except the sign of Jonah the prophet. ⁴⁰You see, just as Jonah was in the belly of a sea monster for three days and three nights, so the son of Adam will be in the bowels of the earth for three days and three nights."

Luke 11:14–16, 29–30
➡ Mark 8:11–12

¹⁴Jesus was driving out a demon that was mute, and when the demon had departed the mute man spoke. And the crowds were amazed. ¹⁵But some of them said, "He drives out demons in the name of Beelzebul, the head demon." ¹⁶Others were testing him by demanding a sign from heaven.

²⁹As more and more people were crowding around him, he began to say, "This generation is an evil generation. It demands a sign, but it will be given no sign except the sign of Jonah. ³⁰For just as Jonah was a sign for the Ninevites, so will the son of Adam be a sign for this generation."

GNaz 21 ➡ Mark 8:11–12
The Jewish gospel does not have: three d[ays and three nights].
Variant to Matthew 12:40

Mark 8:1–10
The words quoted from Jesus in the story of the feeding of the crowd are all context-bound (N2); they are neither aphorisms nor parables (J2) and so could not have circulated independently (O2). They were designated black by common consent.

The parallel story of the loaves and fish for five thousand is found in Mark 6:35–44 and parallels. ■

Mark 8:11–12
Sources. Two versions of this saying entered the tradition at different points (A1). The Q version is found in Matt

Bread and Leaven

Saying	Percentage R	P	G	B	Wgt. Av.
Mk 8:15	11	16	37	37	.33 **G**
Mt 16:6,11	5	0	58	37	.25 **B**
Lk 12:1	0	0	61	39	.20 **B**
Mk 8:17–21	0	5	11	84	.07 **B**
Mt 16:8–11	0	5	11	84	.07 **B**

[14]They forgot to bring bread and had nothing with them in the boat except one loaf. [15]Then he started giving them directives: "Look," he says, "watch out for the leaven of the Pharisees and the leaven of Herod!" [16]They began looking quizzically at one another because they didn't have any bread. [17]And because he was aware of this, he says to them: **"Why are you puzzling about your lack of bread? You still aren't using your heads, are you? You still haven't got the point, have you? Are you just dense? [18]Though you have eyes, you still don't see, and though you have ears, you still don't hear! Don't you even remember [19]how many baskets full of scraps you picked up when I broke up the five loaves for the five thousand?"** They reply to him, "Twelve."

12:39–40//Luke 11:29–30; the Markan version appears in Mark 8:12, which is then copied, with an important addition, in Matt 16:4.

Stages of the tradition. It will be less confusing perhaps if we begin with the tail end of the tradition and work backwards.

Matt 12:40 has been Christianized (W8a): In this version, Jonah's three days and nights in the belly of the whale is compared with Jesus' three days and nights in the bowels of the earth between death and resurrection. This is the meaning given to the sign of Jonah, which Jesus is alleged to have admitted as an exception to the general rule of 'no sign' (Mark 8:12).

Luke 11:30 is a slightly less Christianized version of Matt 12:40, but still in the same category: Jesus is compared with Jonah (W8a), in this instance probably with the preaching of Jonah to the citizens of Nineveh. In both versions, 'son of Adam' refers simply to Jesus as a person and not to an apocalyptic figure (See cameo essay on 'son of Adam,' pp. 78–79).

The key question is whether the earlier version of the saying entailed Jesus' refusal to give any kind of sign—as in Mark

8:12—or whether it joined this refusal to an exception, the sign of Jonah—as in Matt 16:4. Those who hold the Q version to be the earlier believe that Mark was carrying on a polemic against understanding any of Jesus' works as signs and thus makes Jesus' response absolute (W4). In that case, Mark eliminated the reference to Jonah also because he did not want to think of Jesus as merely a prophet.

Those who hold the Mark version to be more original claim that Jesus' refusal to give any sign does not reflect Mark's special interests. Mark elsewhere allows for signs (13:4), as do the other evangelists. A flat refusal is the kind of extreme statement that seems to be characteristic of Jesus (J4).

Attribution. In evaluating this complex tradition, the majority believed that the criticism of 'this generation' sounded more like early Christian preachers after the crucifixion than like anything Jesus may have said (W8a). Such a criticism is put on the lips of Peter by Luke in Acts 2:40 and Paul articulates the same sentiment in Philippians 2:15. As a consequence, the weighted average pulled the Markan version into the gray category, all the other versions into the black. ∎

[20]"When I broke up the seven loaves for the four thousand, how many big baskets full of scraps did you pick up?" And they say, "Seven." [21]And he repeats: "You still don't understand, do you?"

Matt 16:5–12 ➡ Mark 8:14–21

[5]And the disciples came to the other side and they forgot to bring bread. [6]Jesus said to them, "**Look, take care and guard against the leaven of the Pharisees and Sadducees.**" [7]Now they looked quizzically at each other, saying, "We didn't bring any bread." [8]Because Jesus was aware of this, he said, "**Why are you puzzling, you with so little trust, because you don't have any bread? [9]You still aren't using your heads, are you? You** don't remember the five loaves for the five thousand and how many baskets you carried away, do you? [10]Nor the seven loaves for four thousand and how many big baskets you filled?

[11]**How can you possibly think I was talking to you about bread? But guard against the leaven of the Pharisees and Sadducees.**" [12]Then they understood that he was not talking about guarding against the leaven in bread but against the teaching of the Pharisees and Sadducees.

Luke 12:1 ➡ Mark 8:14–21

[1]Meanwhile, a crowd of many thousands had thronged together and were trampling each other. He began to speak first to his disciples: "**Guard against the leaven of the Pharisees,** which is to say, their hypocrisy."

Mark 8:14–21

Stages of the tradition. The exchange between Jesus and his disciples in the boat is a retrospective creation of Mark. The evangelist is reviewing the two accounts of the feeding of the crowd that he has recently related (8:1–10, 6:35–45) and utilizing the disciples' lack of comprehension to prepare for the dire events to come. The context of the saying in Mark 8:15 is therefore Mark's invention (W4), which Matthew has simply taken over. Luke omits this entire exchange because Mark's view of the disciples— they are dense, obtuse—is not acceptable to him (W4).

Attribution. The saying about the leaven of the Pharisees is found in a different context in Luke 12:1 (A2). Some saying about the leaven may be quite old, since Jesus probably uttered the parable of the leaven (Matt 13:33//Luke 13:20–21, given a red designation by the Fellows). The issues here are two: (1) Is the figure used in its established sense, or is it used in a new and odd way? (2) To whom does the saying refer?

Leaven was commonly a symbol for evil (1 Cor 5:7; in Lev 2:11 an offering of bread must be made without leaven), the unleavened for what is sacred or holy. In the parable of the leaven, Jesus turns that symbolism upside down (J5). Here, in Mark 8:15, it is used in the ordinary sense. Moreover, our texts do not agree on the target of the criticism. In Mark it is the Pharisees and Herod, in Matthew the Pharisees and Sadducees, in Luke the Pharisees alone. Since the target of the criticism varies, and since the figure is used in an ordinary sense, most Fellows were prompted to vote gray or black. ■

A Blind Man

Saying	Percentage R	P	G	B	Wgt. Av.	
Mk 8:23,26	0	0	0	100	.00	B

Who Do People Say I Am?

Saying	Percentage R	P	G	B	Wgt. Av.	
Mk 8:27,29	0	0	0	100	.00	B
Mt 16:13,15	0	0	0	100	.00	B
Lk 9:18,20	0	0	0	100	.00	B
Jn 1:42	0	0	0	100	.00	B
Th 13:1,5	0	0	0	100	.00	B

²²They come to Bethsaida, and they bring him a blind person, and plead with him to touch him. ²³He took the blind man by the hand and led him out of the village. And he spat into his eyes, and placed his hands on him, and started questioning him, **"Do you see anything?"** ²⁴When his sight began to come back, the first thing he said was: "I see human figures, as though they were trees walking around." ²⁵Then he put his hands over his eyes a second time. And he opened his eyes, and his sight was restored, and he saw everything clearly. ²⁶And he sent him home, saying, **"Don't bother to go back to the village!"**

²⁷Jesus and his disciples set out for the villages of Caesarea Philippi. On the road he started questioning his disciples, asking them, **"Who do people say I am?"** ²⁸In response they said to him, "⟨Some say⟩ 'John the Baptist,' and others 'Elijah,' but others 'One of the prophets.'" ²⁹But he continued to press them,

---

Matt 16:13–20 ➡ Mark 8:27–30

¹³When Jesus came to the region of Caesarea Philippi, he started questioning his disciples, saying, **"Who do people say the son of Adam is?"** ¹⁴They said, "Some ⟨say⟩ 'John the Baptist,' but others 'Elijah,' and others 'Jeremiah or one of the prophets.'" ¹⁵He says to them, **"What about you, who do you say I am?"** ¹⁶Simon Peter said in response, "You are the Anointed, the son of the living God!" ¹⁷And in response Jesus said to him, "You are to be congratulated, Simon son of Jonah, because flesh and blood did not reveal it to you but my Father who is in heaven. ¹⁸And I add, 'You are Peter, the rock, and on this rock I will build my congregation, and the gates of the underworld will not be able to withstand it. ¹⁹I shall give you the keys of Heaven's domain, and whatever you bind on earth will be bound in heaven and whatever you loose on earth will be loosed in heaven." ²⁰Then he ordered the disciples to tell no one that he was the Anointed.

Luke 9:18–21 ➡ Mark 8:27–30

¹⁸And it so happened once when Jesus was praying alone that the disciples were with him; and he questioned them, saying, **"Who do the crowds say I am?"** ¹⁹They said in response, "⟨Some say⟩ 'John the Baptist,' but others 'Elijah,' and others 'One of the ancient prophets has come back to life.'" ²⁰Then he said to them, **"What about you, who do you say I am?"** And Peter said in response, "God's Anointed!" ²¹Then he warned them, and forbade them to tell this to anyone.

"**What about you, who do you say I am?**" Peter says to him in response, "You are the Anointed!" [30]And he warned them not to tell anyone about him.

John 1:35–42 ➡ Mark 8:27–30

[35]The next day again John was standing with two of his disciples, [36]and seeing Jesus passing he said, "Look, the Lamb of God." [37]And his two disciples heard him speak, and they followed Jesus. [38]And Jesus turned and saw them following and said to them, "What are you looking for?" And they said to him, "Rabbi (which means Teacher), where are you staying?" [39]He said to them, "Come and you'll see." Then they did go and see where he was staying, and they stayed with him that day; it was about four o'clock. [40]Andrew the brother of Simon Peter was one of the two who heard John and followed Jesus. [41]He first found his brother Simon and said to him, "We have found Messiah (which is translated Anointed)." [42]He took him to Jesus. When Jesus saw him he said, "**You are Simon son of John; you shall be called Cephas** (which means Rock)."

Thom 13:1–8 ➡ Mark 8:27–30

[1]Jesus said to his disciples, "**Compare me to something and tell me what I am like.**"

[2]Simon Peter said to him, "You are like a just angel."

[3]Matthew said to him, "You are like a wise philosopher."

[4]Thomas said to him, "Teacher, my mouth is utterly unable to say what you are like."

[5]Jesus said, "**I am not your teacher. Because you have drunk, you have become intoxicated from the bubbling spring that I have tended.**"

[6]And he took him, and withdrew, and spoke three sayings to him.

[7]When Thomas came back to his friends, they asked him, "What did Jesus say to you?"

[8]Thomas said to them, "If I tell you one of the sayings he spoke to me, you will pick up rocks and stone me, and fire will come from the rocks and devour you."

Mark 8:22–26

Attribution. The words attributed to Jesus are context-bound (N2) and so could not have circulated at one time as independent sayings (O2). ■

Mark 8:27–30

Attribution. This scene in Mark and the parallels is a stylized scene replete with Christian motifs (W8a). Similar episodes in Thom 13 and John 1:35–42,

6:66–69 indicate how readily the primitive Christian community invented scenes of this type. The leading disciple or disciples are asked to make the good confession, which they do (note similar examples in John 6:68, 11:27). Their faith becomes the model for the faith of others. The Fellows found it unnecessary to debate the issues: the words attributed to Jesus were designated black by general consent. ■

Son of Adam Must Suffer

Saying	Percentage				Wgt.
	R	P	G	B	Av.
Mk 8:31–33	0	0	16	84	.05 B
Mt 16:21–23	0	4	16	80	.08 B
Lk 9:22	0	0	12	88	.04 B
Mk 9:30–32	0	0	16	84	.05 B
Mt 17:22–23	0	0	16	84	.05 B
Lk 9:43–45	0	4	12	84	.07 B
Mk 10:32–34	0	0	12	88	.04 B
Mt 20:17–19	0	0	12	88	.04 B
Lk 18:31–34	0	0	12	88	.04 B
Mt 26:2	0	0	12	88	.04 B
Lk 17:25	0	4	16	80	.08 B

³¹He started teaching them that the son of Adam must suffer a great deal, and be rejected by the elders and the ranking priests and the scribes, and be killed, and after three days rise. ³²And he would say this openly. And Peter took him aside and began to lecture him. ³³But he turned, noticed his disciples, and reprimanded Peter verbally: **"Get behind me, you Satan, you, because you're not thinking in God's terms, but in human terms."**

Matt 16:21–23 ➡ Mark 8:31–33

²¹From that time Jesus started to demonstrate to his disciples that he must go to Jerusalem, and suffer a great deal at the hands of the elders and ranking priests and scribes, and be killed and, on the third day, be raised. ²²And Peter took him aside and began to lecture him, saying, "May God spare you, master; this surely can't happen to you." ²³But he turned and said to Peter, **"Get behind me, you Satan, you. You are dangerous to me because you are not thinking in God's terms, but in human terms."**

Luke 9:22 ➡ Mark 8:31–33

²²He said, **"The son of Adam must suffer a great deal, be rejected by the elders and ranking priests and scribes, and be killed and, on the third day, be raised."**

Mark 9:30–32 ➡ Mark 8:31–33

³⁰They left there and started going through Galilee, and he did not want anyone to know. ³¹Remember, he was instructing his disciples and telling them: **"The son of Adam is being turned over to human agents, and they will end up killing him. And three days after he is killed he will rise!"** ³²But they never understood this remark, and always dreaded to ask him ⟨about it⟩.

Matt 17:22–23 ➡ Mark 8:31–33

²²And when they had gathered together in Galilee, Jesus said to them, **"The son of Adam is about to be turned over to human agents, ²³and they will end up killing him, and on the third day he will be raised."** And they were very sad.

Luke 9:43–45 ➡ Mark 8:31–33

⁴³And everybody was astounded at the majesty of God. While they all were marveling at everything he was doing, he said to his disciples, ⁴⁴**"Mark well these words: the son of Adam is about to be turned over to human agents."** ⁴⁵But they never understood this remark. It was couched in veiled language, so they would not grasp its meaning. And they always dreaded to ask him about this remark.

Mark 10:32–34 ➡ Mark 8:31–33

³²On the road going up to Jerusalem, Jesus was leading the way, they were apprehensive, and others who were following were frightened. Once again he

took the twelve aside and started telling them what was going to happen to him: ³³**"Look, we're going up to Jerusalem, and the son of Adam will be turned over to the ranking priests and the scribes, and they will sentence him to death, and turn him over to the gentiles, ³⁴and they will make fun of him, and spit on him, and flog him, and kill ⟨him⟩. Yet after three days he will rise!"**

Matt 20:17–19 ➡ Mark 8:31–33

¹⁷And Jesus was going up to Jerusalem and he took the twelve aside privately and on the way he said to them: ¹⁸**"Look, we're going up to Jerusalem, and the son of Adam will be turned over to the ranking priests and scribes, and they will sentence him to death, ¹⁹and turn him over to the gentiles to make fun of, and flog, and crucify. Yet on the third day he will be raised."**

Luke 18:31–34 ➡ Mark 8:31–33

³¹⟨Jesus⟩ took the twelve aside, and said to them: **"Look, we're going up to Jerusalem, and everything written by the prophets about the son of Adam will come true. ³²For he will be turned over to the gentiles, and will be made fun of and insulted. They will spit on him, ³³and flog him, and kill him, Yet after three days he will rise."** ³⁴But they did not understand any of this; this remark was obscure to them, and they did not comprehend its meaning.

Matt 26:2 ➡ Mark 8:31–33

²**"You know that in two days the Passover comes, and the son of Adam will be turned over to be crucified."**

Luke 17:25 ➡ Mark 8:31–33

²⁵**"But first it is necessary that [the son of Adam] suffer many things and be rejected by this generation."**

Mark 8:31–33

Predictions in triplicate. This is the first of three similar predictions of Jesus' suffering, death, and resurrection in the Gospel of Mark. The other two are found in Mark 9:30–32 and 10:32–34. Jesus knows what will happen to him, but the disciples either do not understand (9:32) or are frightened (10:32). Matthew and Luke adopt Mark's formulations as their own, with some revisions.

Stages of the tradition. The earliest version of the "gospel" known to us is that of Paul. He summarizes it in 1 Cor 15:3–5:

> I handed on to you among the very first things
> what I also received as tradition:
>> Christ died for our sins
>>> according to the scriptures,
>> and was buried,
>> and rose on the third day
>>> according to the scriptures.
> He then appeared to Cephas,
> and then to the twelve.

There are two steps in this formulation: Christ died; Christ rose. Both steps take place because the scriptures said they would. The two events are the fulfillment of prophecy. These same terms and formulae are rehearsed in Acts 2:23–24, 3:15, 18, and 13:27–31.

Mark's "gospel" is summarized in his three predictions of the passion of Jesus in 8:31, 9:31, and 10:33–34. These Markan predictions indicate that the author knew the two-step gospel quoted by Paul and was aware that each step was in accordance with scripture. This is the reason Mark composed a narrative gospel that climaxed in the death of Jesus, with the promise of the resurrection. Since these predictions mirror the "proclamation" (Greek: *kerygma*) of the primitive church and accord with Mark's conception of his narrative gospel (W4, W8a), most scholars regard all three as composed by Mark after the events to which they refer (W10). Mark's predictions are of course simply imitated by

Picking Up One's Cross

Saying	Percentage				Wgt.
	R	P	G	B	Av.
Mk 8:34	0	3	29	68	.12 **B**
Mt 16:24	3	3	28	66	.15 **B**
Lk 9:23	0	3	23	74	.10 **B**
Mt 10:38	0	7	20	73	.11 **B**
Lk 14:27	0	6	23	71	.12 **B**
Th 55:2	3	6	16	74	.13 **B**

[34]After he called the crowd together with his disciples, he said to them: "**If any would follow me, they should deny themselves, pick up their cross, and follow me!** [35]**For those who try to save their own life will lose it, but those who lose their life [for my sake and] for the sake of the good news will save it.** [36]After all, what good does it do

---

Matt 16:24 ➡ Mark 8:34

[24]Then Jesus said to his disciples, "**If any would come after me, they should pick up their cross and follow me!**"

Luke 9:23 ➡ Mark 8:34

[23]He would say to everyone, "**If any would come after me, they should deny themselves, pick up their cross daily, and follow me!**"

Matt 10:38 ➡ Mark 8:34

[38]"**And those who do not take their cross and follow after me, are not worthy of me.**"

Luke 14:27 ➡ Mark 8:34

[27]"**Those who do not bear their own cross and come after me, cannot be my disciples.**"

Thom 55:2 ➡ Mark 8:34

[2]"**and whoever does not hate brothers and sisters, and bear the cross as I do, will not be worthy of me.**"

Matt 16:25 ➡ Mark 8:35

[25]"For those who try to save their own life will lose it; and those who lose their own life for my sake will find it."

Luke 9:24 ➡ Mark 8:35

[24]"For those who try to save their own life will lose it; and those who lose their life for my sake, will save it."

Matt 10:39 ➡ Mark 8:35

[39]"Those who find their life will lose it, and those who lose their life for my sake will find it."

Luke 17:33 ➡ Mark 8:35

[33]"Whoever tries to preserve life will destroy it, but whoever destroys it will survive."

John 12:25 ➡ Mark 8:35

[25]"Those who love life lose it, but those who hate life in this world will keep it forever."

Matthew and Luke.

There are no predictions of the passion in either Q or Thomas, since neither mentions Jesus' passion. In John, Jesus makes some cryptic remarks about his "glorification" and his being "lifted up," but he does not make specific predictions such as we find in Mark. ∎

Preface to Mark 8:34–9:1

Three of the six sayings clustered in Mark 8:34–9:1 once circulated indepen-

dently (O2), in all probability, as the following table indicates:

(1) *Picking Up One's Cross*
    Mark: Mark 8:34//Matt 16:24//
           Luke 9:23
    Q: Luke 14:27/Matt 10:38
    Thom: Thom 55:2
(2) *Saving One's Life*
    Mark: Mark 8:35//Matt 16:25//
           Luke 9:24
    Q: Luke 17:33//Matt 10:39
    John: John 12:25

Saving One's Life

Saying	Percentage				Wgt.
	R	P	G	B	Av.
Mk 8:35	18	9	0	73	.24 **B**
Mt 16:25	27	9	18	45	.40 **G**
Lk 9:24	27	9	18	45	.40 **G**
Mt 10:39	27	9	18	45	.40 **G**
Lk 17:33	45	0	18	36	.52 **P**
Jn 12:25	0	30	30	40	.30 **G**

---

(3) *What Profit?*
Mark: Mark 8:36//Matt 16:26a//
         Luke 9:25
(4) *Life's Price*
Mark: Mark 8:37//Matt 16:26b
(5) *Son of Adam Will Be Ashamed*
Mark: Mark 8:38//Matt 16:27//
         Luke 9:26
Q: Luke 12:9//Matt 10:33
(6) *Some Standing Here*
Mark: Mark 9:1//Matt 16:28//
         Luke 9:27

Sayings (1), (2), and (5) appear in both Mark and Q (A1), but they are not clustered in Q (W1). Sayings (1) and (2) were probably not joined in Q, despite the fact that they appear side by side in Matt 10:38–39; Luke records the same two sayings in different contexts (A2), and his location is very likely original. Additionally, Saying (1) is attested in Thom 55:2, and Saying (2) is recorded in John 12:25. In sum, three of the six sayings in Mark's cluster appear unclustered in other sources (W1).

The cluster in 8:34–9:1 is Mark's creation. In so doing, he has possibly also created the double question in 8:36–37, which serves as the fulcrum of his composition; Mark is noted for his doubling technique. ■

Mark 8:34
Sources. This saying is attested by three independent and early sources: Q, Thomas, and Mark (A1). The saying is found in two forms, moreover: the positive version of Mark 8:34//Matt 16:24// Luke 9:23, and a negative version found in Q (Luke 14:27//Matt10:38) and Thom 55:2 (A3).

Attribution. The reference to the cross stands squarely in the way of attributing this saying to the historical Jesus. The admonition to take up one's cross appeals to the fate of Jesus as the standard of obedience, and appears therefore to be relevant to a time when the Christian community was exposed to the fires of persecution (W10). Further, the expectation of the imminent return of Jesus, so characteristic of the earliest community, seems to have faded into the background: picking up one's cross appears to have become a long term proposition (W9a).

For those who think that the saying originated with Jesus, it is a call to radical self-denial and perhaps a warning that association with Jesus entailed a political risk. The difficulty with this interpretation is that there is no evidence that the cross was a recognized symbol of this sort prior to Jesus' death; it became such a symbol only when Paul and Mark made it a focal point of their messages. Paul expounds at length on the significance of the cross, for example, in 1 Cor 1:17–25. The appearance of a version of this saying in Thom 55:2b is startling, to say the very least, since Thomas seems not to know, or not to acknowledge, the crucifixion. ■

Mark 8:35
One core, different performances. The only constant feature among the several versions of this saying is its core: opposing pairs of contrasting verbs and the reference to loss of life. The original wording is beyond recovery (O1).
Attribution. Mark's version exhibits several signs of Christian remodeling:

What Profit?

| Saying | Percentage | | | | Wgt. |
	R	P	G	B	Av.
Mk 8:36	33	0	17	50	.39 G
Mt 16:26a	33	8	17	42	.44 G
Lk 9:25	25	8	17	50	.36 G
2 Clem 6:2	27	9	9	55	.36 G

a person to acquire the whole world and pay for it with life? ³⁷Or, what would a person give in exchange for life? ³⁸**Moreover, those who are ashamed of me and my message in this adulterous and sinful generation, of them the son of Adam will likewise be ashamed when he comes in his Father's glory accompanied by holy angels!"**

Matt 16:26a ➡ Mark 8:36

²⁶"After all, what good will it do if a person acquires the whole world but forfeits life?"

Luke 9:25 ➡ Mark 8:36

²⁵"After all, what good does it do a person to acquire the whole world and lose or forfeit oneself?"

2 Clem 6:2 ➡ Mark 8:36

²"After all, what good does it do if someone acquires the whole world but pays for it with life?"

Matt 16:26b ➡ Mark 8:37

²⁶". . . Or what will a person give in exchange for life?"

Mark adds 'for the sake of the good news,' which is undoubtedly a Christianization; he also has 'for my sake,' in concert with Matt 10:39, 16:25, and Luke 9:24, which also sounds like a Christian addition; finally, the verb he uses is 'save,' a term normally associated with Christian salvation (W8a). For these reasons, the Seminar judged Mark's version the least likely to represent a saying of Jesus.

The relationship of the versions to each other may be observed by comparing their paired verbs:

Mark 8:35//Luke 9:24
    save/lose
    lose/save
Matt 16:25
    save/lose
    lose/find
Matt 10:39
    find/lose
    lose/find
Luke 17:33
    gain/lose
    lose/preserve
John 12:25
    love/lose
    hate/keep

Matt 16:25 is a hybrid: it combines the 'Christian' terminology of Mark 8:35// Luke 9:24 (W8a) with the secular phrasing of Matt 10:39, Luke 17:33. However, Matt 10:39 has the 'for my sake' of the Mark version. Consequently, Luke 9:24, Matt 16:25, 10:39 were all ranked gray. Only Luke 17:33, which is usually traced to Q, drew a pink vote: Luke's terminology does not seem to have echoes of later Christian doctrine. It therefore stands closer to the original form of the saying.

John 12:25 has been remodeled to accommodate the characteristic love/ hate contrast of the Fourth Gospel and was accordingly ranked lower (W4). ∎

Mark 8:36

Attribution. This saying comes from a common stock of proverbial wisdom (O5), although the sentiment was probably not alien to Jesus. The rhetorical question: 'What good does it do?' indicates that it does no good at all if one acquires the world's goods and winds up paying for that acquisition with life. While the saying was undoubtedly drawn from secular wisdom, the ideas in it are

Life's Price

Saying	Percentage				Wgt.
	R	P	G	B	Av.
Mk 8:37	25	8	17	50	.36 **G**
Mt 16:26b	33	0	8	58	.36 **G**

Son of Adam Will Be Ashamed

Saying	Percentage				Wgt.
	R	P	G	B	Av.
Mk 8:38	9	9	12	71	.19 **B**
Mt 16:27	6	6	3	86	.11 **B**
Lk 9:26	9	9	12	71	.19 **B**
Mt 10:32–33	3	9	11	77	.12 **B**
Lk 12:8–9	6	9	18	68	.18 **B**
2 Tim 2:12b	0	9	0	91	.06 **B**
Rev 3:5b	0	6	3	91	.05 **B**
2 Clem 3:2	0	3	9	88	.05 **B**

Matt 16:27 ➡ Mark 8:38
[27]"For the son of Adam is going to come in the glory of his Father with his angels, and then he will reward everyone according to their deeds."

Luke 9:26 ➡ Mark 8:38
[26]"Moreover, whoever is ashamed of me and of my message, of that person will the son of Adam be ashamed when he comes in his glory and the glory of the Father and of the holy angels."

Matt 10:32–33 ➡ Mark 8:38
[32]"Everyone who will acknowledge me in public, I too will acknowledge before my Father who is in heaven. [33]But whoever disowns me in public, I will also disown before my Father who is in heaven."

Luke 12:8–9 ➡ Mark 8:38
[8]"I tell you, everyone who acknowledges me in public, the son of Adam will acknowledge before God's angels. [9]But whoever disowns me in the presence of other people will be disowned in the presence of God's angels."

2 Tim 2:11–13 ➡ Mark 8:38
[11]These are words you can trust: "If we died with him, we will live with him. [12]If we persist, we will reign with him. If we disown him, he will disown us. [13]If we are faithless, he remains faithful, since he cannot disown himself."

Rev 3:5 ➡ Mark 8:38
[5]"The person who is victorious will be robed in white, and I swear I won't blot that person's name out of the book of life. I will acknowledge that person's name in the presence of my Father and his angels."

2 Clem 3:2 ➡ Mark 8:38
[2]He himself also says, "The person who acknowledges me in public I will acknowledge in the presence of my Father."

in accord with what we know of Jesus elsewhere (G5). Gray is an appropriate designation. ■

Mark 8:37
The adage about life's price belongs, like the preceding saying, to the category of common wisdom (O5). Once again, the sentiment was not alien to Jesus, so a gray designation is appropriate. ■

Mark 8:38
Sources and versions. There are two versions, the one recorded by Mark 8:38 and parallels (Luke 9:26, with a partial paraphrase in Matt 16:27), and the other preserved by Q (Matt 10:32–33//Luke 12:8–9). The first promises shame for shame. The second is given a legal twist: acknowledgment for acknowledgment, denial for denial.

Some Standing Here

Saying	Percentage				Wgt.
	R	P	G	B	Av.
Mk 9:1	0	36	28	36	.33 **G**
Mt 16:28	0	4	24	72	.11 **B**
Lk 9:27	4	32	28	36	.35 **G**

9 And he used to tell them: "I swear to you: Some of those standing here certainly won't taste death before they see God's imperial rule set in with power!"

Matt 16:28 ➡ Mark 9:1

²⁸I swear to you: **"Some of those standing here certainly won't taste death before they see the son of Adam's imperial rule arriving."**

Luke 9:27 ➡ Mark 9:1

²⁷"I swear to you, some of those standing here certainly won't taste death until they see God's imperial rule."

It is unclear which version is the earlier, or whether the Q version even mentioned 'the son of Adam': Matthew substitutes 'I' (J8b). The Q version does *not* mention the coming of the son of Adam.

Attribution. This saying draws a strict parallel between the response of people to Jesus on earth and the reception they may expect from 'the son of Adam' at his coming or in heaven. 'The son of Adam' is here an apocalyptic figure who will appear at the end of history and sit in judgment (see the cameo essay on the son of Adam, pp. 78–79). This reference almost certainly excludes the possibility of tracing this saying back to Jesus (W8a).

Mark's version has been influenced by Daniel 7:13–14:

As I looked on, in a night vision, one like a human being [or: son of Adam] came with the clouds of heaven: he reached the Ancient of Days and was presented to him. Dominion, glory and kingship were given to him; all peoples and nations of every language must serve him. His dominion is an everlasting dominion that shall not pass away, and his kingship one that shall not be destroyed.

This influence is to be observed also in 13:26 and 14:41. On each occasion, Mark implies that 'the son of Adam' is Jesus. The 'coming' is derived from Daniel. Mark's allusion to the possibility of being embarrassed by Jesus' words presup-

poses a situation where Jesus is absent (W10): such was the historical situation for Mark and his readers.

The context reflected by the Q version is similar to the one evident in Mark: followers of Jesus are being forced to choose between acknowledging or denying Jesus. The disciples were subject to this dilemma only after Jesus' crucifixion (W10).

Most Fellows of the Seminar view these sayings as formulations shaped by the duress suffered by the church after Jesus' death. ■

Mark 9:1

Attribution. For Mark this saying means two things: (a) God's imperial rule will be manifest apocalyptically—as the direct intervention of God in history at the end of the age; (b) this apocalyptic event will take place within the lifetime of some of Mark's congregation. For Mark, then, the expectation of the imminent arrival of God's rule was still alive (W8a). On these grounds a substantial number of Fellows found it necessary to attribute this formulation to Mark rather than to Jesus.

It is worth noting that both Matthew and Luke rephrase the saying. According to Mark, God's rule 'has set in with power'; according to Matthew, 'God's rule is coming'—at some future date (W4). For Matthew, then, the time has been pushed off into the indefinite future.

²Six days later, Jesus takes Peter and James and John along and leads them off by themselves to a lofty mountain. He was transformed in front of them, ³and his clothes became an intensely brilliant white, whiter than any laundry on earth could make them. ⁴Elijah appeared to them, with Moses, conversing with Jesus. ⁵In response Peter said to Jesus, "Rabbi, it's a good thing we're here. In fact, let's set up three tents, one for you, and one for Moses, and one for Elijah!" ⁶(You see, he didn't know how else to respond, since they were terrified.) ⁷And a cloud moved in and cast a shadow over them, and a voice came out of the cloud: "This is my favored son, listen to him!" ⁸Suddenly, as they looked around, they saw no one, but were alone with Jesus.

Luke eliminates the temporal dimension altogether and has them merely 'see God's imperial rule' (W4).

All three retain the notion that this event or occasion will occur within the lifetime of some of the members of their respective congregations.

The substantial black vote was offset by a substantial pink vote in the tally of Fellows. On what basis did some Fellows vote pink?

One way of reading Mark 9:1 in the context of the ministry of Jesus is to interpret the saying to mean that God's rule was arriving in the exorcism of demons: "If by God's finger I drive out demons, then God's imperial rule has arrived" (Luke 11:20). At the same time, Luke 17:20–21 can be interpreted to mean that God's rule will not be an apocalyptic event, but one that occurs unobserved in the midst of people: "You cannot tell with careful observation when God's rule is coming; nor can people say, 'Look, here it is!' or 'There!' You see, God's rule is among you."

A number of Fellows voted pink on this basis (J5). The resulting weighted average was of course gray. ∎

THE ORIGIN OF
RED LETTER EDITIONS

According to Laurence S. Heely, Jr., publisher of the *Christian Herald*, the idea of a red letter edition originated with Louis Klopsch around the turn of the century.

Mr. Klopsch was born in Germany in 1852 and was brought to America in 1854. He studied journalism at Columbia University. He worked his way up from stock boy to publisher of the American edition of the *Christian Herald.*

The idea of a red letter edition struck Klopsch as he read the words of Luke 22:20: "This cup is the new testament in my blood, which is shed for you." The sentence that provided the name for the second major division of the Bible—the New Testament—also offered Klopsch the idea for printing the words of Jesus in the color of his blood.

The publisher invited scholars in America and Europe "to submit passages they regarded as spoken by Christ while on earth." He thus convened the first Jesus Seminar and produced the first critical red letter edition.

Publishers subsequently abandoned the original limitation—words spoken by Jesus while on earth—and expanded the red sections to all words attributed to Jesus, while on earth, when appearing in visions, as resurrected. Indeed, the Red Letter Edition that supplied much of the information in this note (*The Open Bible*, published by Thomas Nelson, 1975) includes all words attributed to Jesus in whatever state. An edition of the *Revised Standard Version*, publication date unknown, excludes words attributed to Jesus in the Book of Revelation, but includes words spoken to Paul in his visions (for example, Acts 22:6–21). This version was published and copyrighted by World Bible Publishers, Iowa Falls, Iowa. In this instance, as in the case of *The Open Bible*, the publishers do not tell the reader who made the decision to print what in red.

Mr. Klopsch and the twentieth century were anticipated, however, by a fourteenth-century manuscript of the four gospels written in Greek and Latin. In this manuscript, the narrative text is written in vermilion, whereas the words of Jesus, the genealogy of Jesus, and the words of angels are written in crimson. Words of the disciples, of Zechariah, Elizabeth, Mary, Simeon, and John the Baptist appear in blue; the words of the Pharisees, the centurion, Judas Iscariot, and the devil are in black. The idea for a red letter edition had already occurred to some scribe 500 years earlier.

This remarkable copy of the gospels is known as Codex 16 and is housed in the Bibliothèque Nationale in Paris.

⁹And as they were walking down the mountain he instructed them not to describe what they had seen to anyone, until the son of Adam rise from the dead. ¹⁰And they kept it to themselves, puzzling over what this could mean, this 'rising from the dead.' ¹¹And they started questioning him: "The scribes claim, don't they, that Elijah must come first?" ¹²He would respond to them, **"Of course Elijah comes first to restore everything. So, how does scripture claim that the son of Adam will suffer greatly and be the object of scorn?** ¹³**On the other hand, I tell you that Elijah in fact has come, and they had their way with him, just as the scriptures indicate."**

Elijah Must come

Saying	Percentage				Wgt.
	R	P	G	B	Av.
Mk 9:12–13	0	11	17	72	.13 **B**
Mt 17:11–12	0	11	17	72	.13 **B**

Matt 17:10–13 ➡ Mark 9:11–13
¹⁰And the disciples questioned him: "Why do the scribes claim that Elijah must come first?" ¹¹In response he said, **"Elijah does indeed come and will restore everything. ¹²But I tell you that Elijah has already come and they did not recognize him but had their way with him. So also the son of Adam is going to suffer under them."** ¹³Then the disciples understood that he had spoken to them about John the Baptist.

Mark 9:11–13
Attribution. Mark 9:9–13 is a pronouncement story (*chreia*) that climaxes in the saying in 9:12–13. The early Christian community identified John the Baptist with the Elijah who was to come: "Look, I will send Elijah to you before that great and terrible day of the Lord comes" (Mal 4:5). John was identified as the precursor of Jesus in accordance with the prophecy (O5). Moreover, the suffering son of Adam is an early Christian motif and the phrase 'son of Adam' has taken on definite christological meaning (the Anointed, the Christ)(W8a). These features indicate that the story has a Christian imprint, as have the question and answer in vv. 12 and 13. The Fellows agreed by a wide margin in ascribing the entire passage to Mark or the early Christian community. ∎

[14]When they rejoined the disciples, they saw a huge crowd surrounding them and scribes arguing with them. [15]And all of a sudden, when the whole crowd caught sight of him, they were alarmed and rushed up to meet him. [16]He asked them, **"Why are you bothering to argue with them?"** [17]And one person from the crowd answered him, "Teacher, I brought my son to you, because he has a mute spirit. [18]Whenever it takes him over, it knocks him down, and he drools and grinds his teeth and stiffens up. I spoke to your disciples about having them drive it out, but they couldn't." [19]In response he says, **"You distrustful lot, how long will I associate with you? How long will I put up with you? Bring him over to me!"** [20]And they brought him over to him. And when the spirit noticed him, right away it threw him into convulsions, and

The Man with the Mute Spirit

Saying	Percentage			Wgt.
	R	P	G	B	Av.
Mk 9:16,etc.	0	0	0	100	.00 B
Mt 17:17,etc.	0	0	0	100	.00 B
Lk 9:41,etc.	0	0	0	100	.00 B

Matt 17:14–20 ➡ Mark 9:14–29

[14]And when they rejoined the crowd, a person approached and knelt before him [15]and said, "Master, have mercy on my son, because he is epileptic and suffers a lot. For frequently he falls into the fire and often into the water. [16]And I have brought him to your disciples and they weren't able to heal him." [17]In response Jesus said, **"You distrustful and perverted lot, how long will I associate with you? How long will I put up with you? Bring him here to me!"** [18]And Jesus rebuked him and the demon came out of him and the child was healed at that precise moment. [19]Then the disciples came to Jesus privately and said, "Why couldn't we drive it out?" [20]But he says to them, **"Because of your lack of trust. I swear to you, even if you have trust no larger than a mustard seed, you will say to this mountain, 'Move from here to there,' and it will move. And nothing will be beyond you."**

Luke 9:37–43 ➡ Mark 9:14–29

[37]It came to pass on the following day when they came down from the mountain that a huge crowd met him. [38]Suddenly a man from the crowd shouted, "Teacher, I beg you to take a look at my son, for he is my only child. [39]And without warning a spirit takes hold of him, and all of a sudden he screams; it throws him into convulsions and he drools; and it racks his body, leaving him only after a struggle. [40]I begged your disciples to drive it out, but they weren't able to." [41]In response Jesus said, **"You distrustful and perverted lot, how long will I associate with you and put up with you? Bring your son here."** [42]But while the boy was on his way, the demon knocked him down and threw him into convulsions. Jesus rebuked the unclean spirit, healed the boy, and gave him back to his father. [43]And everybody was astounded at the majesty of God.

he fell to the ground, and kept rolling around, foaming at the mouth. ²¹And ⟨Jesus⟩ asked his father, "**How long has he been like this?**" He replied, "Since he was a child. ²²Frequently it has thrown him into fire and into water to destroy him. So if you can do anything, take pity on us and help us!" ²³Jesus said to him, "**What do you mean, 'If you can'? All things are possible for the one who trusts.**" ²⁴Right away the father of the child cried out and said, "I do trust! Help my lack of trust!" ²⁵When Jesus saw that the crowd was about to mob them, he rebuked the unclean spirit, and commands it, "**Deaf and mute spirit, I command you, get out of him and don't ever go back inside him!**" ²⁶And after he shrieked and went into a series of convulsions, it came out. And he took on the appearance of a corpse, so that the rumor went around that he had died. ²⁷But Jesus took hold of his hand and raised him, and there he stood.

²⁸And when he had gone home, his disciples started questioning him privately, "Why couldn't we drive it out?" ²⁹He said to them: "**The only thing that can drive this kind out is prayer.**"

³⁰They left there and started going through Galilee, and he did not want anyone to know. ³¹Remember, he was instructing his disciples and telling them: "**The son of Adam is being turned over to human agents, and they will end up killing him. And three days after he is killed he will rise!**" ³²But they never understood this remark, and always dreaded to ask him ⟨about it⟩.

Mark 9:14–29

All words of Jesus in this story are context-bound and thus are the invention of the narrator (N2). Since they are neither aphorisms or parables (J2), they could not have circulated independently (O2). ∎

Mark 9:30–32
Son of Adam Will Die and Rise

Mark 9:30–32 and parallels, which constitute the second prediction of the passion of Jesus, are considered in the notes on Mark 8:31–33. ∎

Number One

Saying	Percentage				Wgt.
	R	P	G	B	Av.
Mk 9:33	0	0	0	100	.00 B
Mk 9:35	8	24	20	48	.31 G
Mt 23:11	8	20	28	44	.31 G
Lk 9:48b	4	16	24	56	.23 B
Mt 18:4	4	16	24	56	.23 B

³³And they came to Capernaum. When he got home, he started questioning them, "**What were you arguing about on the road?**" ³⁴They fell completely silent, because on the road they had been bickering about who was greatest. ³⁵He sat down and called the twelve and says to them: "If anyone wants to be 'number one,' that person has to be last of all and servant of all!" ³⁶And he

---

Matt 18:1–5 ➡ Mark 9:33–37

¹At that moment the disciples approached Jesus, saying, "Who is greatest in Heaven's domain?" ²And summoning a child, he had her stand in front of them, ³and said, "**I swear to you, if you do not turn and become like children, you will not enter Heaven's domain. ⁴Therefore those who humble themselves like this child are greatest in Heaven's domain. ⁵And whoever accepts one such child in my name, is accepting me.**"

Luke 9:46–48 ➡ Mark 9:33–37

⁴⁶Now an argument broke out among them as to which of them was greatest. ⁴⁷But Jesus, knowing what was on their minds, took a child and had her stand beside him. ⁴⁸He said to them, "**Whoever accepts this child in my name is accepting me. And whoever accepts me accepts the one who sent me. For the one who is least among you is the one who is greatest.**"

Matt 23:11–12 ➡ Mark 9:33–37

¹¹"Now the one who is greater than you shall be your servant. ¹²Whoever exalts himself shall be humbled and whoever humbles himself shall be exalted."

Matt 10:40 ➡ Mark 9:37

⁴⁰The one who welcomes you welcomes me, and the one who welcomes me welcomes the one who sent me."

Luke 10:16 ➡ Mark 9:37

¹⁶"Whoever hears you hears me, and whoever rejects you rejects me, and whoever rejects me rejects the one who sent me."

John 5:22–23 ➡ Mark 9:37

²²"You see, the Father passes judgment on no one, but has turned all judgment over to the son, ²³so everyone will honor the son just as they honor the Father. **Whoever does not honor the son does not honor the Father who sent him.**"

John 12:44 ➡ Mark 9:37

⁴⁴Jesus proclaimed aloud: "**Those who have trust in me, do not have trust in me, but in the one who sent me.**"

John 13:20 ➡ Mark 9:37

²⁰"So help me, the one who welcomes the person I send, welcomes me, and the one who welcomes me, welcomes the one who sent me."

Ign Eph 6:16 ➡ Mark 9:37

¹"**For anyone whom the house manager sends on personal business should be welcomed just as the manager himself.**"

Did 11:4 ➡ Mark 9:37

⁴"**Every apostle who comes to you should be welcomed as ⟨ you would welcome⟩ the Lord.**"

took a child and had her stand in front of them, and he put his arm around her, and he said to them: 37"Whoever accepts a child like this in my name is accepting me. And whoever accepts me is not so much accepting me as the one who sent me."

Accepting a Child

| Saying | Percentage | | | | Wgt. |
	R	P	G	B	Av.
Mk 9:37	0	13	40	47	.22 B
Mt 18:5	0	13	40	47	.22 B
Lk 9:48a	0	13	40	47	.22 B
Mt 10:40	0	27	27	47	.27 G
Lk 10:16	0	27	27	47	.27 G
Jn 5:23b	0	7	13	80	.09 B
Jn 12:44	0	7	13	80	.09 B
Jn 13:20	0	27	33	40	.29 G
IgnEph 6:1	0	7	0	93	.05 B
Did 11:4	0	0	0	100	.00 B

Preface to Mark 9:33–50
Sayings. Nine individual aphorisms are clustered in this passage:
(1) Number One is Last (9:35)
(2) Accepting a Child (9:37)
(3) For and Against (9:40)
(4) Cup of Water (9:41)
(5) Millstone and Sea (9:42)
(6) Hand, Foot, Eye (9:43, 45, 47, 48)
(7) Salted By Fire (9:49)
(8) Salting the Salt (9:50a)
(9) Salt and Peace (9:50b)
The first three aphorisms are embedded in pronouncement stories (*chreiai*), to give them a minimal narrative setting. The remainder are sayings strung together by key word association and by general theme.
Markan cluster. In this passage we can observe how the evangelist clustered aphorisms:
(1) and (2) are both related to the dispute about greatness;
(2), (3), and (4) are clustered on the basis of the key phrases 'in my name' and 'in the name of the Anointed.'
(5) and (6): 'To mislead' and 'to get into trouble' translate the same Greek verb, *skandalizo*, so the link between (5) and (6) is a key word; (5), however, goes back and picks up the theme of 'children' last mentioned in (2).
(6) and (7) are joined because of the common theme, 'fire';
(7), (8), and (9) are clustered around the theme of 'salt.'

Mark has used both theme and key word as the basis for grouping these nine aphorisms.
Matthew and Luke edit Mark. Neither Matthew nor Luke takes over the Markan complex in its entirety.
(1) The first aphorism, 9:35, is duplicated in Mark 10:44//Matt 20:27 (see *Notes*); it is also rephrased by Matthew in 23:11. Luke has a slightly different version in 9:48b.
(2) Mark 9:37 is paralleled in Matt 18:5 and Luke 9:48a, but Matthew adds additional material about 'little children,' which has its parallel in Mark 10:15 (see *Notes*).
(3) Mark 9:38–40 has its parallel in Luke 9:49–50; the aphorism that is embedded in the exchange occurs in Matthew in a different context (12:30).
(4) Mark 9:41 is paralleled in Matt 10:42, again in a different context.
(5) and (6): These aphorisms are taken over by Matthew in 18:6–10, but Matthew has amplified the material; Luke has a parallel only to Mark 9:42 in 17:1–2. Indeed, Luke 17:1–2//Matt 18:6–7 appear to come from Q rather than Mark.
(7), (8), and (9): The sayings about salt in Mark 9:49–50, are parallel to a Q passage in Luke 14:34–35//Matt 5:13, although the Q text lacks aphorisms (7) and (9), which are peculiar to Mark.
These remarks illustrate how complicated the relationships between and among the synoptic gospels sometimes

are. In this instance, Matthew or Luke take some items from Mark, some from Q, and arrange the sayings in clusters in quite different ways.

Thematic unity. A final question concerns the larger thematic unity of Mark 9:33–50. Are the sayings a miscellaneous collection or do they have an underlying thematic unity? The answer to this question depends on how we understand 9:43–48. If these radical sayings are to be interpreted as literally applicable to the individual, then the larger cluster appears not to be unified. If, however, 9:43–48 is a metaphor of the body that symbolizes the Christian community, then the hand, foot, and eye stand for members that cause offense or create problems: they are to be cut off or excluded. In that case, 9:43–48 is a restatement of 9:42 and the entire complex consists of warnings addressed to the community. ■

Mark 9:33–37

Versions. In adapting Mark 9:33–35 to their own purposes, Matthew and Luke have remodeled Mark's text (W4). Luke has rephrased Mark 9:35 in 9:48b. Matthew has apparently substituted the saying in 18:4 for Mark 9:35; Matthew's version of Mark 9:35 appears in Matt 23:11.

Attribution. The context in which this saying appears suggests that it has to do with later controversies about leadership and authority in the Christian communities scattered around the Mediterranean world (W9a). Although it may sound superficially similar to the reversal theme found in the authentic teachings of Jesus (J5), this particular form reflects leadership problems probably unknown to Jesus.

The words attributed to Jesus in Mark 9:33 (no parallels) are context-bound (N2) and so belong to the fabric of the story.

The notes on Mark 10:41–45 are also relevant to this passage. ■

Mark 9:37

Attribution. The saying about accepting a child or accepting the sender is attested in various forms (A2). The versions in Ign Eph 6:1 and Did 11:4 betray the budding bureaucracy of the ancient church: the saying buttresses the protocol for hosting apostles and bishops (W9a).

Ignatius was the bishop of Antioch in Syria early in the second century C.E. He wrote the letter to the Ephesians while on his way to Rome to suffer martyrdom. The Didache is the earliest church order known to us. It was probably compiled early in the second century C.E., partly out of older materials.

The versions of the saying found in John and the Synoptics suggest the context of the church also, although less obviously so. Underneath the saying may be an aphorism about messenger and sender (O3b): to receive a messenger is to receive the one who sent the messenger. The judgment of the Fellows was that all these versions manifest a developed Christian context (W8a) and therefore were not appropriate on the lips of Jesus. ■

³⁸John said to him, "Teacher, we saw someone driving out demons in your name, so we stopped him, because he wasn't one of our adherents." ³⁹Jesus responded: **"Don't stop him! After all, no one who performs a miracle in my name will turn around the next moment and curse me.** ⁴⁰In fact, whoever is not against us is on our side. ⁴¹**By the same token, whoever gives you a cup of water to drink because you carry the name of the Anointed, I swear to you, such persons certainly won't lose their reward!**

For and Against

	Percentage				Wgt.	
Saying	R	P	G	B	Av.	
Mk 9:39	6	6	6	81	.13	**B**
Mk 9:40	13	25	19	44	.35	**G**
Mt 12:30	6	31	19	44	.33	**G**
Lk 9:50b	13	13	31	44	.31	**G**
Lk 11:23	6	31	19	44	.33	**G**
POxy 4:1b	13	13	31	44	.31	**G**

Cup of Water

	Percentage				Wgt.	
Saying	R	P	G	B	Av.	
Mk 9:41	0	0	6	94	.02	**B**
Mt 10:42	0	0	0	100	.00	**B**

Matt 12:30 ➡ Mark 9:40

³⁰"The one who is not with me is against me, and the one who does not gather with me scatters."

Luke 9:49–50 ➡ Mark 9:38–41

⁴⁹John said in response, "Master, we saw someone driving out demons in your name, and we stopped him, because he isn't one of us." ⁵⁰But he said to him, "Don't stop him; In fact, whoever is not against you is on your side."

Luke 11:23 ➡ Mark 9:40

²³"The one who is not with me is against me, and the one who does not gather with me scatters."

POxy1224 4:1–2 ➡ Mark 9:40

¹"And pray for your enemies. The one who is not against us is on our side. ²The one who today is at a distance, tomorrow will be near you."

Matt 10:42 ➡ Mark 9:41

⁴²**"And whoever gives so much as a cup of cold water to one of these little ones, because he is a follower of mine, I swear to you, such persons certainly won't lose their reward."**

Mark 9:38–41

Source. Mark 9:39 is singly attested (Mark//Luke), while Mark 9:40 is triply attested: Mark, Q (Luke 11:23//Matt 12:30), and POxy1224 (A2).

Attribution. The aphorism in 9:40 is proverbial and could apply to any number of situations. The Fellows were evidently not persuaded that there was sufficient reason to ascribe it to Jesus. Mark 9:39 was taken to refer to a time when the Christian community had been formed and the inside/outside lines drawn (W9a). A number of Fellows voted black because they thought the injunction attributed to Jesus here reflected later con-

ditions. Those who voted pink or red did so because the openness or inclusiveness suggested by the remark seemed more appropriate for Jesus than for the later church. In any case, Mark 9:39 is not an aphorism (J2), but belongs to the story of the strange exorcist, and is therefore probably of a piece with that story (context-bound) (N2). ∎

Mark 9:41

Mark 9:41 is a proverb (O5) that has been Christianized (because you carry the name of the Anointed) and is therefore the product, in its present form, of the primitive church (W8a). ∎

Millstone and Sea

Saying	Percentage				Wgt.
	R	P	G	B	Av.
Mk 9:42	7	13	20	60	.22 **B**
Mt 18:6	7	13	20	60	.22 **B**
Lk 17:2	7	13	20	60	.22 **B**
1 Clem 46:8b	0	0	29	71	.10 **B**

Hand, Foot, and Eye

Saying	Percentage				Wgt.
	R	P	G	B	Av.
Mk 9:43,etc.	4	32	28	36	.35 **G**
Mk 9:48	0	0	0	100	.00 **B**
Mt 5:29–30	0	44	24	32	.37 **G**
Mt 18:8–9	0	36	28	36	.33 **G**

Salted by Fire

Saying	Percentage				Wgt.
	R	P	G	B	Av.
Mk 9:49	17	17	0	67	.28 **G**

42And those who mislead one of these little trusting souls would be better off if they were to have a millstone hung around their necks and were thrown into the sea! 43And if your hand gets you into trouble, cut it off! It is better for you to enter life maimed than to go to Gehenna, to the unquenchable fire, with both hands! 45And if your foot gets you into trouble cut it off! It is better for you to enter life lame than to be thrown into Gehenna with both feet! 47And if your eye gets you into trouble, rip it out! It is better for you to enter God's domain one-eyed than to be thrown into Gehenna with both eyes, **48where the worm never dies and the fire never goes out!** 49As you know, everyone there is salted by fire. 50Salt is good ⟨and salty⟩—if salt becomes bland, with what will you renew it? Maintain 'salt' among yourselves and be at peace with each other."

Matt 18:6 ➡ Mark 9:42

6"It is more to the advantage of those who mislead one of these little souls who trust in me to have a millstone hung around their necks and be drowned in the deepest part of the sea!"

Luke 17:2 ➡ Mark 9:42

2"It would be better for them to have a millstone hung around their necks and be thrown into the sea than for them to mislead one of these little ones."

1 Clem 46:8 ➡ Mark 9:42

8Recall what Jesus said: "It is too bad for the fellow! He would be better off not to have been born than to mislead one of my elect. **He would be better off to have a millstone hung around him and to be drowned in the sea than to corrupt one of my elect."**

Matt 5:29–30 ➡ Mark 9:43–47

29"And if your right eye gets you into trouble, rip it out and throw it away! For it is more to your advantage to lose one of your members, than to have your whole body thrown into Gehenna. 30And if your right hand gets you into trouble, cut it off and throw it away! For it is more to your advantage to lose one of your members, than to have your whole body go to Gehenna."

Matt 18:8–9 ➡ Mark 9:43–47

8"If your hand or your foot gets you into trouble, cut it off and throw it away! It is better for you to enter life maimed or lame than to be thrown into the eternal fire with both hands and both feet! 9And if your eye gets you into trouble, rip it out and throw it away! For it is better for you to enter life one-eyed than to be thrown into Gehenna's fire with both eyes."

Salting the Salt

Saying	Percentage				Wgt.
	R	P	G	B	Av.
Mk 9:50a	33	33	8	25	.58 P
Mt 5:13	33	8	42	17	.53 P
Lk 14:34,etc.	42	17	17	25	.58 P

Salt and Peace

Saying	Percentage				Wgt.
	R	P	G	B	Av.
Mk 9:50b	17	8	17	58	.28 G

Matt 5:13 ➡ Mark 9:50a

13"You are the salt of the earth. But if the salt becomes insipid, of what will its saltiness consist? It then has no other use except to be thrown out and crunched underfoot."

Luke 14:34–35 ➡ Mark 9:50a

34"Salt is good ⟨and salty⟩—if salt becomes insipid, with what will it be renewed? 35It is fit neither for the earth nor for the dung-pile; it just gets thrown away. The one who has ears to hear had better listen."

Mark 9:42

Attribution. Like the preceding saying, Mark 9:42 is a proverb (O5) that has been Christianized (W8a). As a proverb it could serve a variety of contexts. One only had to particularize the 'if' clause—'If someone does so and so,—and add the conclusion: 'it were better for that person to have a millstone hung around his or her neck and be tossed into the sea.' As it stands, the saying has been adapted to the situation of the early Christian community (W9a) and is therefore not correctly attributed to Jesus. ■

Mark 9:43, 45, 47

Attribution. This trio of sayings contrasts Gehenna (hell) with God's domain (9:47) and life (9:43, 45). It is thus a saying that concerns the final judgment and eschatological salvation beyond the end of history. As such, it probably does not go back to Jesus.

If it refers to the body of the community metaphorically, as some scholars hold, it reflects the situation of the later church in which it was better—so the saying alleges—for some members to be cut off (excommunicated) than to have the whole collective body damaged (W9a). In that case, too, it does not go back to Jesus.

Some Fellows took the view, however, that such a radical saying as this could echo the voice of Jesus (J4). A marred, incomplete body—abhorrent in society in Jesus' day—was to be preferred to the wanton submission to temptation. The third of the comparisons—the eye—may refer to lust, as Matthew's context indicates. But as the saying stands, it has been remodeled to suit the circumstances of the primitive Christian community (W9a). Gray is therefore an appropriate designation.

Mark 9:48 is a quotation from Isaiah 66:24 (LXX): "And they shall go out and view the limbs of the people who have rebelled against me. There the maggots never die, the fire is never extinguished, and they will be a spectacle for the whole world." The quotation was undoubtedly added by Mark (O5). Neither Matthew nor Luke copy the quotation. ■

Mark 9:49

Attribution. Mark 9:49 was composed by Mark, in the judgment of many Fellows, to link 9:48 to 9:50: the key word 'fire' is repeated and both suggest the fiery judgment to take place at the end of history. Neither Matthew nor Luke reproduce Mark 9:49. Fellows who think there was an eschatological element in the message of Jesus pulled the saying into the gray category. ■

Mark 9:50a

Sources. This saying is attested by both Mark and Q (A2). It is difficult to establish the original form.

Attribution. Matthew's remodeling of it into a metaphor for the Christian presence in the world is clearly secondary (W8a). Some scholars have suggested that the variations in Greek may reflect a common Aramaic original. In any case, salt was commonly used in Palestine in an impure state. If the impurities are greater than the salt, the salt becomes bland or insipid. In Q the conclusion is that such salt is then good for nothing and has to be thrown away. Mark apparently omits this part of the saying in order to link this saying with his conclusion in 9:50b (W4).

The original context of the saying has been lost so it is impossible to determine what it meant on the lips of Jesus. ■

Mark 9:50b

Attribution. The conclusion (9:50b) to this long complex (9:33–50) was probably created by Mark to round it off (W4). The final words are the equivalent of a benediction. Some Fellows take the view, however, that the formulation could have originated with Jesus since we are reasonably certain one salt saying goes back to Jesus (Mark 9:50a) and the peace wish was a common sentiment. ■

10 And from there he gets up and goes to the territory of Judea [and] across the Jordan, and once again crowds gather around him. As usual, he started teaching them. ²And [Pharisees approach him and], to test him, they ask whether it is permitted for a husband to divorce his wife. ³In response he puts a question to them: **"What did Moses command you?"** ⁴They replied: "Moses allowed one to prepare a writ of abandonment and thus to divorce the other party." ⁵Jesus said to them: "He gave you this injunction because you are obstinate. ⁶However, in the beginning, at the creation, 'God made [them] male and female.' ⁷For this reason, a man will leave his father and mother [and stick to his wife], ⁸and the two will become one person,' so they are no longer two individuals but 'one person.' ⁹Therefore those God has coupled together, no one else should separate."

Moses and Divorce

| | Percentage | | | | Wgt. |
Saying	R	P	G	B	Av.
Mk 10:5b–6	15	20	45	20	.43 G
Mt 19:4–6,8	15	20	45	20	.43 G
Mk 10:7–9	5	35	25	35	.37 G

Matt 19:3–8 ➡ Mark 10:2–9
³And the Pharisees approached him and, to test him, they ask whether it is permitted [for a husband] to divorce his wife for any reason. ⁴In response he puts a question to them: "Have you not read that in the beginning, 'the creator made them male and female,' ⁵and said, 'for this reason, a man will leave his father and mother and stick to his wife, ⁶so they are no longer two individuals but one.' Therefore those God has coupled together, no one else should separate." ⁷They say to him, "Why did Moses order a written release and separation?" ⁸He says to them, "Because you are obstinate Moses permitted you to divorce your wives, but from the beginning it was not so."

Mark 10:2–9, 10–12
Jesus is credited with some counsel against divorce in at least three early independent sources: Mark, Q, and Paul in his first letter to the Corinthians (A1). Substantial variation between and among the sources indicates disagreement among early Christians about what Jesus said or how his words were to be interpreted (W6). The lengthy attempt at clarification in that section of Hermas called the Mandates or Commandments shows how difficult it was to clarify the issues.

Divorce was permitted in the Jewish law (Deut 24:1–4): a man may not remarry a woman he has divorced if she was subsequently married to someone else, whether or not her second husband had died. And when a husband divorces a wife, he must give her a bill of divorce. In the exchange with the Pharisees in Mark 10:2–9//Matt 19:3–8, the role of Jesus and the Pharisees seems to be reversed: the Mosaic law as interpreted by the Pharisees is permissive of divorce, while Jesus rules against divorce categorically. Jesus does not abrogate the law as he

Against Divorce

Saying	Percentage				Wgt.
	R	P	G	B	Av.
Mk 10:11-12	28	17	28	28	.48 G
Mt 19:9	0	30	25	45	.28 G
Mt 5:32	10	15	20	55	.27 G
Lk 16:18	28	17	28	28	.48 G
1Cor 7:10,11	28	17	28	28	.48 G
HM 4.1:6,etc.	13	25	19	44	.35 G

[10]And once again, as usual, when they got home, the disciples questioned him about this. [11]And he says to them: "Whoever divorces his wife and marries another commits adultery against her; [12]and if she divorces her husband and marries another, she commits adultery."

Matt 19:9 ➡ Mark 10:10-12

[9]"Now I say to you, whoever divorces his wife, except for infidelity, and marries another commits adultery."

Matt 5:31-32 ➡ Mark 10:10-12

[31]"They say, 'whoever divorces his wife, let him give her a bill of divorce.' [32]But I say to you, everyone who divorces his wife, except for a matter of infidelity, makes her the victim of adultery; and whoever marries a divorced woman commits adultery."

Luke 16:18 ➡ Mark 10:10-12

[18]"Everyone who divorces his wife and marries another commits adultery; and the one who marries a woman divorced from her husband commits adultery."

1 Cor 7:10-11 ➡ Mark 10:10-12

[10]"To the married I give charge, not I but the Lord, that the wife should not separate from her husband [11](but if she does, let her remain single or else be reconciled to her husband)—and that the husband should not divorce his wife."

---

appears to do in other instances (for example, sabbath observance, Mark 2:27-28, unclean foods, Mark 7:15), but advocates a position more stringent than the law.

The variations in the reports make it exceptionally difficult to establish the earliest tradition. Matthew (19:9) allows infidelity as the one exception to the categorical prohibition. Does this exception go back to Jesus, or is it Matthew's accommodation to the difficulty of enforcing the prohibition in the early Christian community (O4)? Mark, Luke, and Paul treat divorce from the perspective of both the husband and the wife; Matthew limits his treatment to the perspective of the husband. Neither Luke nor Paul mentions scriptural authority for Jesus' injunction, while Mark (and Matthew) quotes Gen 1:27 and 2:24 ("he made them male and female," and "the two

shall become one person") (O5).

In the debate over whether or not the categorical injunction against divorce can be traced back to Jesus, some Fellows argued that widespread attestation, including the very early testimony of Paul, is very strong evidence for authenticity (A1, A2). Moreover, an injunction difficult for the early community to practice is usually taken as evidence of originality (W9b). The legal fencing skill exhibited by Jesus in the Markan account is alleged by some Fellows to be characteristic of Jesus (J1). And Jesus' stringent interpretation can be interpreted as protection of women, who, as divorcees, were socially disadvantaged: they could not remarry and could not readily support themselves, so many were forced to turn to prostitution to survive (J4).

Against these arguments, other Fellows advanced the following considera-

Herm Man 4.1:1–11 ➡ Mark 10:10–12
⁴I say to him, "Permit me to ask you a few questions." "**Go ahead,**" he replies. "Sir," I continue, "if someone has a wife who is faithful in the Lord, and he catches her in some infidelity, does the husband commit a sin if he continues to live with her?" ⁵"**So long as he remains ignorant,**" says he, "**the husband does not sin. But if the husband knows about her sin and she does not repent but persists in her infidelity and the husband continues to live with her, he becomes guilty of her sin and a partner in her adultery.**" ⁶"What," I ask, "does the husband do then, if his wife persists in this passionate affair?" "He should divorce her," he replies, "and the husband should live alone. For if he divorces his wife and marries another, he also commits adultery himself." ⁷"Sir," I continue, "if after the divorce the wife repents and wants to return to her husband, should he not take her back?" ⁸"**Yes,**" he replies. "**If the husband does not take her back, he commits a sin and**

brings a great sin down on himself. But it is necessary to welcome back the sinner who repents, although not frequently for there is but one repentance for God's slaves. Consequently, since repentance is a possibility, the husband should not marry. This is the proper course of action for the wife and for the husband." ⁹"**Not only is it adultery,**" he says, "**if a man defiles his body, but whoever behaves like a heathen also commits adultery. Consequently, if anyone continues such practices, and does not repent, leave him and do not live with him. If you do not, you are a partner in his sin.** ¹⁰For this reason, you are enjoined to live alone, whether husband or wife. For repentance is always a possibility in such cases." ¹¹"**I am not,**" he continues, "**therefore, providing an excuse by drawing the matter to a close in this way, but giving the sinner the opportunity to sin no more. There is someone who can provide the cure for previous sin. For he is the one who has authority over everything.**"

tions. Mark's construction is artificial: there is nothing in Mark 10:2–9 that Mark could not have readily created. The variations in the tradition suggest that it was a secondary creation (W6). The argument in Mark is tied to the Hebrew scriptures, which casts doubt on its authenticity (O5). Jesus was not a legal authority and did not engage in debates over fine points of the law (a general question answered negatively by Fellows on another occasion). The categorical prohibition, in fact, makes it tougher on women rather than offering them protection. And, finally, it is difficult to reconcile an injunction of this order with Jesus' attitude

elsewhere towards the law, particularly his willingness to be permissive.

Matthew's versions of the injunction (5:32, 19:9) were taken to be farther from Jesus than the versions found in Mark, Luke, and Paul. The settings provided by Mark and Matthew were considered secondary (W2). However, the vote was fairly evenly divided on whether the prohibition of divorce went back to Jesus in some proximate form. Although the weighted average fell into the gray zone, the distribution of the vote shows that the Fellows of the Seminar were of a divided mind on this issue. ∎

Children in God's Domain

Saying	Percentage				Wgt.	
	R	P	G	B	Av.	
Mk 10:14	16	36	36	12	.52	**P**
Mt 19:14	16	36	36	12	.52	**P**
Lk 18:16	16	36	36	12	.52	**P**
Mk 10:15	8	36	36	20	.44	**G**
Mt 18:3	4	48	24	24	.44	**G**
Lk 18:17	8	40	32	20	.45	**G**
Jn 3:3,5	0	8	48	44	.21	**B**
Th 22:2	4	50	29	17	.47	**G**
Th 22:4–7	0	0	0	100	.00	**B**

¹³And they would bring children to him so he could lay hands on them, but the disciples scolded them. ¹⁴Then Jesus grew indignant when he saw this and said to them: "Let the children come up to me, don't try to stop them. After all, God's domain is peopled with such as these. ¹⁵I swear to you, whoever doesn't accept God's imperial rule the way a child would, certainly won't be able to get in ⟨his domain⟩!" ¹⁶And he would put his arms around them and bless them, and lay his hands on them.

Matt 19:13–15 ➡ Mark 10:13–16

¹³Then little children were brought to him so he could lay his hands on them and pray, but the disciples scolded them. ¹⁴Now Jesus said, "Let the children alone. Don't try to stop them from coming up to me. After all, Heaven's domain is peopled with such as these." ¹⁵And he laid his hands on them and went away from there.

Luke 18:15–17 ➡ Mark 10:13–16

¹⁵They would even bring infants to him so he could lay hands on them. But when the disciples saw it, they scolded them. ¹⁶Jesus called for the infants and said, "Let the children come up to me, and don't try to stop them. After all, God's domain is peopled with such as these. ¹⁷"I swear to you, whoever doesn't accept God's imperial rule the way a child would, surely won't be able to get in ⟨his domain⟩!"

Matt 18:3 ➡ Mark 10:15

³. . . and said, "I swear to you, if you do not turn and become like children, you will not enter Heaven's domain."

Thom 22:1–7 ➡ Mark 10:13–16

¹Jesus saw some babies nursing. ²He said to his disciples, "These nursing babies are like those who enter the kingdom."

³They said to him, "Then shall we enter the kingdom as babies?"

⁴Jesus said to them, "When you make the two into one, and when you make the inner like the outer and the outer like the inner, and the upper like the lower, ⁵and when you make male and female into a single one, so that the male will not be male nor the female be female, ⁶when you make eyes in place of an eye, a hand in place of a hand, a foot in place of a foot, an image in place of an image, ⁷then you will enter [the kingdom]."

John 3:3–5 ➡ Mark 10:13–16

³In response Jesus said to him, "I swear to you, No one can perceive God's empire, without being reborn from on high." ⁴Nicodemus says to him, "How can a person be reborn at an advanced age? It isn't possible to enter the womb of one's mother and be born a second time, is it?" ⁵Jesus came back: "I swear to you, one cannot get into God's empire without being conceived of both water and spirit."

Mark 10:13–16

The saying in Mark 10:14 is taken over by Matthew and Luke, but is attested nowhere else. Mark 10:15 has its immediate parallel in Luke 18:17; Matthew has moved this saying to a new context in 18:1–4. The versions in John 3:3, 5 and Thom 22:2 are "cousins" of Mark 10:15.

Mark 10:14 concerns the status of children under God's rule or in God's domain. Mark 10:15 and parallels all exhibit the idea of "entering ⟨God's domain⟩" and thus concern rites of initiation—this context is made clear by the Gospel of John.

In support of Mark 10:14, some Fellows pointed to the dramatic reversal of the child's traditional status in ancient societies as silent non-participants (J5). This perspective agrees with Jesus' sympathy for those who were marginal to society or outcasts (compare the beatitudes recorded in Luke 6:20–21). It is possible that Mark's story is based on some actual incident in the life of Jesus. However, most Fellows agreed that the words in Mark are probably not an exact reproduction of something Jesus said (O1, W4). Nevertheless, the saying in Mark drew a pink designation.

The saying in Mark 10:15 undoubtedly circulated independently during the oral period (O2). However, the idea of "entering God's domain" suggested that the saying had been drawn into the context of baptism (note John 3) and thus had to do with the rites of initiation into the Christian community (W9a). If this is the original context, Fellows reasoned that the saying could not go back to Jesus, since Jesus was not, in all probability, an institution builder. Other Fellows suggested that the saying had probably been remodelled in the course of its transmission and therefore may have been similar in content to the saying in Mark 10:14 (W4). Upon reconsideration, Thom 22:2 received the highest weighted average of the five versions of Mark 10:15, although it did not quite make it into the pink category. ■

Preface to Mark 10:17–31

This complex is composed of a pronouncement story and loosely related miscellaneous dialogues. The whole has been created by Mark out of materials that came down to him in the tradition (W1, W2).

The initial pronouncement story (10:17–22) begins with a question about eternal life. The question of wealth emerges only at the end of the story. Jesus advises the man with money that he should sell his possessions and follow him (10:21). This conclusion provides Mark with the opportunity to append a series of sayings about how hard it is for those with great wealth to get into God's domain (10:23–27) (W2).

Mark then follows with the other side of the coin: those who have left everything to follow Jesus will receive substantial rewards (10:28–30). The discussion closes with a proclamation about the inversion of rank (10:31). ■

The Man with Money

| Saying | Percentage | | | | Wgt. |
	R	P	G	B	Av.
Mk 10:18	7	27	40	27	.38 G
Mt 19:17a	0	7	27	67	.13 B
Lk 18:19	7	27	40	27	.38 G
Mk 10:19	7	20	27	47	.29 G
Mt 19:17b,etc.	7	20	27	47	.29 G
Lk 18:20	7	20	27	47	.29 G
Mk 10:21	13	27	40	20	.44 G
Mt 19:21	13	27	40	20	.44 G
Lk 18:22	13	27	40	20	.44 G
GNaz 6	0	0	0	100	.00 B

[17]As he was traveling along the road, someone ran up, knelt before him, and started questioning him, "Good teacher, what do I have to do to inherit eternal life?" [18]Jesus said to him: "Why do you call me good? No one is good except for the one God. [19]You know the commandments: 'Do not murder, do not commit adultery, do not steal, do not give false testimony, do not defraud, honor your father and mother.'" [20]He said to him: "Teacher, I have observed all these things since I was a child!" [21]Jesus loved him at first sight and said to him: "You are missing one thing: make your move, sell whatever you have and give ⟨the proceeds⟩ to the poor, and you will have treasure in heaven. And then come, follow me!" [22]But stunned by this advice, he went away dejected, since he had a lot of money.

Matt 19:16–22 ➡ Mark 10:17–22

[16]And just then someone came and said to him, "Teacher, what good do I have to do to have eternal life?" [17]He said to him, **Why do you ask me about the good? One alone is good;** and if you want to enter life, observe the commandments." [18]He said to him, "Which ones?" Then Jesus said, "You shall not murder, you shall not commit adultery, you shall not steal, you shall not give false testimony, [19]honor your father and mother, and you shall love your neighbor as yourself." [20]The young man said to him, "I have observed all these; what do I still lack?" [21]Jesus said to him, "If you wish to be perfect, make your move, sell your possessions and give ⟨the proceeds⟩ to the poor and you will have treasure in heaven. And then come, follow me!" [22]When the young man heard this advice, he went away dejected since he had a lot of money.

Luke 18:18–23 ➡ Mark 10:17–22

[18]Someone from the ruling class asked him, "Good teacher, what do I have to do to inherit eternal life?" [19]Jesus said to him, "Why do you call me good? No one is good except for the one God. [20]You know the commandments: 'Do not commit adultery, do not kill, do not steal, do not give false testimony, honor your father and mother.'" [21]And he said, "I have observed all these since I was a child." [22]When Jesus heard this, he said to him, "You are still lacking one thing. Sell everything you have and distribute ⟨the proceeds⟩ among the poor, and you will have treasure in heaven. And then come, follow me!" [23]But when he heard this, he became very sad, for he was extremely rich.

GNaz 6 ➡ Mark 10:17–22

The second rich man said to him, "Master, What good thing should I do to live?" He said to him, "**Sir, observe the Law and the Prophets.**" He retorted, "I have observed them." He said to him "**Come, sell everything you own and distribute it to the poor and come, follow me.**" But the rich man began to scratch his head and it did not please him. And the Lord said to him, "**How can you say that you observe the Law and the Prophets? For it is written in the Law: Love your neighbor as yourself, and behold, many of your brothers, sons of Abraham, are clothed in filth, dying of hunger, and your house is full of good things and nothing at all passes out of it to them.**" And turning he said to Simon, his disciple who was sitting with him, "Simon, son of Jonah, it is easier for a camel to pass through the eye of a needle than for a rich person to enter the kingdom of the heavens."

Mark 10:17–22

This pronouncement story contains three distinct sayings attributed to Jesus:

(1) a claim that God is the sole "good" (10:18);

(2) a rehearsal of commandments governing social relationships (10:19);

(3) a call to swap earthly for heavenly treasure as the condition for following Jesus (10:21).

In Mark's version, Jesus is particularly sympathetic to the young man (10:21); the other versions omit this detail.

Acts 2:43–47, 4:32–37, and 5:1–6 indicate that some members of the early church did sell their property so that no member was left in want. Some scholars are of the opinion that the Markan story reflects a similar situation and thus was created in and for the early community (W9a). The Seminar decided, however, to consider the three sayings in Mark individually and attempt to determine whether particular elements could be traced back to Jesus.

(1) The claim that only God is good could have been made by any Jew or by any Greek influenced by Plato. Some Fellows thought it improbable that a Christian would have invented Jesus' refusal to be called 'good' (10:18). Matthew was apparently bothered by this refusal and so rephrased Jesus' question (19:17a). While the majority of Fellows saw Jesus' attempt to refocus attention on God rather than on himself as generally in line with Jesus' disposition, most doubted that this saying had an existence independent of the story (O2, N2). It therefore drew a gray designation. Since Matthew is a revision of Mark's account, it is even farther removed from Jesus (W4). The parallel in the Gospel of the Nazarenes is dependent on Matthew and so is a third-hand version at best.

(2) The second saying rehearses Old Testament commandments that any Jew or Christian could have been expected to know (O5). The reference to honoring parents, however, seemed to some to be out of line with Jesus' attitude towards his family (Mark 3:31–35, 10:30) and the Q saying in Luke 14:26//Matt 10:37 regarding hating father and mother. In any case, citing the commandments is scarcely a distinctive statement (J3, O5).

(3) The injunction to sell everything and follow him seemed to many Fellows to be consonant with Jesus' teaching about wealth, as found, for example, in the parables of the pearl and the treasure (Matt 13:44–46//Thom 109, 76), both of which were traced to Jesus (G5). And the idea of divesting oneself of earthly treasure is found in a Q saying (Luke 12:33//Matt 6:19–20), which some Fellows find compatible with Jesus' teaching (G5). However, the promise of heavenly treasure in 10:21 and parallels as a reward for giving up wealth is almost certain to be a later modification (W3). As a consequence, the saying attracted no more than a gray designation. ■

Eye of a Needle

Saying	Percentage				Wgt.
	R	P	G	B	Av.
Mk 10:23	16	40	36	8	.55 P
Mt 19:23	12	40	36	12	.51 P
Lk 18:24	12	40	40	8	.52 P
HS 9.20:1–4	0	8	36	56	.17 B
Mk 10:24	4	36	32	28	.39 G
Mk 10:25	28	40	28	4	.64 P
Mt 19:24	32	44	16	8	.67 P
Lk 18:25	32	40	20	8	.65 P
GNaz 6	16	36	16	32	.45 G
Mk 10:27	0	0	0	100	.00 B
Mt 19:26	0	0	8	92	.03 B
Lk 18:27	0	0	0	100	.00 B

²³After looking around, Jesus says to his disciples, "How difficult it is for those who have money to enter God's domain!" ²⁴The disciples were amazed at his words. In response Jesus repeats what he had said, "Children, how difficult it is to enter God's domain! ²⁵It's easier for a camel to squeeze through a needle's eye, than for a wealthy person to get into God's domain!" ²⁶And they were very perplexed, wondering to themselves, "Well then, who can be saved?" ²⁷Jesus looks them in the eye and says: "**For mortals it's impossible, but not for God; after all, everything's possible for God.**" ²⁸Peter started

---

Matt 19:23–26 ➡ Mark 10:23–27

²³Jesus said to his disciples, "I swear to you, it is very difficult for the rich to enter Heaven's domain. ²⁴And again I say to you, It's easier for a camel to squeeze through a needle's eye, than for a wealthy person to get into God's domain." ²⁵When the disciples heard, they were quite perplexed and said, "Well then, who can be saved?" ²⁶Jesus looked them in the eye, and said to them, "**For mortals this is impossible; for God everything's possible.**"

Luke 18:24–27 ➡ Mark 10:23–27

²⁴Jesus looked at him he became very sad, and said, "How difficult it is for those who have money to enter God's domain! ²⁵It's easier for a camel to pass through a needle's eye, than for a wealthy person to get into God's domain." ²⁶Those who heard this said, "Well then, who can be saved?" ²⁷But he said, "**What's impossible for mortals is possible for God.**"

Mark 10:23–27

This complex exhibits four sayings attributed to Jesus:

(1) "How difficult it is for those who have money to enter God's domain." (Mark 10:23)

(2) "Children, how difficult it is to enter God's domain." (Mark 10:24)

(3) "It's easier for a camel to squeeze through a needle's eye, than for a wealthy person to get into God's domain." (Mark 10:25)

(4) "For mortals it's impossible, but not for God; after all, everything's possible for God." (Mark 10:27)

The second (Mark 10:24) repeats the first (Mark 10:23) without specific reference to those who have money. Both

Matthew and Luke have omitted the second, weaker form. The third is a 'hard' saying: a camel can more readily squeeze through a needle's eye than a wealthy person can get into God's domain (J4, J6). The fourth softens the third by making all things possible with God (O4).

Mark is the sole source of this complex. Matthew and Luke copy him with some minor variations. The Gospel of the Nazarenes is dependent on Matthew, so its witness is secondary. Mark probably put this complex together himself.

(1) *It is difficult . . .*

The complex opens with a general statement to the effect that it is difficult for a person with money to get into God's domain. Such a saying is not memorable

Herm Sim 9.20:1–4

➡ Mark 10:26–27

¹The believers who come from the third mountain, the one with thorns and thistles, are like this: some of them are rich, while others are involved in many business affairs. The thorns represent the rich, the thistles those who are involved in various kinds of business. ²Those who are involved in many and various business matters do associate with God's servants, but are choked by their work and are led astray. The rich, on the other hand, find it hard to associate with God's servants, since they fear they will be asked for something by them. Such persons will find it difficult to enter God's domain. ³For just as it is tough to walk barefooted on thorns, so it is hard for such persons to get into God's domain. ⁴Yet repentance is a possibility for all these persons, provided it comes quickly, so they can retrace their steps during those days when they accomplished nothing and do some good. If they repent and do some good, they will be alive where God is concerned. But if they remain wedded to their business, they will be handed over to those women, who will put them to death.

GNaz 6 ➡ Mark 10:23–27

The second rich man said to him, "Master, What good thing should I do to live?" He said to him, "Sir, observe the law and the prophets." He retorted, "I have observed them." He said to him "Come, sell everything you own and distribute it to the poor and come, follow me." But the rich man began to scratch his head and it did not please him. And the Lord said to him, "How can you say that you observe the Law and the Prophets? For it is written in the Law: Love your neighbor as yourself, and behold, many of your brothers, sons of Abraham, are clothed in filth, dying of hunger, and your house is full of good things and nothing at all passes out of it to them." And turning he said to Simon, his disciple who was sitting with him, "Simon, son of Jonah, it is easier for a camel to pass through the eye of a needle than for a rich person to enter the kingdom of the heavens."

---

in itself (J1); indeed, it is a common sentiment. However, taken in conjunction with the third saying, it gains additional force.

(3) *It is easier for a camel* . . .

Graphic exaggeration is typical of many genuine parables and aphorisms of Jesus (J6). And a humorous hyperbole of this sort is more likely to have come from Jesus than from a more serious-minded follower of his.

The comic disproportion between the camel and the needle's eye presented difficulties to the Christian community from the very beginning (W6). Some Greek scribes substituted the Greek word rope (*kamilon*) for the term camel (*kamelon*) to reduce the contrast, while some modern but misguided interpreters have claimed that the 'needle's eye' was the name of a narrow gate or pass, which a camel would find it difficult but not impossible to pass through. The fact that this saying has been surrounded by attempts to soften it suggest that it was probably original with Jesus (O4).

(4) *For mortals it's impossible* . . .

This proverb was probably appended by Mark as the means of qualifying the categorical nature of the preceding saying (O4).

The question for Fellows of the Seminar turned on whether or not this complex was created in its entirety during the period the primitive community was being formed (W9a). It clearly reflects the

Hundredfold Reward

Saying	Percentage				Wgt.
	R	P	G	B	Av.
Mk 10:29-30	0	40	13	47	.31 G
Mt 19:29	0	40	13	47	.31 G
Lk 18:29-30	0	40	13	47	.31 G
Mt 19:28	0	13	13	73	.13 B
ApJas 4:1-2	0	7	13	80	.09 B

lecturing him, "Look here, we left everything and followed you!" ²⁹Jesus said: "I swear to you, there is no one who has left home, or brothers, or sisters, or mother, or father, or children, or farms on my account and on account of the good news, ³⁰who won't receive a hundredfold now, in the present time, homes, and brothers, and sisters, and mothers, and children, and farms— including persecutions—and in the age to come, eternal life. ³¹Many of the first will be last, and of the last many will be first."

Matt 19:27-29 ➡ Mark 10:28-30
²⁷In response Peter said to him, "Look here, we left everything and followed you! What do we get out of it?" ²⁸Jesus said to them, **"Make no mistake, you who have followed me, when the son of Adam is seated on his throne of glory in the renewal ⟨of creation⟩, you also will be seated on twelve thrones and sit in judgment on the twelve tribes of Israel.** ²⁹And everyone who has left homes or brothers or sisters or father or mother or children or farms, on account of my name, will receive a hundredfold and inherit eternal life."

Luke 18:28-30 ➡ Mark 10:28-30
²⁸Then Peter said, "Look here, we have left what we had and followed you!" ²⁹And he said to them, "Make no mis-

take, there is no one who has left home, or wife, or brothers, or parents, or children, for the sake of God's imperial rule, ³⁰who won't receive many times as much in the present age, and in the age to come, eternal life."

ApJas 4:1-2 ➡ Mark 10:28-30
¹I answered and said to him, "Lord, we can obey you if you want, for we have left our fathers behind us, and our mothers, and our villages, and have followed you. Give us the means, then, not to be tested by the evil Devil."

²The Lord answered and said, **"If you are not receiving a part of the gift while you are being tempted by Satan, what is your merit in doing the will of the father?"**

struggle over who was to be admitted to that community. On the one hand, Jesus congratulates the poor in the beatitudes (Luke 6:20), since God's domain belongs to them. If Jesus thought the kingdom belonged to the poor, he probably also thought that it did not belong to the rich. The first and third sayings thus could well go back to Jesus.

On the other hand, all of these sayings could reflect the attempt to define the social borders of the Christian commu-

nity. It is possible that all of them were generated in the matrix of that attempt. This possibility led a few Fellows to vote gray or even black.

On balance, Fellows were of the opinion that the first and third sayings did echo the voice of Jesus. ∎

Mark 10:28-30
This saying promises abundance to those who have abandoned property and family in response to Jesus' summons. In

First and Last

	Percentage				Wgt.
Saying	R	P	G	B	Av.
Mk 10:31	33	17	17	33	.50 G
Mt 19:30	33	17	17	33	.50 G
Mt 20:16	42	17	17	25	.58 P
Lk 13:30	25	25	17	33	.47 G
POxy654 4:2	36	18	18	27	.55 P
POxy654 4:3	0	0	0	100	.00 B
Th 4:2	27	18	18	36	.45 G
Th 4:3	0	0	0	100	.00 B
Barn 6:13a	9	18	27	45	.30 G

Matt 19:30 ➡ Mark 10:31

30"Many of the first will be last, and of the last many will be first."

Matt 20:16 ➡ Mark 10:31

16"The last will be first and the first last."

Luke 13:30 ➡ Mark 10:31

30"And look out! Some who are first will be last, and those who are last will be first."

POxy654 4:2–3 ➡ Mark 10:31

2"For many of the first will be last, and the last first, 3and they will become one."

Thom 4:2–3 ➡ Mark 10:31

2"For many of the first will be last, 3and will become a single one."

Barn. 6:13a ➡ Mark 10:31

13Once again I will indicate to you how [the Lord] speaks about us. In more recent times, he renewed the creative process. For the Lord says, "Please note, I am making the last things like the first things."

---

its full form—the present form in Mark and parallels—it fits the situation of the primitive community: many had abandoned their family ties, their property, their social position, in order to become followers of the new way (W9a). The promise of reward was enticing to them. On this reading, Fellows were agreed that the promises in Mark 10:29–30 could not be attributed to Jesus.

The question arose, however, whether the saying has not been edited to suit the aspirations of the community (W3). If one were to eliminate the last two phrases in Mark 10:29 ("on my account and on account of the good news") and the last two in Mark 10:30 ("including persecutions—and in the age to come, eternal life") the saying could well have come from Jesus. The rewards on this reading would be metaphorical: 'brother, sisters, etc.' could refer to the acquisition of new friends in Jesus' circle of disciples (J7). This possibility induced some Fellows to give the saying a pink designation. There were no red votes.

The majority opinion was predominantly negative, however, partly because Fellows had agreed not to attempt to reconstruct sayings as the basis for assessment. ■

³²On the road going up to Jerusalem, Jesus was leading the way, they were apprehensive, and others who were following were frightened. Once again he took the twelve aside and started telling them what was going to happen to him: ³³**"Look, we're going up to Jerusalem, and the son of Adam will be turned over to the ranking priests and the scribes, and they will sentence him to death, and turn him over to the gentiles, ³⁴and they will make fun of him, and spit on him, and flog him, and kill ⟨him⟩. Yet after three days he will rise!"**

Matt 20:17–19 ➡ Mark 10:32–34

¹⁷And Jesus was going up to Jerusalem and he took the twelve aside privately and on the way he said to them: ¹⁸**"Look, we're going up to Jerusalem, and the son of Adam will be turned over to the ranking priests and scribes, and they will sentence him to death, ¹⁹and turn him over to the gentiles to make fun of, and flog, and crucify. Yet on the third day he will be raised."**

Luke 18:31–34 ➡ Mark 10:32–34

³¹⟨Jesus⟩ took the twelve aside, and said to them: **"Look, we're going up to Jerusalem, and everything written by the prophets about the son of Adam will come true. ³²For he will be turned over to the gentiles, and will be made fun of and insulted. They will spit on him, ³³and flog him, and kill him, Yet after three days he will rise."** ³⁴But they did not understand any of this; this remark was obscure to them, and they did not comprehend its meaning.

Mark 10:31

The saying about the 'first and last' is triply attested (A1):

(1) Mark 10:31//Matt 19:30 (Mark)
(2) Matt 20:16//Luke 13:30 (Q)
(3) POxy654 4:2//Thom 4:2 (Thom)

The three sources have slightly different versions:

(1) First, last/last, first
(2) Last, first/first, last
(3) First, last/last, first/become one

The third segment of the Thomas version reflects a gnostic motif that appears elsewhere in Thomas (22, 23, 106) (W3). Without this motif, the version preserved by the Greek version of Thomas corresponds to the form in Mark 10:31.

The radical reversal of roles is characteristic of other sayings and parables of Jesus (J5). The texture of this saying—conciseness, chiastic pattern, first/last//last/first—suggests Jesus as the originator (J1). However, for many Fellows the fact that Mark has taken the edge off the saying by limiting the reversal to 'many' of the first indicates that the original aphorism has been softened (O5). Luke even reduces it to 'some.' The only 'clean' version is found in Matt 20:16: here the reversal is categorical. For this reason, the Matthean version in 20:16 drew the highest ranking—pink. ∎

Mark 10:32–34

Son of Adam Will Die and Rise. This passage is treated under Mark 8:31–33. ∎

³⁵Then James and John, the sons of Zebedee, come up to him, and say to him, "Teacher, we want you to do for us whatever we ask!" ³⁶He said to them: **"What do you want me to do for you?"** ³⁷They reply to him: "In your glory, let one of us sit at your right hand, and the other at your left." ³⁸Jesus said to them: **"You have no idea what you're asking for. Can you drink that cup that I'm drinking, or undergo the baptism I'm undergoing?"** ³⁹They said to him: "We can!" Jesus said to them: **"The cup I'm drinking you'll be drinking, and the baptism I'm undergoing you'll be undergoing, ⁴⁰but as for sitting at my right or my left, that's not mine to grant, but belongs to those for whom it's been reserved."**

Request for Precedence

Saying	Percentage				Wgt.
	R	P	G	B	Av.
Mk 10:38	7	0	27	67	.16 B
Mt 20:22	7	0	27	67	.16 B
Lk 12:50	3	6	9	82	.10 B
Mk 10:39–40	7	7	20	67	.18 B
Mt 20:23	7	7	20	67	.18 B

Matt 20:20–23 ➡ Mark 10:35–40

²⁰Then the mother of the sons of Zebedee came to him with her sons, bowed down before him, and asked him for a favor. ²¹He said to her, "What do you want?" She said to him, "Tell me that these, my two sons, may sit one at your right hand and one at your left in your domain?" ²²In response Jesus said, **"You have no idea what you're asking for. Can you drink the cup that I am about to drink?"** They said to him, "We can!" ²³He says to them, **"You'll be drinking the same cup I am but as for sitting at my right or my left, that's not mine to grant, but belongs to those for whom it's been reserved by my Father."**

Luke 12:50 ➡ Mark 10:39–40

⁵⁰**I have a baptism to be baptized with; and what pressure I am under until it is over!**

Mark 10:35–40

After presenting the most detailed of his three predictions of Jesus' passion, Mark introduces a scene in which the dialogue anticipates Jesus' last supper. Matthew reproduces while editing Mark's account (he omits reference to Jesus' baptism) (W4). Luke omits this dialogue. A story of two prominent disciples attempting to grab power is not likely to have been invented after the crucifixion—except that Mark does not depict the original disciples in a good light, but pictures them as obtuse, dim-witted, and unsupportive of Jesus' actions. This story seems to fit that particular Markan interest and so could have been invented by him.

The single element that could have circulated independently as a saying is the sentence about Jesus' baptism (O2). This reference is omitted by Matthew but reported by Luke in another context (12:50). In this saying, Jesus is not looking back to an earlier baptism but forward to something still to come. Several Fellows thought this saying was not likely to have been invented after Jesus' death. But the majority held the view that this reference, like the remainder of the story, is a Markan creation. Luke simply held the reference to baptism for use in another context. ∎

Number One is Slave

Saying	Percentage				Wgt.
	R	P	G	B	Av.
Mk 10:42–45	12	20	24	44	.33 **G**
Mt 20:25–28	4	12	28	56	.21 **B**
Lk 22:25–27	12	16	20	52	.29 **G**

⁴¹When they learned of it, the ten began to get testy with James and John. ⁴²So, calling them aside, Jesus says to them: "You know how those who supposedly rule over the gentiles lord it over them, and how their strong men tyrannize them. ⁴³It's not going to be like that among you! Among you, whoever wants to become great must be your servant, ⁴⁴and whoever among you wants to be 'number one' must be everybody's slave. ⁴⁵After all, the son of Adam didn't come to be served, but to serve, even to give his life as a ransom for many."

Matt 20:24–28 ➡ Mark 10:41–45

²⁴And when they learned of it, the ten became testy with the two brothers. ²⁵And calling them aside, Jesus said, "You know how the rulers of the gentiles lord it over them, and how their strong men tyrannize them. ²⁶It is not going to be like that among you! Among you, whoever wants to become great, will be your servant, ²⁷and whoever among you wants to be 'number one' must be your slave. ²⁸After all, the son of Adam didn't come to be served, but to serve, even to give his life as a ransom for many."

Luke 22:24–27 ➡ Mark 10:41–45

²⁴Then a rivalry arose among them over which of them should be considered the greatest. ²⁵He said to them, "The kings of the gentiles lord it over them; and those in power are called 'benefactors.' ²⁶But not so with you; rather, the greatest among you must behave as a beginner, and the leader as one who serves. ²⁷For who is greater, the one who reclines at table or the one who serves? Isn't it the one who reclines? But among you I function as one who serves."

Mark 10:41–45

In the judgment of Fellows, the aphoristic story in Mark 10:35–45 is largely the work of Mark. It goes together with Mark's critical views of the first disciples (cf. Mark 9:33–37). Matthew has taken over Mark's complex, and so has Luke, except that Luke has carried out a more extensive rewriting than Matthew. In so doing, Luke has eliminated some of Mark's theological interpretation (cf. Luke 22:27 with Mark 10:45) and thus moved the complex closer to something Jesus might have said. There is a bit of irony in Luke's move: by removing Mark's interpretation of Jesus' death as a ransom, Luke unwittingly creates a version less inimical to Jesus.

The sayings in Mark 10:42–44 and their parallels probably vaguely reflect something Jesus might have said: those who aspire to greatness must become servants, and those who want to be 'number one' must become slaves. Yet these sayings are so intimately bound up with the leadership struggles that ensued in the Christian communities that it is impossible to untangle them (W9a). As a consequence, Fellows decided to designate the complex in Mark and Luke gray, but put the counterparts in Matthew and John into the black category.

⁴⁶Then they come to Jericho. As he was leaving Jericho with his disciples and a sizable crowd, Bartimaeus, the son of Timaeus, a blind beggar, was sitting alongside the road. ⁴⁷When he learned that it was Jesus the Nazarene, he began to shout: "You son of David, Jesus, have mercy on me!" ⁴⁸And many kept yelling at him to shut up, but he shouted all the louder, "You

---

In any case, the saying in Mark 10:45 is clearly Mark's creation (W4, W7), then borrowed by Matthew. Luke didn't like the theology contained in Mark's version and so rewrote it to suit himself (W4, W7).

The *Notes* on Mark 9:33–37 and parallels are also relevant to these sayings. ■

Blind Bartimaeus

Saying	Percentage				Wgt.
	R	P	G	B	Av.
Mk 10:49,etc.	0	0	0	100	.00 B
Mt 20:30,etc.	0	0	0	100	.00 B
Lk 18:41,etc.	0	0	0	100	.00 B
Mt 9:28,etc.	0	0	0	100	.00 B

son of David, have mercy on me!" ⁴⁹And Jesus stopped and said, "**Tell him to come over here!**" They called to the blind man, "Be brave, get up, he's calling you!" ⁵⁰So he threw off his cloak, and jumped to his feet, and went over to Jesus. ⁵¹In response Jesus said, "**What do you want me to do for you?**" The blind man said to him: "Rabbi, I want to see again!" ⁵²And Jesus said to him: "**Be on your way, your trust has cured you.**" And right away he regained his sight, and he started following him on the road.

Matt 20:29–34 ➠ Mark 10:46–52

²⁹And as they were leaving Jericho, a huge crowd followed him. ³⁰There were two blind men sitting beside the road. When they learned that Jesus was going by, they shouted, "Have mercy on us, Master, you son of David." ³¹The crowd yelled at them to shut up, but they shouted all the louder, "Have mercy on us, Master, you son of David." ³²And Jesus stopped and called out to them, "**What do you want me to do for you?**" ³³They said to him, "Master, open our eyes!" ³⁴Then Jesus took pity on them, touched their eyes, and right away they regained their sight, and followed him.

Luke 18:35–43 ➠ Mark 10:46–52

³⁵One day as he was approaching Jericho, a blind man was sitting by the side of the road begging. ³⁶Hearing a crowd passing through, he asked what was going on. ³⁷They told him, "Jesus the Nazarene is going by." ³⁸Then he shouted, "Jesus, you son of David, have mercy on me!" ³⁹Those in the lead kept yelling at him to shut up, but he kept shouting all the louder, "You son

of David, have mercy on me!" ⁴⁰Jesus stopped and ordered them to guide the man over. When he came near, ⟨Jesus⟩ asked him, ⁴¹"**What do you want me to do for you?**" He said, "Master, I want to see again." ⁴²Jesus said to him, "**Then use your eyes, your trust has cured you.**" ⁴³And immediately he regained his sight. He then began to follow him, praising God all the while. And everyone who saw it gave God the praise.

Matt 9:27–31 ➠ Mark 10:46–52

²⁷And when Jesus went on from there, two blind men followed him, crying out, "Have mercy on us, son of David." ²⁸When ⟨Jesus⟩ arrived home, the blind men came to him. Jesus says to them, "**Do you trust that I can do this?**" They reply to him, "Yes, master." ²⁹Then he touched their eyes, saying, "**Let your trust be a measure of your cure.**" ³⁰And their eyes were opened. Then Jesus scolded them, saying, "See that no one finds out about it." ³¹But they went out and spread the news of him throughout that whole territory.

Mark 10:46–52

There is no detachable saying in this story; all statements attributed to Jesus are context-bound (N2). For that reason

the designation was black by consensus. For a further explanation of this point, see the discussion of Mark 1:21–28. ∎

THE TIME LINE OF THE GOSPELS AND MANUSCRIPTS

25 C.E.   50   75   100   125   150   175   200   225   250   275   300   325

30 — Death of Jesus

50 — Q written

60 — Thomas written

70 — Fall of Jerusalem / Mark written

90 — Matthew written / Council of Jamnia / Luke written

100 — John written

125 — Earliest surviving gospel fragments (𝔓52 & PEger2)

200 — Earliest surviving fragments of Thomas (POxy1 & POxy655) / Earliest surviving fragments of Matthew (𝔓64, 𝔓67, 𝔓77) / Earliest surviving fragment of Luke (𝔓75) / Early surviving fragments of John (𝔓66) / Earliest surviving fragment of Peter (POxy2949)

225 — Earliest surviving fragment of Mark (𝔓45)

300 — Earliest surviving complete codex of New Testament (Sinaiticus) (ℵ)

313 — Edict of Constantine

Entry Into Jerusalem

	Percentage				Wgt.
Saying	R	P	G	B	Av.
Mk 11:2–3	0	0	0	100	.00 **B**
Mt 21:2–3	0	0	0	100	.00 **B**
Lk 19:30–31	0	0	0	100	.00 **B**
Lk 19:40	0	0	4	96	.01 **B**

11 When they get close to Jerusalem, near Bethphage and Bethany at the Mount of Olives, he sends off two of his disciples ²with the instructions, **"Go into the village across the way, and right after you enter it, you will find a colt tied up, one that has never been ridden. Untie it and bring it here. ³If anyone questions you, 'Why are you doing this?' tell them, 'Its master has need of it and he will send it back here right away.'"**

⁴They set out and found a colt tied up at the door out on the street, and they untie it. ⁵Some of the people standing around started saying to them, "What do you think you're doing, untying that colt?" ⁶But they said just what Jesus had told them to say, so they left them alone.

⁷So they bring the colt to Jesus, and they throw their cloaks over it; then he got on it. ⁸And many people spread their cloaks on the road, while others cut leafy branches from the fields. ⁹Those leading the way and those following kept shouting, "'Hosanna! Blessed is the one who comes in the name of the Lord!' ¹⁰Blessed is the coming kingdom of our father David! 'Hosanna' in the highest!"

¹¹And he went into Jerusalem to the temple area and took stock of everything, but since the hour was already late, he returned to Bethany with the twelve.

Mark 11:1–11

Attribution. The words ascribed to Jesus in the story of the entry into Jerusalem are neither an aphorism nor a parable (J2), and so could not have circulated independently (O2). The words are integral to the story and thus are context-bound (N2). As a consequence, the Fellows of the Jesus Seminar designated them black by general consent.

The saying in Luke 19:40 was considered separately. It is attested only by Luke (A1). The vote was almost unanimous: the words are probably an invention of Luke.

The question whether this story reflects a historical incident in the life of Jesus will be on the agenda for the second phase of the Jesus Seminar. ■

Matt 21:1–11 ➡ Mark 11:1–11

¹When they got close to Jerusalem, and came to Bethphage at the Mount of Olives, then Jesus sent two disciples ²with the instructions, **"Go into the village across the way, and right away you will find a donkey tied up, and a colt with her. Untie ⟨them⟩ and bring ⟨them⟩ to me. ³And if anyone says anything to you, you will say, 'their master has need of them and he will send them back right away.'"** ⁴This happened that the word spoken through the prophet might be fulfilled: ⁵"Tell the daughter of Zion, Look, your king comes to you humble and mounted on a donkey and on a colt, foal of a beast of burden."

⁶Then the disciples went and did as Jesus instructed them, ⁷and brought the donkey and colt and they placed their cloaks on them and he sat on top of them. ⁸The enormous crowd spread their cloaks on the road, and others cut branches from the trees and spread them on the road. ⁹The crowds leading the way and those following kept shouting, "Hosanna to the son of David! Blessed is the one who comes in the name of the Lord! 'Hosanna' in the highest." ¹⁰And when he entered into Jerusalem all the city shook, saying, "Who is this?" ¹¹The crowds said, "This is the prophet Jesus who is from Nazareth of Galilee!"

Luke 19:28–40 ➡ Mark 11:1–11

²⁸When he had said this, he went on ahead, on his way up to Jerusalem. ²⁹And it so happened as he got close to Bethphage and Bethany, at the mountain called Olives, that he sent off two of the disciples, ³⁰with the instructions, **"Go into the village across the way. As you enter, you will find a colt tied there, one that has never been ridden. Untie it and bring it here. ³¹If anyone asks you, 'Why are you untying it?' This is what you will say: 'Its master has need of it.'"** ³²So those who were designated went off and found it just as he had told them.

³³As they were untying the colt, its owners said to them, "Why are you untying the colt?" ³⁴And they said, "Its master has need of it."

³⁵So they brought it to Jesus. They threw their cloaks on the colt and had Jesus mount it. ³⁶And as he went along, they spread their cloaks on the road. ³⁷As he drew near the slope of the Mount of Olives, the whole crowd of disciples began to rejoice and shout praise to God for all the miracles they had seen. ³⁸They were saying, "Blessed is the king who comes in the name of the Lord! Peace in heaven and glory in the highest!" ³⁹Some of the Pharisees in the crowd said to him, "Teacher, rebuke your disciples." ⁴⁰But he answered, **"I tell you, if these folks were silent, the stones would cry out."**

The Fig Tree Without Figs

Saying	Percentage				Wgt.
	R	P	G	B	Av.
Mk 11:14	0	0	0	100	.00 B
Mt 21:19	0	0	0	100	.00 B

The Temple as Hideout

Saying	Percentage				Wgt.
	R	P	G	B	Av.
Mk 11:17	6	22	17	56	.26 G
Mt 21:13	6	22	17	56	.26 G
Lk 19:46	6	22	17	56	.26 G
Jn 2:16	6	22	17	56	.26 G

¹²On the next day, as they were leaving Bethany, he got hungry. ¹³So when he spotted a fig tree in the distance, with leaves on it, he went up to it expecting to find something on it. But when he got right up to it, he found nothing on it except leaves. (You see, it wasn't 'time' for figs.) ¹⁴And he reacted by saying: "**May no one so much as taste your fruit again!**" And his disciples were listening.

¹⁵They come to Jerusalem. And he went into the temple and began driving out the vendors and the buyers in the temple area, and he turned the tables of the moneychangers upside down, and the chairs of the pigeon merchants, ¹⁶and he wouldn't even let anyone carry a container through the temple area. ¹⁷Then he started teaching and would say to them: "Is it not written, 'My house will be called a house of prayer for all peoples'?—but you have made it 'a hideout for crooks'!" ¹⁸And the ranking priests and the scribes heard this and kept looking for a way to get rid of him. (The truth is that they stood in fear of him, and that the whole crowd was astonished at his teaching.) ¹⁹And when it grew dark, they made their way out of the city.

Matt 21:18–19 ➡ Mark 11:12–14

¹⁸Early in the morning, as he was returning to the city, he got hungry. ¹⁹And so when he spotted a single fig tree on the way, he came up to it, and found nothing on it except leaves, and he says to it, "**May you never bear fruit again!**" And the fig tree instantly withered.

Mark 11:12–14, 20–21

Attribution. The words ascribed to Jesus are once again context-bound (N2); they cannot be detached from the narrative and so could not have circulated separately during the oral period (O2).

Whether or not this story reports an actual event in the life of Jesus will be on the agenda for the second phase of the Jesus Seminar. ■

Mark 11:15–17

Historical circumstance. The text of this passage proved to be difficult to evaluate as it stands. After extended discussion of this and other related texts, members of the Seminar took a poll on two related questions:

(1) Jesus performed some anti-temple act;

(2) Jesus spoke some anti-temple word.

Matt 21:12–13 ➡ Mark 11:15–17

¹²And Jesus went into [God's] temple and drove out all the vendors and the buyers in the temple area and he turned the tables of the moneychangers upside down, and the chairs of the pigeon merchants. ¹³Then he says to them, "It is written, 'My house will be called a house of prayer,' but you have made it 'a hideout for crooks'!"

Luke 19:45–46 ➡ Mark 11:15–17

⁴⁵Then he entered the temple area and began driving out the vendors. ⁴⁶He says to them, "It is written, 'My house will be a house of prayer'; but you have made it a 'hideout for crooks'!"

John 2:13–17 ➡ Mark 11:15–17

¹³It was almost time for the Jewish Passover, so Jesus went up to Jerusalem. ¹⁴In the temple precincts he came upon people selling oxen, sheep, and pigeons; money-changers were seated ⟨in their stalls⟩. ¹⁵And he made a whip out of cords and drove the whole bunch out of the temple area, along with both sheep and oxen. Then he knocked over the money-changers' tables, and set their coins flying. ¹⁶Then he told the pigeon merchants: "Get these ⟨birds⟩ out of here! Stop turning my Father's house into a public market." ¹⁷His disciples recalled the words of Scripture: "Passion for your house will devour me."

Approximately 68% of the Fellows answered the first question affirmatively; the affirmative vote rose to 70% on the second question. Two-thirds of the Fellows are thus convinced that Jesus both did and said something that could have been understood as an act or a word directed against the temple cult in Jerusalem. The problem that arises is that the texts which record such an event may in fact obscure it to a certain degree, so that the evaluation of the texts turns out differently than an assessment of the event or some words presumably connected with such an event.

Attribution. Mark 11:17 is a complex quotation in which phrases from both Isaiah 56:7 and Jeremiah 7:11 are conflated to form a new quotation. The text being cited is the Greek Old Testament, the Septuagint (LXX), not the Hebrew Bible. This technique of mixing scriptural quotations was a common practice of Jewish scribes and of the evangelists in the first century. Jesus probably did not quote scripture in Greek, much less conflate quotations. In any case, the mixed

citation suggests that these words were probably coined by Mark or some other early Christian interpreter (O5). Confirmation of this possibility is provided by John, who also mixes quotations: he alludes to Zechariah 14:21 in 2:16 and quotes Psalm 69:9 in 2:17 (O5).

The conclusion to be drawn is that there is no saying in Mark 11:17 that once circulated independently (O2). The interpretation of an act of Jesus by reference to scripture is probably the work of the evangelist (O5). Nevertheless, Fellows did agree that Jesus probably said something on an occasion like the one depicted here, but the words he spoke have been lost.

Jesus' act in the temple was undoubtedly intended as a prophetic gesture, such as the one made by Jeremiah when he put a wooden yoke around his neck to forecast the coming conquest of Nebuchadnezzar and the ensuing bondage. A majority of Fellows agree that Jesus performed some such anti-temple act as that depicted in Mark, although we cannot be certain of the details. ∎

Mountains Into the Sea

Saying	Percentage				Wgt.
	R	P	G	B	Av.
Mk 11:23	0	30	35	35	.32 G
Mt 21:21	0	30	35	35	.32 G
Mt 17:20	0	30	40	30	.33 G
Lk 17:5–6	9	17	26	48	.29 G
Th 48	4	29	29	38	.33 G
Th 106	4	29	29	38	.33 G
Core	12	42	19	27	.46 G

20As they were walking along early one morning, they saw the fig tree withered from the roots up. 21And Peter remembered and says to him: "Rabbi, look, the fig tree you cursed has withered up!" 22In response Jesus says to them: **"Have trust in God.** 23I swear to you, those who say to this mountain, 'Up with you and into the sea!' and do not waver in their conviction, but trust that what they say will happen, that's the way it will be. 24This is why I keep telling you, trust that you will receive everything you pray and ask for, and that's the way it will turn out. 25And when you stand up to pray, if you are holding anything against anyone, forgive them, so your father in heaven may forgive your misdeeds."

Matt 21:20–22 ➡ Mark 11:20–25
20And when the disciples saw this, they marveled: "How did the fig tree wither up so quickly?" 21In response Jesus said to them, "I swear to you, if you have trust and do not doubt, not only can you do this to the fig tree but you can say to this mountain, 'Up with you and into the sea!' and that's how it will happen; 22and everything you pray and ask for, if you trust, you will receive it."

Matt 17:20 ➡ Mark 11:23
20But he says to them, "Because of your lack of trust. I swear to you, even if you have trust no larger than a mustard seed, you will say to this mountain, 'Move from here to there,' and it will move. And nothing will be beyond you."

Luke 17:5–6 ➡ Mark 11:23
5The apostles said to the Lord, "Enlarge our trust!" 6And the Lord said, "If you had trust no larger than a mustard seed, you could say to this mulberry tree, 'Be uprooted and be planted in the sea,' and it would obey you."

Thom 48 ➡ Mark 11:23
Jesus said, "If two make peace with each other in a single house, they will say to the mountain, 'Move from here!' and it will move."

Thom 106:1–2 ➡ Mark 11:23
1Jesus said, "When you make the two into one, you will become children of humankind, 2and when you say, 'Mountain, move from here!' it will move."

John 14:13–14 ➡ Mark 11:24
13"Whatever you ask in my name, I will do, so the Father can be glorified in the son. 14If you ask anything in my name, I will do ⟨it⟩."

John 15:7 ➡ Mark 11:24
7". . . ask for whatever you want and it will be done for you."

John 15:16 ➡ Mark 11:24
16 ". . . so that whatever you ask of the Father in my name, he may give ⟨it⟩ to you."

Ask and Receive

Saying	Percentage				Wgt. Av.
	R	P	G	B	
Mk 11:24	7	20	47	27	.36 G
Mt 21:22	7	20	47	27	.36 G
Jn 14:13–14	0	0	47	53	.16 B
Jn 15:7b	0	0	47	53	.16 B
Jn 15:16b	0	0	47	53	.16 B
Jn 16:23,etc.	0	0	47	53	.16 B

Forgiveness for Forgiveness

Saying	Percentage				Wgt. Av.
	R	P	G	B	
Mk 11:25	14	36	36	14	.50 G
Mt 6:14–15	7	36	43	14	.45 G
Lk 6:37	7	71	7	14	.57 P
1 Clem 13:2	7	71	7	14	.57 P
Pol Phil 2:3	7	71	7	14	.57 P
Pol Phil 6:2	7	14	50	29	.33 G

John 16:23–24, 26 ➡ Mark 11:24

23"When that day comes, you won't have any more questions for me. So help me, if you ask the Father for anything in my name, he will give it to you. 24Up till now you have asked nothing in my name. Ask and you will receive that you may be full of joy. . . . 26when that day comes, you will make requests in my name . . ."

Matt 6:14–15 ➡ Mark 11:25

14"If you forgive other persons their misdeeds, your Father in the heavens will forgive yours also. 15But if you don't forgive other people, your father won't forgive you."

Luke 6:37 ➡ Mark 11:25

37". . . Forgive, and you'll be forgiven."

1 Clem 13:2 ➡ Mark 11:25

2. . . "The measure you give will be the measure you get."

Pol Phil 2:3 ➡ Mark 11:25

3. . . "The measure you give will be the measure you get back."

Pol Phil 6:2 ➡ Mark 11:25

2"If we beg the Lord to forgive us, we ourselves should also practice forgiveness."

Mark 11:20–25

Forms and sources. The saying about 'moving mountains' must have been popular among early Christians. It is known in three distinct forms (A3) in three different sources (A1).

The first form, Mark 11:23//Matt 21:21, is derived from Mark. It is linked to a second saying about the power of prayer (Mark 11:24//Matt 21:22).

In the second form, the saying begins with an if-clause with reference to faith as a grain of mustard seed, which gives the power to move the mountain. Luke's movable object is a tree rather than a mountain. Matthew adds a generalization: nothing will then be impossible for you.

The third version, preserved by Thomas, links unity or peace with the ability to move mountains. The Thomas version looks to be rather simpler than the versions recorded by the Synoptics (O3a). The reference in 1 Cor 13:2, although not attributed to Jesus, indicates that the connection between faith and moving mountains was widespread in the early tradition (A3).

Attribution. Fellows decided to vote on a hypothetical core saying about moving mountains, stripped of embellishments like those found in Mark 11:22b, on the view that a simpler form might represent something Jesus probably said (O3a). The weighted average rose only to .46, which left it short of the pink range. However, 54% of the Fellows voted either red or pink.

Although widely attested, the saying was not stable during its transmission, appearing now in this form, now in that, without a clearly discernible pattern. Such instability led many Fellows to doubt that it had a firm place in the early tradition, in spite of Paul's reference to the concept.

Beyond that problem, Fellows were not convinced the saying could be given an interpretation that was consonant with what we know of Jesus from other sayings and parables (G5). The suggestion that mountains represented the foundations of the cosmos and served as the pillars of the earth and sky and so could stand for 'changing the face of the world' in some metaphorical sense did not commend itself to everyone. Those who voted black (and possibly gray) took it rather as a commonplace adopted by Mark and the other evangelists for specifically religious contexts, such as prayer and exorcism. ■

Mark 11:24

Attestation. The saying about the power of prayer is attested by Mark 11:24 with its parallel in Matthew 21:22; the saying also appears in various guises in the Gospel of John (A1).

Attribution. Most Fellows were convinced that this formulation reflects the situation in primitive Christian circles, in which the continuing interest in exorcism, healing, and various other demonstrations, was linked to prayer (W9a). The sentiment, in any case, was common and therefore not distinctive of Jesus (J3).

The Fellows who voted red or pink on the Markan version argued that this admonition was comparable to the confidence expressed in the petitions of the Lord's Prayer which Fellows designated pink (they so designated four individual petitions, although not the prayer as a whole: Luke 11:2–4). They thought it also comparable to the trust in God as provider that Jesus instilled in his followers (Matt 6:26– 30)(G5). ■

Mark 11:25

Attribution. The petition in the Lord's Prayer for forgiveness (Matt 6:12) was given a pink designation by Fellows. The saying here about forgiveness seems entirely coherent with that other petition (G5). For this reason, Fellows were inclined to ascribe the saying to Jesus.

The Markan form, however, is linked to prayer, which is the theme Mark uses to cluster sayings in 11:22–25 (W1). Since this theme appears to be secondary to the saying, Mark 11:25 was given a slightly lower ranking (W3). The form in Matthew appears to be a commentary on the prayer petition in the Lord's Prayer, since it follows immediately on that prayer (W4). It is also formulated in Matthew's language. These features caused it to fall further into the gray spectrum. The version in Polycarp's letter to the Philippians 6:2 also has the cast of a commentary (W3), and so was designated gray.

With these qualifications, the majority of the Fellows agreed that the saying originated with Jesus in some proximate form. ■

Mark 11:27–33

Attribution. Mark 11:27–33 is a pronouncement story or *chreia.* The words attributed are in the style of a retort or rejoinder and so sound like Jesus must have sounded on such occasions. However, they do not take the form of a parable or an aphorism (J2). It is difficult, as a consequence, to imagine how they could have been transmitted during the oral period, except as a part of this story (N2). Furthermore, this story is only singly attested (A1). Fellows designated the words black on the grounds that they were probably the invention of the storyteller. The question whether this story reflects a historical incident will form part of the agenda of the Jesus Seminar in its second phase. ■

²⁷They come once again to Jerusalem. As he walks around in the temple area, the ranking priests and scribes and elders come up to him ²⁸and start questioning him: "By what authority are you doing these things?" or, "Who gave you the authority to do these things?" ²⁹But Jesus said to them: **"I have one question for you. If you answer me, then I will tell you by what authority I do these things.** ³⁰**Tell me, was the baptism of John heaven sent or was it of human origin? Answer me that."** ³¹And they argued among themselves, saying, "If we say 'heaven sent,' he'll say, 'Then why didn't you trust him?' ³²But if we say 'Of human origin . . . !'" They were afraid of the crowd. (You see, everybody considered John a genuine prophet.) ³³So they answered Jesus by saying, "We can't tell." And Jesus says to them: **"Neither am I going to tell you by what authority I do these things!"**

By What Authority?

Saying	Percentage				Wgt.
	R	P	G	B	Av.
Mk 11:29,etc.	0	0	0	100	.00 **B**
Mt 21:24,etc.	0	0	0	100	.00 **B**
Lk 20:3,etc.	0	0	0	100	.00 **B**

Matt 21:23–27 ➡ Mark 11:27–33

²³And when he came to the temple area, the ranking priest and elders of the people approached him while he was teaching, and asked, "By what authority are you doing these things?" and "Who gave you this authority?" ²⁴In response Jesus said to them, **"I have one question for you. If you answer me, I will tell you by what authority I do these things.** ²⁵**The baptism of John, what was its origin? Was it heaven sent or was it of human origin?"** And they argued among themselves, saying, "If we say 'heaven sent,' he'll say to us, 'Why didn't you trust him?' ²⁶And if we say 'Of human origin . . .!' We are afraid of the crowd." (Remember, everybody considered John a prophet.) ²⁷So they answered Jesus by saying, "We can't tell." He replied to them in kind, **"Neither am I going to tell you by what authority I do these things!"**

Luke 20:1–8 ➡ Mark 11:27–33

¹One day as he was teaching the people in the temple area and speaking of the good news, the ranking priests and the scribes approached him along with the elders, ²and asked him, "Tell us, by what authority are you doing these things? Who gave you this authority?" ³He answered them, **"I will ask you a question too; tell me,** ⁴**was John's baptism heaven sent or was it of human origin?"** ⁵And they argued among themselves, saying, "If we say, 'heaven sent,' he'll say, 'Why didn't you trust him?' ⁶But if we say, 'Of human origin,' the people will all stone us, for they are convinced John was a prophet." ⁷So they answered that they did not know its origin. ⁸And Jesus said to them, **"Neither am I going to tell you by what authority I do these things!"**

The Tenants

Saying	Percentage				Wgt.
	R	P	G	B	Av.
Mk 12:1–8	0	9	64	27	.27 G
Mt 21:33–39	0	9	64	27	.27 G
Lk 20:9–15a	0	9	64	27	.27 G
Th 65:1–7	14	64	14	9	.61 P

12 And he began to speak to them in parables. "Someone planted a vineyard, put a hedge around it, dug a winepress, built a tower, leased it to farmers, and went abroad. ²In due time he sent a slave to the farmers to collect his share of the vineyard's crop from them. ³But they grabbed him, beat him, and sent him away empty-handed. ⁴So once again he sent another slave to them, but they attacked him and abused him. ⁵Then he sent another, and this one they killed; many others followed, some of whom they beat, others of whom they killed. ⁶He still had one more, a son who was the apple of his eye. This one he finally sent to them, with the thought,

Matt 21:33–39 ➡ Mark 12:1–8

³³"Hear another parable. There once was a landlord who planted a vineyard, put a hedge around it, dug a winepress in it, built a tower, leased it out to farmers, and went abroad. ³⁴Now when harvest time drew near, he sent his slaves to the farmers to collect his crop. ³⁵And the farmers grabbed his slaves, and one they beat and another they killed, and another they stoned. ³⁶Again he sent other slaves, more than the first time, and they did the same thing to them. ³⁷Then finally he sent his son to them, with the thought, 'This son of mine they will respect.' ³⁸But when the farmers recognized the son they said to one another, 'This fellow's the heir! Come on, let's kill him and we will have his inheritance!' ³⁹And they grabbed him, threw him outside the vineyard, and killed him."

Luke 20:9–15a ➡ Mark 12:1–8

⁹Then he began to tell the people this parable. "Someone planted a vineyard, leased it to farmers, and went abroad for an extended time. ¹⁰In due time he sent a slave to the farmers, to get his share of the vineyard's crop. But the farmers beat him and sent him away empty-handed. ¹¹He repeated his action by

sending another slave; but they beat him up too, and abused him, and sent him away empty-handed. ¹²And he sent yet a third slave; but they wounded him and threw him out. ¹³Then the owner of the vineyard asked himself, 'What should I do? I know, I will send my son, the apple of my eye. Perhaps they will respect him.' ¹⁴But when the farmers recognized him, they said one to another, 'This fellow's the heir! Let's kill him so the inheritance will be ours!' ¹⁵So they threw him outside the vineyard and killed him."

Thom 65:1–7 ➡ Mark 12:1–8

¹He said, "A [. . .] person owned a vineyard and leased it to some farmers, so they could work it and he could collect its crop from them. ²He sent his slave that the farmers might give him the vineyard's crop. ³They grabbed him, beat him, and almost killed him. So the slave returned and told his master. ⁴His master said, 'Perhaps he did not know them.' ⁵He sent another slave, and the farmers beat that one as well. ⁶Then the master sent his son and said, 'Perhaps they will show my son some respect.' ⁷But because the farmers knew that he was the heir to the vineyard, they grabbed him and killed him."

'This son of mine they will respect.' [7]But those farmers said to one another, 'This fellow's the heir! Come on, let's kill him and the inheritance will be ours!' [8]So they grabbed him, and killed him, and threw him outside the vineyard. [9]**What will the owner of the vineyard do? He will come in person, and destroy those farmers, and give the vineyard to others.** [10]**Haven't you read this scripture, 'A stone that the builders rejected, this has become the keystone. [11]It was the Lord's doing and is admired in our eyes'?"** [12]⟨His opponents⟩ kept looking for some opportunity to seize him, but they were still afraid of the crowd, since they realized that he had aimed

The Rejected Stone

Saying	Percentage				Wgt.
	R	P	G	B	Av.
Mk 12:9–11	0	0	0	100	.00 B
Mt 21:40–43	0	0	0	100	.00 B
Lk 20:15b–18	0	0	0	100	.00 B
Th 66	0	0	0	100	.00 B
Barn 6:4a	0	0	0	100	.00 B

Matt 21:40–43 ➡ Mark 12:9–11
[40]**"When the owner of the vineyard comes, what will he do to those farmers then?"** [41]They said to him, "These extremely evil ones he will destroy and lease out the vineyard to other farmers who will deliver their produce to him at the proper time."

[42]Jesus says to them, "Haven't you read in the scriptures, 'A stone that the builders rejected, this has become the keystone. It was the Lord's doing and is admired in our eyes'? [43]Therefore I say to you, God's domain will be taken away from you and given to a nation that bears its fruit."

Luke 20:15b–18 ➡ Mark 12:9–11
[15]"... What then will the owner of the vineyard do to them? [16]He will come and destroy those farmers, and give the vineyard to others." When they heard this, they said, "God forbid!" [17]But Jesus looked them straight in the eye and said, "**What then does this scripture mean: 'A stone that the builders rejected, this has become the keystone'?** [18]Everyone who falls over that stone will be smashed to pieces, and anyone on whom it falls will be crushed."

Thom 66 ➡ Mark 12:9–11
Jesus said, "**Show me the stone that the builders rejected: that is the keystone.**"

Barn 6:4a ➡ Mark 12:9–11
[4]Again the prophet says, "**A stone that the builders rejected, this has become the keystone.**"

Mark 12:1–8, 9–11
Development of the tradition. The synoptic versions (Matthew, Mark, Luke) clearly have been reworked to form an allegory of the history of salvation, culminating in the rejection and death of Jesus (W3). The landlord (God) establishes a vineyard and leases it out to tenant farmers. He sends his servants (the prophets) to the tenants to collect the rent, but they treat the servants shamefully. Finally, he sends his (beloved) son, whom the wicked tenants kill. The Christian listener knows that God has vindicated his son by raising him from the dead, but the allegorized parable does not provide for that vindication, except indirectly in the quotation from Psalm 118:22–23 about the rejected keystone. The reference to the Psalm was undoubtedly added at the time the parable was allegorized (O5).

the parable at them. So they left him there and went on their way.

[13]And they send some of the Pharisees and the Herodians to him to trap him with a riddle. [14]They come and say to him, "Teacher, we know that you are honest and impartial, because you pay no attention to appearances, but instead you teach God's way forthrightly. Is it permissible to pay the poll tax to the Roman emperor or not? Should we pay or should we not pay?" [15]But he saw through their trap, and said to them: **"Why do you provoke me like this? Let me have a look at a coin."** [16]They handed him a denarius, and he says to them, **"Whose picture is this? Whose name is on it?"** They said, "The emperor's." [17]Jesus said to them: "Pay to the emperor whatever belongs to the emperor, and to God whatever belongs to God!" And they were dumbfounded at him.

God and the Emperor

Saying	Percentage				Wgt.
	R	P	G	B	Av.
Mk 12:17	50	45	5	0	.82 R
Mt 22:21	50	45	5	0	.82 R
Lk 20:25	50	45	5	0	.82 R
Th 100:2–4	50	45	5	0	.82 R
EgerG 3:5–6	0	0	0	100	.00 B

The version in Thomas demonstrates that the parable once circulated without allegorical traits. Indeed, the Thomas version parallels Matthew 21:33b–39, Mark 12:1b–8, Luke 20:9b–15a, but without allegorical traits. We may be confident, therefore, that Thomas is closer to the original version (O3a).

Attribution. The following allegorical elements are not found in the simpler version of Thomas: (a) the allusions to Isa 5:1–7 (planted a vineyard, put a hedge around it, dug a winepress, built a tower) are missing from Thomas (O5). (b) Only single servants are sent—not the groups of Matthew. (c) No one is killed prior to the son; in Matthew some are killed in each group. (d) No mention is made of throwing the son outside the vineyard (a reference, presumably, to Jesus' death outside the walls of Jerusalem) (W10). (e) There is no concluding question addressed to the hearers and therefore no punishment of the tenants (J7). To be sure, some of these traits are missing from Mark and Luke as well. It is Matthew who has carried the allegorization

to its ultimate degree. Nevertheless, it is striking that there are no allegorical traits in Thomas.

The Fellows of the Seminar were of the opinion that a version of this parable without allegorical overtones could be traced to Jesus. There were absentee landlords in Galilee in Jesus' day, and there were peasants who were unhappy with their lot. The tenants acted resolutely to take possession of the vineyard by getting rid of the only heir (G2). If Jesus told this parable, he did so as a story vindicating the successful execution of a murder. From a moral perspective, the parable of the Tenants is perhaps no different than the parable of the Unjust Steward (Luke 16:1–7) (G5).

Aspects of the story were too much of a temptation to the early Christian mind: it seized on the possibilities and turned it into an allegory of the history of salvation. Initially, the quotation from the Psalm moved the parable in the direction of allegory, and then the parable itself was reshaped to reflect the well-known scenario (W3, W4, W8a). ∎

Matt 22:15–22 ➡ Mark 12:13–17

[15]Then the Pharisees went and conferred on how to entrap him with a riddle. [16]And they send their disciples with the Herodians to him, and say, "Teacher, we know that you are honest and that you teach God's way forthrightly, and are impartial because you pay no attention to appearances. [17]Tell us therefore what you think: Is it permissible to pay the poll tax to the Roman emperor or not? [18]Jesus knew how devious they were, and said, **"Why do you provoke me, you phonies?** [19]**Let me see the coin used to pay the poll tax."** And they handed him a denarius. [20]And he says to them, **"Whose picture is this? Whose name is on it?"** [21]They say to him, "The emperor's." Then he says to them, "Pay to the emperor whatever belongs to the emperor, and to God whatever belongs to God!" [22]And upon hearing his reply, they were dumbfounded. and they withdrew from him and went away.

Luke 20:19–26 ➡ Mark 12:13–17

[19]The scribes and the ranking priests wanted to lay hands on him then and there, but they were afraid of the people, since they realized he had aimed this parable at them. [20]So they kept him under surveillance, and sent spies, who pretended to be sincere, in order to lay a verbal trap for him, so they could turn him over to the authority and jurisdiction of the governor. [21]They asked him, "Teacher, we know that what you speak and teach is correct, that you show no favoritism, but instead teach God's way forthrightly.

[22]Is it permissible for us to pay taxes to the Roman emperor or not?" [23]But he perceived their cunning, and said to them, [24]**"Show me a coin. Whose likeness does it bear? And whose name is on it?"** They said, "The emperor's." [25]So he said to them, "Then pay to the emperor whatever belongs to the emperor, and to God whatever belongs to God!" [26]And so they were unable to catch him in anything he said in front of the people; they were dumbfounded at his answer and fell silent.

Thom 100:1–4 ➡ Mark 12:13–17

[1]They showed Jesus a gold coin and said to him, "The Roman emperor's people demand taxes from us."

[2]He said to them, "Give the emperor whatever belongs to the emperor, [3]give God whatever belongs to God, [4]**and give me what is mine."**

EgerG 3:1–6 ➡ Mark 12:13–17

[1]They come to him and put him to the test by examination. [2]They ask, "Teacher, Jesus, we know that you are from God, since the things you do put you above all the prophets. [3]Tell us, then, is it permitted to pay to rulers what is due them? Should we pay them or not?" [4]Jesus knew what they were up to, and became indignant. [5]Then he said to them, **"Why do you pay me lip service as a teacher, but pay no attention to what I say? [6]How accurately Isaiah prophesied about you when he said, 'This people honor me with their lips, but their heart stays far away from me; they worship me in vain, [because they insist on teachings that are human] commandments . . ."**

Mark 12:13–17

Sources. This is one of the few pronouncement stories (*chreiai*) that preserves an isolable saying of Jesus. That the saying once circulated independently is demonstrated by the Gospel of

Thomas where it is recorded without narrative context (O2). Unfortunately, the Egerton Gospel attests the narrative framework of Mark 12:13–17, but attaches a different aphoristic conclusion. The upshot is that we cannot be

¹⁸And some Sadducees come up to him—those who claim there is no resurrection—and they start questioning him. ¹⁹"Teacher," they said, "Moses wrote for our benefit, 'If someone's brother dies and leaves his widow childless, his brother is obligated to take the widow as his wife and produce offspring for his brother.' ²⁰There were seven brothers; now the first took a wife but left no offspring when he died. ²¹So the second married her but died without leaving offspring, and the third likewise. ²²In fact, all seven ⟨married her but⟩ left no offspring. Finally, the wife also died. ²³In the res-

---

Matt 22:23–33 ➡ Mark 12:18–27

²³On that day, the Sadducees came to him—-those who claim there is no resurrection—and questioned him. ²⁴"Teacher," they said, "Moses said, 'If someone dies without children, his brother is obligated to marry his widow and raise offspring for his brother.' ²⁵There were seven brothers among us; and the first married and died. And since he produced no offspring, he left his widow to his brother. ²⁶The second brother did the same thing, and the third, and so on, through the seventh brother. ²⁷Finally the wife also died. ²⁸So then, in the resurrection whose wife, of the seven, will she be? Remember, they had all had her." ²⁹In response Jesus said to them, "You have missed the point again, all because you underestimate both the scriptures and the power of God. ³⁰After all, at the resurrection they will neither marry nor get married, but are like heaven's angels. ³¹As for the resurrection of the dead, haven't you read God's word to you: ³²'I am the God of Abraham and the God of Isaac and the God of Jacob.' He is not God of the dead, only of the living." ³³And when the crowd heard, they were stunned by his teaching.

---

certain that the synoptic context for the story is original (W2). In any case, the words ascribed to Jesus in Mark 12:15, 16; Matt 22:18–19, 20; Luke 20:24 are context-bound (N2) and so could not have circulated independently (O2).

It was agreed that the final words in the Thomas version are secondary: "and give me what is mine" (W3). This addition is to be printed in black.

Attribution. Everything about this pericope commends its authenticity. Jesus' retort to the question of taxes is a masterful bit of enigmatic repartee (J7). He avoids the trap laid for him by the question without really resolving the issue: he doesn't advise them to pay the tax and he doesn't advise them not to pay the tax; he advises them to know the difference between the claims of emperor and the claims of God. Nevertheless, the early Christian interpretation of this story affirmed the Christian obligation to pay the tax (O4, W9a). Paul struggled with this issue (Rom 13:1–7) and came out on the side of expedience: pay everyone their proper dues, including the civil authorities, who have received their appointment from God. ∎

urrection, after they rise, whose wife will she be? Remember, all seven had her as wife!" [24]Jesus said to them: "You've missed the point again, haven't you, all because you underestimate both the scriptures and the power of God. [25]After all, when men and women rise from the dead, they neither marry nor are given in marriage, but are like heavens' angels. [26]As for whether or not the dead rise, haven't you read in the book of Moses, how God spoke to him from the bush: 'I am the God of Abraham and the God of Isaac and the God of Jacob'? [27]He is not God of the dead, only of the living—you're constantly missing the point!"

Whose Wife Will She Be?

Saying	Percentage				Wgt.
	R	P	G	B	Av.
Mk 12:24–27	7	13	40	40	.29 G
Mt 22:29–32	7	13	40	40	.29 G
Lk 20:34–38	7	13	40	40	.29 G

Luke 20:27–40 ➡ Mark 12:18–27

[27]Some of the Sadducees came up to him—those who deny there is a resurrection—[28]and asked a question. "Teacher," they said, "Moses wrote for our benefit, 'If someone's brother dies, leaving a wife but no children, his brother is obligated to take the widow as wife and produce offspring for his brother.' [29]Now there were seven brothers; the first took a wife, and died childless. [30]Then the second [31]and the third married her, and so on. All seven ⟨married her but⟩ left no children when they died. [32]Finally, the wife also died. [33]So then, in the resurrection whose wife will the woman be? Remember, all seven had her as wife." [34]And Jesus said to them, "The children of this age marry and are given in marriage; [35]but those who are deemed worthy of participating in the coming age, and in the resurrection from the dead, will neither marry nor be given in marriage. [36]They can no longer die, for they are like angels; they are children of God and children of the resurrection. [37]That the dead are raised, Moses demonstrates in the passage about the bush: he calls the Lord 'the God of Abraham, the God of Isaac, and the God of Jacob.' [38]So He is not God of the dead, but of the living; for to him they are all alive." [39]And some of the scribes answered, "Well said, Teacher." [40]And they no longer dared to ask him anything else.

Mark 12:18–27

History of the tradition. The debate over the resurrection is a close knit composition. The words attributed to Jesus cannot be isolated from their narrative context (N2). The concluding proof in Mark 12:26–27 was probably added by Mark; it could not have been a saying that originally circulated independently (O2). The style is that of a rabbinic debate (discussion of a problem posed by scripture), which was not characteristic of Jesus (J6, J7), but belongs to the later Palestinian community, when the church was in direct conflict with Pharisees and other groups. The Sadducees are made the opponents because they traditionally opposed the concept of a resurrection.

Attribution. This exchange betrays the situation of the Christian community when theological debate was well developed (W9a). ∎

Which Commandment?

| Saying | Percentage | | | | Wgt. |
	R	P	G	B	Av.
Mk 12:29-31	0	40	53	7	.44 G
Mk 12:34	0	33	27	40	.31 G
Mt 22:37-40	0	33	60	7	.42 G
Lk 10:28	0	14	29	57	.19 B

[28]And one of the scribes approached when he heard them arguing, and because he saw how skillfully Jesus answered them, he asked him, "Of all the commandments, which is the most important?" [29]Jesus answered: "The first is, 'Hear, Israel, the Lord your God is one Lord, [30]and you are to love the Lord your God with all your heart and all your soul [and all your mind] and with all your energy.' [31]The second is this: 'You are to love your neighbor as yourself.' There is no other commandment greater than these." [32]And the scribe said to him, "That's a fine answer, Teacher. You have correctly said that God is one and there is no other beside him. [33]And 'to love him with all one's heart and with all one's mind and with all one's energy'

Matt 22:34–40 ➡ Mark 12:28–34

[34]When the Pharisees learned that he had silenced the Sadducees, they conspired against him. [35]And one of them, a lawyer, asked him to test him: [36]"Teacher, which commandment in the law is the greatest?" [37]He replied to him, "'You are to love the Lord your God with all your heart and all your soul and all your mind.' [38]This is the greatest and preeminent commandment. [39]And the second is like it: 'You are to love your neighbor as yourself.' [40]On these two commandments the whole of the law and the prophets hangs."

Luke 10:25–29 ➡ Mark 12:28–34

[25]On one occasion, a lawyer stood up to test him with a question. "Teacher, what must I do to inherit eternal life?" [26]He said to him, "How do you read what is written in the Law?" [27]And he answered, "You shall love the Lord your God with all your heart, with all your soul, with all your strength, and with all your mind; and your neighbor as yourself." [28]Jesus said to him, "You have answered correctly; do this and you will live."

[29]But wanting to justify himself, he said to Jesus, "But who is my neighbor?"

Mark 12:28–34

Development of the tradition. Like the preceding pericope, this story, too, is a unitary composition: the words of Jesus are of a piece with the dialogue in which they are embedded (N2).

Mark has provided a minimal narrative framework in vv. 28 and 34, in which a friendly scribe poses the question. The scribe is hostile in the narrative frame provided by Matthew. Luke has used the exchange to furnish a narrative context for the parable of the Good Samaritan

(10:25–29). This variety in setting demonstrates that the narrative framework provided by each of the evangelists is secondary (W2).

Attribution. The content of the dialogue is by no means original. Questions about the greatest commandment were regularly posed by every student of the Torah, and every rabbi had a ready answer, probably not unlike the one ascribed to Jesus here (O5). In any case, Jesus' response is a collage of scriptural references: Deut 6:4–5, Lev 19:18. The

and 'to love one's neighbor as oneself' is greater than all the burnt offerings and sacrifices put together." [34]And when Jesus saw that he answered him sensibly, he said to him, "You are not far from God's domain." And from then on no one dared question him.

[35]And during the time Jesus was teaching in the temple area, he would pose this question: **"How can the scribes claim that the Anointed is the son of David? [36]David himself said under the influence of the holy spirit, 'The Lord said to my lord, "Sit here on my right, until I make your enemies grovel at your feet."' [37]David himself calls him 'lord,' so how can he be his son?"** And a huge crowd would listen to him with delight.

Whose Son Is the Anointed?

Saying	Percentage				Wgt.
	R	P	G	B	Av.
Mk 12:35-37	0	5	21	74	.11 B
Mt 22:41-45	0	5	21	74	.11 B
Lk 20:41-44	0	5	21	74	.11 B
Barn 12:10-11	0	0	6	94	.02 B

Matt 22:41-46 ➡ Mark 12:35-37

[41]When the Pharisees gathered together, Jesus asked them, [42]**"What do you think about the Anointed? Whose son is he?"** They said to him, "David's." [43]He said to them, **"How then does David call him 'lord,' while speaking under the influence of the spirit? [44]The Lord said to my lord, "Sit here on my right, until I make your enemies grovel at your feet."' [45]If therefore David called him 'lord,' how can he be his son?"** [46]And no one could provide an answer to his question. And from that day on no one dared to ask him a question.

Luke 20:41-44 ➡ Mark 12:35-37

[41]Then he said to them, **"How can they say that the Anointed is the son of David? [42]For David himself says in the book of Psalms, 'The Lord said to my lord, "Sit on my right, [43]until I make your enemies grovel at your feet."' [44]Since David calls him 'lord,' how can he be his son?"**

Barn 12:10-11 ➡ Mark 12:35-37

[10]Consider "Jesus" again, not as a son of Adam, but as a son of God, who appeared in the flesh as a type. Since they are going to say that Christ is David's son, David himself prophesies, since he fears and understands the error of sinners, "The Lord said to my lord, 'Sit here on my right, until I make your enemies your footstool.'" [11]And again, Isaiah speaks in a similar manner: "The Lord tells my Anointed, my Lord, whose right hand I hold, that the nations will obey him, and ⟨he says,⟩ 'I will demolish the power of kings.'" Notice how David refers to him as 'Lord'; he does not call him 'son.'

latter is quoted by Paul (Gal 5:14) without reference to Jesus.

The majority of the Fellows thought that the ideas in this exchange represented Jesus' own views; the words, however, were those of the young church. Those who voted pink argued that Jesus might have affirmed the interpretation of the law given by Hillel, a famous rabbi who was contemporary with Jesus. ■

Mark 12:35-37

History of the tradition. When Jesus initiates a dialogue or debate, we have a good indication that we are dealing with a secondary composition (J8a). The rea-

Scribes in Long Robes

| Saying | Percentage | | | | Wgt. |
	R	P	G	B	Av.
Mk 12:38–39	25	42	25	8	.61 P
Lk 20:45–46	25	42	25	8	.61 P
Mt 23:5–7	17	33	42	8	.53 P
Lk 11:43	17	33	42	8	.53 P

³⁸During the course of his teaching he would say: "Look out for the scribes who like to parade around in long robes, and insist on being addressed properly in the marketplaces, ³⁹and prefer important seats in the synagogues and the

---

Luke 20:45–46 ➡ Mark 12:38–39
⁴⁵Within earshot of the people Jesus said to the disciples, ⁴⁶"Be on guard against the scribes who like to parade around in long robes, and who love to be addressed properly in the marketplaces, and who prefer important seats in the synagogues and the best couches at banquets."

Matt 23:5–7 ➡ Mark 12:38–39
⁵"They perform all their deeds so others will notice them. They make their phy-

lacteries wide and the fringes ⟨on their robes⟩ long. ⁶They love the best couches at banquets and important seats in the synagogues. ⁷⟨They love⟩ to be greeted in marketplaces and addressed as 'Rabbi' by others."

Luke 11:43 ➡ Mark 12:38–39
⁴³"It's too bad for you Pharisees! You love the front seat in synagogues and respectful greetings in marketplaces."

---

son for this is twofold: (a) In the healing stories, he does not offer to heal people; he waits until they approach him. His approach to argument and debate must have been comparable: he probably did not seek to engage his opponents, but waited until they questioned or criticized him. He was also sometimes questioned by his disciples and other friendly inquirers. In both healing and debate, Jesus appears to have been a passive participant. (b) The church would have been inclined, subsequently, to represent Jesus as making pronouncements on a variety of topics. The direct way to this end would have been to have Jesus raise the issue himself.

For Fellows' views on this subject as expressed in replies to general questions, consult the data under Mark 2:23–28.

The words of Jesus in Mark 12:35–37 and parallels are context-bound (N2) and thus did not circulate independently at one time.

Attribution. To begin with, the Old Testament text cited in this pericope is Psalm 110:1, a favorite in early Christian christological speculation (note Acts 2:34–35, Hebrews 1:13, 10:12–13) (O5). Further, it is difficult to think of a plausible context for this piece of sophistry during Jesus' life (G2). What would be the point of demonstrating that the Messiah was not the son of David? By some stretch of the imagination it could be supposed that Jesus was carrying on a polemic against the notion of a Davidic messiah. Yet it is unlikely that Jesus' own lineage through David would have been introduced into the tradition so readily if he had himself carried on a polemic against the idea. It is more likely, in the view of most scholars, that it comes from a segment of the church in which there was some tension between the messiah as the son of man (a heavenly figure) and the messiah as the son of David (a political, royal figure) (W9a). Admittedly, there is very little evidence for such tension, but there is even less evidence for such a debate in Jesus' own time. ∎

best couches at banquets. ⁴⁰They are the ones who prey on widows and their families, and recite long prayers for appearance' sake. These people will get a stiff sentence!"

Those Who Prey on Widows

Saying	Percentage				Wgt.
	R	P	G	B	Av.
Mk 12:40	21	21	36	32	.44 G
Mt 23:14	0	5	16	79	.09 B
Lk 20:47	21	21	26	32	.44 G

Matt 23:14 ➡ Mark 12:40
¹⁴**"It's too bad for you, scribes and Pharisees, you phonies! You prey on widows and their families and recite long prayers for appearance' sake. For this reason you will get a stiff sentence!"**

Luke 20:47 ➡ Mark 12:40
⁴⁷"They are the ones who prey on widows and their families, and recite long prayers for appearance' sake. These people will get a stiff sentence!"

Mark 12:38–39

Sources. Luke 20:46 reproduces Mark 12:38b–39 almost word for word. On the other hand, Luke 11:43 is from Q, which Matthew also takes over but expands in 23:5–7: verse 5 and the second part of verse 7 seem to be Matthean additions. There are thus two sources for this complex, Mark and Q (A1).

Attribution. The Q saying is directed against the Pharisees, whereas the Markan form takes aim at some anonymous scribes. In the judgment of the Fellows, the Markan version is the older and more likely to be attributable to Jesus: there were certainly scribes in Galilee in Jesus' day; the indictment of Pharisees may reflect the later controversies between Christians and emerging Pharisaic Judaism.

The Markan version may be understood as an indictment of a certain type of scribe—those whose piety was on parade and who insisted on certain social advantages, such as proper address and the best couches at banquets. This kind of public performance is not unknown in other societies among the learned who have been deprived of political power and wealth. The scribal parade of pomp and circumstance is a plausible setting for Jesus' biting criticism (G2). ∎

Mark 12:40

Sources. The criticism of the scribes is continued in Mark 12:40 and parallels. Mark is the sole source of this saying, unlike the preceding items.

Attribution. While a plausible setting could be imagined for the ministry of Jesus (G2)—the abuse of the public position of scribes to exploit widows and their families—the majority of Fellows were inclined to the view that this setting was more likely characteristic of the later church (W9a). The red and pink votes were prompted by the comparison of this saying with other sayings of Jesus in which he acts as an advocate for the poor (G5). The gray and black votes were inspired by the incongruity of linking preying on widows with long prayers, and by the moralizing conclusion.

Matthew's reference to both scribes and Pharisees and the epithet 'hypocrites' or 'phonies' were regarded as Matthean additions: they reflect the conflict between Christians and Pharisees in Matthew's community in Matthew's day. As a consequence, Matt 23:14 as a whole was designated black. ∎

Widow's Pittance

Saying	Percentage				Wgt.
	R	P	G	B	Av.
Mk 12:43	0	60	20	20	.47 G
Mk 12:44	0	27	47	27	.33 G
Lk 21:3	0	60	20	20	.47 G
Lk 21:4	0	27	47	27	.33 G

[41]And when he sat across from the treasury, he would observe the crowd dropping money into the collection box. And many wealthy people would drop large amounts in. [42]Then one poor widow came and put in two small coins, which is a pittance. [43]And he motioned his disciples over and said to them: "I swear to you, this poor widow has contributed more than all those who dropped something into the collection box! [44]After all, they were all donating out of their surplus, whereas she, out of her poverty, was contributing all she had, her entire livelihood!"

Luke 21:1–4 ➡ Mark 12:41–44

[1]He looked up and observed the rich dropping their donations into the collection box. [2]Then he saw a needy widow put in two small coins, [3]and he said, "I swear to you, this poor widow has contributed more than all of them! [4]After all, they all made donations out of their surplus, whereas she, out of her poverty, was contributing her entire livelihood, which was everything she had."

Mark 12:41–44

Sources. We are dependent solely on Mark for this story. Luke reproduces and edits the Markan version (W4); Matthew omits it.

Attribution. This story has many parallels, one in the Buddhist tradition, another in the Rabbinic literature, and still another in ancient Greek literature. It was therefore not original with Jesus (O5). In addition, the words of Jesus are part and parcel of the story so they cannot be detached; they are context-bound (N2). This story is another example of how a widespread sentiment is attributed to Jesus (O5): the small sacrifices of the poor are more pleasing to God and the gods than are the extravagant contributions of the rich. ∎

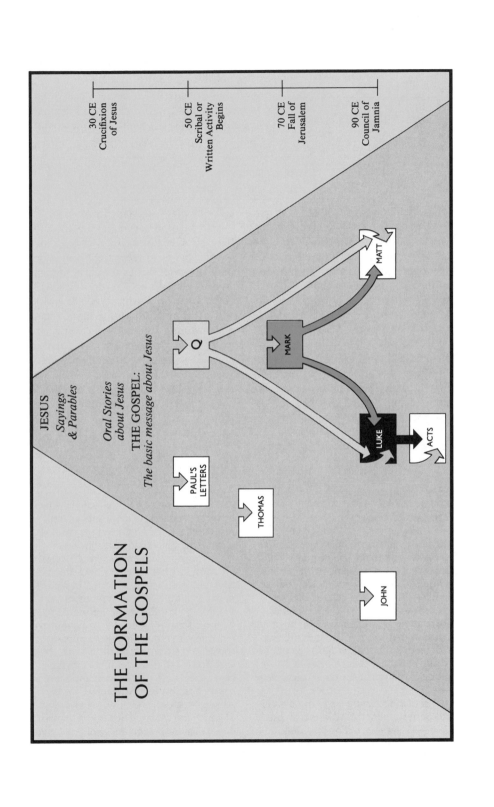

THE FORMATION
OF THE GOSPELS

JESUS
Sayings
& Parables

Oral Stories
about Jesus
THE GOSPEL:
The basic message about Jesus

Q

MARK

MATT

LUKE

ACTS

PAUL'S
LETTERS

THOMAS

JOHN

30 CE
Crucifixion
of Jesus

50 CE
Scribal or
Written Activity
Begins

70 CE
Fall of
Jerusalem

90 CE
Council of
Jamnia

Temple's Destruction

Saying	Percentage				Wgt.
	R	P	G	B	Av.
Mk 13:2	31	23	12	35	.50 G
Mt 24:2	21	29	14	36	.45 G
Lk 21:6	18	25	21	36	.42 G
Lk 19:44b	4	22	33	41	.30 G

13 And as he was going out of the temple area, one of his disciples remarks to him, "Teacher, look, what magnificent stones and what wonderful buildings!" ²And Jesus replied to him, "Take a good look at these monumental buildings! You may be sure one stone won't remain on another! They will all certainly be knocked down!"

Matt 24:1-2 ➡ Mark 13:2

¹And Jesus left the temple area, and was about to depart, when his disciples came to him and pointed out the sacred buildings. ²In response he said to them, "Yes, take a good look at all this! I swear to you, there certainly won't remain here one stone on another that won't be knocked down."

Luke 21:5-6 ➡ Mark 13:2

⁵When some were speaking about how the temple was adorned with fine masonry and decorations, he said, ⁶"As for these things that you now admire, the time will come when there will not remain here one stone on another that won't be knocked down."

Luke 19:41-44 ➡ Mark 13:2

⁴¹As he approached and saw the city he wept over it, ⁴²saying, "If only you —yes, you—had recognized today the path to peace! But as it is, it is hidden from your eyes. ⁴³For the days will come upon you when your enemies will build up a rampart alongside you and surround you, and hem you in on every side, ⁴⁴and smash you to the ground, you and your children within you. They will not leave one stone upon another within you, because you have not recognized the time of your visitation."

Preface to Mark 13
The Little Apocalypse

An apocalypse. The focus of Mark 13 is the events that are to take place at the end of history, when the son of Adam will appear on the clouds and gather God's chosen people from the ends of the earth (13:26–27). This and related themes make it sound much like the Book of Revelation, which also predicts signs and portents that will precede the end. For this reason, the chapter has been dubbed 'the little apocalypse' (revelation is simply a translation of the Greek term, apocalypse).

There is a second reason the chapter has been termed 'the little apocalypse.' Some scholars have proposed that Mark

had at his disposal a written source which he incorporated into his gospel as Jesus' response in 13:5–37. One of the reasons for making this proposal is that Jesus' long reply does not answer the disciples' question in 13:4. Jesus' opening prediction that the (sacred) buildings in Jerusalem would be destroyed prompts the disciples to inquire when that would happen. Jesus responds by listing numerous things that must happen before the son of Adam appears on the clouds. His speech has the character of a long digression. The theory that Mark made use of a source has now been discarded, for the most part, and replaced by the view that Mark himself constructed this discourse out of disparate elements, in order to give expression to his own views on the subject of eschatology ('last things').

Jesus' last discourse. A notable feature of early Christian instruction is that teaching about last things (termed 'eschatology') occurs at the conclusion of the catechism or manual of instruction. The earliest such manual known to us is the Didache, a second-century C.E. compendium of teaching. The final chapter, 16, is devoted to just such instruction in eschatology. Paul tended to put such instruction toward the close of his letters, for example, in 1 Thess 5:1–13 and 1 Cor 15. Similarly, there is a Q apocalypse that is reproduced in Luke 17:22–37, even though Luke also copies Mark's apocalypse (Mark 13 // Luke 21). The Q apocalypse also occurs at the end of Q.

It is thus fitting that Mark should gather together sayings about last things and shape them into the last public discourse Jesus was to give. The passion narrative begins in chapter 14, and Jesus does not thereafter speak at length publicly.

Outline of Jesus' last discourse. It is notoriously difficult to create an entirely satisfactory outline of the contents of Mark 13:3–37. Yet some sections and themes are clear. The following is a loose outline.

1. Early Signs (3–8)
   (a) Bogus messiahs (5–6)
   (b) Wars and rumors of wars (7–8)
2. Persecution of Disciples (9–13)
3. Devastation in Jerusalem (14–23)
   (a) 'Devastating desecration' (14–20)
   (b) Bogus messiahs (21–23)

4. Devastation in the Cosmos (24–31)
   (a) Heavenly portents (24–25)
   (b) Son of Adam comes on clouds (26–27)
   (c) Analogy of the fig tree (28–29)
   (d) In this generation (30–31)
5. Concluding Admonitions (32–37)
   (a) No one knows the hour (32)
   (b) Stay alert! (33–37)

Date. The author's admonition to the reader in v. 14 indicates that Mark is writing for his own people in his own time. The concluding warnings in vv. 33–37 are thus meant for his own generation. Scholars are inclined to think that these features provide clues to the time Mark composed his gospel. His focus on the destruction of the temple and Jerusalem points to a date close to the siege and fall of Jerusalem in 66–70 C.E. Whether one places the date just before or just after the fall of Jerusalem depends on whether the sayings anticipate events about to happen or whether they reflect events that have just taken place. In either case, scholars are generally of the opinion that the content of the discourse does not go back to Jesus. There are, however, some important exceptions to this generalization. ■

Mark 13:1–2

Source and form. It is difficult to know whether Jesus is referring to the temple complex in Mark or to the city as a whole. When Matthew and Luke copy Mark 13:1–2, they make the reference to the temple itself definite.

Luke records a saying in 19:44 that is a partial parallel to Mark 13:2. Luke's

³And as he was sitting on the Mount of Olives across from the temple, Peter would ask him privately, as would James and John and Andrew: ⁴"Tell us," when will these things take place, and what will be the sign when all these things are about to be accomplished?" ⁵And

---

version has the city of Jerusalem as its reference.

Luke 19:44 and Mark 13:2 provide evidence that such a saying may have circulated as a separate item at one time, without a specific reference (A2). If this is not the case, the sole source for the saying is Mark.

The form of Mark 13:2 is that of a prophetic oracle. Apart from the context in Mark and Luke, we would not know whether to take the reference to falling stones literally or figuratively. In Mark 12:10, the author has Jesus quote Psalm 118 about the rejected stone becoming the keystone—obviously a metaphorical use of the term. In the present context, however, the saying in Mark has to do with the destruction of the buildings of the city, including the temple.

Markan context. Mark places this saying between Jesus' debates in the temple (chapter 12) and his warnings about the impending devastation (13:5–37), while Jesus is seated opposite the temple on the Mount of Olives (13:3). There is no explicit mention of the temple or its destruction in the rest of chapter 13. In chapter 14, Mark introduces false witnesses at Jesus' trial who claim that he said he would destroy the temple (vv. 57–59). A similar saying is attributed to Jesus in John 2:19. But the interpretation in John indicates that Jesus was speaking of his body, not the temple (vv. 20–22). Could Mark 13:2 have been the basis of this tradition? Mark 13:2 is the only saying recorded in Mark that might have been the basis of the charge made in Mark 14:57–59.

Attribution. In a separate poll, seventy percent of the Fellows agreed that Jesus spoke some word against the temple. The question is whether that word is approximately represented by Mark 13:2.

The Fellows of the Seminar were sharply divided on whether or not this saying goes back to Jesus. The weighted average was exactly .50, although the red/pink votes outnumbered the gray/black votes 54/47.

After the destruction of Jerusalem in 70 C.E., Christians regularly interpreted the fall of the city and the temple cult as divine punishment for the rejection of Jesus. This trend alone prompted many to doubt that the saying could be traced back to Jesus. Moreover, some Fellows reasoned that Jesus, who was from outlying Galilee, would scarcely have been concerned with the temple and its cult, and so is not likely to have spoken about it.

On the other side, the temple was the center not only of the sacrificial cult, but also of the banking system, of the meat industry, and of political power in Jesus' day. In view of Jesus' concern for the poor, it is likely that he would have been interested in the role the temple played in the economic life of the people. Further, the reference to false testimony given at Jesus' trial suggests that this saying—or one like it—was not invented by the evangelist.

The versions in Matthew and Luke were given a lower rating than the Markan form because they were considered revisions of Mark. The cousin in Luke 19:44b has a different context and the saying has been remodeled to suit that context. It was accordingly given a gray designation. ■

Jesus would say to them, "Stay alert, otherwise someone might just lead you astray! ⁶For many will come in my name and claim, 'I'm the one!' and they will delude many people. ⁷When you hear of wars and rumors of wars, don't be afraid. These are ordained, but it is not yet the end. ⁸For nation will rise against nation and empire against empire; there will be earthquakes everywhere; there will be famines. These things mark the beginning of the final agonies. ⁹But you look

Deception and Strife

Saying	Percentage				Wgt.
	R	P	G	B	Av.
Mk 13:5–8	3	6	16	74	.13 **B**
Mt 24:4–8	0	7	14	79	.09 **B**
Lk 21:8–11	3	3	10	84	.09 **B**

Matt 24:3–8 ➡ Mark 13:3–8

³As he was sitting on the Mount of Olives, the disciples came to him privately, and said, "Tell us, when will these things take place, and what will be the sign of your coming and end of the age?" ⁴And in response Jesus said to them: "Stay alert, otherwise someone might just lead you astray! ⁵For many will come in my name, and claim, 'I am the Anointed!' and they will delude many people. ⁶You are going to hear about wars and rumors of wars. See that you are not afraid. For these are ordained, but it is not yet the end. ⁷For nation will rise against nation and empire against empire and there will be famines and earthquakes everywhere. ⁸Now all these things mark the beginning of the final agonies."

Luke 21:7–11 ➡ Mark 13:3–8

⁷And they asked him, "Teacher, when will these things take place, and what will be the sign when these things are about to happen?" ⁸He said, "Stay alert! Do not be led astray. For many will come in my name and claim, 'I'm the one!' and, 'The time is near!' Don't follow them! ⁹And when you hear of wars and insurrections, do not panic. For these things are ordained to take place first, but the end will not come at once."

¹⁰Then he went on to say to them, "Nation will rise against nation, and empire against empire; ¹¹there will be powerful earthquakes, and famines and plagues everywhere; there will be terrifying events and important portents from heaven."

Mark 13:3–8

Most scholars recognize a striking correlation between this passage and the description of the events preceding the Jewish–Roman war of 66–70 c.e. by the Jewish historian Josephus, who wrote just after the fall of Jerusalem. In his *Jewish War* 6.285–287, 300–309, he tells of false prophets who led many astray, and in 5.21–26 he describes the famine that came over Jerusalem when the store houses were burned. Of course, he also narrates the burning of the temple

(6.250–266). Josephus provides parallels to other passages in Mark's 'little apocalypse.'

Some scholars have argued that the events mentioned in Mark 13:5–8 are based on traditional Jewish apocalyptic predictions—predictions with which Jesus might have been acquainted. Other scholars doubt there is any precedent for the theme of bogus messiahs. Fellows of the Jesus Seminar were decisively of the opinion that these sayings do not go back to Jesus. ■

Persecution and Testimony

Saying	Percentage				Wgt.
	R	P	G	B	Av.
Mk 13:9	0	7	17	77	.10 B
Mt 10:17–18	0	7	10	83	.08 B
Lk 21:12–13	0	10	7	83	.09 B

Gospel and Eschaton

Saying	Percentage				Wgt.
	R	P	G	B	Av.
Mk 13:10	0	7	13	80	.09 B
Mt 24:14	0	7	7	87	.07 B

out for yourselves! They will turn you over to councils, and beat you in synagogues, and haul you up before governors and kings, on my account, so you can make your case to them. ¹⁰Yet the good news must first be announced to all peoples. ¹¹And when they arrest you to lock you up, don't be worried about what you should say. Instead, whatever occurs to you at the moment, say that. For it is not you who are speaking but the holy spirit. ¹²And brother will turn in brother to be put to death, and a father his child, and children will rise up against their parents and kill them. ¹³And you will be hated by everyone because of my name. Those who hold out to the end will be saved!

Matt 10:17–22 ➡ Mark 13:9–13

¹⁷"And beware of people for they will turn you over to the council and in the synagogues they will scourge you. ¹⁸And you will be brought before governors and even kings for my sake so you can make your case to them and to the gentiles." ¹⁹"And when they lock you up, don't worry about how you will speak or what you will say, for at that moment you will be given what to say. ²⁰For it is not you who are speaking but your Father's spirit speaking in you." ²¹"Brother will turn in brother to be put to death, and a father his child, and children will rise up against their parents and kill them. ²²And you will be hated by everyone because of my name. But those who hold out to the end will be saved."

Luke 21:12–19 ➡ Mark 13:9–13

¹²"But before all these things ⟨take place⟩, they will lay their hands on you, and persecute you, and turn you over to synagogues and deliver you to prisons, and you will be brought before kings and governors on account of my name. ¹³This will give you a chance to make

your case." ¹⁴"So make up in your minds not to rehearse your defense in advance, ¹⁵for I will give you the words and wisdom which none of your adversaries will be able to resist or refute." ¹⁶"You will be turned in, even by parents and brothers and relatives and friends; and they will put some of you to death. ¹⁷And you will be hated by everyone because of my name. ¹⁸Yet not a hair on your head will be harmed. ¹⁹By your perseverance you will secure your lives."

Luke 12:11–12 ➡ Mark 13:11

¹¹"And when they bring you into synagogues and before rulers and authorities, do not worry about how you will defend yourself or what you will say. ¹²The holy spirit will teach you at that moment what you must say."

John 14:25–26 ➡ Mark 13:11

²⁵"I have told you these things while I am still with you. ²⁶The paraclete, the holy spirit, which the Father will send in my name, will teach you everything and remind you of everything I told you."

Spirit Under Trial

Saying	Percentage				Wgt.
	R	P	G	B	Av.
Mk 13:11	0	17	17	67	.17 **B**
Mt 10:19–20	3	10	20	67	.17 **B**
Lk 21:14–15	3	6	16	74	.13 **B**
Lk 12:11–12	3	10	10	76	.14 **B**
Jn 14:25–26	3	6	10	81	.11 **B**

Hatred and Patience

Saying	Percentage				Wgt.
	R	P	G	B	Av.
Mk 13:12–13	3	10	3	83	.11 **B**
Mt 24:9–13	0	7	7	87	.07 **B**
Mt 10:21–22	3	7	10	80	.11 **B**
Lk 21:16–19	3	3	20	73	.12 **B**
Did 16:4–5	0	3	10	86	.06 **B**

Matt 24:9–14 ➡ Mark 13:11–13

9"Then they will turn you over for torture, and will kill you, and you will be hated by all the heathen because of my name. 10And then many will be misled, and they will betray one another and hate one another. 11And many false witnesses will appear and delude many. 12And as lawlessness spreads, mutual love will grow cool. 13But those who hold out to the end will be saved!" 14"And this good news of Heaven's imperial rule will have been proclaimed in the whole inhabited world, so you can make your case to all gentiles, and then the end will come."

Did 16:4–5 ➡ Mark 13:12–13

4"For as lawlessness increases, they will hate each other, and engage in persecution and betrayal. And then the cosmic deceiver will appear as a son of God. He will perform signs and wonders, and the whole earth will fall into his hands. He will commit wanton acts, the likes of which have not occurred since the world began. 5Then created beings will be brought to trial by fire, and many will be misled and destroyed. But those who persist in their faith will be saved by the accursed one himself."

Mark 13:9–13

Attribution. The sayings in Mark 13:9–13 and parallels all reflect detailed knowledge of events and ideas that took place or developed after Jesus' death (W10): trials and persecutions of the followers of Jesus, the call to preach the gospel to all nations, advice to offer spontaneous testimony, and the prediction that families would be turned against each other are features of later Christian existence (W9a). The note about children betraying their parents may be an allusion to the terrible calamities that took place during the siege of Jerusalem (66–70 C.E.). Fellows were almost unanimous in their judgment that none of these sayings was based on anything Jesus himself said. ■

Time for Flight

Saying	Percentage				Wgt.
	R	P	G	B	Av.
Mk 13:14a	9	12	15	64	.22 B
Mk 13:14b–20	3	3	3	90	.07 B
Mt 24:15–22	0	3	7	90	.04 B
Lk 21:20–24	0	0	10	90	.03 B

[14]"When you see the 'devastating desecration' standing where it must not (the reader had better figure out what this means), then the people in Judea should head for the hills; [15]no one on the roof should go downstairs; no one should enter the house to retrieve anything; [16]and no one in the field should turn back to get a coat. [17]It's too bad for the women who are pregnant, and for those who are nursing in those days! [18]Pray that none of this happens in winter! [19]For those days will see distress the likes of which have not occurred since God created the world until now, and will never occur again. [20]And if the Lord had not cut short the days, no human being would have survived! But he did shorten the days for the sake of the chosen people whom he selected.

Matt 24:15–22 ➡ Mark 13:14–20

[15]"When therefore you see the 'devastating desecration' (as described by Daniel the prophet) standing in the holy place (the reader had better consider this carefully), [16]then the people in Judea should head for the hills; [17]no one on the roof should go downstairs to retrieve anything; [18]and no one in the field should turn back to get a coat. [19]It's too bad for the women who are pregnant, and for those who are nursing in those days! [20]Pray that your flight may not take place in winter or on the sabbath day. [21]For there will be a great distress the likes of which have not occurred since creation until now, and will never occur again. [22]And if those days had not been cut short, no human being would have survived. But for the sake of the chosen people, those days will be cut short."

Luke 21:20–24 ➡ Mark 13:14–20

[20]"When you see Jerusalem surrounded by armies, know then that she will be laid waste soon. [21]Then the people in Judea should head for the hills, and those inside the city flee it, and those out in the countryside not reenter it. [22]For these are days of retribution, to bring to pass everything that was predicted. [23]It's too bad for the women who are pregnant and for those who are nursing in those days! For there will be great distress in the land and wrath ⟨will fall⟩ upon this people. [24]They will fall by the edge of the sword, and be taken prisoner ⟨and scattered⟩ in all the pagan countries, and Jerusalem will be overrun by heathen, until the period allotted to the heathen has run its course."

Mark 13:14–20

This passage appears to be more directly related to the question posed by Peter, James, and John in v. 4 than are the intervening verses (5–13). The warnings of the previous section are now raised to the level of a red alert: it's the time for immediate evacuation.

Sources. Matt 24:15–22 and Luke 21:20–24 are based on Mark, their common source, although each modifies Mark to a greater or lesser extent.

(a) The reference in Mark 13:14 and Matt 24:15 is to the desecration of the temple, but the parallel in Luke has changed the crisis to the siege of Jerusalem. Of course, the one is related to the other.

(b) Luke omits Mark 13:15–16 because he has already recorded that warning in Luke 17:31—a passage he may have taken from Q (see the Preface to Mark 13 above).

(c) The Q apocalypse (Luke 17:22–31) also consists of a series of similar warnings, but the Q text makes no reference to either the desecration of the temple or the destruction of Jerusalem.

(d) Scholars currently regard both the Mark apocalypse and the Q apocalypse as composed of independent sayings or clusters of sayings taken from a variety of sources.

Historical references.

(a) The 'devastating desecration' mentioned in Mark 13:14 was a phrase coined in Jewish apocalyptic speculation long before Jesus. In Matthew, it is clearly an allusion to Daniel 11:31, 12:11, where it refers to the desecration of the altar before the temple in Jerusalem. An event fitting this description is recorded in 1 Macc 1:54–64: Antiochus Epiphanes erected a 'devastating desecration' on the altar where burnt offerings were made, probably in the form of an image of Zeus but fashioned in his own likeness. This event took place in 167 B.C.E. and led to the Maccabean revolt.

(b) There is no evidence that the altar before the temple was similarly desecrated in Jesus' time. After the temple was destroyed in 70 C.E., Roman soldiers celebrated their victory by raising their standards, which bore the image of the emperor, on the holy place. Scholars are inclined to the view that Mark 13:14 was inspired by this event (W10).

Conclusion. Because some Fellows were persuaded that Jesus could have issued a warning against a ruler who exalted himself to the status of a god, the Seminar voted on Mark 13:14a separately. The result was a weighted average of .22—black. Most Fellows doubted that warnings to flee like those found in this passage could be realistically ascribed to Jesus. In addition, the references to cosmic turmoil in 13:19–20 are so typical of apocalyptic language, both Jewish and Christian, that the language could have come from just about anyone (O5). ■

When and Where

Saying	Percentage				Wgt.	
	R	P	G	B	Av.	
(1)						
Mk 13:21	14	18	7	61	.29	G
Mk 13:22	7	4	7	81	.12	B
Mk 13:23	0	11	4	86	.08	B
Mt 24:23	14	18	7	61	.29	G
Mt 24:24	4	4	7	85	.09	B
Mt 24:25	0	11	4	85	.09	B
Mt 24:11–12	0	0	0	100	.00	B

[21]And then if someone says to you, 'Look, here is the Anointed,' or 'Look, there he is!' don't count on it! **[22]For bogus messiahs and false prophets will show up, and they will provide portents and miracles so as to delude, if possible, even the chosen people. [23]But you be on your guard! Note that I always warn you about these things in advance.**

Matt 24:23–28 ➠ Mark 13:21–23
[23]"Then if someone says to you, 'Look, here is the Anointed' or 'he's over here,' don't count on it! **[24]For bogus messiahs and false prophets will show up, and they will offer great portents and miracles so as to delude, if possible, even the chosen people. [25]Look, I have warned you in advance."** [26]"Therefore if they should say to you, 'See, he is in the wilderness,' don't go out there; 'See, he is in the secret room,' don't count on it. [27]For just as a bolt of lightning flashes in the east and lights up the sky all the way to the west, so will be the coming of the son of Adam. **[28]For wherever there is a corpse, there the vultures will gather."**

Matt 24:11–12 ➠ Mark 13:21–23
[11]**"And many false witnesses will appear and delude many. [12]And as lawlessness spreads, mutual love will grow cool."**

Luke 17:20–24 ➠ Mark 13:21–23
[20]When he was asked by the Pharisees when God's imperial rule would come, he answered them, "You cannot tell with careful observation when God's imperial rule is coming; [21]nor can people say, 'Look, here it is!' or 'Over there!' because look: God's imperial rule is among you."

[22]And he said to the disciples, "The time will come when you will yearn to see one of the days of the son of Adam, and you will not see it. [23]And people will say to you, 'Look, there it is!' or 'Look, here it is!' Do not go; do not pursue it." [24]"For just as lightning flashes and lights up the sky from one end to the other, so will the son of Adam be in his day."

Luke 17:37 ➠ Mark 13:21–23
[37]Then they asked him, "Where, Lord?" And he said to them, "Vultures will gather wherever there's a body."

POxy654 3:1–3 ➠ Mark 13:21–23
[3]Jesus says, "If your leaders say to you, 'Look, the kingdom is in heaven,' the birds of heaven will precede you. [2]If they say that it is under the earth, the fish of the sea will enter, preceding you. [3]And the kingdom of God is within you and outside you."

Thom 3:1–3 ➠ Mark 13:21–23
[1]Jesus said, "If your leaders say to you, 'Look, the kingdom is in heaven,' then the birds of heaven will precede you. [2]If they say to you, 'It is in the sea,' then the fish will precede you. [3]Rather, the kingdom is within you and it is outside you."

(2)

Mt 24:26	14	11	11	64	.25	B
Mt 24:27	0	34	14	51	.28	G
Mt 24:28	0	16	41	44	.24	B
Lk 17:22	25	4	25	46	.36	G
Lk 17:23	10	14	21	55	.26	G
Lk 17:24	6	34	11	49	.32	G
Lk 17:37	3	16	41	41	.27	G

(3)

Lk 17:20–21	16	56	12	16	.57	P
POxy 3:1–3	4	43	21	32	.39	G
Th 3:1–3	14	27	32	27	.42	G
Th 113:2–4	14	50	36	0	.59	P
Th 51:2	0	0	0	100	.00	B

Thom 113:2–4 ➡ Mark 13:21–23

²"It will not come by watching for it.
³It will not be said, 'Look over here!' or
'Look over there!' ⁴Rather, the kingdom
of the Father is spread out upon the
earth, and people do not see it."

Thom 51:2 ➡ Mark 13:21–23

²He said to them, "**What you look for
has come, but you do not know it.**"

Mark 13:21–23
Sources. There are three distinct
groups of sayings in the array gathered in
Mark 13:21–23.

(1) The first consists of Mark 13:21–
25//Matt 24:23–25, for which Mark is the
source. Matt 24:11–12 belongs with this
first group.

(2) The second group is made up of
Matt 24:26–28//Luke 17:23–24, 37, for
which Q is the source.

(3) The third group consists of Luke
17:20–21 with related sayings in Thom
3:1 (both Greek and Coptic), 113:2, and
51:2.

The subject of the first group is the
appearance of bogus messiahs and false
prophets, while the second cluster concerns the arrival of the son of Adam on
the clouds at the end of history. The third
group refers to the coming of God's imperial rule.

Mark knows only the first group, for
which he is the source. However, the
Seminar considered the second and third
clusters at the same time, since some
verbal similarities made that necessary.

The variation in wording and subject
matter makes it extremely difficult to
identify one of these sayings or cluster of
sayings as the source for all the others.
Indeed, the three groups may have originated separately even though they share
some of the same language.

Attribution. The appearance of bogus
messiahs and false prophets is a common
theme in apocalyptic expectations. That
is also the case with speculation about the
appearance of the messiah or son of
Adam in the last days. Since the majority
of the Fellows of the Seminar thought
that Jesus spoke about neither, these sayings were generally designated either gray
or black. Gray indicates that some Fellows thought that something Jesus said
may underlie the sayings in their present
form.

The original question, in the judgment
of most Fellows, concerned the location
or appearance of God's imperial rule.
Jesus spoke of God's reign as present and
accessible—there for those to see who
had two good eyes. Thom 113:2–4 was
judged to be closer to the original form of
the saying because God's reign is portrayed as spread out on the earth, there
for all to see. That is *not* how gnostic
Christians viewed God's kingdom, as a
rule. Luke's version (17:20–21) was a
close second, however. Thomas 3:1–3
and POxy654 3:1–3 are parodies of those
who take references to the location of
God's rule or kingdom literally. While
the majority thought this notion might be
in line with Jesus' thinking (G5), they
doubted that the wording could be traced
back to Jesus (O1). ■

Coming of the Son of Adam

Saying	R	P	G	B	Wgt. Av.	
Mk 13:24–25	6	0	9	84	.09	**B**
Mt 24:29	6	0	9	84	.09	**B**
Lk 21:25–26	6	0	9	84	.09	**B**
Mk 13:27	3	6	9	81	.10	**B**
Mt 24:31	3	6	9	81	.10	**B**
Mt 24:29–31	0	6	9	86	.07	**B**
Lk 21:25–28	0	6	9	86	.07	**B**
Did 16:6–8	0	0	11	89	.04	**B**
Mk 13:26	9	3	15	73	.16	**B**
Mt 24:30	0	11	9	80	.10	**B**
Lk 21:27	0	14	6	80	.11	**B**
Did 16:8	0	3	9	88	.05	**B**

(Percentage: R P G B)

**24“But in those days, after that tribulation, the
sun will be darkened, and the moon will not give
off her glow, 25and the stars will fall from the
sky, and the heavenly forces will be shaken!
26And then they will see the son of Adam coming
on the clouds with great power and splendor.
27And then he will send out his messengers and
will gather the chosen people from the four
winds, from the ends of the earth to the edge of
the sky!**

Matt 24:29–31 → Mark 13:24–27

**29“Then at once after the tribulation
of those days the sun will be darkened,
and the moon will not give off her glow,
and the stars will fall from the sky, and
the heavenly forces will be shaken!
30And then the sign of the son of Adam
will appear in the sky, and then every
tribe of the earth will mourn, and they
will see the son of Adam coming on
clouds of the sky with great power and
splendor. 31And he will send out his
messengers with a mighty trumpet call,
and they will gather his chosen people
from the four winds, from one end of the
sky to the other.”**

Luke 21:25–28 → Mark 13:24–27

**25“And there will be portents in sun
and moon and stars, and on the earth
nations will be dismayed in their confusion at the sound and surge of the sea.
26People will expire from fear and from
the expectation of what is descending
on the civilized world, for the heavenly
forces will be shaken! 27And then they
will see the son of Adam coming on
clouds with great power and splendor.
28Now when these things begin to happen, stand tall and lift up your heads,
because your deliverance is closing in!”**

Did 16:6–8 → Mark 13:24–27

6“Next, the signs of what is true will
appear. First, there will be a sign consisting of an opening in the skies. Second, a sign consisting of the sound of a
trumpet. The third sign will be a resurrection of the dead. 7But not of all the
dead. Rather, as it is written, “The
Lord will come and the saints with
him.” 8Next, the world will see the
Lord coming on clouds in the sky.

Mark 13:24–27

Sources. This oracle is based on eschatological imagery found in various Old Testament prophecies (Isa 13:10, Ezek 32:7, Joel 2:10, 31, Dan 7:13–14). This same imagery appears in other Christian writings without reference to a saying of Jesus: Acts 2:19–20, 2 Thess 1:7, 2 Pet 3:7, Rev 1:7, and 8:10–12. The language in Did 1:6–8, though reminiscent of this same imagery, is not directly ascribed to Jesus. Daniel 7:13–14 is undoubtedly the primary source of the oracle.

Attribution. The prediction in Mark 13:26 and parallels anticipates the coming of the son of Adam on clouds with great power and glory—without any reference to Jesus as the son of Adam.

²⁸"Note the analogy to be drawn from the fig tree. When its branch is already in bud and leaves come out, you know that summer is near. ²⁹So, when you see these things take place, you ought to realize that he is near, just outside your door. ³⁰**I swear to you, this generation certainly won't pass away before all these things take**

Fig Tree's Lesson

	Percentage				Wgt.	
Saying	R	P	G	B	Av.	
Mk 13:28–29	19	33	4	44	.42	**G**
Mt 24:32–33	27	27	12	35	.49	**G**
Lk 21:29–31	27	23	23	27	.50	**G**
Mk 13:30	4	8	8	79	.13	**B**
Mt 24:34	4	8	8	79	.13	**B**
Lk 21:32	4	8	8	79	.13	**B**

Matt 24:32-34 ➡ Mark 13:28-30

³²"Note the analogy to be drawn from the fig tree. When its branch is already in bud and leaves come out, you know that summer is near. ³³So, when you see all these things, you ought to realize that he is near, just outside your door." ³⁴**"I swear to God, this generation certainly won't pass away before all these things take place!"**

Luke 21:29-32 ➡ Mark 13:28-30

²⁹And he told them a parable: "Observe the fig tree, or any other kind of tree. ³⁰When they once put out foliage, you can see for yourselves that summer is already near. ³¹So, when you see these things happening, you will know that God's imperial rule is near." ³²**I swear to you, this generation certainly won't pass away before it all takes place!"**

This curious omission has led some scholars to imagine that Jesus spoke this prophecy about the son of Adam figure as someone entirely distinct from himself. For that reason, the Seminar decided to vote on this verse and its parallels separately. In order to test all the possibilities, they also voted on other parts of the complex in Mark separately. The result was fairly consistent: every part of the oracle was designated black. It is the opinion of most critical scholars that Mark intends his readers to understand 13:26 and other parts of the oracle as addressed to them (W7)—not as something Jesus addressed to his disciples decades earlier. ■

Mark 13:28-30

The analogy of the fig tree utilizes a concrete natural image like many other sayings and parables of Jesus (J7). However, this saying does not exploit the image in a surprising or unusual way as Jesus often does elsewhere (J5). For Jews, the fig tree was a symbol of abundant

blessings and peace in the land of promise (Deut 8:7–8, 1 Kings 4:25). While it is mentioned in some descriptions of the new age (Mic 4:4), it is not a typical apocalyptic image. The figure most suited to symbolize the nearness of the end was that of the harvest. The reference here to the closeness of summer in this context seems quite out of place. Indeed, in Luke 21:31 the analogy is connected with the appearance of God's rule, rather than with the coming of the son of Adam, as in Mark and Matthew. Many Fellows hold the view that the Lukan context was the original one.

The analogy of the fig tree was designated pink in all three synoptic versions at an early meeting of the Seminar. Upon reconsideration three years later, Fellows designated all three versions gray.

The promise that all these things would come to pass in the current generation was again taken by most Fellows as Mark's address to his own audience (W7), rather than as something Jesus said earlier to his disciples. ■

My Words Eternal

| Saying | Percentage | | | | Wgt. |
	R	P	G	B	Av.
Mk 13:31	4	8	16	72	.15 **B**
Mt 24:35	4	8	16	72	.15 **B**
Lk 21:33	4	8	16	72	.15 **B**

Only the Father

| Saying | Percentage | | | | Wgt. |
	R	P	G	B	Av.
Mk 13:32	3	24	21	52	.26 **G**
Mt 24:36	3	24	21	52	.26 **G**

place! ³¹**The earth will pass away and so will the sky, but my words will never pass away!**

³²"As for that day or that hour: no one knows, not even heaven's messengers, nor even the son, no one, except the Father.

³³**Be on guard! Stay alert! For you never know what time it is.** ³⁴It's like a person who takes a

---

Matt 24:35 ➡ Mark 13:31
³⁵**"The earth will pass away and so will the sky, but my words will never pass away!"**

Luke 21:33 ➡ Mark 13:31
³³**"The earth will pass away and so will the sky, but my words will never pass away!"**

Matt 24:36 ➡ Mark 13:32
³⁶"As for that day: no one knows, not even heaven's messengers, nor even the son, no one, except the Father alone."

Matt 24:42 ➡ Mark 13:33
⁴²**"Therefore, stay alert since you never know on what day your landlord returns."**

Matt 25:13 ➡ Mark 13:33
¹³**"Therefore stay alert because you do not know the day or the hour."**

Luke 12:40 ➡ Mark 13:33
⁴⁰**"You too must be ready; for the son of the son of Adam is coming when you least expect it."**

Luke 21:36 ➡ Mark 13:33
³⁶**"Be alert at all times, praying that you may have strength to escape all these things that will happen and to stand before the son of Adam."**

Luke 12:35–38 ➡ Mark 13:34–36
³⁵"Keep your shirt on and your lamps burning. ³⁶Be like those who are waiting for their master to come home from a wedding, ready to open the door for him as soon as he arrives and knocks. ³⁷Those slaves are to be congratulated whom the master finds alert when he arrives. I swear to you, he will put on an apron, seat them at the table, and proceed to serve them. ³⁸If he gets home around midnight, or even around 3 a.m., and finds them so, they are to be congratulated!"

Did 16:1 ➡ Mark 13:34–36
¹ Stay alert for your life's sake! Don't let your lamps go out! Don't let your shirt hang loose! Rather, be prepared since you don't know the time our Lord is to come.

Mark 13:31

This is a Jewish oath to affirm the truth of accompanying statements. The allusion to the earth and sky passing away is probably the reason it was included in this complex. It also functions as part of

the dramatic conclusion to the whole cluster.

Some Fellows thought it possible that Jesus might have made use of this type of graphic exaggeration. At times, he does reinforce his statements with oaths (Note

trip and puts slaves in charge, each with a task, and enjoins the doorkeeper to be alert. [35]Therefore, stay alert! For you never know when the landlord returns, maybe at dusk, or at midnight, or when the rooster crows, or maybe early in the morning. [36]He may return suddenly and find you asleep. [37]**What I'm telling you, I say to everyone: Stay alert!**"

Readiness	*andReturn*				
	Percentage				Wgt.
Saying	R	P	G	B	Av.
Mk 13:33	4	4	11	81	.10 B
Mt 24:42	0	0	0	100	.00 B
Mt 25:13	4	4	11	82	.10 B
Lk 12:40	3	17	23	57	.22 B
Lk 21:36	0	4	7	89	.05 B
Did 16:1	0	4	4	92	.04 B
Mk 13:34–36	7	55	10	28	.47 G
Lk 12:35–38	4	63	11	22	.49 G
Did 16:1a	4	11	26	59	.20 B

Mark 8:12 SV). If this affirmation had appeared in another context, it might well have attracted a higher designation. In its Markan context, however, it cannot be understood as something Jesus might have said with reference to the preceding statements. In addition, its content is scarcely distinctive enough to warrant attributing it directly to Jesus rather than to a disciple of his who wanted to underscore the reliability of Jesus' teaching. ∎

Mark 13:32
Context. This saying strikes the reader as odd in its present context. Jesus' last discourse is designed to tell the disciples when the end of history will occur. Yet in this saying Jesus admits that he does not know; only the Father knows.
Problems. It is doubtful that Jesus would have used the term son to refer to himself, yet in this context it can only mean Jesus (W8a). Nevertheless, a later believer would probably not have invented a saying in which Jesus claims that he does not have knowledge of that most important of dates—the time of his return (W11). Perhaps this is the reason Luke omits the saying altogether. At the same time, the Seminar was in general agreement that Jesus probably did not pretend to make chronological predictions, if he spoke about the end at all. And all are agreed that Jesus referred to God as Father. A final problem has to do with what time the day and the hour refers to. It could have been Jesus' original response to the disciples question

about the time the temple would be destroyed (Mark 13:4). In that case it might well be based on something Jesus actually said. But most Fellows were dubious that Jesus was responsible for the present wording. ∎

Mark 13:33–36
Sources. Admonitions to watch and be on guard are common in early Christian literature, often in an apocalyptic context. Note, for example, 1 Thess 5:1–11, where Paul writes an extended series of admonitions of just this sort.
On the other hand, the synoptic gospels preserve several parables involving a landlord's return. These are drawn from two independent sources (Mark 12:1–11 and parallels; Luke 12:42–46 and parallel is from Q, as well as the parable of the Entrusted Money, Luke 19:11–27 and parallel) and possibly a third (Luke 12:35–38 may be from special Luke, perhaps an oral source). The text under consideration has Mark as its source.
Attribution. Few members of the Jesus Seminar thought that Jesus advised his followers to prepare for his own return, although all were agreed that the image of the returning landlord could well go back to Jesus. As a consequence of the latter, Mark 13:34–36 attracted a higher vote than the other sayings in this passage. On balance, however, the Seminar rejected all of the complex as atypical of Jesus. ∎

14 Now it was two days until the Passover and the feast of Unleavened Bread. And the ranking priests and the scribes were looking for some way to arrest him by trickery and kill him. [2]For their motto was: "Not during the festival, otherwise the people will riot."

[3]When he was in Bethany in the house of Simon the leper, he was just reclining there, and a woman came in carrying an alabaster jar of myrrh, of pure and expensive nard. She broke the jar and poured ⟨the myrrh⟩ on his head. [4]Now some were annoyed ⟨and thought⟩ to themselves: "What good purpose is served by this waste of myrrh? [5]For she could have sold the myrrh for more than thirty denarii and given ⟨the money⟩ to the poor." And they were angry with her. [6]Then Jesus said, **"Let her alone! Why bother her? She has done a good deed for me. [7]For you have the poor with you always, and whenever you want you can do good for them, but me you won't always have. [8]She did what she could—she anticipates in anointing my body for burial. [9]So help me, wherever the good news is announced in all the world, what she has done will also be told in memory of her!"**

Matt 26:6–13 ➡ Mark 14:3–9

[6]While Jesus was in Bethany in the house of Simon the leper, [7]a woman who had an alabaster jar of very expensive myrrh came to him and poured it over his head while he was reclining ⟨at table⟩. [8]When they saw this, the disciples were annoyed, and said, "What good purpose is served by this waste? [9]For she could have sold it for a good price and given ⟨the money⟩ to the poor." [10]But Jesus perceived ⟨their complaint⟩ and said to them, **"Why bother the woman? For she has done a good deed for me. [11]For you have the poor with you always; but me you won't always have. [12]For, by pouring this myrrh on my body she has made me** ready for burial. [13]**So help me, wherever this good news is announced in all the world, what she has done will be told in memory of her."**

Luke 7:36–50 ➡ Mark 14:3–9

[36]One of the Pharisees invited him to eat with him; he entered the Pharisee's house, and reclined at the table. [37]And behold, there was a woman in the city who was a sinner. When she learned that he was having dinner at the Pharisee's house, she brought an alabaster jar of myrrh, [38]and stood weeping behind him at his feet. Her tears wet his feet, and she wiped them dry with her hair; she kissed his feet, and anointed them with the myrrh.

³⁹The Pharisee who had invited him saw this and said to himself, "If this man were a prophet, he would know who this is and what kind of woman is touching him, for she is a sinner." ⁴⁰And Jesus answered him, **"Simon, I have something to say to you."** "Teacher," he said, "Say it." ⁴¹**"A certain moneylender had two debtors; one owed five hundred denarii, and the other fifty.** ⁴²**Since neither could pay, he forgave both debts. Now which of them will love him more?"** ⁴³Simon answered, "I suppose, the one for whom he forgave the larger debt." And he said to him, **"You are right."** ⁴⁴Then turning to the woman, he said to Simon, **"Do you see this woman? I entered your house and you gave me no water for my feet; yet she has washed my feet with her tears and dried them with her hair.** ⁴⁵**You gave me no kiss, but she has not stopped kissing my feet since I arrived.** ⁴⁶**You did not anoint my head with oil, but she has anointed my feet with myrrh.** ⁴⁷**For this reason, I tell you, her sins, which are many, are forgiven, for she loves much. But the one who is forgiven little, loves little."** ⁴⁸And he said to her **"Your sins are forgiven."** ⁴⁹Then those who were at table with him began to say to themselves, "Who is this who even forgives sins?" ⁵⁰And he said to the woman, **"Your trust has cured you; go in peace."**

John 12:1–8 ➡ Mark 14:3–9
¹Six days before Passover Jesus came to Bethany, where Lazarus lived, whom Jesus had raised from the dead. ²They gave him a dinner; Martha did the serving, and Lazarus was one of those who reclined ⟨at table⟩ with him. ³Mary brought in a pound of expensive perfume made from pure nard and anointed Jesus' feet and wiped them with her hair. The house was filled with the fragrance. ⁴Judas Iscariot, one of his disciples (the one who was going to turn him in), says, "Why wasn't this perfume sold for three hundred pieces of silver and the proceeds given to the poor?" ⁶He said this, not out of any concern for the poor, but because he was a thief. He was in charge of the common purse, and now and again would embezzle monies put in. ⁷Jesus then said, **"Let her alone. Let her keep it for the time I am to be embalmed.** ⁸**[The poor you have with you always, but me you won't always have with you.]"**

Ign Eph 17:1 ➡ Mark 14:3–9
¹For this reason the Lord let his head be anointed: in order that he might breathe incorruptibility on the church.

Mark 14:3–9
Sources. It is difficult to determine whether Mark is the source of the other three versions of this pronouncement story (the reference in Ignatius' letter to the Ephesians is simply an allusion to this or a similar event). Except for Matthew, who is copying Mark, Luke and John have constructed very different versions. Luke inserts a parable into the midst of his version (vv. 41–43) and orients the narrative to that parable. The woman who anoints Jesus is of questionable repute, as she is likely to have been had she intruded into a symposium (a banquet) made up entirely of men and performed this action. John sets the same story in Bethany with Mary, Martha, and Lazarus. The affinity of these stories with each other is unmistakable. Yet it is just possible that Luke and John had other sources for their versions (A1).

Aphorisms. There are three possible independent aphorisms in this story:

Passover Preparation

Saying	Percentage				Wgt.
	R	P	G	B	Av.
Mk 14:13–15	4	4	24	68	.15	B
Mt 26:18	4	4	12	80	.11	B
Lk 22:8,etc.	4	4	24	68	.15	B
GEbi 7	0	0	8	92	.03	B

[10]And Judas Iscariot, one of the twelve, went off to the ranking priests to turn him over to them. [11]When they heard, they were delighted, and promised to pay him in silver. And he started looking for some way to turn him in at the appropriate moment.

[12]On the first day of Unleavened Bread, when they would sacrifice the Passover lamb, his disciples say to him, "Where do you want us to go and get things ready for you to celebrate the Passover?" [13]He sends two of his disciples and says to them, **"Go into the city, and a person carrying a waterpot will meet you. Follow him,** [14]**and whatever place he enters say to the master of the house, 'The teacher says, "Where is my guest room where I can celebrate Passover with my disciples?"'** [15]**And he'll show you a large upstairs room that has been arranged. That's the place you're to get ready for us."** [16]And the disciples left, went into the city, and found it exactly as he had told them; and they got ready for Passover.

(a) "She has done a good deed" (v. 6); (b) "For you have the poor with you always" (v. 7); (c) "Wherever the good news is announced in all the world, what she has done will also be told in memory of her" (v. 9).

The third possibility is evidently an internal reference to the Gospel of Mark—the woman has been memorialized in Mark's story. Moreover, the interpretation of the anointing as an anointing in advance for Jesus' death is possible only for those who already know the outcome of the gospel: Jesus dies, but he is raised before his body can be anointed for burial.

The second aphoristic statement is perhaps based on Deut 15:11: "The needy will never disappear from the country." In any case, the saying seems to clash with the sage who said, "Congratulations, you poor!" (Luke 6:20).

If the original story portrayed a disreputable woman interrupting a symposium to anoint Jesus with some precious perfume, Jesus might have responded, "You have done a good (or beautiful) thing." The Greek adjective, *kalon,* could mean either. Such a response is possible for a sage like Jesus, whose clever reply covers both his own embarrassment and averts further criticism of the woman.

Attribution. The Fellows of the Jesus Seminar were of the opinion that the original form of the story was beyond recovery. As a consequence, they also doubted that any of the words preserved by the evangelists could be attributed to Jesus. ∎

Matt 26:17–19 ➡ Mark 14:12–16

[17]On the first ⟨day⟩ of Unleavened Bread, the disciples came to Jesus, and said, "Where do you want us to make preparations for you to celebrate the Passover?" [18]He said, "**Go into the city to so-and-so and say to him, 'The teacher says, "My time is near, I will keep the Passover at your place with my disciples."'**" [19]And the disciples did as Jesus instructed them and they got ready for Passover.

Luke 22:7–13 ➡ Mark 14:12–16

[7]The day of Unleavened Bread arrived, when the Passover ⟨lambs⟩ had to be sacrificed. [8]So he sent Peter and John, with these instructions: "**Go and prepare the Passover so we may eat.**" [9]They said to him, "Where do you want us to prepare it?" [10]He said to them, "**Look, when you enter the city, a person carrying a waterpot will meet you. Follow him into the house he enters,** [11]**and say to the master of the house, 'The Teacher says to you, "Where is the guest room where I can celebrate the Passover with my disciples?"'** [12]And he will show you a large

upstairs room; There you're to get ready." [13]They set off and found things just as he had told them; and they got ready for Passover.

GEbi 7 ➡ Mark 14:12–16

But on their own accord they disfigure the proper sequence of the truth and alter the saying, as is plain to all from the reading attached, and have the disciples say:

"**Where do you want us to prepare for you to eat the passover?**" and evidently (they have) him answer: "**Surely I would desire to eat flesh with you at this Passover, would I?**"

Will their deceit not be detected, inasmuch as the sequence makes obvious that the *mū* and the *ēta* have been added? For instead of saying "I have eagerly desired" they add the additional word, *mē* ["not"]. Now in fact he said, "**I have eagerly desired to the Passover with you,**" but by adding the word "flesh" they deceive themselves, and acting wickedly they say, "**I do not desire to eat flesh with you at this Passover.**"

Epiphanius, *Haer.* 30.22.4

Mark 14:12–16

Source. Mark is the sole source of this story; he is copied by both Matthew and Luke. The fragment from the Gospel of the Ebionites does not provide any additional information.

Sayings and attribution. Nothing in

this narrative can be isolated as an aphorism that can be attributed to Jesus (J7); story and words are integral to each other (N2). If Mark created the narrative in his own words, he undoubtedly also composed the words ascribed to Jesus (W7). ∎

Better Not Born

Saying	Percentage				Wgt.
	R	P	G	B	Av.
Mk 14:18–21	4	4	20	72	.13 B
Mt 26:21–24	4	0	20	76	.11 B
Lk 22:21–22	0	4	16	80	.08 B
1 Clem 46:8a	4	4	4	88	.08 B
HVis 4.2:6b	0	0	4	96	.01 B

[17]When evening comes, he arrives with the twelve. [18]And as they reclined at table and were eating, Jesus said, "**So help me, one of you who is eating with me will turn me in!**" [19]They began to fret and to say to him one after another, "I'm not the one, am I?" [20]But he said to them, "**It is one of the twelve, the one who is dipping into the bowl with me.** [21]**The son of Adam departs just as the scriptures predict, but it's too bad for the one through whom the son of Adam is turned in! It would be better for that man if he had never been born!**"

Matt 26:21–24 ➡ Mark 14:17–21
[21]and they were eating. He said, "**So help me, one of you will turn me in.**" [22]And they were very vexed and each one began to say to him, "I am not the one, am I, Master?" [23]In response he said, "**The one who dips his hand in the bowl with me, he will turn me in!** [24]**The son of Adam departs just as the scriptures predict, but it's too bad for the person through whom the son of Adam is turned in. It would be better for that person if he had never been born!**"

Luke 22:21–22 ➡ Mark 14:18–21a
[21]Yet look! The one who is going to turn me in shares this table with me. [22]The son of Adam goes to meet his destiny; yet it is too bad for the person responsible for turning him in."

1 Clem 46:8 ➡ Mark 14:18–21
[8]Remember the words of the Lord Jesus, for he said, "**It is too bad for that man. It would be better for him if he had never been born.**"

Herm Vis 4.2:6b ➡ Mark 14:18–21
[6]. . . "**It will be too bad for those who hear these injunctions and fail to obey them. It would be better for them if they had not been born.**"

Mark 14:17–21
Aphorism. Most of the words attributed to Jesus in Mark 14:17–21 are context-bound (N2) and so are the product of the storyteller. The only possible exception to this generalization is the woe pronounced upon the betrayer in Mark 14:21b and parallels, a woe that is reproduced in 1 Clem 46:8 and in HermVis 4.2:6a (A1). Its appearance in these multiple independent sources indicate that the saying once circulated independently (O2).

Attribution. The saying attributed to Jesus in Mark 14:21b and parallels is a woe-oracle, modeled on prophetic woe-oracles in the Old Testament. It assumes the betrayal is an accomplished fact—it looks back on the outcome of the betrayal, as it were—and Jesus is identified as the son of Adam—the heavenly figure who comes in judgment—in v. 21a. This son of Adam goes out, moreover, just as scripture predicts, which means that Mark's own interpretation of events is guiding his hand (W7, W2). While one of the disciples may have betrayed Jesus, and while Jesus may have been aware of that betrayal, this oracle was introduced into the passion narrative by Mark (O5). It cannot, therefore, have originated with Jesus. ■

Mark 14:22–26

The tradition of the final supper Jesus ate with his disciples is extremely complex. Christian investment in the significance of the meal was high from the beginning, and remains high, which tends to complicate and obscure the history of the tradition. It is not possible in this context to set out all the issues and problems; we must be content with observations that account for the gray and black averages in the vote.

Sources. Paul's account in his first letter to the Corinthians is an early and an independent version of the Christian common meal. Mark's account is copied by Matthew; Luke's version differs at so many points from the Markan that some scholars believe it stems from another source. John substitutes the foot washing scene for the last supper. The summary in the Didache reflects a later time when the eucharist is already established as a Christian sacrament.

The Last Supper and the Passover Meal. Historically, one might expect Jesus to have eaten the Passover with his disciples on the occasion before his death. Luke 22:15 points to that desire on Jesus' part, and the Fourth Gospel reports that Jesus went to Jerusalem on three different earlier occasions for Passover (2:13, 23; 6:4, 13:1). Yet none of the evangelists describes a Passover celebration. And the report in Mark 14:22–25 is not a description of a Passover meal:

bitter herbs are not mentioned, and there is no liturgy connected with the eating of the Passover lamb. Indeed, the evangelists do not appear to be interested in a Passover meal as such, only in a memorial meal Jesus ate with his disciples. This curious disinterest in the Jewish meal Jesus might have eaten with his disciples suggests that the last supper has already been transposed into a cultic meal by Christian practice and theological interpretation.

Markan context and interpretation. Mark conceives the Last Supper as a ceremony (a) related to the feeding stories (6:30–44, 8:1–10), (b) to the anointing of Jesus at Bethany (14:3–9), (c) and to his own theological interpretation of the meaning of Jesus' death (note 14:25 and 10:45 in particular).

(a) The disciples do not understand about 'the bread' in the feeding stories (6:52, 8:14–21), a mystery that is not cleared up until Mark comes to the Last Supper: 'the bread' is really Jesus' body, which he gives as a ransom for many (10:45).

John, too, links the supper to the feeding stories. Language characteristic of the eucharist pervades the long discourse on bread from heaven in John 6:48–58, which interprets the feeding story in 6:1–14. For the Last Supper John substitutes the foot washing scene (13:1–20).

(b) The woman anoints Jesus' body in

Supper and Eucharist

Saying	Percentage				Wgt.
	R	P	G	B	Av.
Mk 14:22,etc.	0	16	44	40	.25 G
Mt 26:26–29	0	0	40	60	.13 B
Lk 22:15–20	0	0	48	52	.16 B
Jn 6:51–58	0	0	4	96	.01 B
1 Cor 11:23–25	0	16	36	48	.23 B
Did 9:1–4	0	0	4	96	.01 B

²²And as they were eating, he took a loaf, gave a blessing, broke it into pieces and gave it to them. And he said, "Have some, this is my body!" ²³And he took a cup, gave thanks and gave it to them, and they all drank from it. ²⁴And he said to them: "This is my blood of the covenant, which has been poured out for many! ²⁵So help me, I certainly won't drink again from the fruit of the vine until that day when I drink it for the first time in God's domain!" ²⁶And they sang a hymn and left for the Mount of Olives.

Matt 26:26–29 ➡ Mark 14:22–25

²⁶As they were eating, Jesus took a loaf, gave a blessing, broke it into pieces. And he gave it to the disciples, and said, "Have some and eat, this is my body." ²⁷And he took a cup and giving thanks, he gave it to them, saying, "Drink from it, all of you, ²⁸for this is my blood of the covenant, which has been poured out for many for the forgiveness of sins. ²⁹Now I tell you, From now on I certainly won't drink from this fruit of the vine until that day when I drink it for the first time with you in my Father's domain."

---

advance for burial (14:8), and her good deed will be rehearsed as a memorial to her wherever the gospel is proclaimed. 'The bread' and the body thus represent Jesus' death—his absence. The disciples will participate in Jesus' death by eating the bread at the Last Supper (14:22), in a ceremony that recalls the feeding of the multitudes earlier: breaking, blessing, and distributing the loaves.

(c) Mark has prepared his readers for Jesus' death by his creation of the three predictions of the passion (8:31–33, 9:30–32, 10:32–34). The cup is the climax of the Last Supper on Mark's view because it represents Jesus' redemptive sacrifice (14:24) and anticipates Jesus' return as the son of Adam (14:25). This interpretation fills out the predictions of the passion, as it were, by giving Jesus' death a sacrificial twist and, at the same time, providing a cultic cup that anticipates Jesus' return.

Mark links 'the cup' with Jesus' death in 14:26, and earlier, in 10:39, Mark has him tell those who aspire to positions of power that they will drink from his 'cup,' which they all in fact do in 14:23: "and they all drank from it." The 'cup' thus embodies the entire gospel for Mark: the death, burial, and resurrection of Jesus, together with his return as the son of Adam.

Attribution. Some of the Fellows were of the opinion that a genuine saying of Jesus might lie behind 14:25: Jesus may have suggested that he would share a common meal with his followers sometime in the future when God's imperial rule had arrived. But most Fellows were convinced that the supper tradition has been so overlaid with Christianizing elements and interpretation (W8a) that it is impossible to recover anything of an original event, much less original words spoken by Jesus. Nevertheless, the Seminar readily conceded the possibility that Jesus may have performed some symbolic acts during table fellowship with his followers. And those symbolic acts may have involved bread and wine or perhaps fish. ■

Luke 22:15–20 ➡ Mark 14:22–25

[15]He said to them, "I have desperately desired to celebrate this Passover with you before I die. [16]For I tell you, I certainly won't eat it until such a time as it is fulfilled in God's domain." [17]Then he took a cup, gave thanks, and said, "Take this and share it among yourselves. [18]For I tell you, from now on I certainly won't drink of the fruit of the vine until God's domain is established." [19]And he took a loaf, gave thanks, broke it into pieces, gave it to them, and said, "This is my body which is given for you. Do this as my memorial." [20]And in the same way, the cup after dinner, saying, "This cup is the new covenant in my blood, which is poured out for you."

John 6:51–58 ➡ Mark 14:22–25

[51]"I am the living bread that comes down from the sky. Whoever eats this bread will live forever. And the bread that I will give for the life of the world is my own body." [52]At this point "The Jews" began to argue among themselves, saying, "How can this fellow give us his body to eat?" [53]Accordingly, Jesus told them: "I swear to God, If you do not eat the body of the son of Adam and do not drink his blood, you have no life in yourselves. [54]Whoever eats my body and drinks my blood possesses eternal life, and that one I will raise up on the last day. [55]For my body is real food, and my blood real drink. [56]Whoever eats my body and drinks my blood is a part of me and I am a part of him. [57]The Father of life sent me, and I have life because of the Father. Just so, whoever consumes me will have life because of me. [58]This is the bread that comes down from the sky. Unlike our ancestors who ate and then died, whoever eats this bread will live forever."

1 Cor 11:23–25 ➡ Mark 14:22–25

[23]For I received from the Lord what I also delivered to you, that the Lord Jesus on the night when he was betrayed took bread, [24]and when he had given thanks, he broke it, and said, "This is my body which is for you. Do this in remembrance of me." [25]In the same way also the cup, after supper, saying, "This cup is the new covenant in my blood. Do this, as often as you drink it, in remembrance of me."

Did 9:1–4 ➡ Mark 14:22–25

[1]Concerning the eucharist, this is how you are to conduct it: [2]First, concerning the cup, "We thank you, our Father, for the sacred vine of David, your child, whom you made known to us through Jesus, your child. To you be glory forever." [3]Then concerning the fragments ⟨of bread⟩: "We thank you, our Father, for the life and knowledge that you made known to us through Jesus, your child. To you be glory forever. [4]Just as this loaf was scattered upon the mountains but was gathered into a unity, so your church should be gathered from the ends of the earth into your domain. Yours is the glory and the power through Jesus Christ forever."

Peter's Betrayal Foretold

| Saying | Percentage | | | | Wgt. |
	R	P	G	B	Av.
Mk 14:27–31	0	4	20	76	.09 B
Mt 26:31–34	0	0	24	76	.08 B
Lk 22:31–34	0	0	24	76	.08 B
Jn 13:36–38	0	0	16	84	.05 B
FayyumFrag	0	0	16	84	.05 B

[27]And Jesus says to them, "**You will all be provoked to fall away, for it is written, 'I will strike the shepherd and the sheep will be scattered!'** [28]**But after I'm raised I'll go ahead of you to Galilee.**" [29]Peter said to him, "Even if they are all provoked to fall away, I won't!" [30]And Jesus says to him, "**So help me, tonight before the rooster crows twice you will disown me three times!**" [31]But he repeated it with more bravado, "If they force me to die with you, I will never disown you!" And they took the same oath, all of them.

Matt 26:31–35 ➡ Mark 14:27–31

[31]Then Jesus says to them, "**All of you will be provoked to fall away because of me on this night, for it is written, 'I will strike the shepherd and the sheep of his flock will be scattered!'** [32]**But after I'm raised, I'll go ahead of you to Galilee.**" [33]In response Peter said to him, "If everyone is provoked to fall away because of you, I'll never be provoked to fall away." [34]Jesus said to him, "**So help me, tonight before the rooster crows you will disown me three times!**" [35]Peter says to him, "Even if they force me to die with you, I will never disown you!" And all of the disciples took the same oath, all of them.

Luke 22:31–34 ➡ Mark 14:27–31

[31]"**Simon, Simon, look out, Satan is after all of you, to winnow you like wheat. [32]But I have prayed for you that your trust may not give out. And you, when you have come back, strengthen your brothers.**" [33]He said to him, "Master, you I'm prepared to follow to prison and to death." [34]He said, "**Let me tell you, Peter, the rooster will not crow tonight until you deny knowing me three times.**"

John 13:36–38 ➡ Mark 14:27–31

[36]Simon Peter says to him, "Master, where are you going?" Jesus replied [to him], "**Where I now go you can't follow. You will follow later.**" [37]Peter says to him, "Master, why can't I follow you now? I'll give up my life for you." [38]Jesus responded, "⟨You say⟩ **you'll give up your life for me? So help me, the rooster certainly won't crow before you disown me three times.**"

Fayyum Fragment ➡ Mark 14:27–31

. . . while he was going out, he said "**This night you will all desert me, as it is written, 'I will strike the shepherd and the sheep will be scattered.'**" Then Peter said, "Even if they all do, I will not." Jesus says, "**Before the rooster crows twice, you will this day disown me three times.**"

Mark 14:27–31

Words of Jesus. There are three groups of words attributed to Jesus in this passage.

(a) The prediction that the disciples will all be provoked to fall away (14:27).

(b) The promise that Jesus will precede them to Galilee after his resurrection (14:28).

(c) The prediction that Peter will deny Jesus before the cock crows (14:30).

Attribution.

(a) The first group of words (Mark 14:27) is inspired by Zech 13:7: "O sword! You should be raised against my shepherds, and against my leaders," says the Lord Almighty. "Strike my shepherds and scatter my sheep, and I will lift my hand against my shepherds." The sword raised against Jesus at his arrest (Mark 14:48) and the flight of the disciples attracted part of this messianic oracle (O5). Or, it is possible that the prophecy prompted the creation of the story.

(b) The second saying (Mark 14:28) goes together with the scene at the empty tomb (Mark 16:7), where the youth reminds the women of this promise. Luke omits this saying because his resurrection appearances are not located in Galilee. This saying, like the predictions of the passion, is most probably a Markan creation. It is intrusive in the story that concerns the prophetic prediction of Zechariah, the oath of Peter, and the saying of Jesus.

(c) Peter responds in v. 28 to the prophesy recorded in v. 27 by taking an oath (v. 30). Jesus assures Peter that he will not keep that oath.

This passage goes together with Mark 14:54, 66–72—the account of Peter's triple denial in the courtyard. It is possible that these narratives are part of a polemic against Peter, constructed by those who opposed Peter's leadership in the early church. Remnants of such a polemic are found in Mark 8:33 ("Get behind me, Satan"), Matt 14:28–31 (Peter doubts and sinks in the water). And in Thom 12, James the Just is the leader of the church, not Peter. Luke modifies the story so that Peter is vindicated in part: he is presented as failing but also as being restored (Luke 22:31–34). The story may well be older than Mark, but it probably arose at a time when there was contention among the potential leaders of the church.

The saying attributed to Jesus, however, may be older than the story. It is recorded in a different context in the Gospel of John (13:38) (A2). The saying may have a proverbial background (O5), and it may have involved the motif of the rooster crowing, but as it stands, it is a prophetic curse: Peter will deny Jesus as inevitably as the rooster will crow. Such curses undoubtedly functioned in early Christian circles to include and exclude persons from the community (W9a). In any case, the saying put in the mouth of Jesus belongs to a context in which the role of Peter is being devalued.

In sum, none of the words attributed to Jesus in this passage are likely to go back to Jesus. Like most of the sayings in the passion narrative, they were created as a part of the narrative (N2). ∎

Prayer Against Temptation

Saying	Percentage				Wgt.
	R	P	G	B	Av.
Mk 14:32,etc.	0	12	16	72	.13 B
Mt 26:36,etc.	0	8	12	80	.09 B
Lk 22:40,etc.	0	12	8	80	.11 B
Jn 12:27	0	0	8	92	.03 B
PolPhil 7:1–2	0	0	8	92	.03 B

³²And they come to a place the name of which was Gethsemane, and he says to his disciples, "**Sit down here while I pray.**" ³³And he takes Peter and James and John along with him, and he began to be apprehensive and full of anguish. ³⁴He says to them, "**I'm so sad I could die. You stay here and be alert!**" ³⁵And he would move on a little, fall on the ground, and pray that the crisis might pass him by, if possible. ³⁶And he would say, "***abba*** **(Father), all things are possible for you! Take this cup away from me! But it's not what I want ⟨ that matters ⟩, but what you want.**" ³⁷And he returns and finds them sleeping, and he says to Peter, "**Simon, are you sleeping? Couldn't you stay awake for one hour?** ³⁸**Be alert and pray that you are not put to the test! Though the spirit is willing, the flesh is weak.**" ³⁹And once again he went away and prayed, saying the same thing. ⁴⁰And once again he came and found them sleeping, since their eyes had become very heavy, and they didn't know what to say to him. ⁴¹And he comes a third time and says to them, "**You may as well sleep on now and get your rest. It's all over! The**

Mark 14:32–42

Attribution. In this scene, Jesus speaks to the three intimate disciples in vv. 32, 34, 37–38, 41–42. In v. 36 a prayer is attributed to Jesus, although no one else is present to overhear it (N3).

Mark has probably composed the prayer for Jesus (W7), which Mark anticipates in v. 35 and then has Jesus repeat in v. 39. Since there were no witnesses, Mark, or the tradition before him, must have imagined what Jesus said. For his part, Matthew slightly alters Mark's version (26:39) and then composes a second prayer for Jesus (26:42) (N2, W7). Luke also modifies Mark's prayer in his version (22:42) (W4). These variations and additions illustrate how loosely the evangelists treated even written discourse, to say nothing of oral tradition they may

have received. The prayer in the garden, consequently, received a black designation.

The allusion to the Lord's Prayer in Mark 14:38 ("Do not put us to the test") was designated black by the Seminar, in concert with its gray designation of that petition in Luke 11:4//Matt 6:13.

The words of Jesus addressed to the disciples are integral to the story, for the most part, and are thus context-bound (N2). The one possible exception, "Though the spirit is willing, the flesh is weak" (Mark 14:38b), is proverbial in character and could have been spoken by almost anyone (O5).

The Seminar was accordingly content to place the entire complex in the black category. ∎

time has come! Look, the son of Adam is being turned over to heathen. ⁴²Get up, let's go! See for yourselves! Here comes the one who is going to turn me in."

Matt 26:36–46 ➡ Mark 14:32–42

³⁶Then Jesus comes with them to a place called Gethsemane, and he says to the disciples, "**Sit down here while I go over there and pray.**" ³⁷And taking Peter and the two sons of Zebebee, he began to be dejected and full of anguish. ³⁸He says to them, "**I'm so sad I could die. You stay here with me and be alert!**" ³⁹And he went a little way and fell on his face, and prayed, "**My Father, if it is possible, let this cup pass me by! Yet it's not how I want it ⟨that matters⟩, but how you want it.**" ⁴⁰And he returns to the disciples and finds them sleeping, and he says to Peter, "**Couldn't you stay awake for one hour with me? ⁴¹Be alert, and pray that you are not put to the test! Though the spirit is willing, the flesh is weak.**" ⁴²Again for a second time he went away and prayed, "**My Father, if it is not possible for this ⟨cup⟩ to pass ⟨me⟩ by unless I drink it, let your will prevail!**" ⁴³And once again he came and found them sleeping, since their eyes were heavy. ⁴⁴And leaving them again, he went away and prayed, saying again the same words for a third time. ⁴⁵Then he comes to the disciples and says to them, "**Are you still sleeping and taking a rest? Look, the time is at hand! The son of Adam is being turned over to heathen. ⁴⁶Get up, let's go! See for yourselves! Here comes the one who is going to turn me in.**"

Luke 22:39–46 ➡ Mark 14:32–42

³⁹Then he left and went, as usual, to the Mount of Olives; and the disciples

followed him. ⁴⁰When he arrived at the place he said to them, "**Pray that you are not put to the test.**" ⁴¹And he withdrew from them about a stone's throw away, knelt down and began to pray, ⁴²"**Father, if you so choose, take this cup away from me! Yet not my will, but yours, be done.**" ⁴⁵And when he got up from his prayer and returned to the disciples, he found them asleep, weary from grief. ⁴⁶He said to them, "**Why are you sleeping? Get up and pray that you are not put to the test.**"

John 12:27 ➡ Mark 14:32–42

²⁷"**Now my soul is in turmoil. But what shall I say? 'Father, save me from this hour'? No, it was precisely for this hour that I came!**"

Pol Phil 7:1–2 ➡ Mark 14:32–42

¹Everyone who does not acknowledge that Jesus the Anointed has come in the flesh is an antichrist. Whoever does not accept the testimony of the cross belongs to the devil. And whoever twists the Lord's sayings to suit his own desires and claims there is neither resurrection nor judgment, is a true relative of Satan. ²We should therefore abandon the idle speculations and false teachings of the crowd and return to the word that was passed down to us from the beginning: we should be sober in prayer, we should stick to our fasts, and in our prayers we should ask the all-seeing God not to lead us to the test, just as the Lord indicated. Of course, the spirit is willing, but the flesh is weak.

Jesus Arrested

| Saying | Percentage | | | | Wgt. |
	R	P	G	B	Av.
Mk 14:48–49	4	16	28	52	.24 **B**
Mt 26:50,etc.	4	4	32	60	.17 **B**
Lk 22:48,etc.	0	8	24	68	.13 **B**
Jn 18:4,etc.	0	8	12	80	.09 **B**

⁴³And right away, while he was still speaking, Judas, one of the twelve, arrives, and with him a crowd, dispatched by the ranking priests and the scribes and the elders, wielding swords and clubs. ⁴⁴Now the one who was to turn him in had arranged a signal with them, saying, "The one I'm going to kiss is the one you want. Seize him and escort him safely away!" ⁴⁵And right away he arrives, comes up to him, and says, "Rabbi," and kissed him. ⁴⁶And they seized him and held him fast. ⁴⁷One of those standing around drew his sword and struck the high priest's slave and cut off his ear. ⁴⁸In response

---

Matt 26:47–56 ➡ Mark 14:43–50

⁴⁷And while he was still speaking, suddenly Judas, one of the twelve, came and with him a great crowd wielding swords and clubs dispatched by the ranking priests and elders of the people. ⁴⁸Now the one who was to turn him in had arranged a sign with them, saying, "The one I'm going to kiss is the one you want. Seize him!" ⁴⁹And he came right up to Jesus, and said, "Hello, Rabbi," and kissed him. ⁵⁰But Jesus said to him, **"Friend, why are you here?"** Then they came and seized him and held him fast. ⁵¹At that moment one of those with Jesus lifted his hand, drew his sword, struck the high priest's slave, and cut off his ear. ⁵²Then Jesus says to him, **"Put your sword back where it belongs. For everyone who takes up the sword will be done in by the sword. ⁵³Or do you suppose that I am not able to call on my Father, who would put more than twelve legions of angels at my disposal? ⁵⁴How then would the scriptures be fulfilled that say these things are ordained?"** ⁵⁵At that moment Jesus said to the crowds, **"Have you come out to take me with swords and clubs as though you were apprehending a common crook? I would sit there day**

after day in the temple area teaching and you didn't lift a hand against me." ⁵⁶All of this happened in order that the writings of the prophets might be fulfilled. Then all the disciples deserted him and ran away.

Luke 22:47–53 ➡ Mark 14:43–50

⁴⁷Suddenly, while he was still speaking, a crowd appeared with the one known as Judas, one of the twelve, leading the way. He came up to Jesus to kiss him. ⁴⁸But Jesus said to him, **"Judas, would you turn in the son of Adam with a kiss?"** ⁴⁹And when those around him saw what was going to happen, they said, "Master, should we use our swords? ⁵⁰And one of them struck the high priest's slave and cut off his right ear. ⁵¹But Jesus responded, **"Stop! That's enough!"** And he touched his ear and healed him. ⁵²Then Jesus said to the ranking priests and temple officers and elders who had come for him, **"Have you come out with swords and clubs as though you were apprehending a common crook? ⁵³When I was with you every day in the temple area, you did not lay a hand on me. But this is your hour, and the authority darkness affords."**

Jesus said to them, "**Have you come out to take me with swords and clubs as though you were apprehending a common crook? ⁴⁹I was with you day after day teaching in the temple area and you didn't lift a hand against me. But the scriptures must be fulfilled!**" ⁵⁰And they all deserted him and ran away.

John 18:2–11 ➡ Mark 14:43–50
²But because Jesus had often gone there before with his disciples, Judas, who was going to turn him in, knew the place too. ³So it wasn't long before Judas arrived, bringing with him the company of Roman soldiers and some of the police from the ranking priests and the Pharisees, with their lamps and torches and weapons.

⁴Jesus, of course, knew just what would happen to him, so he went right up to them and says, "**Who are you looking for?**" ⁵"Jesus the Nazarene," was their reply. "**That's me,**" says Jesus. And all the while Judas, the one who was to turn him in, was standing there with them. ⁶But as soon as he said, "That's me," they all retreated and fell to the ground. ⁷So Jesus asked them again, "**Who are you looking for?**" "Jesus the Nazarene," they said. ⁸"**I told you that that's me,**" Jesus answered, "**so if it's me you're looking for, let the others go.**" ⁹(This was so the prediction he had given might come true: "**I lost none—not one of those you put in my care.**") ¹⁰Simon Peter had brought along a sword, and now he drew it; he hit the high priest's slave, who was called Malchus, and cut off his right ear. ¹¹"**Put the sword back in it's scabbard,**" said Jesus to Peter. "**Won't you let me drink from the cup that my Father has given me?**"

Mark 14:43–50
Sayings. A close comparison of the four versions of the arrest episode indicates that the evangelists have taken great liberties in reporting (or not reporting) the words of Jesus (N2, W4).

Jesus' address to Judas varies (compare Matt 26:50 with Luke 22:48). In John, Jesus does not address Judas, but the temple police accompanying Judas (18:4). The verbal exchange of John 18:4–5 is repeated in 7–8, with the notice in v. 9 that this was to fulfill scripture— another suggestion that much of the passion narrative was inspired by texts from scripture (O5). Matthew expands Mark's episode of the sword by adding words attributed to Jesus (26:52–54) (W7); Luke follows suit, but reports different words (22:51) (W4). John provides still another response to the sword incident (John 18:11).

The single possibility of an isolatable saying ascribed to Jesus is the one found in Mark 14:48–49a, with parallels in Matt 26:55 and Luke 22:52–53a.

Sources. Matthew and Luke are obviously dependent on Mark as in many other instances. What they add to the account is therefore of little historical value. We cannot be sure that John has a separate source for this incident. In any case, John sustains a very free relationship to the sayings tradition overall.

Attribution. There are two reasons why Fellows were hesitant to attribute Mark 14:48–49a directly to Jesus. First, the phrase that follows in both Mark and Matthew suggests that the time and place of the arrest was to fulfill scripture; the evangelists may have some text in mind that we do not recognize (O5). Second,

⁵¹And a youth was following him, wearing a shroud over his nude body, and they grab him. ⁵²But he dropped the shroud and ran away naked.

⁵³And they brought Jesus before the high priest, and all the ranking priests and elders and scribes assemble. ⁵⁴Peter followed him at a distance until he was inside the courtyard of the high priest, and was sitting with the attendants and keeping warm by the fire. ⁵⁵The ranking priests and the whole Council were looking for evidence against Jesus in order to issue a death

---

Mark 15:27–30 ➡ Mark 14:55–61a
²⁷And with him they crucify two rebels, one on his right and one on his left. ²⁹Those passing by kept taunting him, wagging their heads, and saying, "Ha! You who would destroy the temple and rebuild it in three days, ³⁰save yourself and come down from the cross!"

Matt 26:59–63a ➡ Mark 14:55–61a
⁵⁹The ranking priests and the whole Council were looking for false testimony against Jesus so they might issue a death sentence; ⁶⁰but they couldn't find many perjurers to come forward. But finally, two persons came forward ⁶¹and said, "This fellow said, **'I'm able to destroy the temple of God and within**

three days rebuild it.'" ⁶²And the high priest got up, and questioned him, "Don't you have something to say? Why do these people testify against you?" ⁶³But Jesus was silent. And the high priest said to him, "I adjure you by the living God: Tell us if you are the Anointed, the son of God!"

Matt 27:38–40 ➡ Mark 14:55–61a
³⁸Then they crucified with him two rebels, one on his right and one on his left. ³⁹Those passing by kept taunting him, wagging their heads, and saying, ⁴⁰"You who would destroy the temple and rebuild it in three days, save yourself, if you're God's son, come down from the cross!"

---

there is nothing aphoristic, or memorable, about the words attributed to Jesus (J1). Rather, while the words are realistic and may reflect the actualities of Jesus' teaching openly and regularly in Jerusalem, there is no reason the disciples would have remembered precisely those words. There is this additional consideration: these words add nothing significant to the stock of sayings and parables ascribed to Jesus in the gospels. ∎

Mark 14:55–61a
Preliminary observations.
(1) Scholars have long debated wheth-

er the synoptic account of Jesus' trial by the temple authorities is historically plausible. In a special poll on this question, 97% of the Fellows agreed that the Jewish trial was a figment of the Christian imagination.

(2) Even if Jesus was tried by Jewish authorities, his followers were certainly not present. Statements made in the absence of those providing testimony is not historically verifiable (N3).

(3) The words ascribed to Jesus in Mark 14:58//Matt 26:61 are reported secondhand as hearsay evidence by Jesus' opponents. Only in John 2:19 and Thom

sentence, but they couldn't find any. [56]Although many gave false evidence against him, their stories didn't agree. [57]And some people stood up and testified falsely against him: [58]"We have heard him saying, 'I'll destroy this temple made with hands and in three days I'll build another, not made with hands!'" [59]Yet even then their stories did not agree. [60]And the high priest got up and questioned Jesus: "Don't you have some answer to give? Why do these people testify against you?" [61]But he was silent and refused to answer.

Temple and Jesus

Saying	Percentage				Wgt.
	R	P	G	B	Av.
Mk 14:58	0	24	32	44	.27 G
Mk 15:29	0	16	32	52	.21 B
Mt 26:61	0	12	20	68	.15 B
Mt 27:40	0	8	16	76	.11 B
Jn 2:19	0	8	16	76	.11 B
Acts 6:14	0	4	16	80	.08 B
Th 71	4	8	24	64	.17 B

John 2:13–22 ➡ Mark 14:55–61a

[13]It was almost time for the Jewish Passover, so Jesus went up to Jerusalem. [14]In the temple precincts he came upon people selling oxen, sheep, and pigeons; money changers were seated ⟨in their stalls⟩. [15]And he made a whip out of cords and drove the whole bunch out of the temple area, along with both sheep and oxen. Then he knocked over the money changers' tables, and sent their coins flying. [16]Then he told the pigeon merchants: "Get these ⟨birds⟩ out of here! Stop turning my Father's house into a public market." [17]His disciples recalled the words of scripture: "Passion for your house will devour me."

[18]To this 'the Jews' responded, "What sign are you going to show us ⟨as warrant⟩ for doing these things?"

[19]In response Jesus said to them, "**Destroy this temple and in three days I will resurrect it.**" [20]'The Jews' said, "It took forty-six years to erect this temple, and you are going to re-erect it in three days?" [21]Actually he was talking about the temple of his body. [22]After he had been raised from the dead, his disciples recalled that he had said this and believed the scripture and the prediction Jesus had made.

Acts 6:14 ➡ Mark 14:55–61a

[14]We have heard him say that this Jesus the Nazarene will destroy this place and change the regulations Moses handed down to us.

Thom 71 ➡ Mark 14:55–61a

Jesus said, "**I will destroy [this] house, and no one will be able to build it [. . .].**"

71 is the statement put directly on the lips of Jesus.

Sources. It is surprising that we are dealing in this instance with a saying attributed to Jesus by hostile parties, except for John 2:19 and Thom 71.

What is the basis for this report?

The saying is attributed to Jesus twice in Mark (14:58 and 15:29). The only possible basis for the ascription recorded in Mark is the saying in Mark 13:4: "There certainly won't remain one stone

on another . . ." Yet that saying makes no reference to rebuilding in three days, nor does it distinguish a temple made of stone from one not made with human endeavor. In short, there in no basis in the Gospel of Mark for the claim made by Jesus' opponents that he would destroy the temple and in three days raise another, metaphorical temple.

Matthew is copying in both cases. Luke omits this part of the passion story in his gospel, but alludes to the saying in

Priest's Question

| Saying | Percentage | | | | Wgt. |
	R	P	G	B	Av.
Mk 14:62	0	4	16	80	.08 **B**
Mt 26:64	0	0	20	80	.07 **B**
Lk 22:67-69	0	4	20	76	.09 **B**

Once again the high priest questioned him and says to him, "Are you the Anointed, the son of the Blessed One?" 62Jesus replied, "**I am! And you will see the son of Adam sitting at the right hand of Power and coming with the clouds of the sky!**" 63Then the high priest tore his vestments and says, "Why do we still need witnesses? 64You have heard the blasphemy! What do you think?" And they all concurred in the death penalty. 65And some began to spit on him, and to put a blindfold on him, and punch him, and say to him, "Prophesy!" And the guards abused him as they took him into custody.

Matt 26:63-68 → Mark 14:61b-65

63But Jesus was silent. And the high priest said to him, "I adjure you by the living God: Tell us if you are the Anointed, the son of God!" 64Jesus says to him, "**If you say so. But I tell you, from now on you will see the son of Adam sitting at the right hand of Power and coming on the clouds of the sky.**" 65Then the high priest tore his cloak, and said, "He has blasphemed! Why do we still need witnesses? See, now you have heard the blasphemy. 66What do you think?" In response they said, "He deserves to die!" 67Then they spit in his face, and punch him and struck him, 68saying, "Prophesy for us, you Anointed, you! Who is it that struck you?"

Luke 22:66-71 → Mark 14:61b-65

66When day came, the elders of the people, together with both ranking priests and scribes, met in assembly. They had him brought before their Council, and they interrogated him: 67"If you are the Anointed, tell us." But he said to them, "**If I tell you, you certainly won't believe me. 68If I ask you a question, you certainly won't answer. 69But from now on the son of Adam will be seated at the right hand of the power of God.**" 70And they all said, "So you, are you the son of God?" He said to them, "**You're the ones who say so.**" 71And they said, "Why do we still need witnesses? We have heard it ourselves from his own lips."

Acts 6:14, again as a secondhand report. The Acts reference could well be dependent on Mark.

The version in John may come from an independent source. At all events, the form in John is highly developed in that the temple is interpreted as Jesus' body and the saying thus made to refer to his death and resurrection (W8a).

The form in Thomas perhaps represents the most primitive form (O3a). But there is insufficient context in Thomas to be able to determine what the saying meant originally.

Attribution. Some Fellows thought that a saying in which Jesus forecast the destruction of the present temple and its replacement by another temple not erected by human endeavor might conceivably go back to Jesus. For this reason, Mark 14:58 drew the highest weighted average. The version in Thomas at-

⁶⁶And while Peter was below in the court-yard, one of the high priest's slave women comes over, ⁶⁷and sees Peter warming himself; she looks at him closely and says, "You too were with that Nazarene, Jesus!" ⁶⁸But he denied it, saying, "I don't know or understand what you're saying!" And he went outside into the forecourt. ⁶⁹And when the slave woman saw him, she once again began to say to those standing nearby, "This fellow is one of them!" ⁷⁰But once again he denied it. And a little later, those standing nearby would again say to Peter, "You really are one of them, since you also are a Galilean!" ⁷¹But he began to curse and swear, "I don't know the fellow you're talking about!" ⁷²And just then a rooster crowed a second time, and Peter remembered what Jesus had told him: "Before a rooster crows twice you will disown me three times!" And he broke down and started to cry.

---

tracted the only red votes, but because the text in Thomas is fragmentary, many Fellows were hesitant to designate it anything other than black.

In general, the opinion prevailed that the saying, whatever its original form, had been remodeled to conform to the three day interval between Jesus' death and resurrection and was thereby made to conform to the kerygmatic perspective of the later church (W8a). ■

Mark 14:61b–65
Words of Jesus. The words attributed to Jesus in this passage should be divided into two groups.

(a) The first group concerns Jesus' immediate answer to the high priest: "I am" (Mark) or "If you say so" (Matthew). Luke rewrites: "If I tell you, you certainly won't believe me."

(b) The second group promises that the son of Adam will sit at the right hand of Power and come with or on clouds of the sky. Mark and Matthew have essen-tially the same version; Luke again modifies.

Attribution.

(a) Matthew's version sounds more like the reticent, evasive Jesus (J8), or of a person on trial. Mark has Jesus say flatly that he is the Anointed, the son of the Blessed One (God). Luke's answer is evasive like Matthew's and thus more in the spirit of Jesus, so far as we can determine it (J7, J8). But all these responses, like the one following, are undoubtedly the work of the evangelists (W7), since none of Jesus' disciples were present to hear and report his responses (N3).

(b) The substance of the second group of words is derived from Dan 7:13–14 and Ps 110:1 (O5). As observed earlier, words about the coming of the son of Adam are probably not from Jesus, especially when the reference is based on Daniel 7 (See the discussion of Mark 13:26 above for additional remarks.) ■

| Saying | Percentage | | | | Wgt. |
	R	P	G	B	Av.
Mk 15:2	4	12	16	68	.17 B
Mt 27:11	4	12	16	68	.17 B
Lk 23:2–3	8	8	20	64	.20 B
Jn 18:33–38a	0	0	12	88	.04 B

15 And right away, at daybreak, the ranking priests, after consulting with the elders and scribes and the whole Council, bound Jesus and led him away and turned him over to Pilate. ²And Pilate questioned him: "*You* are the King of the Jews?" And in response he says to him, "**If you say so.**" ³And the ranking priests started a long list of accusations against him. ⁴Again Pilate tried questioning him: "Don't you have some answer to give? You see what a long list of charges they bring against you!" ⁵But Jesus still did not respond, so Pilate was baffled.

Matt 27:11 ➡ Mark 15:2
¹¹Jesus stood before the governor, and the governor questioned him, "*You* are the King of the Jews?" Jesus said, "**If you say so.**"

Luke 23:2–3 ➡ Mark 15:2
²They began to accuse him, saying, "We have found this one to be a corrupting influence on our nation, opposing the payment of taxes to Caesar, and claiming that he himself is an anointed king." ³Pilate questioned him, "*You* are the King of the Jews?" In response he said to him, "**If you say so.**"

John 18:33–38a ➡ Mark 15:2
³³Then Pilate came back into the praetorium. He addressed Jesus, "You, are you King of 'the Jews'?" "**Is this your own idea,**" answered Jesus, "**or**

have other people told you this about me?" ³⁵"Am I a Jew?!" countered Pilate. "It is your people and your ranking priests who have handed you over to me. What have you done?" ³⁶Jesus responded, "**Mine is not a secular government. If my government were secular my companions would fight, so that I not be turned over to 'the Jews.' But as it is, my government does not belong to the secular domain.**" ³⁷"You are a king, then?" said Pilate. Jesus replied, "**Do you say that I am a king? This is what I was born for, and this is why I came into the world: to bear witness to the truth. Everyone who comes from the truth can hear my voice.**" ³⁸"What is the truth?" says Pilate. When he had said this, he again came out to 'the Jews.' "I find no basis for any charge," he said.

Mark 15:2
Sources. The question of 'sources' must here be posed differently. It is not a question of whether Mark is the written source of the other three versions, but whether there is a narrative 'source' that inspired the development of quoted speech.
   Pilate asks Jesus, "*You* are the king of the Jews?" in disbelief (Mark 15:2, Matt

27:11, Luke 23:3, John 18:33). The wording of the question agrees with the inscription or sign put on the cross: "The King of the Jews" (with slight variation: Mark 15:26, Matt 27:37, Luke 23:38, John 19:19). Pilate is presumably the author of the inscription (John 19:19) and also of the question. When 'the Jews' see the sign, they respond: "Don't write, 'The King of the Jews,' but 'This man

⁶At each festival it was the custom for him to set one prisoner free for them, whichever one they requested. ⁷And one called Barabbas was being held with the insurgents who had committed murder during the uprising. ⁸And when the crowd arrived, they began to demand that he do what he usually did for them. ⁹And in response Pilate said to them, "Do you want me to set the King of the Jews free for you?" ¹⁰After all, he realized that the ranking priests had turned him over out of envy. ¹¹But the ranking priests incited the crowd to get Barabbas set free for them instead. ¹²But in response Pilate would again say to them, "What do you want me to do with the fellow you call 'the King of the Jews'?" ¹³And they in turn shouted, "Crucify him!" ¹⁴Pilate kept saying to them, "Why? What has he done wrong?" But they shouted all the louder, "Crucify him!" ¹⁵And because Pilate was always looking to satisfy the crowd, he set Barabbas free for them, had Jesus flogged, and then turned him over to be crucified.

¹⁶And the soldiers led him away to the courtyard, that is, the praetorium, and they called the whole company together. ¹⁷And they dressed him in purple and crowned him with a garland woven of thorns. ¹⁸And they began to salute him: "Greetings,'King of the Jews'!" ¹⁹And they kept striking him on the head with a staff, and spitting on him; and they would get down on their knees and bow down to him.

---

said, "I am the King of the Jews."'" In this brief exchange, we can observe the birth of direct speech put on the lips of Jesus but generated ultimately by the words Pilate coined originally.

Jesus is never recorded elsewhere as referring to himself as a king. The 'source' of the phrase is actually Pilate, if we accept the account at face value.

Words of Jesus. The response of Jesus is ambiguous. The Greek phrase (*su legeis*) may be translated in a variety of ways: "You say so," "If you say so," "The words are yours," "Whatever you say," "You said it, I didn't," or something similar. This type of ambiguity, or evasiveness, goes together with Jesus' posture during the trial, including his silence. It is tempting to claim that these may be the very words of Jesus. Unfortunately, they are inspired by the question, which, as we have just observed, was created by Pilate. Since the context determines the meaning in this case, the majority of Fellows were inclined to vote black or gray. ∎

²⁰And when they had made fun of him, they stripped off the purple and put his own clothes back on him. And they lead him out to crucify him.

²¹And they conscript someone named Simon of Cyrene, who was coming in from the country, the father of Alexander and Rufus, to carry his cross.

²²And they bring him to the place Golgotha (which means "Place of the Skull"). ²³And they tried to give him wine mixed with myrrh, but he didn't take it. ²⁴And they crucify him, and they divide up his garments, casting lots to see who would get what. ²⁵It was 9 o'clock in the morning when they crucified him. ²⁶And the inscription, which identified his crime, read,

---

Matt 27:38–44 ➡ Mark 15:27–32

³⁸Then they crucified with him two rebels, one on his right and one on his left. ³⁹Those passing by kept taunting him, wagging their heads, and saying, ⁴⁰"You who would destroy the temple and rebuild it in three days, save yourself, if you're God's son, come down from the cross!" ⁴¹Likewise the ranking priests made fun of him along with the scribes and elders; they would say, ⁴²"Others he saved, but he can't save himself! He's the King of Israel; he should come down from the cross here and now and we'll trust in him. ⁴³He trusted in God, so God should rescue him now if he holds him dear. For he said, **'I'm God's son.'"** ⁴⁴In the same way the rebels who were crucified with him would abuse him.

Luke 23:32–43 ➡ Mark 15:27–32

³²Two others, who were criminals, were also led away with him to be put to death.

³³And when they came to the place called "The Skull," there they crucified him with the criminals, one on his right and the other on his left. ³⁴They divided up his garments after they cast lots. ³⁵And the people stood around, looking on. And the rulers were sneering at him, "Others he saved; he should save himself if he is God's Anointed, the Chosen One!" ³⁶The soldiers also made fun of him, coming up and offering him sour wine, ³⁷and saying, "If you are the King of the Jews, save yourself!" ³⁸There was also an inscription over him, 'This is the King of the Jews.' ³⁹One of the criminals hanging there kept treating him irreverently, "Aren't you the Anointed? Save yourself and us!" ⁴⁰But the other ⟨criminal⟩ rebuked him, "Don't you even fear God, since you are under the same sentence? ⁴¹We are getting justice, since we are getting what we deserve. But this man has done nothing improper." ⁴²And he implored, "Jesus, remember me when you come into your domain." ⁴³And ⟨Jesus⟩ said to him, **"I swear to you, today you'll be with me in paradise."**

'The King of the Jews.' ²⁷And with him they crucify two rebels, one on his right and one on his left. ²⁹Those passing by kept taunting him, wagging their heads, and saying, "Ha! You would destroy the temple and rebuild it in three days, ³⁰save yourself and come down from the cross!" ³¹Likewise the ranking priests had made fun of him to each other, along with the scribes; they would say, "Others he saved, but he can't save himself! ³²'The Anointed,' 'the King of Israel,' should come down from the cross here and now, so that we can see and trust for ourselves!" Even those being crucified along with him would abuse him.

Taunts

	Percentage				Wgt.
Saying	R	P	G	B	Av.
Mk 15:29	0	8	20	72	.12 B
Mt 27:40,43	0	4	16	80	.08 B
Lk 23:43	0	4	24	72	.11 B

GPet 4:1–5 ➡ Mark 15:27–32
¹And they brought two criminals and crucified the Lord between them. But he himself remained silent, as if in no pain. ²And when they set up the cross, they put an inscription on it, "This is the King of Israel." ³And they piled his clothing in front of him; then they divided it among themselves, and gambled for it. ⁴But one of those criminals reproached them and said, "We're suf-

fering for the evil that we've done, but this fellow, who has become a savior of humanity, what wrong has he done to you?" ⁵And they got angry at him and ordered that his legs not be broken so he would die in agony.

John 19:18 ➡ Mark 15:27–32
¹⁸Here they crucified him, and with him two others—one on each side and Jesus in the middle.

Mark 15:27–32
Words of Jesus. In this narrative segment, four sets of words are attributed to Jesus.

(a) The saying about destroying and rebuilding the temple in three days is attributed indirectly to Jesus by those passing by (Mark 15:29, Matt 27:40). This saying was discussed above, under Mark 14:58.

(b) The saying, "I'm God's son," is likewise attributed to Jesus by the ranking priests, scribes, and elders (Matt 27:43).

(c) "Father, forgive them, for they don't know what they're doing" is ascribed to Jesus in Luke 23:34, according to some manuscripts, but omitted in many others.

(d) "I swear to you, today you'll be

with me in paradise" (Luke 23:43).
Attribution.

(a) The first saying takes the form of an indirect statement in Mark 15:29; it was given as a direct quotation in Mark 14:58. Fellows designated Mark 14:58 gray, Mark 15:29 black because of this difference. See the *Notes* on Mark 14:58 for further details, and consult the remarks on various forms of quoted speech *Rules of Evidence,* under N1.

(b) The saying, Matt 27:43, is another example of how people around Jesus create direct speech for Jesus. Jesus does not elsewhere in the synoptic gospels claim to be God's son; others make that claim for him. In the Gospel of John, of course, Jesus makes this claim for himself (for example, 10:36). Members of the Seminar were of the opinion that this

Jesus' Dying Words

Saying	Percentage				Wgt.
	R	P	G	B	Av.
Mk 15:34	4	20	16	60	.23 B
Mt 27:46	8	12	20	60	.23 B
Lk 23:46	0	4	8	88	.05 B
Jn 19:28,30	4	4	4	88	.08 B
GPet 5:5	0	8	4	88	.07 B

[33]And when noon came, darkness blanketed the whole earth until mid-afternoon. [34]And at 3 o'clock in the afternoon Jesus shouted in a loud voice, "*Eloi, Eloi, lema sabachthani*" (which means "My God, my God, why did you abandon me?"). [35]And when some of those standing nearby heard, they would say, "Listen, he's calling Elijah!" [36]And someone ran and filled a sponge with sour wine, fixed it on a pole, and offered him a drink, saying, "Let's see if Elijah comes to take him down !" [37]But Jesus let out a

---

Matt 27:45–50 ➡ Mark 15:33–37

[45]Beginning at noon darkness blanketed the entire earth until mid-afternoon. [46]And about 3 o'clock in the afternoon Jesus shouted out in a loud voice, saying, "*Eli, Eli, lema sabachthani*" (which means, "My God, my God, why did you abandon me?") [47]When some of those standing there heard, they would say, "This fellow's calling Elijah!" [48]And immediately one of them ran and took a sponge filled with sour wine and fixed it on a pole and offered him a drink. [49]But the rest would say, "Let's see if Elijah comes to take him down." [50]Jesus again shouted in a loud voice and stopped breathing.

Luke 23:36, 44–46 ➡ Mark 15:33–37
[36]The soldiers also made fun of him, coming up and offering him sour wine,
. . .

[44]It was already about noon, and darkness blanketed the whole earth until mid-afternoon, [45]during an eclipse of the sun. The curtain of the temple was torn down the middle. [46]Then Jesus cried out with a loud cry and said, "**Father, into your hands I entrust my spirit!**" Having said this he breathed his last.

John 19:28–30 ➡ Mark 15:33–37
[28]Now that he knew that matters had run their course, so the scripture might come true, he says, "**I'm thirsty.**" [29]A bowl full of vinegar was sitting there, and so they took a sponge full of the sour wine, put it on hyssop, and brought it to his mouth. [30]When Jesus had taken some sour wine, he said, "**It's all over.**" His head sank, and he gave up his spirit.

---

title was conferred upon Jesus by the early Christian community and does not go back to Jesus (W8a).

(c) The saying in Luke 23:34 was probably inspired by the Lord's Prayer. In any case, the saying is not found in a number of important manuscripts and so probably does not belong to the original text of Luke (it is easier to explain its addition to Luke, than it is to explain its omission).

(d) The saying in Luke 23:43 was probably inspired by Luke 22:28–30, where Jesus tells his disciples that his Father has appointed a kingdom for him and there he will reign. The term paradise occurs only here in the gospels and thus is not found on the lips of Jesus elsewhere. This saying seems out of character for Jesus.

The Seminar coded all of these sayings black. ■

great shout and breathed his last. [38]And the curtain of the temple was torn in two from top to bottom! [39]When the centurion standing opposite him saw that he had died like this, he said, "This man really was God's son!" [40]Now some women were observing this from a distance, among whom were Mary of Magdala, and Mary the mother of James the younger and Joses, and Salome. [41]⟨These women⟩ had regularly followed and assisted him when he was in Galilee, along with many other women who had come up to Jerusalem in his company.

[42]And when it had already grown dark, since it was preparation day (the day before the sabbath), [43]Joseph of Arimathea, a respected member of the council, who himself was anticipating God's imperial rule, appeared, and dared to go to Pilate and request the body of Jesus. [44]And Pilate was surprised that he had died so soon.

GPet 5:1–6 ➡ Mark 15:33–37
[1]It was midday and darkness covered the whole of Judea. They were confused and anxious for fear the sun had set since he was still alive. ⟨For⟩ it is written that, "The sun must not set upon one who has been executed." [2]And one of them said, "Give him vinegar mixed with something bitter to drink." And they mixed it and gave it to him to drink. [3]And they fulfilled all things and brought to completion the sins on their head. [4]Now many went about with lamps, and, thinking that it was night, they laid down. [5]And the Lord cried out, saying, **"My power, (my) power, you have abandoned me."** When he said this, he was taken up. [6]And at that moment, the veil of the Jerusalem temple was torn in two.

Mark 15:33–37
Words of Jesus. Four different utterances are attributed to the dying Jesus.

(a) "My God, my God, why did you abandon me?" is taken from Ps 22:1 (Mark 15:34, Matt 27:46).

(b) "Father, into your hands I entrust my spirit!" is inspired by Ps 31:5 (Luke 23:46).

(c) "I'm thirsty" (John 19:28) was probably suggested by Ps 69:21.

(d) "It's all over" (John 19:30) echoes Job 19:25–27 (LXX).

Attribution. All the words attributed to Jesus as he dies are taken from scripture, principally the Psalms (O5). Psalm 22:1 appears first in the tradition; it occurs in the same Psalm from which the theme of dividing Jesus' clothes comes (Ps 22:18). Luke probably thought the lament of Ps 22:1 was too harsh to put on the lips of Jesus, so substituted words more suitable to the course of his own gospel (W4). John adopted a different course but stayed with the tradition of quoting scripture as the final gasp of Jesus (O5).

All of these sayings are of course the work of the individual evangelists. ■

He summoned the centurion and asked him whether he had been dead for long. [45]And when he had been briefed by the centurion, he granted the body to Joseph. [46]And he bought a shroud and took him down and wrapped him in the shroud, and placed him in a tomb that had been hewn out of rock, and rolled a stone up against the opening of the tomb. [47]And Mary of Magdala and Mary the mother of Joses noted where he had been laid to rest.

16 And when the sabbath day was over, Mary of Magdala and Mary the mother of James and Salome bought spices so they could go and embalm him. [2]And very early on the first day of the week they got to the tomb just as the sun was coming up. [3]And they had been saying to themselves, "Who will help us roll the stone away from the opening of the tomb?" [4]And they look up and see that the stone has been rolled away! (For in fact the stone was very large.) [5]And when they went into the tomb, they saw a youth sitting on the right, wearing a white robe, and they were apprehensive. [6]He says to them,

---

Matt 28:1–10 → Mark 16:1–8

[1]After the sabbath day, at first light on the first day of the week, Mary of Magdala and the other Mary came to inspect the tomb. [2]And just then there was a strong earthquake. You see, an angel of the Lord had come down from the sky, had arrived ⟨at the tomb⟩, had rolled away the stone, and was sitting on it. [3]The messenger gave off a dazzling light, and wore clothes as white as snow. [4]Now those who kept watch were paralyzed with fear, and looked like corpses themselves. [5]In response the messenger said to the women, "Don't be frightened! For I know you are looking for Jesus who was crucified. [6]He is not here! You see, he was raised, just as he said. Come, see the spot where he was lying. [7]And go quickly, tell his disciples that he was raised from the dead. See here, he is going ahead of you to Galilee. There you will see him. Now I have told you so." [8]And they hastened from the tomb, full of apprehension and an overpowering joy, and ran to tell his disciples.

[9]And then Jesus met them saying, "Rejoice!" They came up and took hold of his feet and made obeisance to him. [10]Then Jesus says to them, "**Do not be afraid. Go, make your announcement to your brothers so that they may depart for Galilee and there they will see me.**"

"Don't be alarmed! You are looking for Jesus the Nazarene who was crucified. He was raised, he is not here! Here is the spot where they put him! [7]But go and tell his disciples, including 'Rock,' he is going ahead of you to Galilee! There you will see him, just as he told you." [8]And once they got outside, they ran away from the tomb, because great fear and excitement gripped them. And they didn't breathe a word of it to anyone: talk about terrified . . .

Jesus and Galilee

Saying	Percentage				Wgt.
	R	P	G	B	Av.
Mk 16:7	0	4	12	84	.07 **B**
Mt 28:10	0	0	8	92	.03 **B**
Lk 24:7	0	4	8	88	.05 **B**

Luke 24:1–11 ➡ Mark 16:1–8

[1]But on the first day of the week, they went to the tomb at daybreak, bringing the spices they had prepared. [2]They found the stone rolled back from the tomb, [3]but when they went inside they did not find the body of the Lord Jesus. [4]And it so happened, while they were uncertain about what to do, suddenly, two men appeared in dazzling clothing and stood beside them. [5]They were frightened and prostrated themselves on the ground; the men said to them, "Why do you seek the living among the dead? [6][He is not here—he was raised.] Remember what he told you, while he was still in Galilee: [7]"The son of Adam must be turned over to villains, be crucified, and on the third day come back to life." [8]And they recalled what he had said. [9]And returning from the tomb, they related everything to the eleven and to everybody else. [10]The group included Mary of Magdala and Joanna and Mary the mother of James, and the rest of the women with them. They related their story to the apostles, [11]but their story struck them as nonsense, so they refused to believe the women.

Mark 16:1–8

Words of Jesus. Once again we find words attributed to Jesus indirectly in both Mark and Luke. Matthew, however, quotes Jesus directly in 28:10.

(a) In Mark 16:7, the youth in a white robe who appeared at the tomb instructs the women to go and tell his disciples that he is going to Galilee and there you will see him, "just as he told you." The last phrase is a reference to Mark 14:28, discussed above.

In the parallel in Matt 28:7, the same words are spoken by the angel, but this time attributed to the angel directly, and not to an earlier statement of Jesus.

(b) In Matt 28:10, the same words are quoted directly from Jesus.

(c) In contrast, Luke has two men in dazzling garments appear to the women at the tomb and remind them of Jesus' prediction that he would be crucified and on the third day come back to life (Luke 24:6–7). The reference is to the two predictions of the passion in Luke 9:18–22 and 18:31–34.

Attribution. By definition, words ascribed to Jesus after his death are not subject to historical verification. Many in the early Christian world, and in the Christian world now, believed and believe that Jesus spoke and speaks directly to human beings after his death. Such claims are beyond the limits of historical assessment (N4).

In the gospel tradition, however, words spoken by Jesus during his life are sometimes transferred to him after his resurrection (the Gospel of Thomas, for example, assigns all sayings to the "liv-

⁹[[Now after he arose at daybreak on the first day of the week, he appeared first to Mary of Magdala, from whom he had driven out seven demons. ¹⁰She went and told those who were close to him, who were mourning and weeping. ¹¹But when those folks heard that he was alive and had been seen by her, they didn't believe it.]]

¹²[[A little later he appeared to two of them in a different guise as they were walking along, on their way to the country. ¹³And these two returned and told the others. They did not believe them either.]]

¹⁴[[Later he appeared to the eleven as they were reclining ⟨at a meal⟩. He reproached them for their lack of trust and obstinacy, because they did not believe those who had seen him after he had been raised. ¹⁵And he said to them: **"Go out into the whole world and announce the good news to every creature. ¹⁶Whoever trusts and is baptized will be saved. The one who lacks trust will be condemned. ¹⁷These are the signs that will accompany those who have trust: they will drive out demons in my name; they will speak in new tongues; ¹⁸they will pick up snakes with their hands; and even if they swallow poison, it certainly won't harm them; they will lay their hands on those who are sick, and they will get well."**]]

Comission and Promise

Saying	Percentage				Wgt.
	R	P	G	B	Av.
Mk 16:15–18	0	0	0	100	.00 **B**

ing" Jesus, which probably means the risen Jesus). Words supposedly spoken by the resurrected Jesus are also occasionally moved to a point in his life. Consequently, the Jesus Seminar decided in some instances to evaluate such words as though they were spoken by a historical figure.

The uncertainty surrounding the speaker of the words reported in Mark 16:7 (with reference to Mark 14:28), Matt 28:7, and 28:10 casts doubt on their attribution to Jesus at this point in the narrative. The earlier evaluation of Mark 14:28 by Fellows has already labelled this saying black.

Similarly, the recollection of Jesus' prediction of his death in Luke 24:6–7 depends on the assessment of those predictions earlier in Luke: they were all designated black, since they are shaped by the early Christian kerygma (gospel) (W8a). For discussion, see the *Notes* on Mark 8:31–34. ■

[19][[The Lord Jesus, after he said these things, was taken up into the sky and sat down at the right hand of God. [20]Those ⟨to whom he had spoken⟩ went out and made their announcement everywhere, and the Lord worked with them and certified what they said by means of accompanying signs.]]

[21][[They promptly reported all the instructions they had been given to Peter and his companions. Afterwards Jesus himself, using them as agents, broadcast the sacred and imperishable message of eternal salvation from one end of the earth to the other.]]

Mark 16:15–18

Source. Mark 16:9–21 (the longer and shorter endings to the Gospel of Mark) did not form a part of the original text of Mark. These verses are not found in the best manuscripts. Further, the vocabulary and style of the two endings differ markedly from the rest of the Gospel.

Attribution. Words ascribed to Jesus after his death are not subject to historical verification (N4). The words recorded in Mark 16:15–18 reflect the early Christian world mission as variously formulated by Matthew (28:16–20), Luke (24:44–48), John (20:19–23), and Acts (1:8)—all of which are composed in the language of the respective evangelists (W4). ■

EARLIEST GREEK MANUSCRIPTS
OF THE GOSPEL OF MARK

The earliest manuscripts of Greek Mark are listed in chronological order. Since many ancient manuscripts are fragmentary the contents of each is listed. Also provided are the place and date of discovery and the present location. The final piece of information concerns the first appearance of the variants provided by each in a critical edition of the Greek New Testament.

The five earliest witnesses to the text of Mark have all been discovered in the last 150 years and have been included in critical editions for the most part only in the twentieth century.

$\mathfrak{P}^{45}$ Chester Beatty Papyrus I

Contents: Mark 4:36–9:31; 11:27–12:28
Date of manuscript: 200–250 C.E.
Discovery: Unknown; purchased in
   1930–1931
Current location: Chester Beatty
   Collection, Dublin
Added to critical edition: Nestle[16] 1936

PDura[10] (0212)

Contents: Mark 15:40, 42
Date of manuscript: Third century C.E.
Discovery: Dura-Europos (Iraq), 1933
Current location: Yale University
First published: 1935
Added to critical edition: Nestle[26] 1979

$\mathfrak{P}^{88}$

Contents: Mark 2:2–26
Date of manuscript: Fourth century C.E.
Discovery: Date and location unknown
Current location: Catholic University,
   Milan
First published: 1972
Added to critical edition: Nestle[26] 1979

‫א‬, Codex Sinaiticus

Contents: Complete Gospel of Mark
Date of manuscript: Fourth century C.E.
Discovery: Monastery of St. Catherine
   (Sinai), 1844
Current location: British Museum,
   London
First published: 1908, 1911
Added to critical edition: Tischendorf,
   1869–1872

B, Codex Vaticanus

Contents: Complete Gospel of Mark
Date of manuscript: Fourth century C.E.
Discovery: Unknown
Current location: Vatican Library
First published: 1868–1872
Added to critical edition: Westcott and
   Hort, 1881

FURTHER READING

The place to begin the study of Mark and parallel texts is with the proper study instruments.

STUDY INSTRUMENTS

Funk, Robert W., ed. *New Gospel Parallels.* Vol. 1,2: *Mark.* Rev. ed. Sonoma, CA: Polebridge Press, 1990.

> The editor has revised the first edition of *New Gospel Parllels* by breaking the gospels into short lines (called cola) and matching them up wherever possible. The reader can tell at a glance what the gospels have in common and where they differ. Vol. 1, 2 contains only the Gospel of Mark, of course, with all its parallels in both canonical and extracanonical gospels. Vol. 1,1: Matthew and Vol. 1,3: Luke will follow.
>
> *New Gospel Parallels* makes use of the new Scholars Version of the gospels.

Crossan, J. Dominic, ed. *Jesus Parallels.* Sonoma, CA: Polebridge Press, 1991.

> This is the revised and enlarged edition of *Sayings Parallels.* Prof. Crossan has added the deeds of Jesus to the inventory and arranged the entire corpus of texts in a new, easy to use configuration. *Jesus Parallels* covers all surviving texts containing information about Jesus that can be dated to 300 c.e. or earlier.

Miller, Robert J., ed. *The Complete Gospels. Annotated Scholars Version.* Sonoma, CA: Polebridge Press, 1991.

> This volume contains all the gospel records from the first three centuries in a new translation to be known as Scholars Version. The translators have provided brief introductions to each gospel, together with notes on the text.

Cameron, Ron, ed. *The Other gospels: Non-Canonical Gospel Texts.* Philadelphia: The Westminster Press, 1982.

> A convenient, useful compendium of non-canonical gospels. The author has provided lucid, compact introductions to each of the texts.

Schmidt, Daryl D. *The Gospel of Mark.* The Scholars Bible 1. Sonoma, CA: Polebridge Press, 1991. Introduction and Notes with Greek text and Scholars Version on facing pages.

The new Scholars Version is laid out on right hand pages facing the Greek text on left hand pages for the benefit of the student. The author has prepared an extensive introduction to Mark, along with explanatory notes on difficult passages or problems of translation.

Kloppenborg, John S., et al. *Q–Thomas Reader.* Sonoma, CA: Polebridge Press, 1990.

This handy volume contains the texts of Q and the Gospel of Thomas in translation. Each is preceded by a lucid introduction. The Coptic text of Thomas is included for reference.

Kloppenborg, John S. *Q Parallels: Synopsis, Critical Notes, & Concordance.* Sonoma, CA: Polebridge Press, 1988.

This volume is the basic instrument for the study of Q. It presents all Q texts, with all parallels, in both original languages and translation. The author has incorporated brief scholarly notes for each section.

RULES OF EVIDENCE

The author has utilized all the papers produced by Fellows of the Jesus Seminar over a six-year period in formulating the rules of evidence for determining what Jesus really said. However, the following have been particularly useful in organizing the rules systematically.

Boring, M. Eugene. "Criteria of Authenticity: The Lucan Beatitudes as a Test Case." *Forum* 1,4 (1985) 3–38.
Patterson, Stephen J. "Fire and Dissension: Ipsissima Vox Jesu in Q 12:49, 51–53?" *Forum* 5,2 (1989) 121–39.
Vaage, Leif E. "Q¹ and the Historical Jesus: Some Peculiar Sayings (7:33–34; 9:57–58; 59–60; 14:26–27)." *Forum* 5,2 (1989) 159–76.
Funk, Robert W. "Unraveling the Jesus Tradition: Criteria and Criticism." *Forum* 5,2 (1989) 31–62.

THE GOSPEL OF MARK
Sayings, Parables, & Anecdotes

Bultmann, Rudolf. *History of the Synoptic Tradition.* Trans John Marsh. Rev. ed. San Franciso: Harper & Row, 1963.
Crossan, J. Dominic. *In Fragments: The Aphorisms of Jesus.* San Francisco: Harper & Row, 1983; Sonoma: Polebridge Press, 1990.
Crossan, J. Dominic. *In Parables: The Challenge of the Historical Jesus.* San Francisco: Harper & Row, 1976; Sonoma: Polebridge Press, 1990.
Funk, Robert W. *Jesus as Precursor.* Rev. ed. Edited by Edward F. Beutner. Sonoma: Polebridge Press, 1991.
Kelber, Werner H. *The Oral and the Written Gospel. The Hermeneutics of Speaking and Writing in the Synoptic Tradition.* Philadelphia: Fortress Press, 1983.

Koester, Helmut. *Ancient Christian Gospels: Their History and Development.* Philadelphia: Trinity Press International, 1990.

Mack, Burton L. *A Myth of Innocence. Mark and Christian Origins.* Philadelphia: Fortress Press, 1988.

Mack, Burton L. and Vernon K. Robbins. *Patterns of Persuasion in the Gospels.* Foundations & Facets. Sonoma: Polebridge Press, 1989.

Scott, Bernard Brandon. *Hear Then the Parable. A Commentary on the Parables.* Philadelphia: Fortress Press, 1988.

Sellew, Philip. *Dominical Discourses: Oral Clusters in the Jesus Sayings Tradition.* Minneapolis: Fortress Press, 1991.

PASSION NARRATIVE

Crossan, J. Dominic. *The Cross that Spoke. Origins of the Passion Narrative.* San Francisco: Harper & Row, 1988; Sonoma: Polebridge Press, 1990.

Kelber, Werner H., ed. *The Passion in Mark: Studies on Mark 14–16.* Philadelphia: Fortress Press, 1976.

RED LETTER EDITIONS

Funk, Robert W., et al. *The Parables of Jesus: Red Letter Edition.* Sonoma: Polebridge Press, 1988.

Smith, Mahlon H. *The Sayings Gospel Q: Red Letter Edition.* Sonoma: Polebridge Press, in preparation.

Patterson, Stephen J. *The Gospel of Thomas: Red Letter Edition.* Sonoma: Polebridge Press, in preparation.

Dewey, Arthur J. *The Gospel of Matthew: Red Letter Edition.* Sonoma: Polebridge Press, in preparation.

Miller, Robert J. *The Gospel of Luke: Red Letter Edition.* Sonoma: Polebridge Press, in preparation.

Fortna, Robert T., and Julian V. Hills. The *Gospel of John: Red Letter Edition.* Sonoma: Polebridge Press, in preparation.

Funk, Robert W., and Roy W. Hoover. *The Five Gospels: Red Letter Edition.* Sonoma: Polebridge Press, 1991.

CRITICAL SCHOLARSHIP

Fellows of the Jesus Seminar are critical biblical scholars. What does it mean to be a critical scholar of the Bible?

Critical in popular usage suggests someone who is excessively critical, judgmental, or inclined to find fault unnecessarily. Among scholars, critical scholarship means to "exercise careful judgment" or "render judicious evaluation," and this is the dictionary definition. Literary criticism is the careful, painstaking, judicious reading and interpretation of literary works. Art criticism performs a similar function on works of art. Biblical criticism involves this same type of scholarly endeavor. What makes a biblical critic different from other kinds of biblical interpeters?

1. Critical scholars employ the critical methodologies pertinent to their fields of study. In the biblical field, scholars must be able to read the Bible in its original languages—Hebrew, Aramaic, Greek. They must also be trained as historians: they know how to gather data from texts and other artifacts unearthed by archaeologists, and they know how to organize and interpret such data. Because they must deal with handwritten manuscripts, biblical scholars must know textual criticism—how to locate and evaluate variant readings in their sources. Since the Bible is also literature, they must know literary criticism as it pertains to biblical texts. Since they are historians of religious movements and institutions, they must know something of the social-scientific method. Other disciplines or fields of study for which critical biblical scholars have regular need include archaeology, linguistics, philosophy and theology, and computer science.

2. Critical scholars make themselves accountable to an established body of knowledge and theory. Biblical scholars must be acquainted with the history of biblical scholarship: they must be able to show how their work corrects or improves upon previous work done on the same topic and problem. They must know the theories and methods they employ in their research, and be able to defend those procedures. This responsibility rests on a knowledge of the basic reference works in the field and of the standard critical literature.

3. Critical scholars must of course know the Bible intimately. But they must also know the relevant comparative literature for their fields of specialization. If they are specialists in Proverbs or Ecclesiastes, for example, they must know the wisdom literature of the Ancient Near East. If they

concentrate on the Book of Revelation, to be qualifed as competent, they must be acquainted with the vast array of apocalyptic literature in late antiquity. The study of comparative literature often involves other ancient languages such as Latin and Coptic for the New Testament, and Babylonian, Ugaritic, Sumerian, Egyptian, and other exotic tongues for the Old Testament.

4. Critical scholars practice their craft by submitting their work to the critical assessment of peers. Untested work is held in low esteem.

5. Critical scholars measure their work by the standards and criteria common to all scholarship. That is what makes scholarly work critical: the acceptance and use of established standards and criteria.

6. Special pleading is not admissible. Theological position or church doctrine cannot be advanced as the basis for critical historical evaluation. To be sure, scholars are human and subject to hidden prejudice. The only means they have of protecting themselves against the intrusion of private proclivities is to insist that every fact, every theory, stand the test of examination by other scholars with different private interests but common standards.

Critical biblical scholars reflect a broad spectrum of religious belief, including agnosticism and atheism. However, the majority of them come from mainline churches, Protestant and Catholic, and from Judaism, principally the Reformed and Conservative traditions. The Jesus Seminar draws its members from the U.S.A. and Canada, and from Europe. It has one member who lives in Peru.

Fellows of the Jesus Seminar, like other critical scholars of the Bible, have been trained in the great universities of the world and in denominational seminaries. The roster of active Fellows with their pedigrees speaks for itself.

FELLOWS
of
The Jesus Seminar

Harold Attridge, University of Notre Dame
A.B., Boston College
M.A., Cambridge University
Ph.D., Harvard University
Special study: Hebrew University of Jerusalem

William Beardslee, Center For Process Studies
A.B., Harvard University
M.A., Union Theological Seminary
B.D., New Brunswick Theological Seminary
Ph.D., University of Chicago
Special study: University of Bonn

George R. Beasley-Murray
A.B., Jesus College, Cambridge University
M.Th., Kings College, London University
D.D., London University; Cambridge
University
Special study: Jesus College, Cambridge; Kings
College, London

Edward F. Beutner, Santa Clara University
A.B., St. Francis Seminary, Milwaukee
M.A., St. Louis University
Ph.D., Graduate Theological Union, Berkeley

Sterling Bjorndahl, Camrose Lutheran
University College
A.B., Luther College, University of Regina
M.A., Claremont Graduate School
M.Div., Lutheran Theological Seminary,
Saskatoon
Ph.D., Claremont Graduate School
(candidate)

Marcus Borg, Oregon State University
A.B., Concordia College
M.Th., Oxford University
D.Phil., Oxford University
Special study: Union Theological Seminary,
NYC; University of Tübingen

Willi Braun, Centre for Religious Studies,
University of Toronto
A.B., University of Manitoba
M.A., University of St. Michael's College
Ph.D., University of Toronto (candidate)

Ron Cameron, Wesleyan University
A.B., Western Kentucky University
M.T.S., Harvard Divinity School
Ph.D, Harvard University
Special study: University of Manchester,
University of Tübingen

Bruce D. Chilton, Bard College
A.B., Bard College
M.Div., The General Theological Seminary
Ph.D., Cambridge University (St, John's
College)
Special study: Institutum Judaicum
Delitzschanum, Münster

Wendy J. Cotter C.S.J., University of St.
Michael's College
M.A., University of St. Michael's College

John Dominic Crossan, DePaul University
D.D., Maynooth College, Ireland
Special study: Biblical Institute, Rome; Ecole
Biblique, Jerusalem

Jon Daniels, Defiance College
A.B., Wesleyan University
M.T.S., Harvard Divinity School
Ph.D., Claremont Graduate School

Jon F. Dechow, Westar Institute
B.A., Concordia Seminary, St. Louis
M.Div., Concordia Seminary, St. Louis
Ph.D., University of Pennsylvania

Arthur J. Dewey, Xavier University
A.B., Boston College
M.Div., Weston School of Theology
Th.D., Harvard University

Dennis C. Duling, Canisius College
A.B., College of Wooster
M.A., University of Chicago
B.D., McCormick Theological Seminary
Ph.D., University of Chicago
Special Study: Heidelberg University; Yale
    University; Yeshiva University

Karl Eklund, Berkley, Massachusetts
B.S., Massachusetts Institute of Technology
M.A., Columbia University
Ph.D., Columbia University

Robert T. Fortna, Vassar College
B.A., Yale University
M.A., Cambridge University
B.D., Church Divinity School of the Pacific
Th.D., Union Theological Seminary, New
    York
Special study: Ecumenical Institute,
    Jerusalem; American School of Oriental
    Research/Albright Institute, Jerusalem

Robert W. Funk, Westar Institute
A.B., Butler University
M.A., Butler University
B.D., Christian Theological Seminary
Ph.D., Vanderbilt University
Special study: Ecumenical Institute,
    Switzerland; American School of Oriental
    Research, Jerusalem; University of
    Tübingen; University of Toronto

Heinz Guenther, Emmanuel College of
    Victoria University
A.B., Kirchl. Hochschule, Wuppertal,
    University of Heidelberg
S.T.M., Union Theological Seminary, New
    York
Th.D., University of Toronto
Special study: University of Hamburg;
    Ecumenical Institute, Bossey, Switzerland;
    Kwansei Gakuin University, Nishinomiya,
    Japan

Stephen L. Harris, California State University,
    Sacramento
A.B., University of Puget Sound
M.A., Cornell University
Ph.D., Cornell University

Charles W. Hedrick, Southwest Missouri State
    University
B.A., Mississippi College
B.D., Golden Gate Southern Baptist Seminary
M.A., University of Southern California
Ph.D., Claremont Graduate School

Ian H. Henderson, McGill University
B.A., University of Manitoba
M.A., McMaster University
B.D., University of St. Andrews
D.Phil., Oxford University
Special study: University of Heidelberg

James D. Hester, University of Redlands
A.B., Eastern Baptist College
B.D., California Baptist Theological Seminary
D.Theol., University of Basel, Switzerland

C.M. Kempton Hewitt, Methodist Theological
    School in Ohio
B.A., Cascade College
B.D., Garrett Evangelical Theological
    Seminary
S.T.M., Yale University Divinity School
Ph.D., University of Durham, England
Special study: University of Basel, Switzer-
    land; Kerk en Wereld, Netherlands; Centro
    de Idioma y Cultura Latinoamericano,
    Mexico

Julian V. Hills, Marquette University
A.B., University of Durham
S.T.M., McCormick Theological Seminary
Th.D., Harvard University
Special study: Westar Institute

Roy Hoover, Whitman College
A.B., Pasadena College
Th.D., Harvard University

Arland Jacobson, Concordia College
B.A., Augustiana College, Sioux Falls
B.D., Lutheran Theological Seminary
Ph.D., Claremont Graduate School
Special Study: Chicago Divinity School

Clayton N. Jefford, St. Meinrad Seminary
A.B., Furman University
M.A., Claremont Graduate School
Th.M.; M.Div., South Eastern Baptist
    Theological Seminary
Ph.D., Claremont Graduate School

Perry Kea, University of Indianapolis
A.B., University of South Carolina
M.A., Vanderbilt University
Ph.D., University of Virginia
Special study: Westar Institute

Karen King, Occidental College
A.B., University of Montana
Ph.D. Brown University
Special study: Freie Universität; Humboldt University, Berlin

John S. Kloppenborg, University of St. Michael's College
B.A., University of Lethbridge
M.A., University of St. Michael's College
Ph.D., University of St. Michael's College

John Lown, National University, San Diego
B.A., Cambridge University
M.A., Cambridge University
M.A., Vanderbilt University
B.D., Nazarene Theological Seminary
Ph.D., Vanderbilt University
Special Study: Publishing Institute of Montana

Loren Mack-Fisher, The Double Bar A Ranch
A.B., University of Oregon
M.A., Butler University
Ph.D., Brandeis University
Special study: Hebrew Union College, Jerusalem; Collège de France

Lane C. McGaughy, Willamette University
A.B., Ohio Wesleyan University
M.A., Vanderbilt University
B.D., Drew Theological Seminary
Ph.D., Vanderbilt University
Special study: University of Tübingen; Harvard Divinity School; Yale Divinity School; Ecumenical Institute, Tantur

Edward J. McMahon II, Texas Christian University
A.B., University of Notre Dame
M.A., Vanderbilt University
Ph.D., Vanderbilt University

Marvin W. Meyer, Chapman College
A.B., Calvin College
M.Div., Calvin Theological Seminary
Ph.D., Claremont Graduate School

J. Ramsey Michaels, S.W. Missouri State University
A.B., Princeton University
B.D., Grace Theological Seminary
Th.M., Westminster Theological College
Th.D., Harvard University

Robert J. Miller, Midway College
B.A., St. John's College
M.A., University of California, Santa Barbara
M.A., Claremont Graduate School
Ph.D., Claremont Graduate School
Special study: Vanderbilt University

Winsome Munro, St. Olaf College
A.B., Witwatersrand University
B.D., Birmingham University
S.T.M., Union Theological Seminary, New York
Ed.D., Teachers College, Columbia University and Union Theological Seminary

Culver H. Nelson, Church of the Beatitudes (UCC)
A.B., University of Redlands
M.A., University of Southern California
L.H.D., University of Redlands
D.D., Pacific School of Religion
D.D., Doane College
Special study: Pacific School of Religion; University of Southern California

Rod Parrott, Disciples Seminary Foundation
B.Th., Northwest Christian College
M.Div., The Graduate Seminary, Phillips University
M.Th., The Graduate Seminary, Phillips University
Ph.D., Claremont Graduate School
Special study: Hebrew Union College; University of Oklahoma

Stephen Patterson, Eden Theological Seminary
A.B., Yankton College
M.A., Claremont Graduate School
M.T.S., Harvard University
Ph.D., Claremont Graduate School
Special study: Heidelberg University

Vernon K. Robbins, Emory University
A.B., Westmar College, Iowa
M.A., University of Chicago
B.D., United Theological Seminary, Ohio
Ph.D., University of Chicago

John J. Rousseau, University of California, Berkeley
Ph.B., University of Paris
M.S., Collège Libre des Sciences Sociales et Economiques, Paris
Cambridge Diploma of English Studies
Ph.D., University of Paris
D.Rel., School of Theology at Claremont
Special study: University of Nevada, Las Vegas; University of Haifa; Pacific School of Religion; Saint George's College, Jerusalem

Daryl D. Schmidt, Texas Christian University
A.B., Bethel College
M.Div., Associated Mennonite Biblical Seminaries
Ph.D., Graduate Theological Union

Bernard Brandon Scott, Phillips Graduate Seminary, Tulsa Center
A.B., St. Meinrad
M.A., Miami University
Ph.D., Vanderbilt University
Special study: Yale University

Philip Sellew, University of Minnesota
A.B., Macalester College
M.Div., Harvard Divinity School
Th.D., Harvard University

Dennis Smith, Phillips Graduate Seminary
A.B., Abilene Christian University
M.A., Abilene Christian University
M.Div., Princeton Theological Seminary
Th.D., Harvard University

Mahlon H. Smith, Rutgers University
A.B., Rutgers University
B.D., Drew University
M.S.L., Pontifical Institute of Medieval Studies, Toronto
Special study: Université Catholique de Louvain, Belgium

Michael G. Steinhauser, Toronto School of Theology
A.B., Cathedral College, Brooklyn
M.A., University of Innsbruck
Th.D., University of Munich

Robert F. Stoops, Jr., Western Washington University
A.B., University of North Carolina, Chapel Hill
M.Div., Harvard Divinity School
Ph.D., Harvard University

W. Barnes Tatum, Greensboro College
A.B., Birmingham Southern College
B.D., Duke University
Ph.D., Duke University
Special study: University of St. Andrews, Scotland

Hal Taussig, St. Joseph's University
A.B., Antioch College
M.Div., Methodist Theological School in Ohio
Ph.D., The Union Institute
Special study: Institut Catholique, Paris; University of Basel, Switzerland

Paul Verhoeven, Brooksfilms
Ph.D., University of Leiden

Wesley Hiram Wachob, Emory University
A.B., South-Eastern Bible College
M.Div., Candler School of Theology, Emory University
Ph.D., Emory University

John L. White, Loyola University of Chicago
A.B., William Jewell College
M.A., Vanderbilt University
B.D., Colgate Rochester Divinity School
Ph.D., Vanderbilt University
Special study: University of Toronto

Walter Wink, Auburn Theological Seminary
A.B., Southern Methodist University
B.D., Union Theological Seminary, New York
Th.D., Union Theological Seminary, New York
Special study: Oxford University; Peace Fellow, U.S. Institute of Peace, Washington D.C.

GLOSSARY

Albright, W. F. W. F. Albright was for many years preeminent among Old Testament scholars. He was a master of many Semitic and modern languages, a superb field archaeologist, and had an encyclopedic command of the entire domain of biblical studies. He is perhaps best known for his *From the Stone Age to Christianity.* He served as Director of the American School of Oriental Research in Jerusalem from 1920–29, and held a distinguished chair of Semitic Studies at Johns Hopkins University from 1929 until his retirement in 1958. He died in 1971.

Apocalypticism. Apocalypticism is the view that history will come to an end and a new age begin following a cosmic catastrophe. Such views are frequently expressed in an apocalypse: a revelation through a heavenly vision of events to come.

Aphorism. Aphorisms and proverbs are striking one-liners. An aphorism is a short, provocative saying that challenges the established, the accepted, view of things. A proverb embodies common sense. A proverb: "Early to bed, early to rise, makes one healthy, wealthy, and wise." An aphorism: "It's not what goes into a person that defiles, but what comes out" (Mark 7:15).

Apology. An apology is the defense or justification of a point of view, usually the Christian perspective. Fellows of the Seminar who are also church leaders and theologians may of course have hidden agendas that they want, subconsciously, to defend. And Fellows may also have secular agendas that prompt them to react against the Christian perspective.

Apostles' Creed. The so-called Apostles' Creed is alleged to have been created by the twelve apostles, each of them contributing one of the twelve articles. In its present form, the creed goes back only to the sixth century c.e., although its content may be much older.

Barnabas, Epistle of. Barnabas is a treatise in letter form, attributed to Barnabas, the companion of Paul. It was written towards the end of the first century c.e.

Bultmann, R. Rudolf Bultmann is undoubtedly the most influential New Testament scholar of the twentieth century. He is famous for his demythologizing proposal, which led to worldwide controversy following the Second World War. His book, *Jesus and the Word,* summarizes his views of the historical Jesus, which were based on the dissimilarity concept. Bultmann died in 1976.

Canon. A collection or authoritative list of books accepted as holy scripture. The canon was determined for Roman Catholics at the Council of Trent in 1546 c.e.; it has never been determined for Protestants, except by common consent and the action of some individual denominations.

C.E., B.C.E. c.e. stands for Common Era, b.c.e. for Before the Common Era. These designations are used rather than the earlier forms (a.d., b.c.) out of deference to those for whom the birth of Jesus marks the beginning of a new era only in a secular sense.

Chalcedon, Council of. The Council of Chalcedon, convened in 451 c.e., adopted a christological formula that emphasized both the divinity and the humanity of Jesus: Jesus was both fully divine and fully human.

Chreia (plural: chreiai). Chreia is the term of hellenistic rhetoricians for what may be called an anecdote or pronouncement story. A chreia is a short story depicting a situation to which a sage or prominent person gives a response, usually in the form of an aphorism or proverb. *Ancient Quotes and Anedotes* is a collection of hundreds of cheiai from hellenistic literature arranged topically.

1 Clement. A letter written from Clement of Rome to the church at Corinth about 95 C.E.

2 Clement. 2 Clement is a sermon attributed to Clement of Rome. It dates from about 150 C.E.

Codex and scroll. The earlier form of the book was the scroll. The codex, which is a stack of sheets the same size bound or tied on one side, replaced the scroll in the first century C.E. because codices were easier to use and store. The modern book is a codex in form.

Critic, critical. To be critical in the popular mind means "to criticize, to find fault with." But the basic meaning of *critical* is "to exercise careful, considered judgment." Biblical critics are critics in the second, positive sense, as are art critics and literary critics. For biblical scholars *critical* also means to exercise judgment independently of all theological dogma.

Didache. A compendium of teachings attributed to the twelve apostles. It was compiled in the early second century C.E., partly out of older materials.

Enlightenment. The Enlightenment refers to a movement in philosophy that advocated the untrammeled use of reason to establish truth. The movement challenged traditional authority, doctrine, and values. Emphasis was placed on the empirical method employed by the sciences. The movement began in the seventeenth century.

Fellow (of the Jesus Seminar). Fellows of the Jesus Seminar have had advanced training in biblical studies. Most of them hold the Ph.D. or equivalent from one of the world's leading institutions. For additional information, consult the appendix: Critical Scholarship and the roster of Fellows.

Galileo. Galileo Galilei (1564–1642), Italian astronomer and physicist, became convinced of Copernicus' theory, through his work with the telescope, that the earth revolves around the sun. He was forced to recant such 'heresies.'

Gnosticism, Gnostic. Gnosticism gets its name from the Greek word *gnosis* meaning knowledge or insight. For gnostics the world is divided into realms of darkness and light. The realm of darkness is the concrete world of sticks and stones, whereas the realm of light is above, completely isolated from the fallen world below. The creator God of the Old Testament is therefore a lesser god, the source of the corrupt creation. *Gnosis* is the means of salvation for the selected few; it is the means of finding one's way back to the realm of light above. In gnostic gospels, it is usually the risen Jesus—the one belonging to the realm of light—that instructs his disciples.

Gospel of Signs. The identification of a signs source for the Gospel of John is based on two prominent miracle stories in John, the miracle at Cana (2:1–11) and the cure of the nobleman's son (4:46–54), which are numbered one and two (2:11, 4:54). Several other miracle stories in John are believed to have derived from this source.

Gospel parallels. In a gospel parallels or synopsis the gospels are arranged in parallel columns with matching materials opposite each other. *New Gospel Parallels* is a synopsis incorporating the texts of all known written gospels.

Hermas. The Shepherd of Hermas consists of Visions, Mandates (Commandments), and Similitudes (Parables). It was composed about 100 C.E. by an unknown author.

Ignatius. Ignatius was bishop of Antioch in Syria. He was arrested and transported to Rome under guard around 110 C.E. On his way he wrote letters to several churches: Ephesians, Magnesians, Trallians, Romans, Philadelphians, Smyrnaeans. He also wrote a letter to Polycarp, bishop of Smyrna.

Josephus. Flavius Josephus was a writer and historian, a near contemporary of Jesus (born 37/38, died after 100 C.E.). He wrote two huge works: *The Jewish War,* which is his account of the events leading up to the destruction of Jerusalem in 70 C.E., and *The Jewish Antiquities,* which is a history of the Jews down to the Roman war, in twenty books. The two works are primary sources of information about the period just before and after Jesus.

Justin. Justin was a Christian apologist who was martyred between 163 and 167 C.E. He composed the First and Second Apologies and the Dialogue with Trypho. These books were produced shortly after 150 C.E.

Kepler, J. Johannes Kepler (1571–1630), German astronomer, established that the planes of all planetary orbits pass through the center of the sun; he also came to the view that the sun was the moving power of the solar system. Kepler is regarded as the founder of modern physical astronomy.

Kerygma. Kerygma is a Greek term meaning proclamation or gospel. New Testament scholars use it as a technical term for the message of the early church and its leaders, such as Paul.

Papyrus. Papyrus is the predecessor of modern paper. It was made from Egyptian reeds that were cut in strips, dried, and glued together to form sheets. Thousands of papyrus documents and fragments have been retrieved from the sands of Egypt during the last one hundred years.

Parable. A parable is a brief narrative or picture. It is also a metaphor or simile drawn from nature or the common life, arresting the hearer by its vividness or strangeness, and leaving the mind in sufficient doubt about its precise application to tease it into active thought.

Parchment. Parchment is made from the skins of animals, usually sheep or goats, prepared to receive writing.

Philostratus. Flavius Philostratus (ca. 170–245) belonged to a literary circle in Rome patronized by Julia Domna, wife of Emperor Septimius Severus. At her suggestion, he wrote the life of Apollonius of Tyana, a contemporary of Jesus.

Polycarp. Polycarp was bishop of Smyrna and a contemporary of Ignatius. His letter to the Philippians actually consists of two letters: chapters 13–14 were written much earlier than chapters 1–12. He suffered martyrdom under Marcus Aurelius, after 160 C.E.

Premise. A premise is a statement on which further conclusions rest. It is worth noting that a premise may be a statement of fact, a hypothesis, or a combination of the two.

Pronouncement story. See Chreia.

Proverb. See Aphorism.

Q. Q stands for the German word *Quelle,* which means source. Q is the source on which Matthew and Luke draw, in addition to Mark.

Rabbinic Judaism. The Judaism centered in Jerusalem and the temple was replaced by rabbinic Judaism following the destruction of the city and temple in 70 C.E. The Council of Jamnia in 90 C.E. laid the groundwork for the development of learning and worship focused in the synagogue. The rabbinic traditions surrounding the Hebrew Bible and codifying law and lore were later gathered into the Mishnah and Gemara, which together make up the Talmud.

Renaissance. The Renaissance (*renaissance* means rebirth) is marked by the revival of learning, the invention of the printing press, and other advances that initiated the modern period. With the Renaissance, attention shifted from the divine to the human, from theological speculation to the sciences. The Renaissance took place during the fourteenth to the sixteenth centuries c.e.

Scholars Version. The Scholars Version is a new translation of the gospels being prepared by members of the Jesus Seminar.

Schweitzer, A. Albert Schweitzer (1875–1965) world renowned organist, biblical scholar, medical doctor, and recipient of the Nobel Peace Prize, gave up a brilliant academic career to found a mission hospital in Africa. He wrote *The Quest of the Historical Jesus* at age 31; it was published in 1906 and remains one of the great critical works on the gospels.

Scroll. See Codex.

ben Sira. Jesus ben Sira taught in Jerusalem ca. 200–175 B.C.E. His teachings were collected into a book called Ecclesiasticus, which was preserved as a part of the Old Testament apocrypha. It belongs to the wisdom tradition of the Old Testament, but it bears the stamp of a highly disciplined individual mind.

Sophia of Jesus Christ. This document is a philosophical-gnostic treatise that takes the form of a revelation discourse in which the risen redeemer instructs the twelve disciples and seven women. It is a Christianized version of a gnostic treatise found at Nag Hammadi under the name of Eugnostos the Blessed. The tractate was probably composed in Egypt in the second half of the first century c.e.

Synoptic. Synoptic means to have a common view. The synoptic gospels, Matthew, Mark, and Luke, share a common view of the ministry of Jesus.

SV. See Scholars Version.

Thomas, Gospel of. The Gospel of Thomas is a new and important source for the sayings and parables of Jesus. See the *Catalogue of Written Gospels* for a description and consult the index for the discussion of Thomas.

Tradition. Tradition is a body of information, customs, beliefs, stories, wisdom, and other material transmitted by word of mouth or in writing from one generation to another. The Jesus tradition is the entire body of lore about Jesus that was transmitted from one generation to another in early Christian communities.

Weighted average. The weighted average is the value assigned to each saying and parable by vote of the Fellows of the Jesus Seminar. Votes are weighted as follows: red is given a value of 3, pink a value of 2, gray a value of 1, and black a value of zero. Each value is multiplied by the number of votes in each category and the sum of values divided by the total number of votes. See *Voting Procedures and Interpetation* for further explanation.

INDEX
of
Rules of Evidence

INDEX
of
Parallel Passages

249